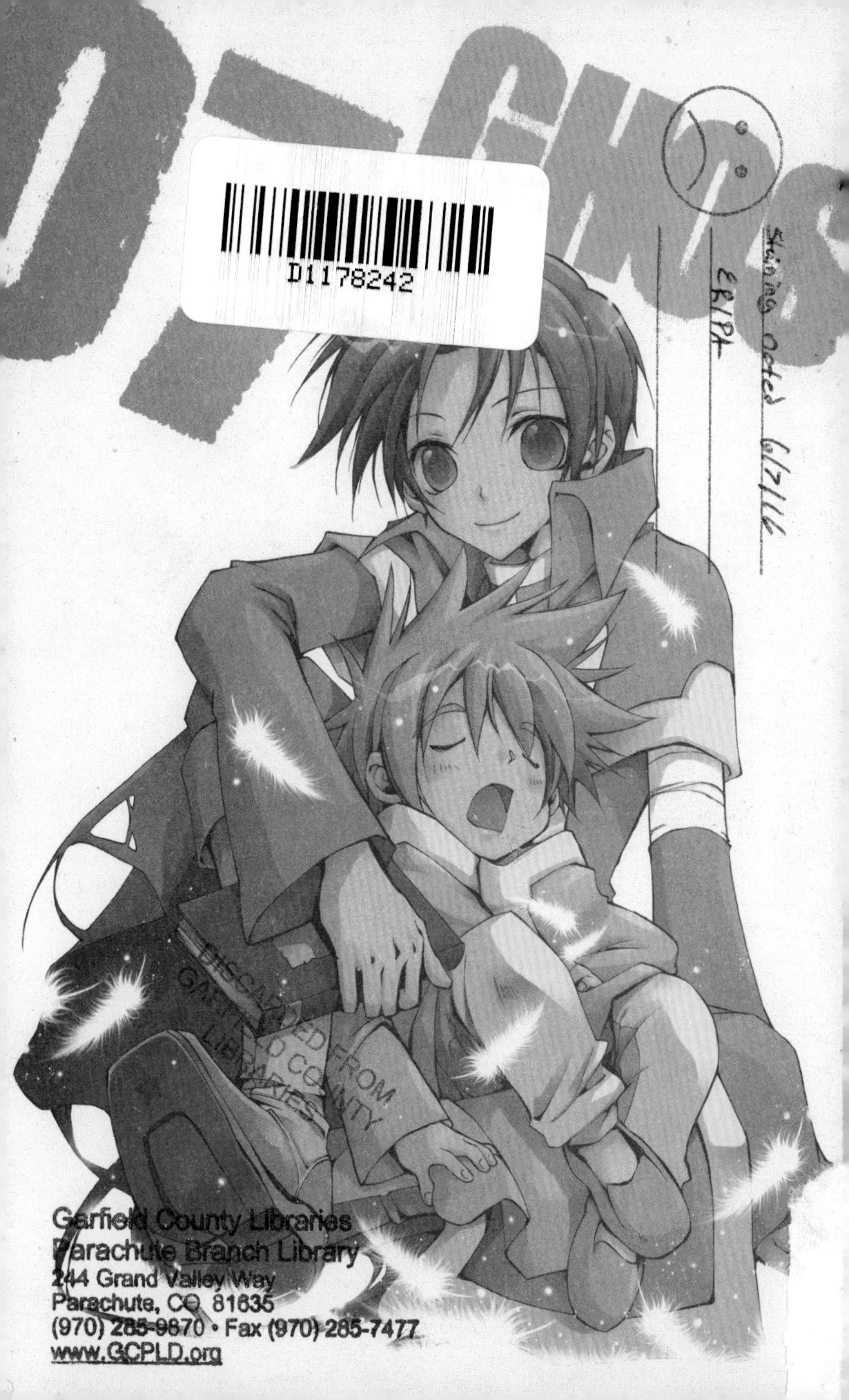

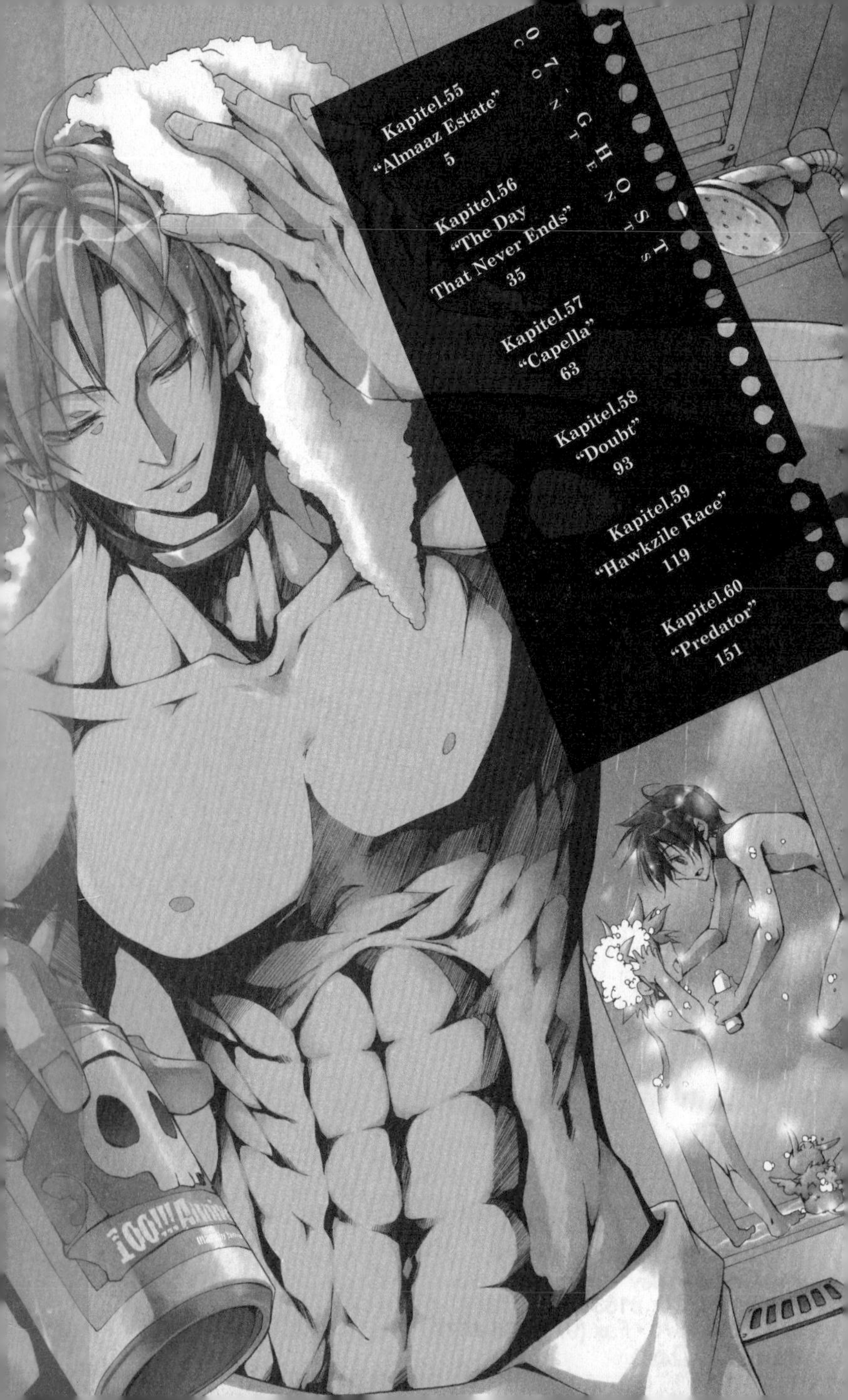

07-GHOST
CONTENTS

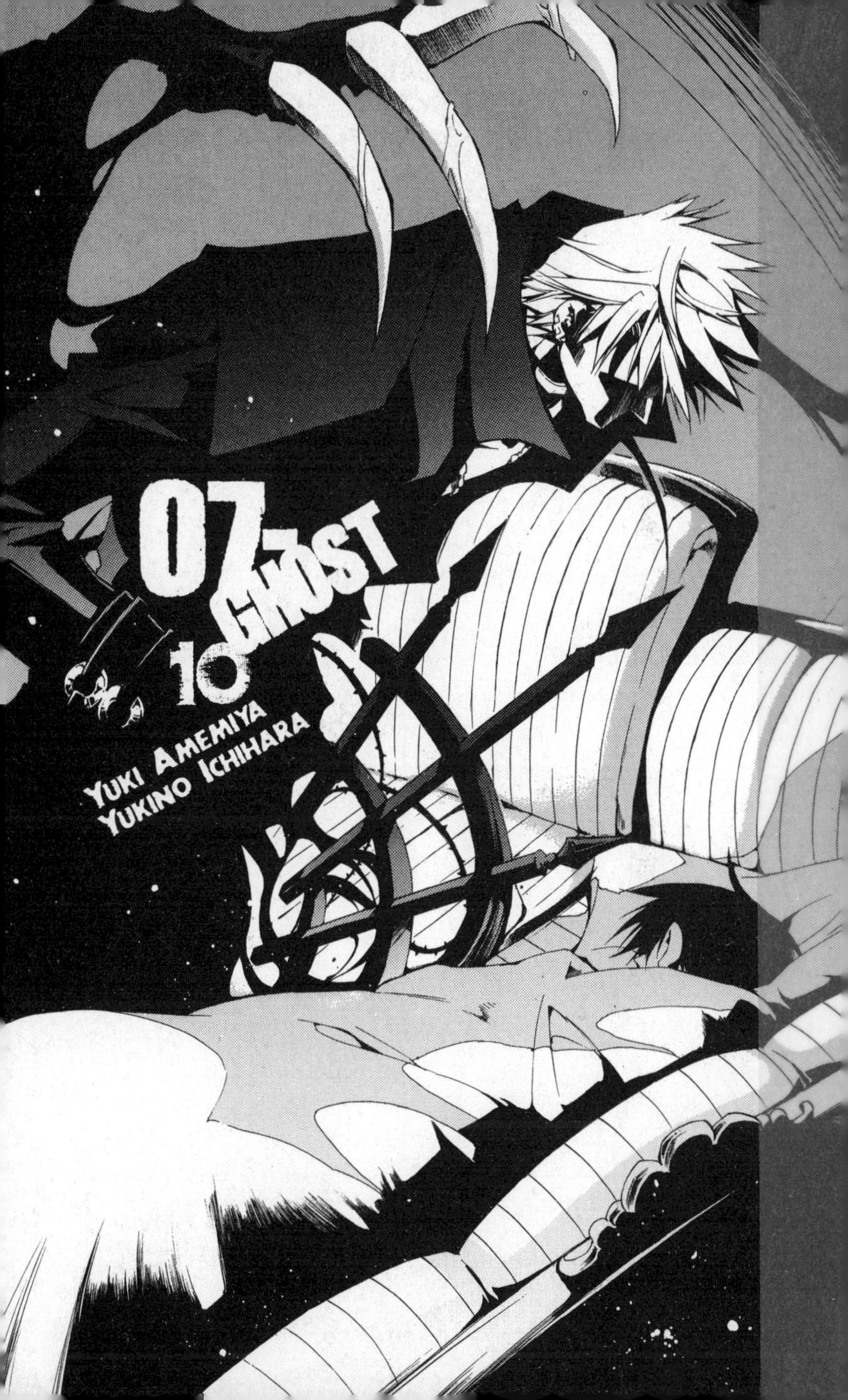
07-GHOST
10
YUKI AMEMIYA
YUKINO ICHIHARA

07 GHOST Characters

One thousand years ago, two equally powerful nations coexisted. One was the Barsburg Empire, protected by the Eye of Rafael. The other was the Raggs Kingdom, protected by the Eye of Mikael. Now that the Raggs Kingdom has been destroyed, things have changed...

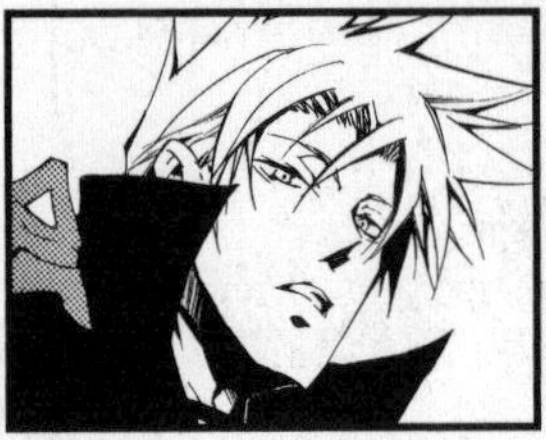

Frau

Bishop who saved Teito when he was fleeing from the academy and now watches over him. He is Zehel of the Seven Ghosts.

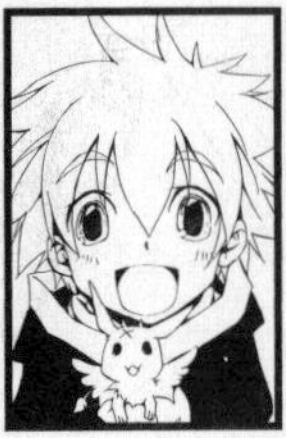

Capella

Child Teito saved from a slave trader.

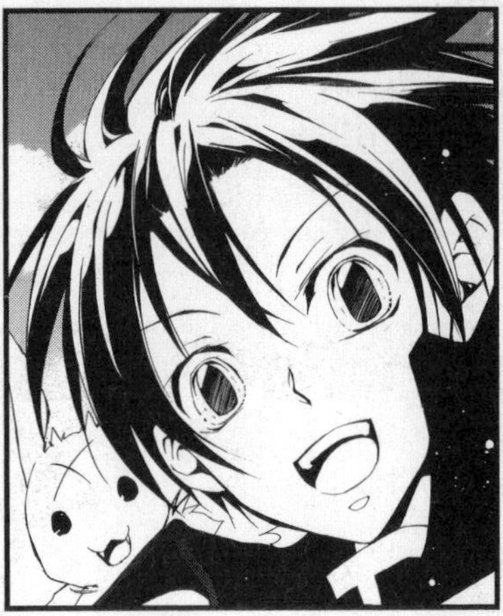

Teito Klein

Born a prince of Raggs, Teito was stripped of his memories and raised as a soldier by the military academy's chairman. He harbored the Eye of Mikael (an artifact said to bring either the world's salvation or destruction) in his right hand until the Black Hawks stole it. Currently Frau's apprentice.

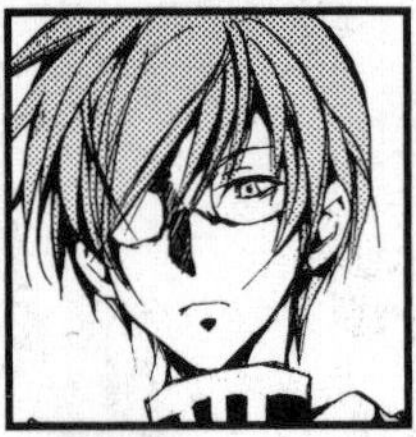

Castor

Bishop who can manipulate puppets. He watches over Teito and is Fest of the Seven Ghosts.

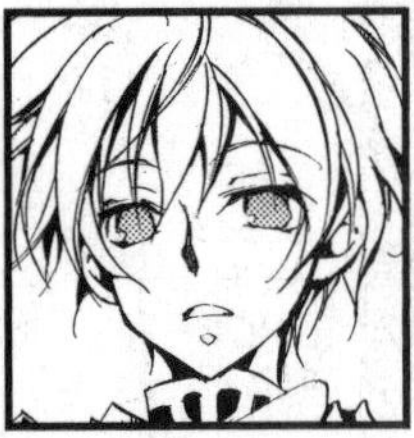

Labrador

Flower-loving bishop with the power of prophecy. He is Prophe of the Seven Ghosts.

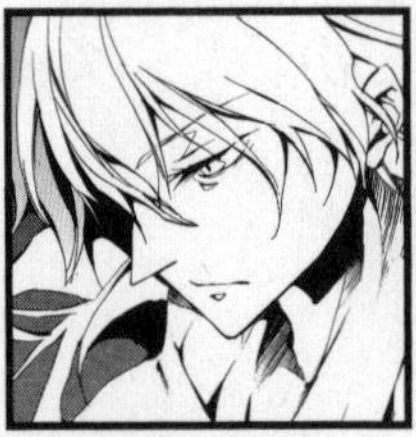

Ayanami

Imperial Army's Chief of Staff. Searching for Teito. His true identity is the evil death god, Verloren.

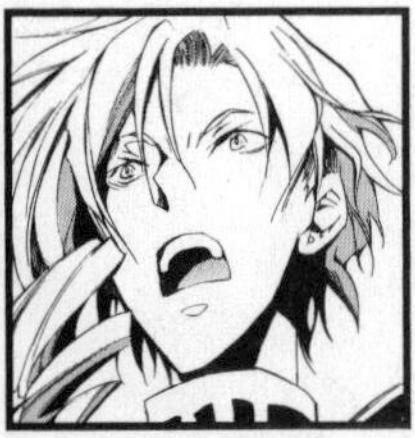

Lance

Bishop with no sense of direction who loves to travel. He is Relikt of the Seven Ghosts.

Story

Teito is a student at the Barsburg Empire's military academy until the day he discovers that his father was the king of Raggs, the ruler of a kingdom the Barsburg Empire destroyed. He runs away, but loses his best friend to the diabolical Ayanami. As a first step in avenging Mikage's death, Teito becomes an apprentice bishop to obtain special privileges. He then embarks on a journey to the "Land of Seele," which holds the key to his past and the truth about the fall of Raggs. He obtains the Cursed Tickets in Districts 4, 5 and 6. On the way, he meets Ouka, a princess who hosts the Eye of Rafael!

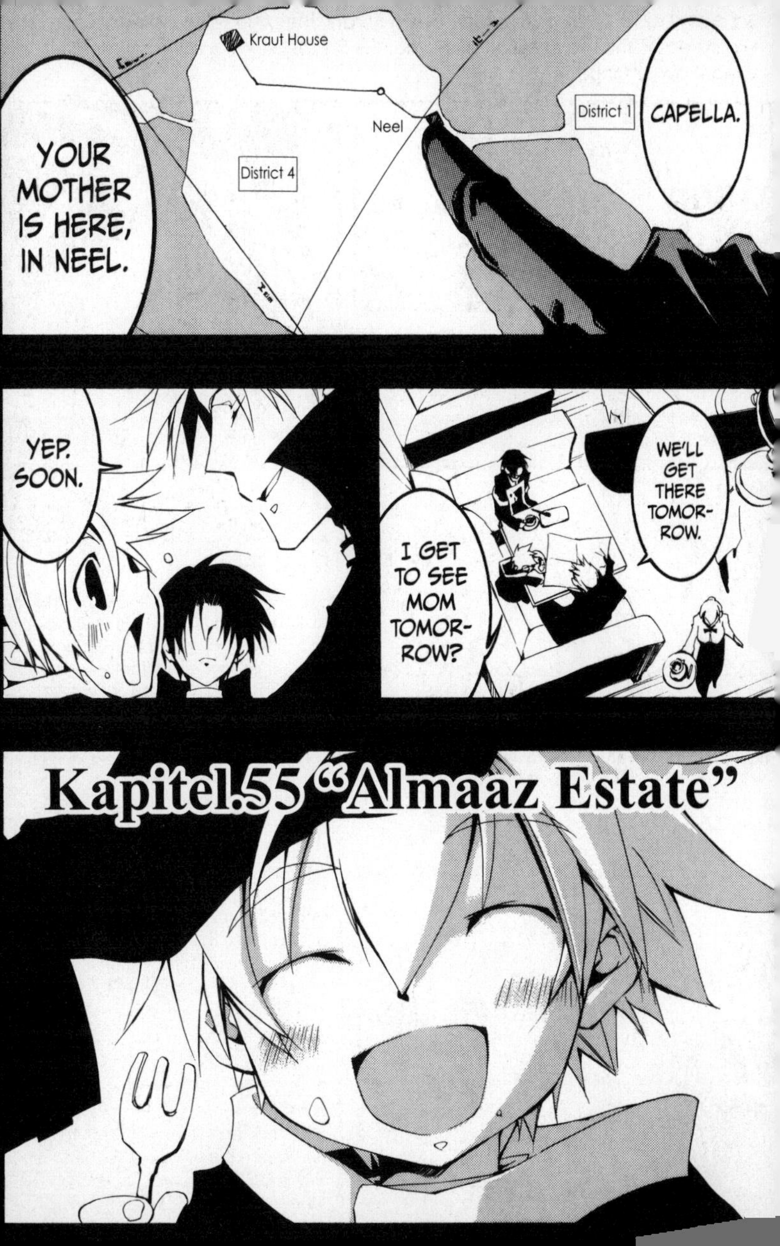
Kraut House
District 1
CAPELLA.
Neel
District 4
YOUR MOTHER IS HERE, IN NEEL.
WE'LL GET THERE TOMOR-ROW.
I GET TO SEE MOM TOMOR-ROW?
YEP. SOON.
Kapitel.55 "Almaaz Estate"

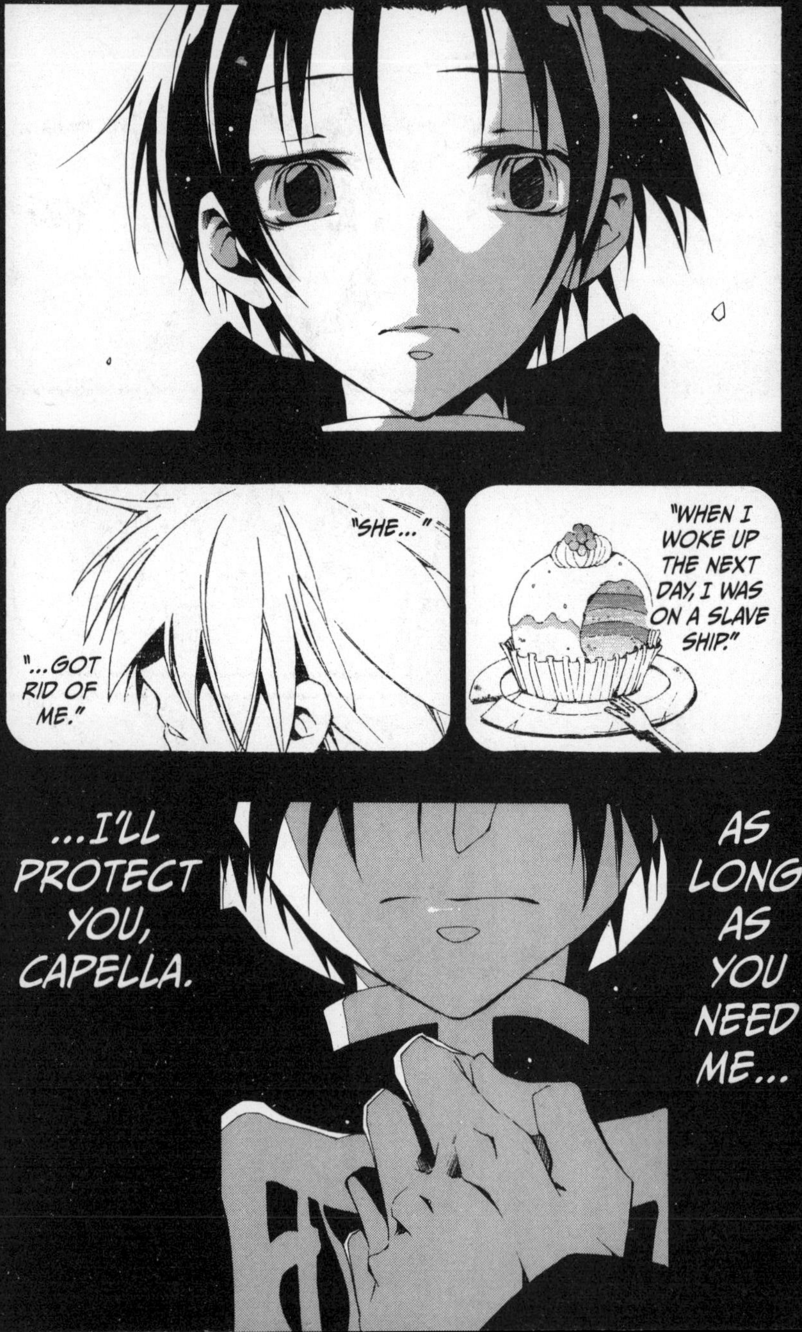
"WHEN I WOKE UP THE NEXT DAY, I WAS ON A SLAVE SHIP."
"SHE..."
"...GOT RID OF ME."
AS LONG AS YOU NEED ME...
...I'LL PROTECT YOU, CAPELLA.

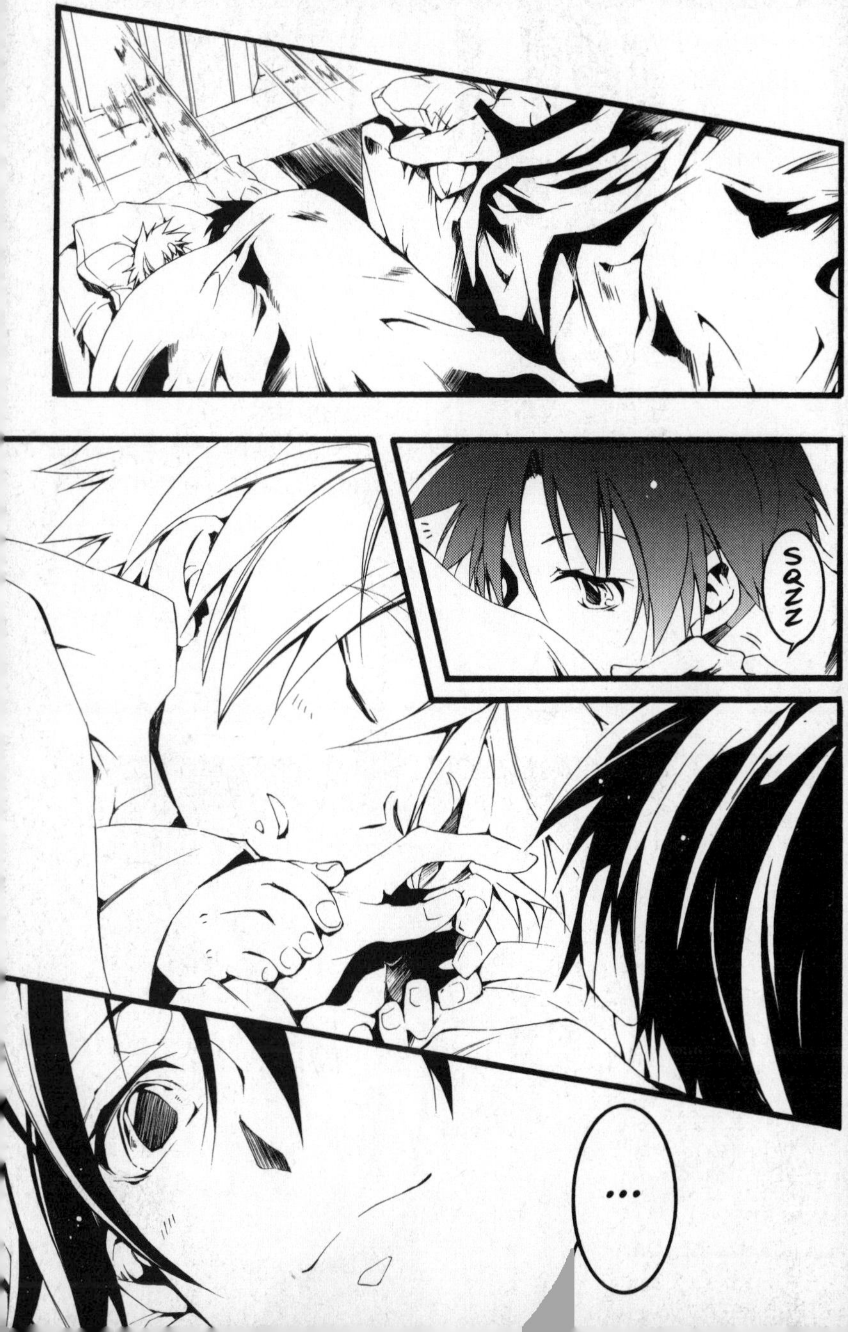
SQZZ
...

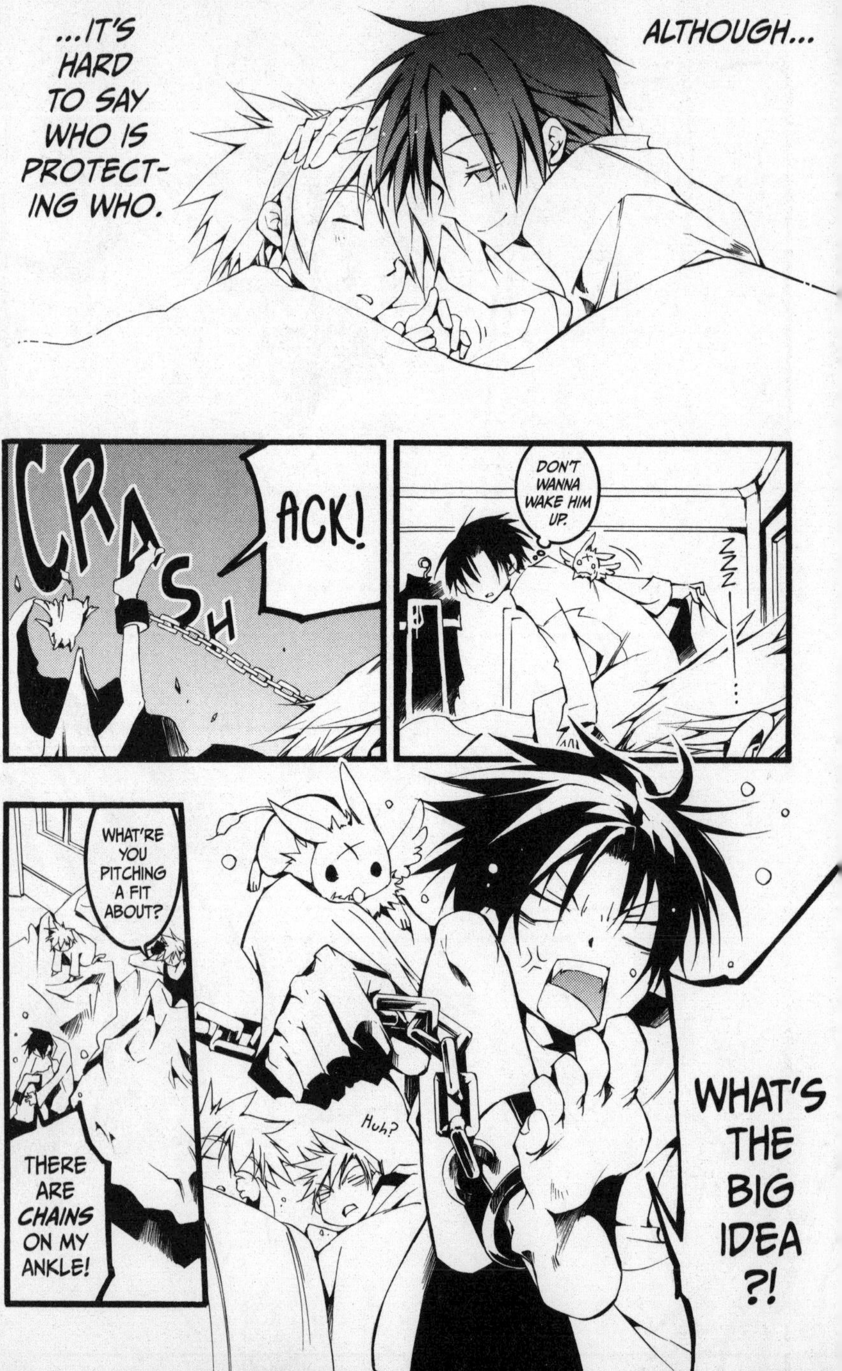
ALTHOUGH...
...IT'S HARD TO SAY WHO IS PROTECTING WHO.
DON'T WANNA WAKE HIM UP.
ZZZ......
ACK!
CRASH
WHAT'S THE BIG IDEA?!
Huh?
WHAT'RE YOU PITCHING A FIT ABOUT?
THERE ARE CHAINS ON MY ANKLE!

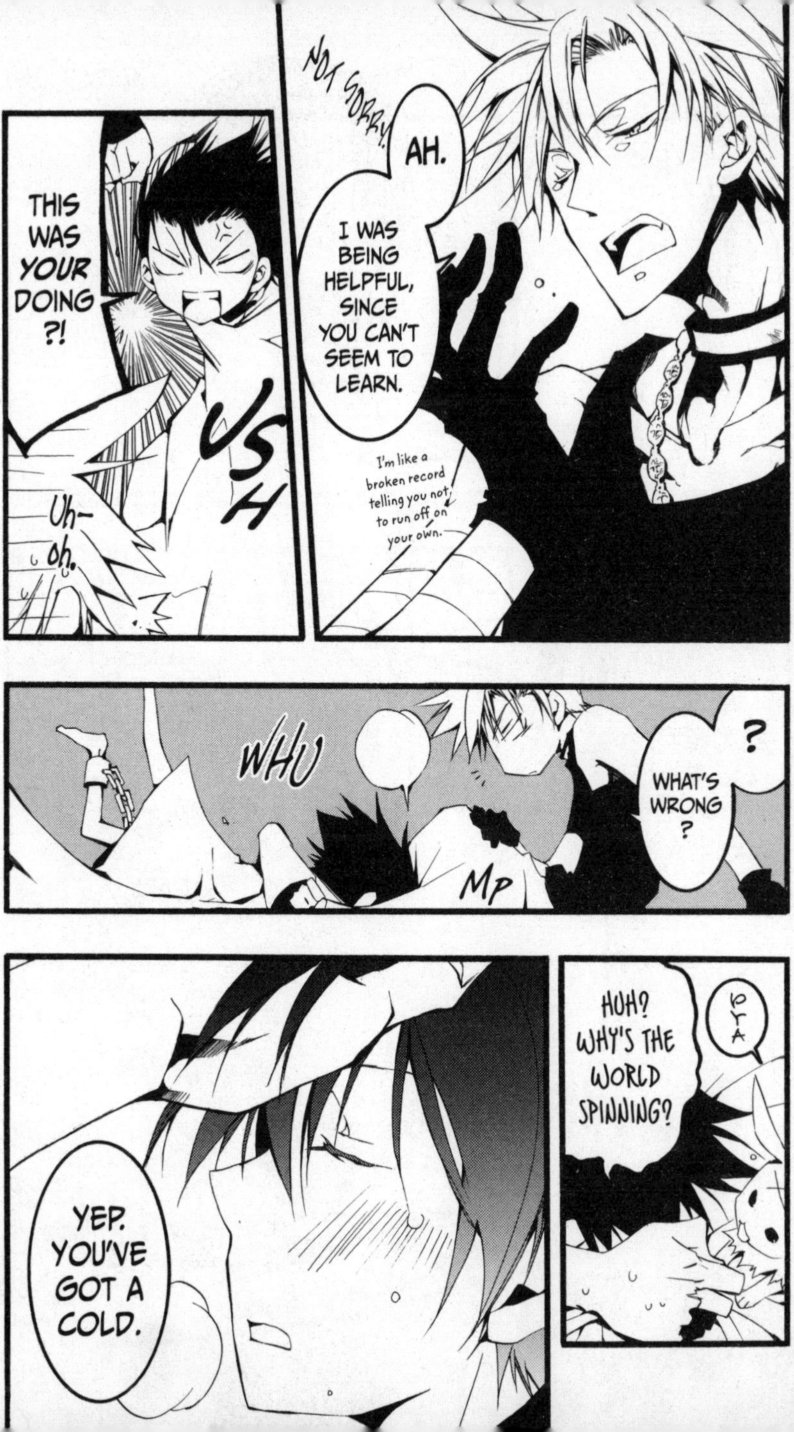
NOT SORRY
AH.
I WAS BEING HELPFUL, SINCE YOU CAN'T SEEM TO LEARN.
I'm like a broken record telling you not to run off on your own.
THIS WAS YOUR DOING?!
USH
Uh-oh.
?
WHAT'S WRONG?
MP
WHU
HUH? WHY'S THE WORLD SPINNING?
YEP. YOU'VE GOT A COLD.

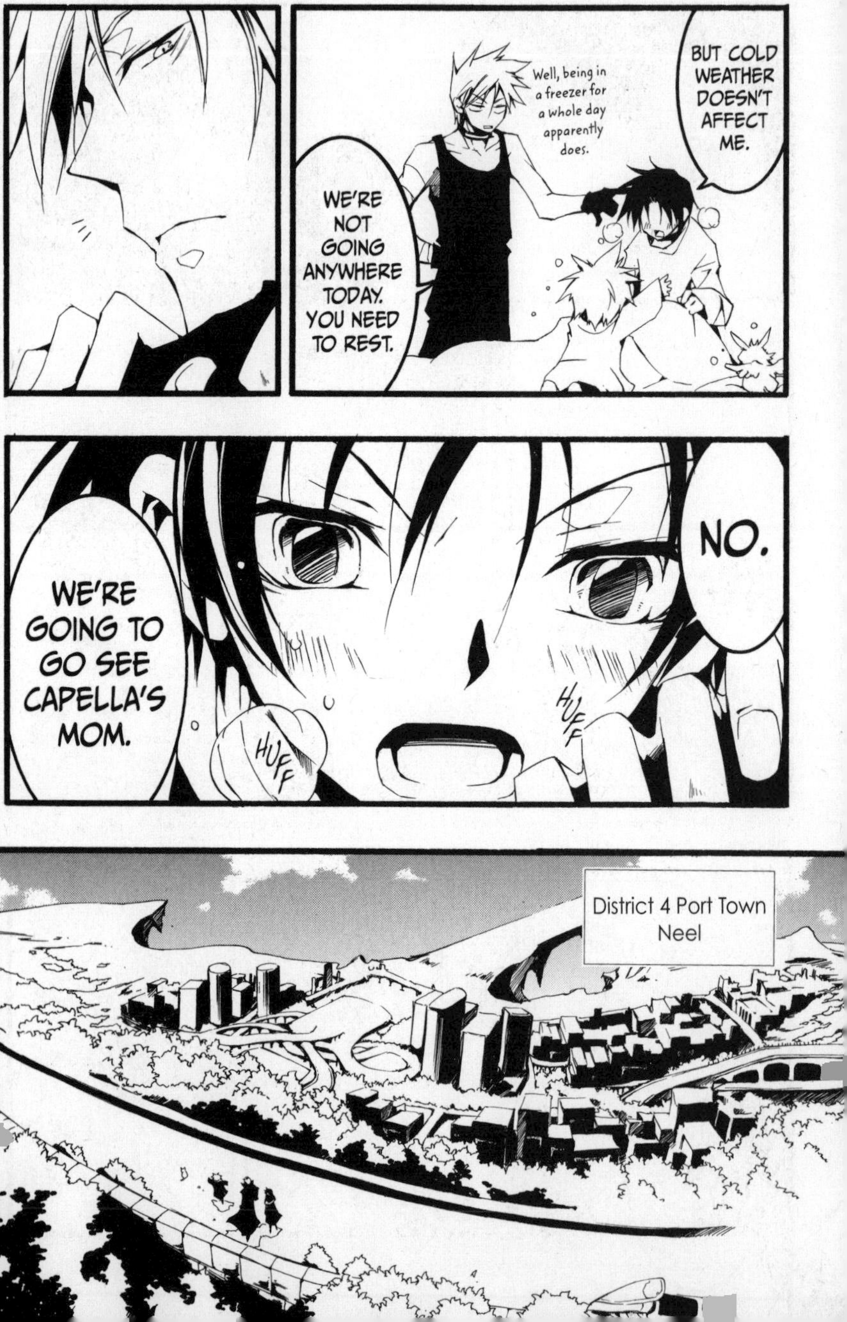
BUT COLD WEATHER DOESN'T AFFECT ME.
Well, being in a freezer for a whole day apparently does.
WE'RE NOT GOING ANYWHERE TODAY. YOU NEED TO REST.
NO.
HUFF
HUFF
WE'RE GOING TO GO SEE CAPELLA'S MOM.
District 4 Port Town Neel

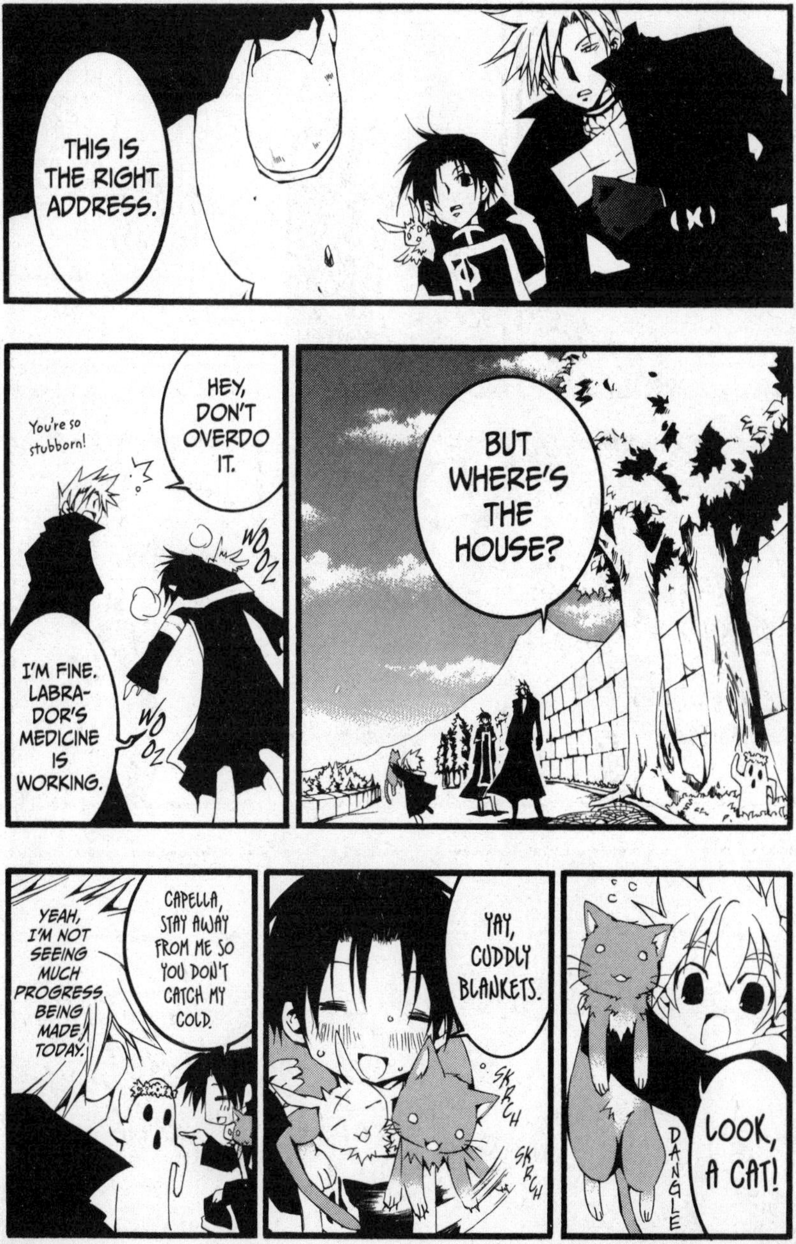
THIS IS THE RIGHT ADDRESS.
BUT WHERE'S THE HOUSE?
HEY, DON'T OVERDO IT.
You're so stubborn!
WOOZ
I'M FINE. LABRADOR'S MEDICINE IS WORKING.
WOOZ
LOOK, A CAT!
DANGLE
YAY, CUDDLY BLANKETS.
SKRCH
SKRCH
CAPELLA, STAY AWAY FROM ME SO YOU DON'T CATCH MY COLD.
YEAH, I'M NOT SEEING MUCH PROGRESS BEING MADE TODAY.

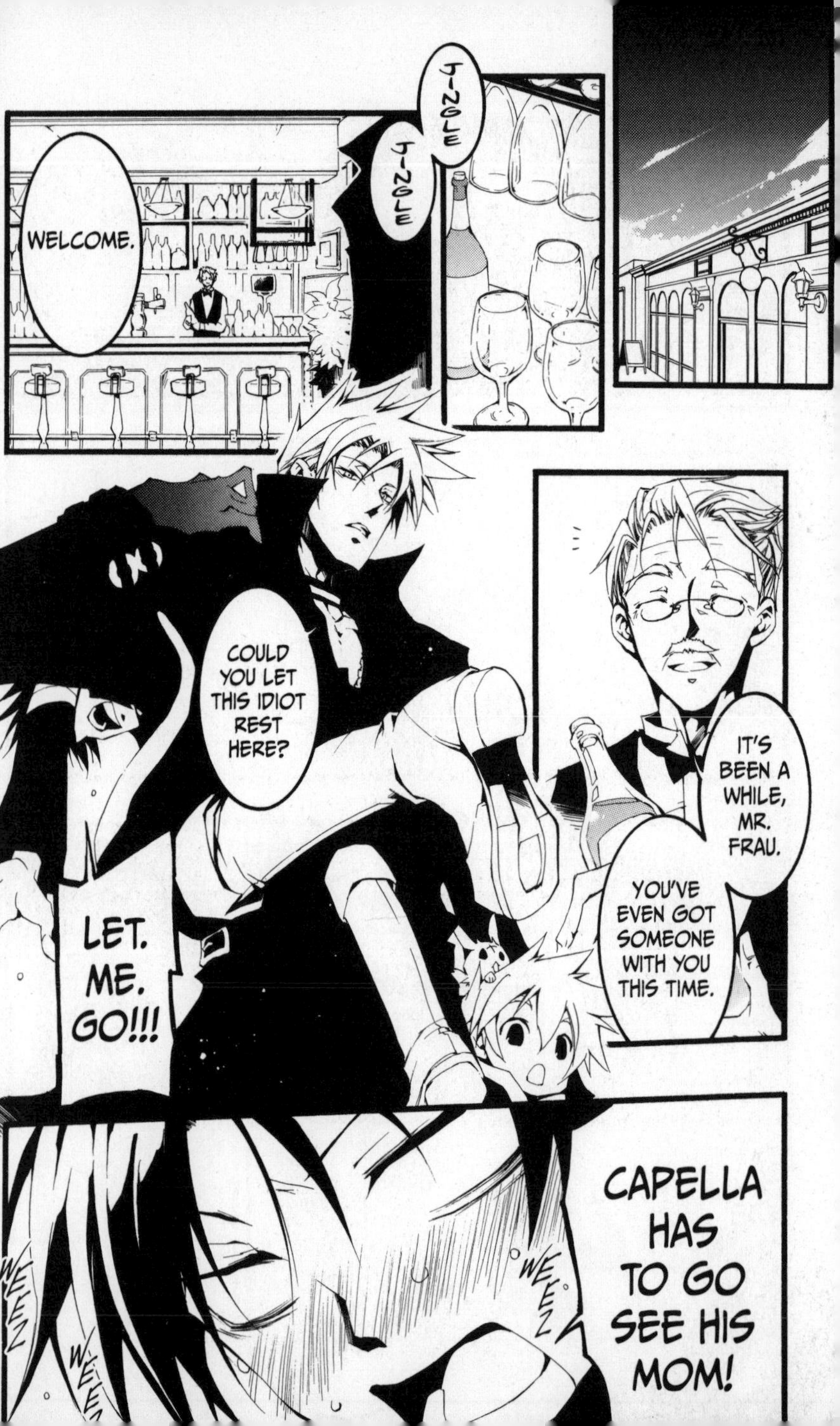
JINGLE
JINGLE
WELCOME.
IT'S BEEN A WHILE, MR. FRAU.
YOU'VE EVEN GOT SOMEONE WITH YOU THIS TIME.
COULD YOU LET THIS IDIOT REST HERE?
LET. ME. GO!!!
CAPELLA HAS TO GO SEE HIS MOM!
WEEZ
WEEZ
WEEZ

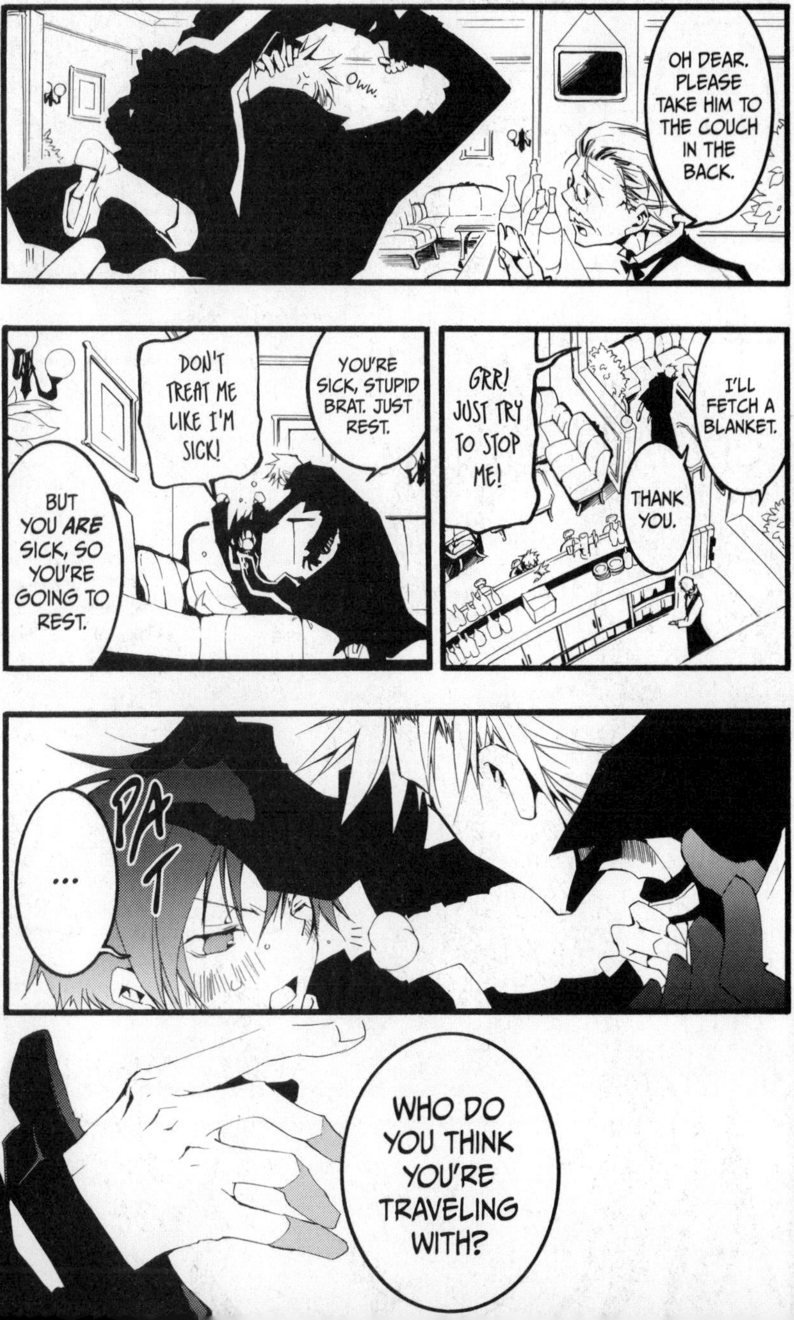
OH DEAR. PLEASE TAKE HIM TO THE COUCH IN THE BACK.
Oww.
I'LL FETCH A BLANKET.
GRR! JUST TRY TO STOP ME!
THANK YOU.
YOU'RE SICK, STUPID BRAT. JUST REST.
DON'T TREAT ME LIKE I'M SICK!
BUT YOU ARE SICK, SO YOU'RE GOING TO REST.
PAT
...
WHO DO YOU THINK YOU'RE TRAVELING WITH?

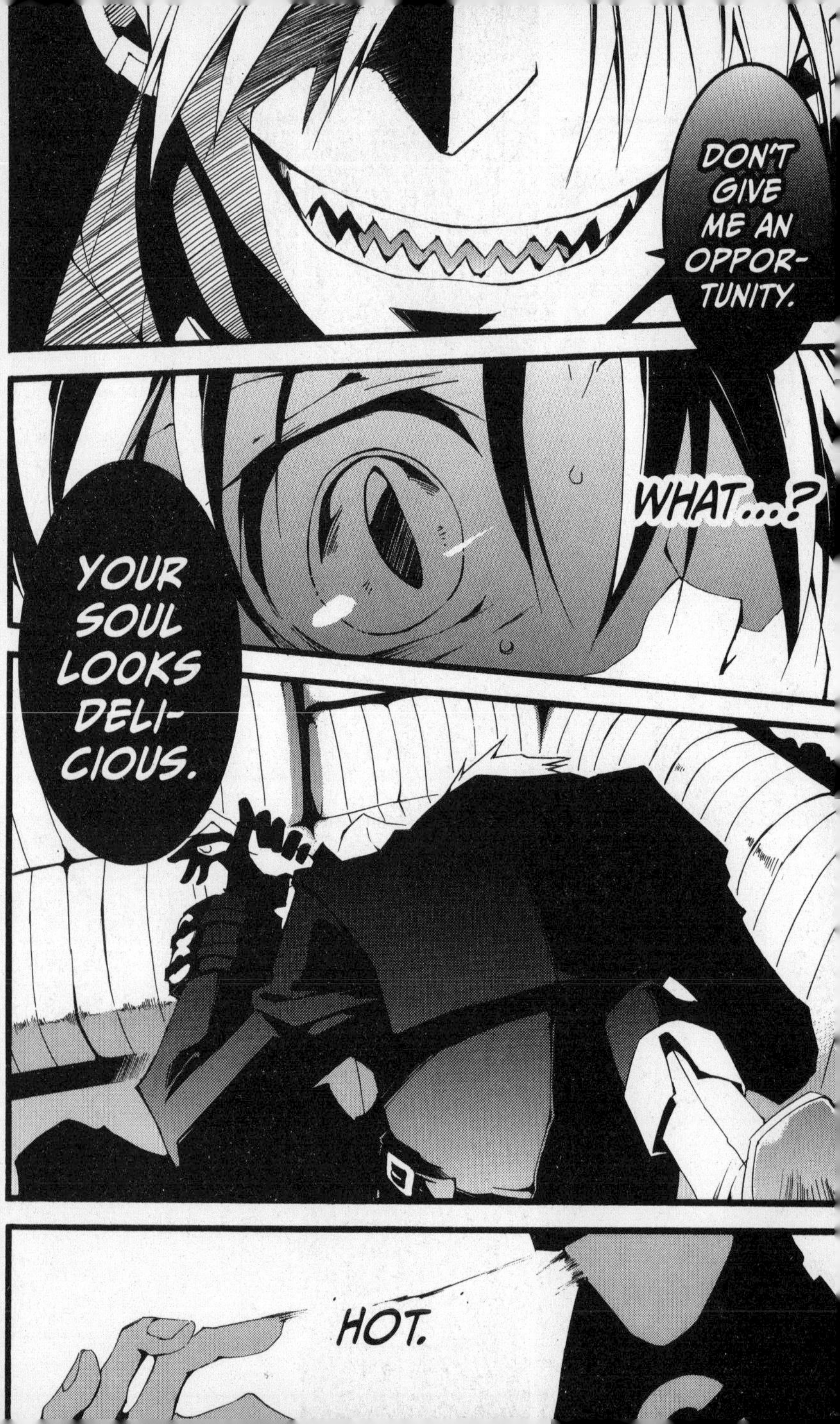
DON'T GIVE ME AN OPPORTUNITY.
WHAT...?
YOUR SOUL LOOKS DELICIOUS.
HOT.

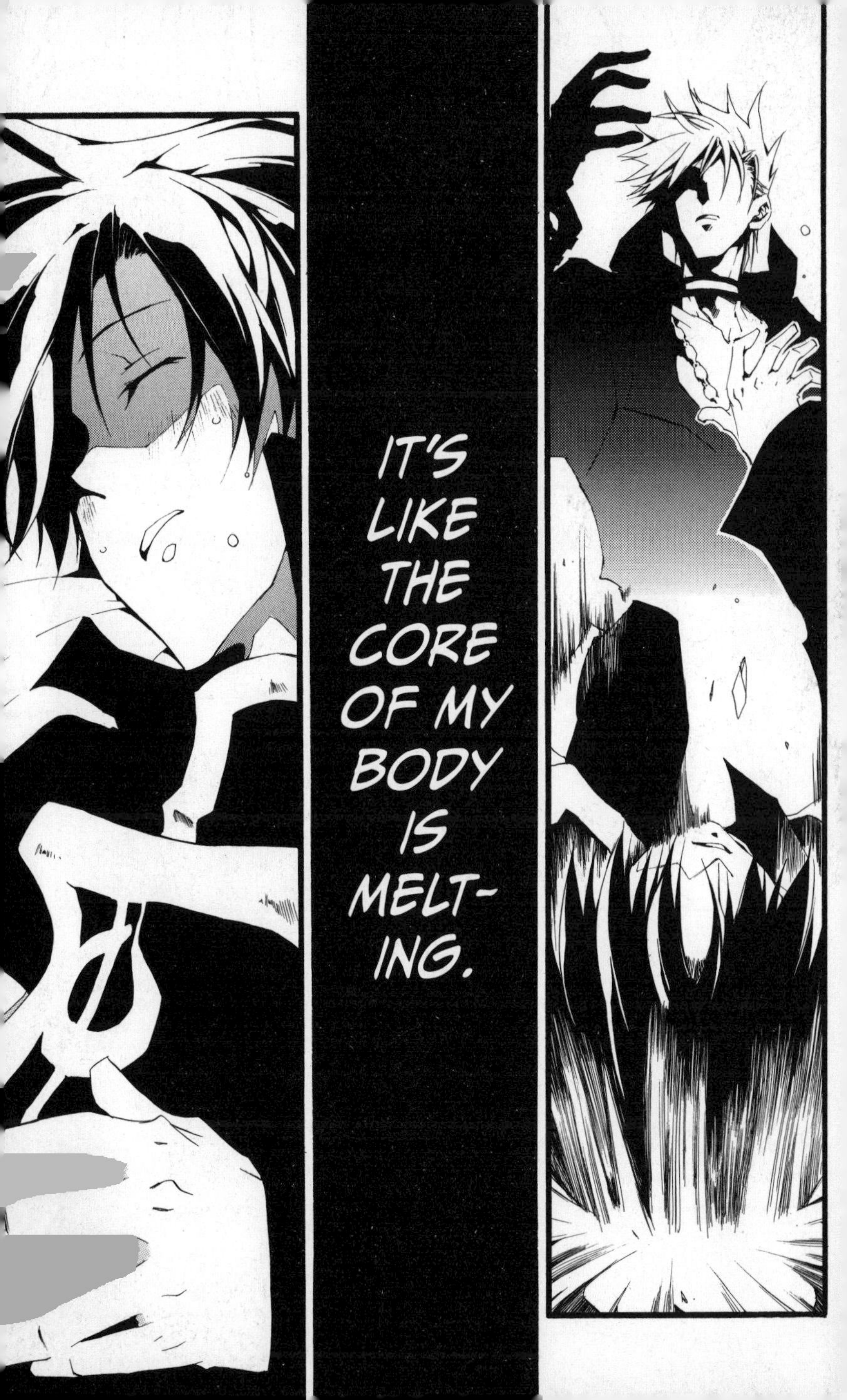
IT'S LIKE THE CORE OF MY BODY IS MELT-ING.

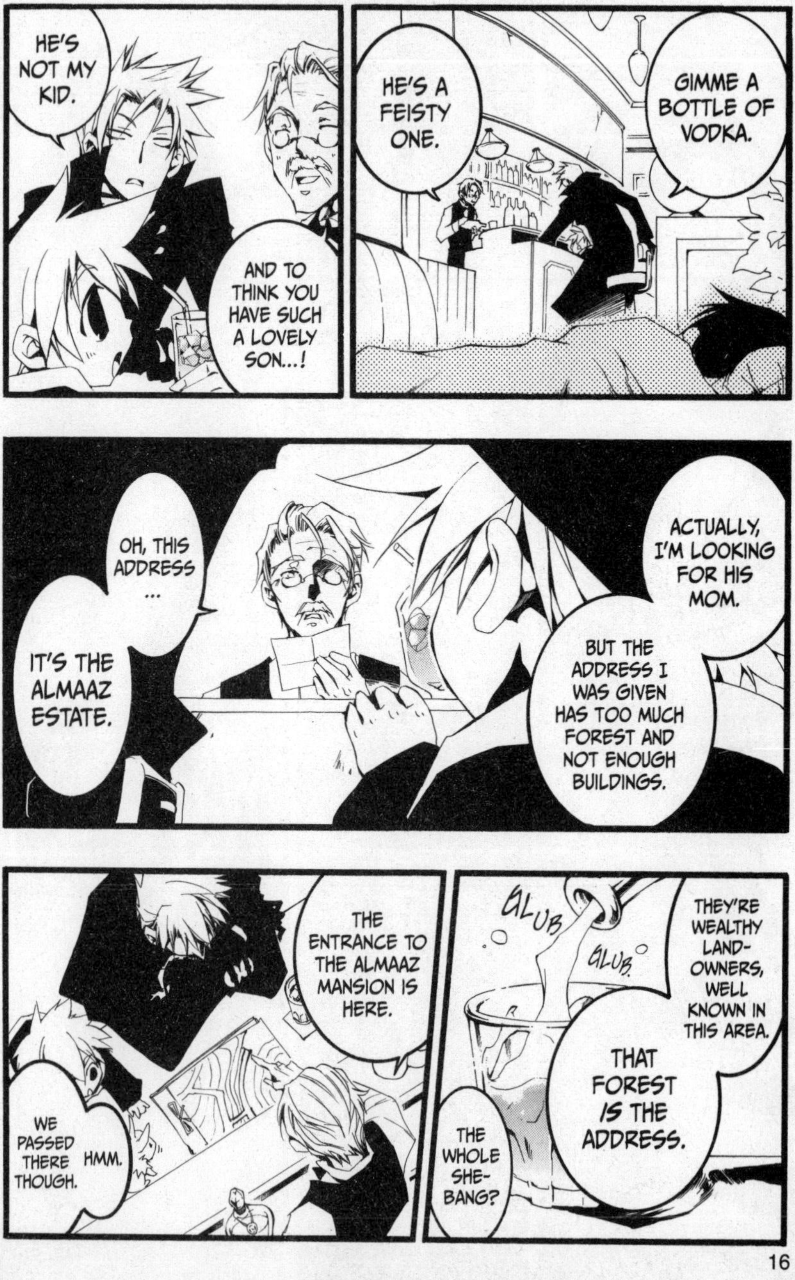
GIMME A BOTTLE OF VODKA.
HE'S A FEISTY ONE.
AND TO THINK YOU HAVE SUCH A LOVELY SON...!
HE'S NOT MY KID.
ACTUALLY, I'M LOOKING FOR HIS MOM.
BUT THE ADDRESS I WAS GIVEN HAS TOO MUCH FOREST AND NOT ENOUGH BUILDINGS.
OH, THIS ADDRESS ...
IT'S THE ALMAAZ ESTATE.
GLUB
GLUB
THEY'RE WEALTHY LAND-OWNERS, WELL KNOWN IN THIS AREA.
THAT FOREST *IS* THE ADDRESS.
THE WHOLE SHE-BANG?
THE ENTRANCE TO THE ALMAAZ MANSION IS HERE.
HMM.
WE PASSED THERE THOUGH.

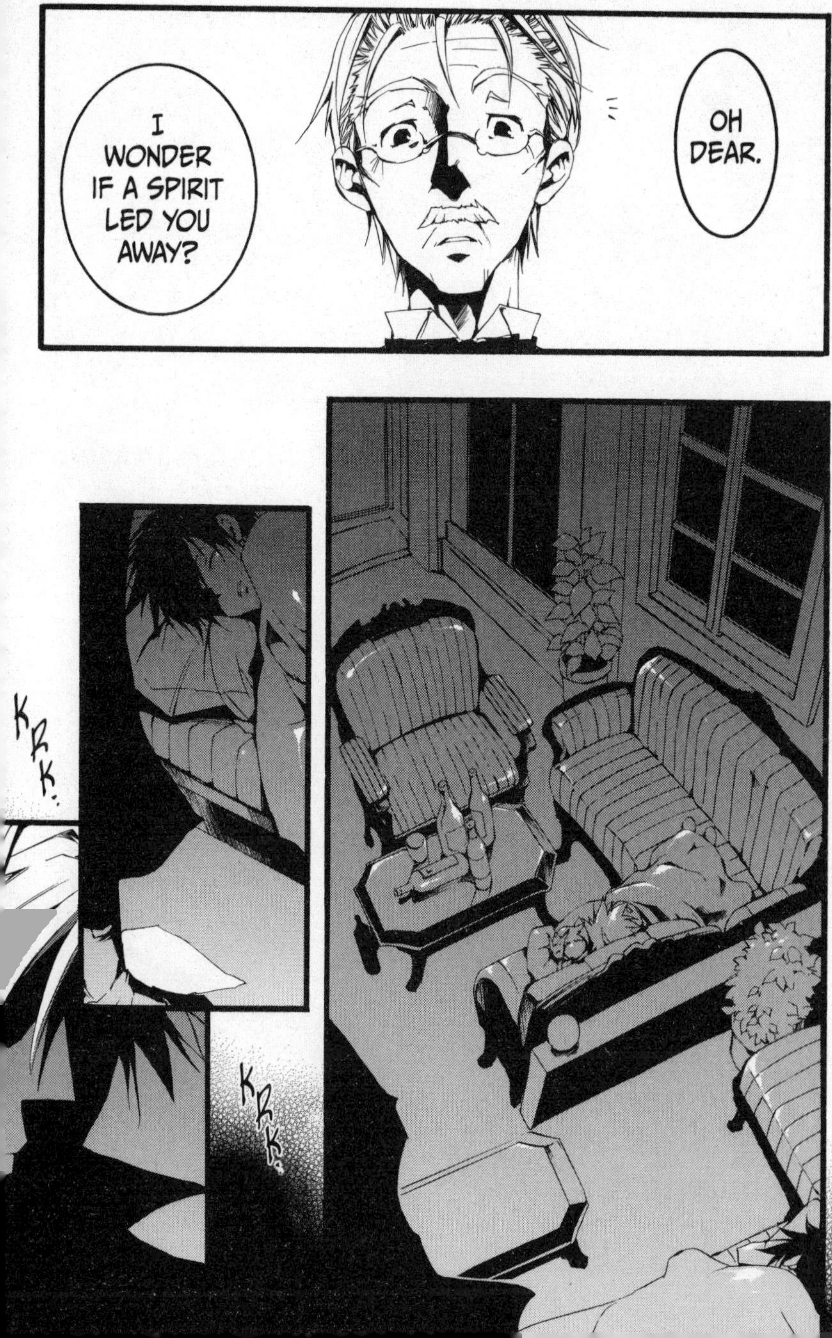
OH DEAR.
I WONDER IF A SPIRIT LED YOU AWAY?
KRK...
KRK...

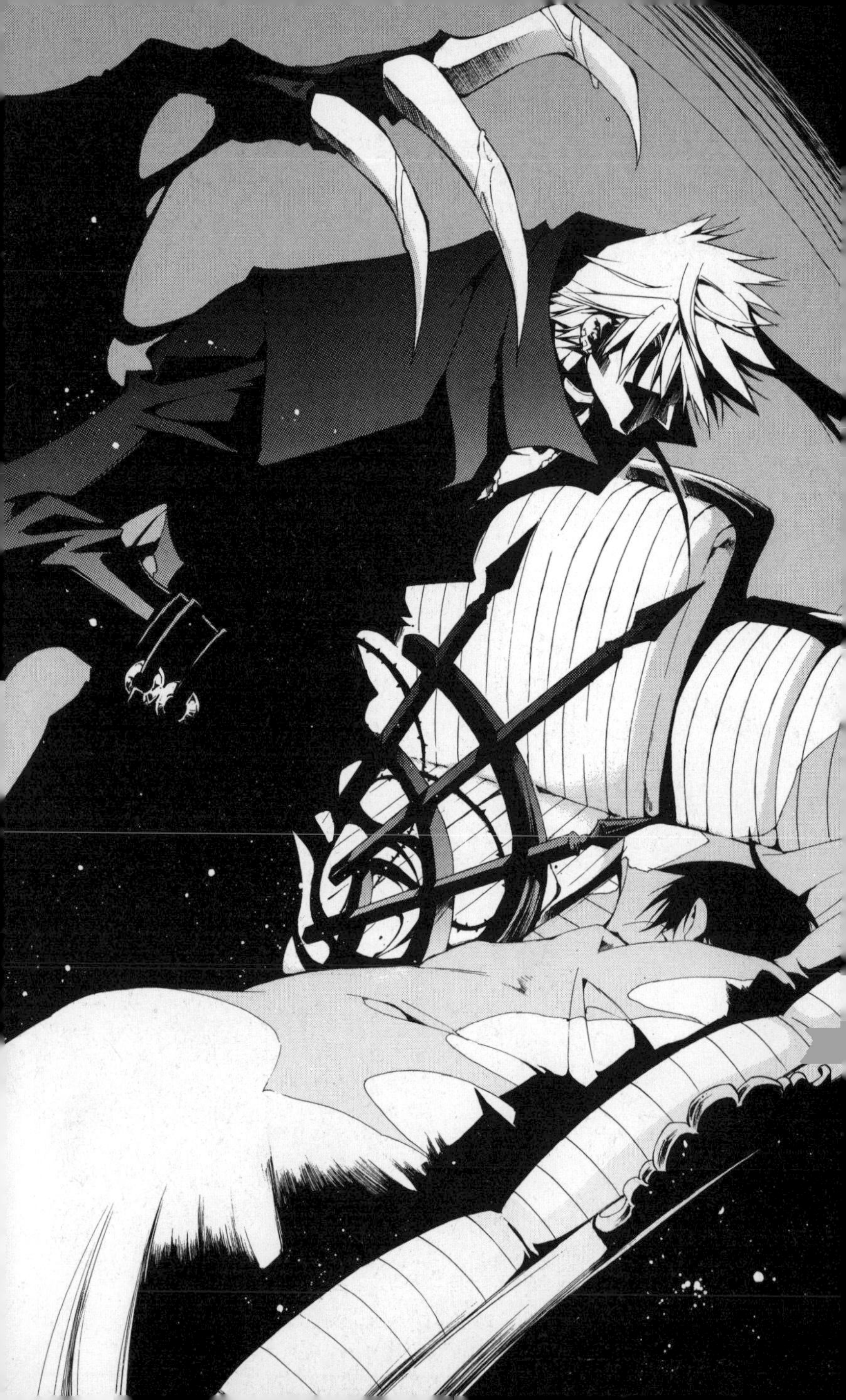

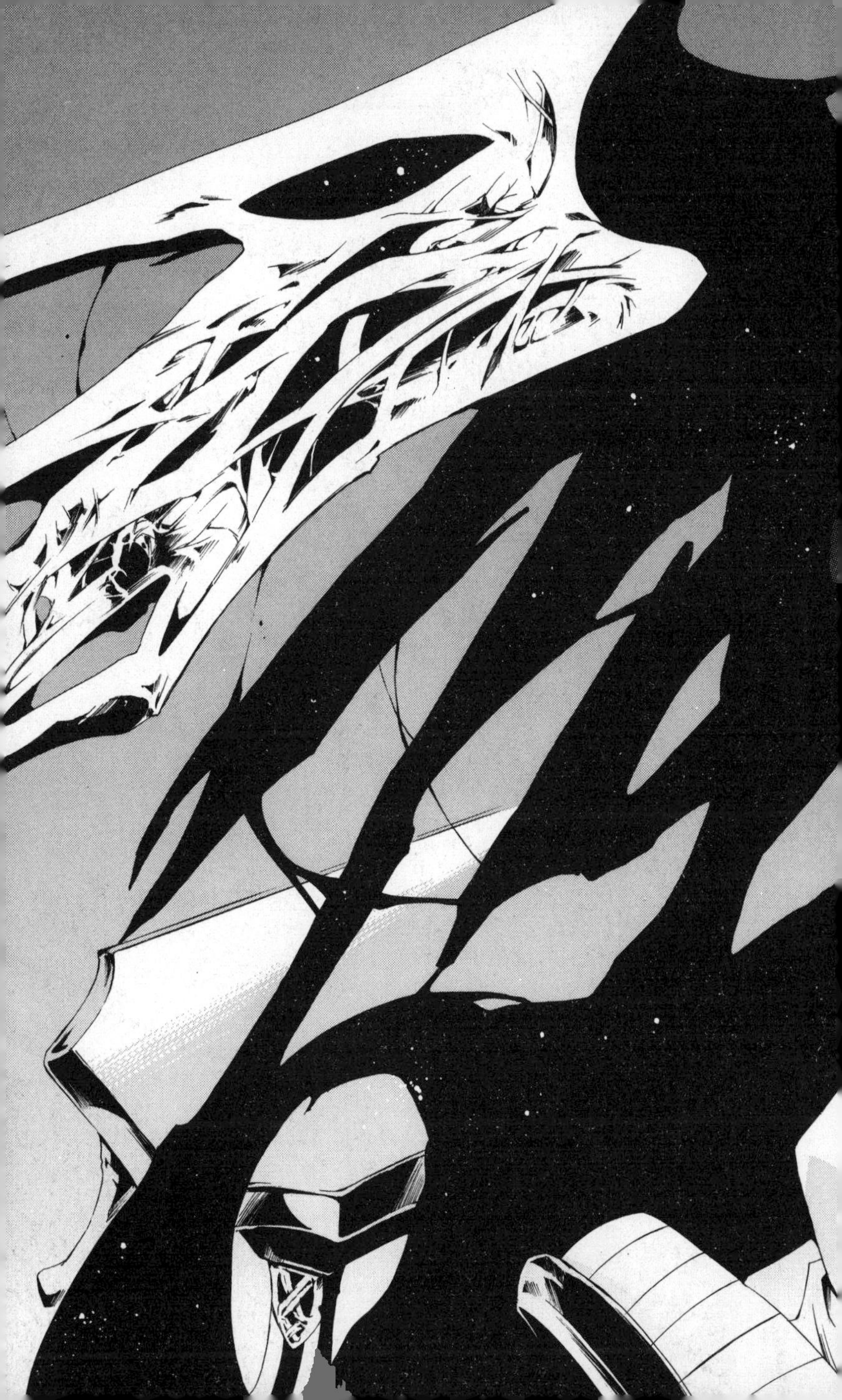

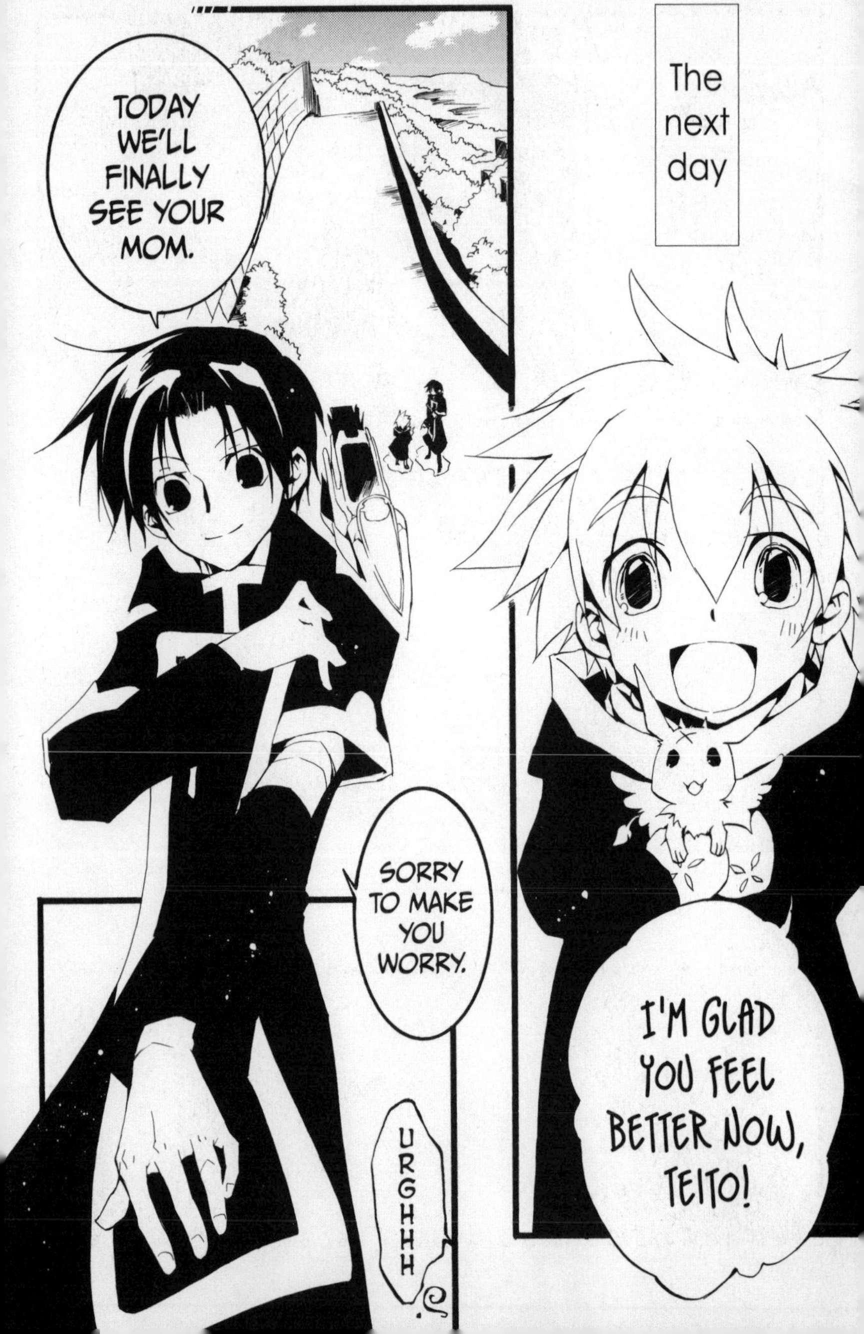
The next day
I'M GLAD YOU FEEL BETTER NOW, TEITO!
TODAY WE'LL FINALLY SEE YOUR MOM.
SORRY TO MAKE YOU WORRY.
URGHHH

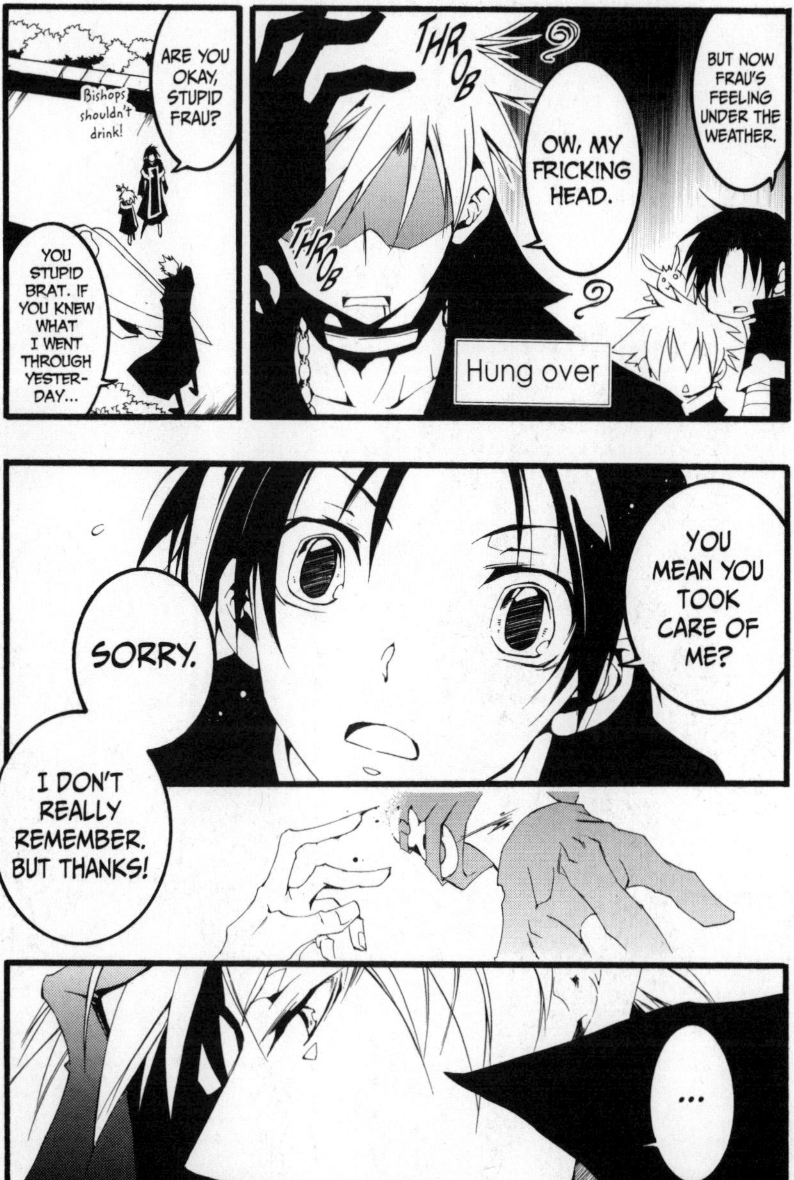

BUT NOW FRAU'S FEELING UNDER THE WEATHER.
THROB
OW, MY FRICKING HEAD.
THROB
Hung over
ARE YOU OKAY, STUPID FRAU?
Bishops shouldn't drink!
YOU STUPID BRAT. IF YOU KNEW WHAT I WENT THROUGH YESTER-DAY...
YOU MEAN YOU TOOK CARE OF ME?
SORRY.
I DON'T REALLY REMEMBER. BUT THANKS!
...

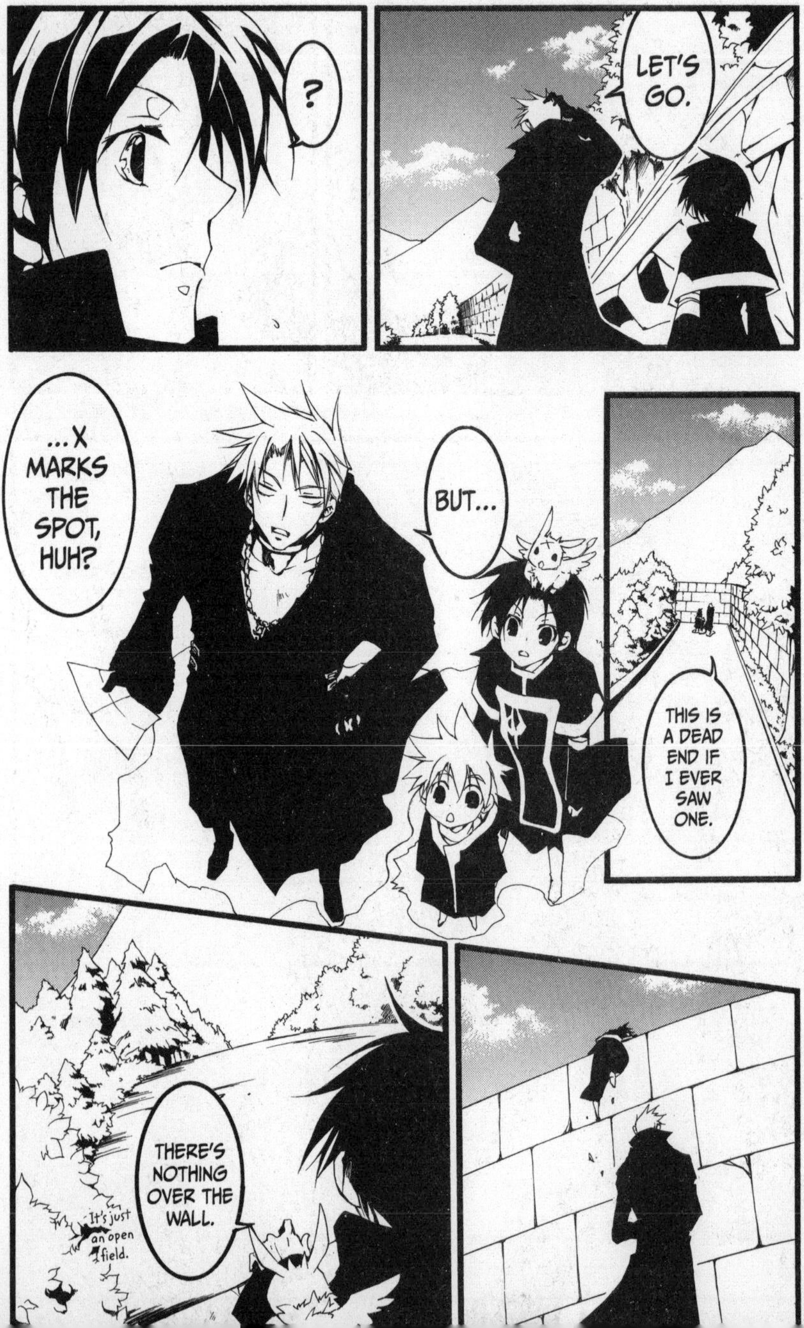
LET'S GO.
?
THIS IS A DEAD END IF I EVER SAW ONE.
BUT...
...X MARKS THE SPOT, HUH?
THERE'S NOTHING OVER THE WALL.
It's just an open field.

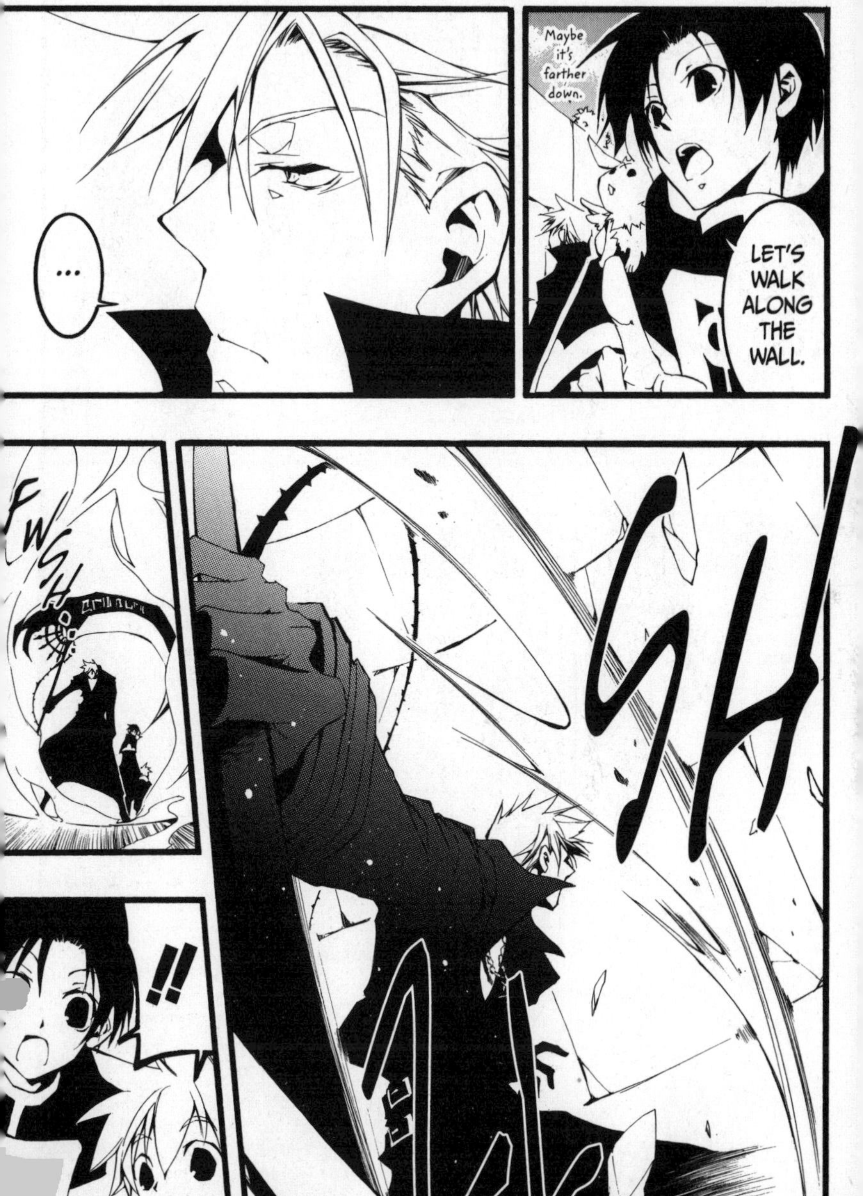
Maybe it's farther down.
LET'S WALK ALONG THE WALL.
...
FWSH
!!

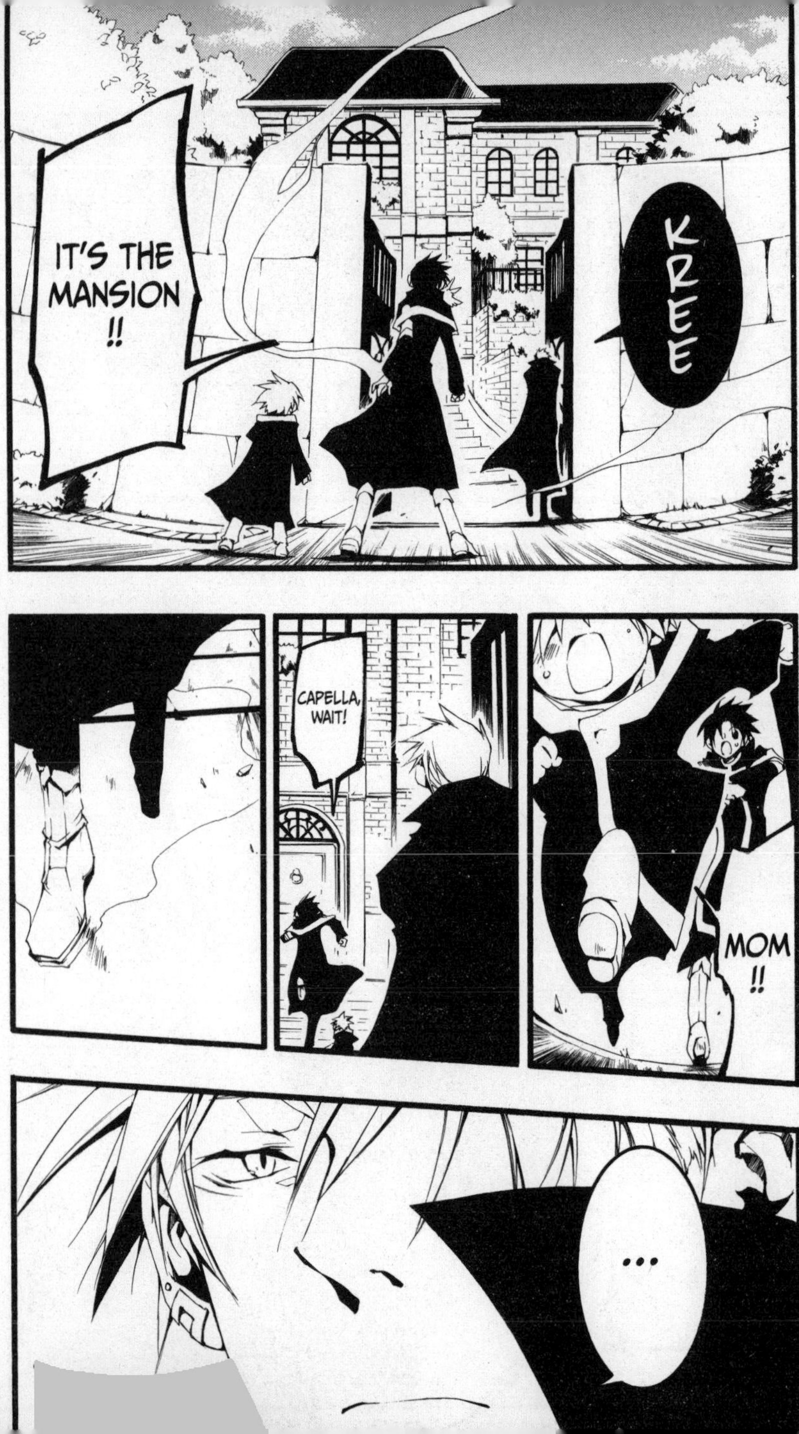
KREE
IT'S THE MANSION !!
MOM !!
CAPELLA, WAIT!
...

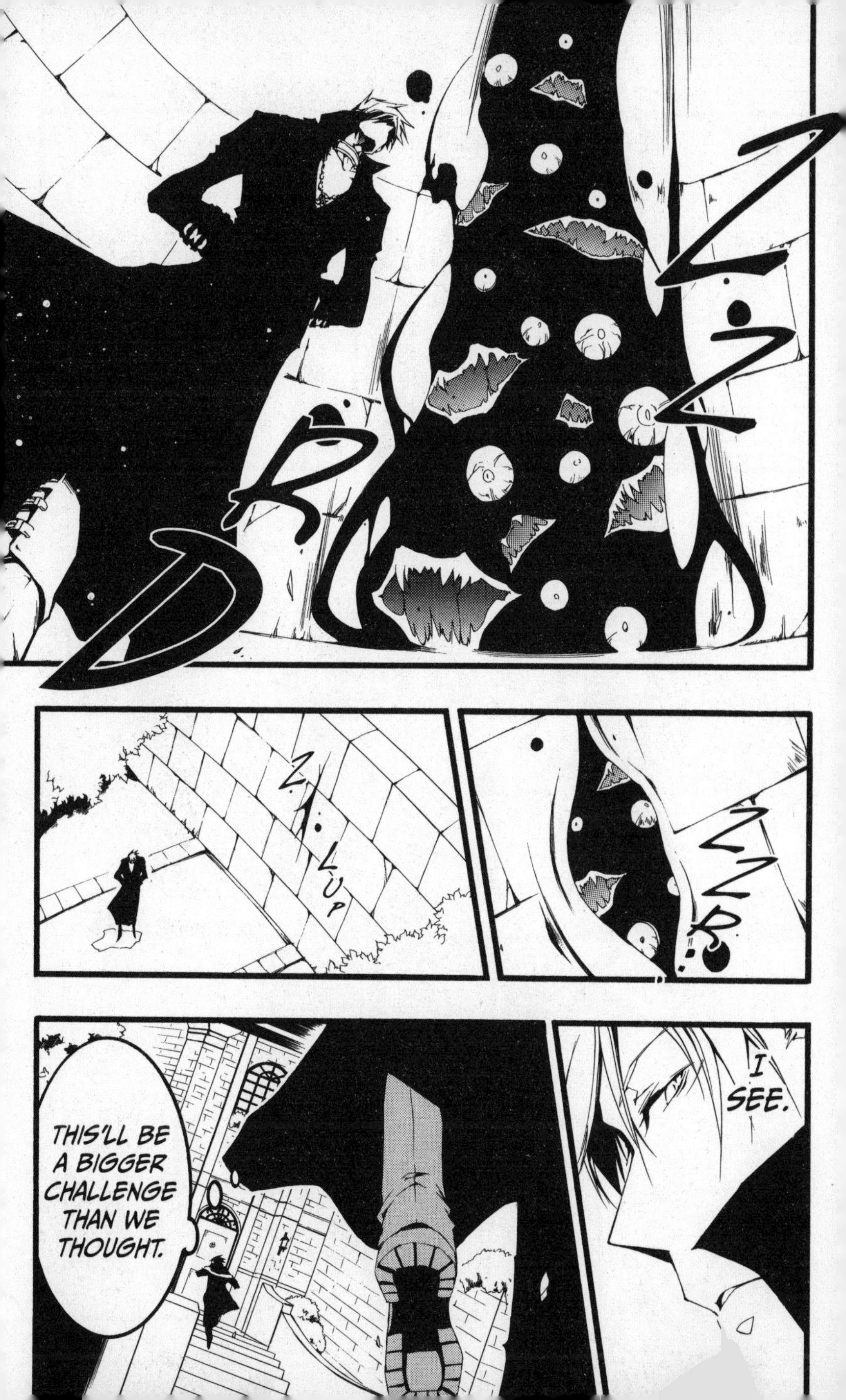
DR
ZZZR
ZLUP
I SEE.
THIS'LL BE A BIGGER CHALLENGE THAN WE THOUGHT.

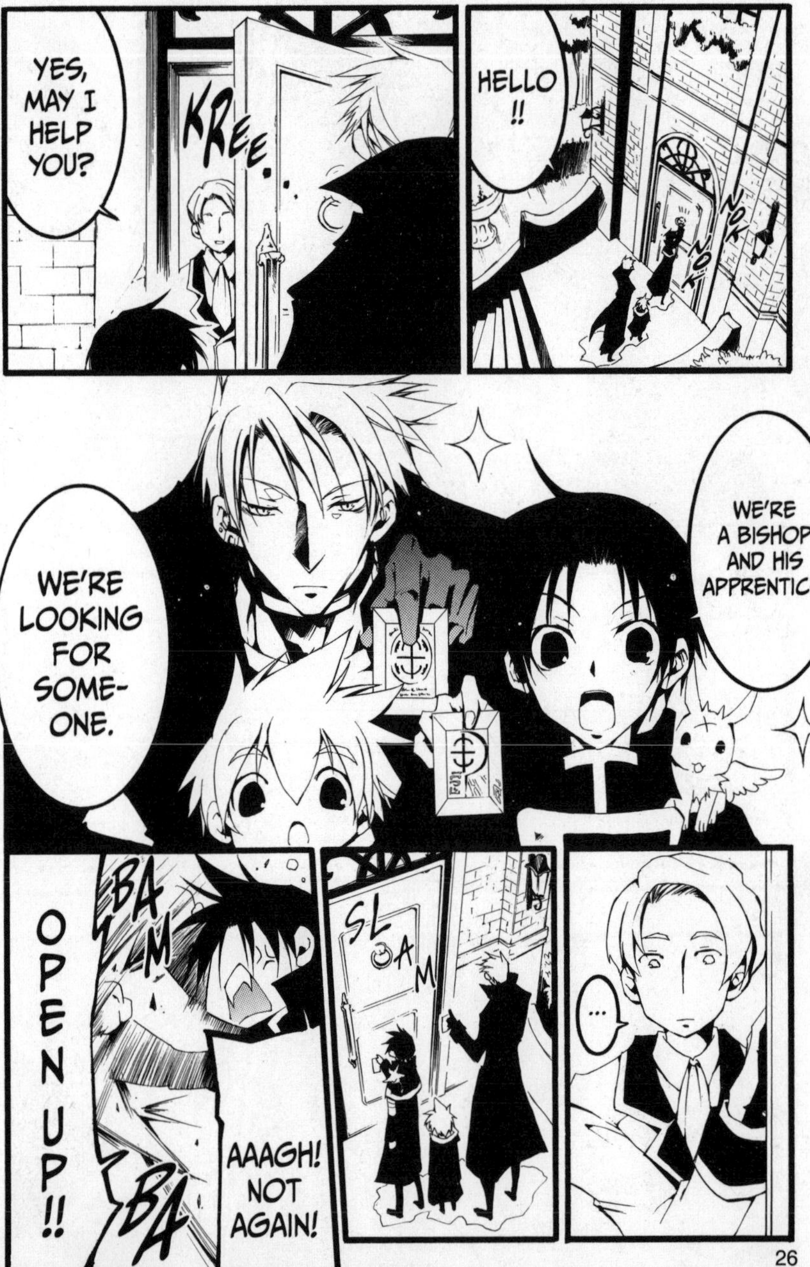
HELLO !!
NOK NOK
KREE.
YES, MAY I HELP YOU?
WE'RE A BISHOP AND HIS APPRENTICE.
WE'RE LOOKING FOR SOME-ONE.
...
SLAM
BAM
OPEN UP!!
AAAGH! NOT AGAIN!
BAM

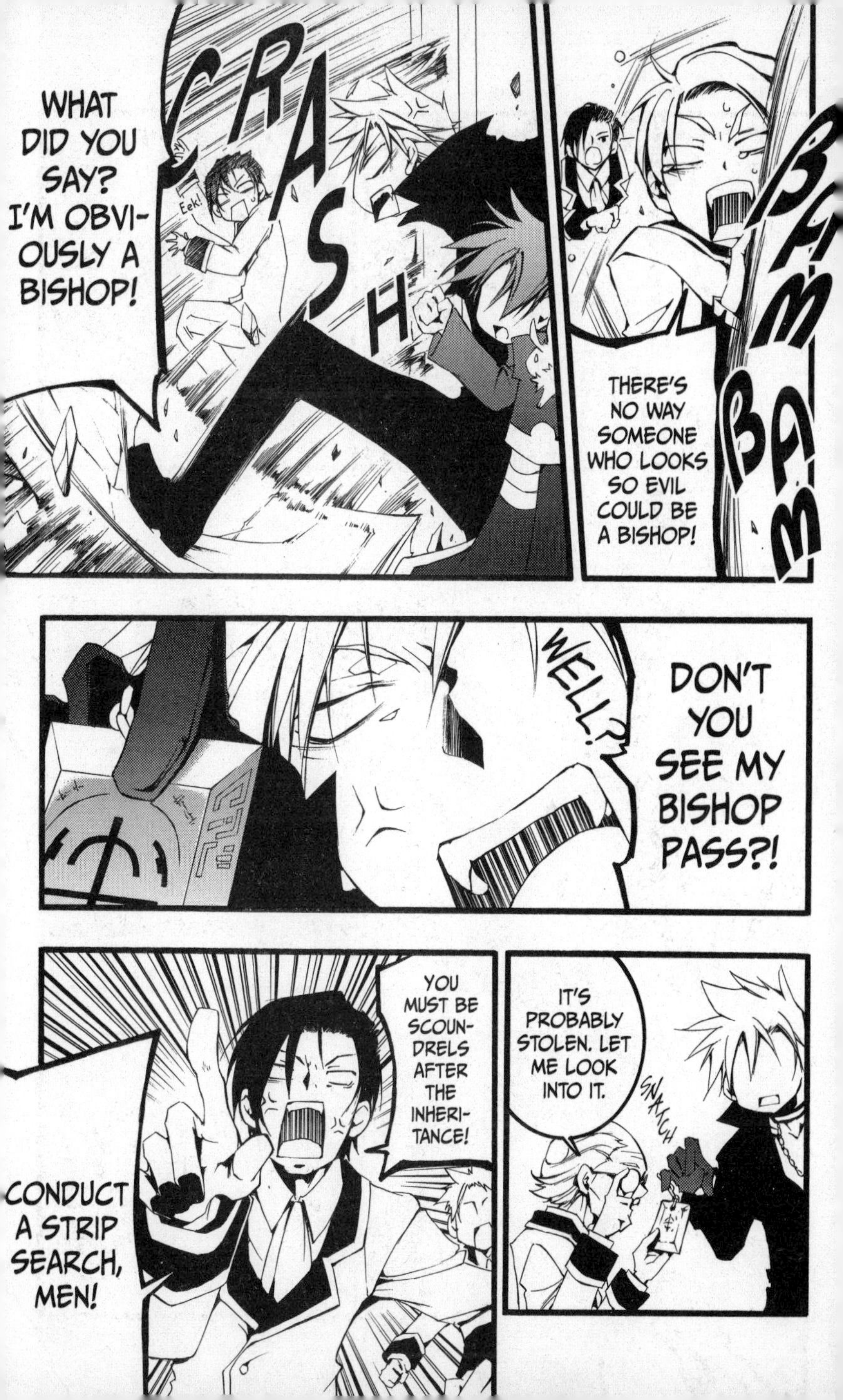
BAM BAM
THERE'S NO WAY SOMEONE WHO LOOKS SO EVIL COULD BE A BISHOP!
CRASH
Eek!
WHAT DID YOU SAY? I'M OBVI-OUSLY A BISHOP!
WELL?!
DON'T YOU SEE MY BISHOP PASS?!
IT'S PROBABLY STOLEN. LET ME LOOK INTO IT.
SNATCH
YOU MUST BE SCOUN-DRELS AFTER THE INHERI-TANCE!
CONDUCT A STRIP SEARCH, MEN!

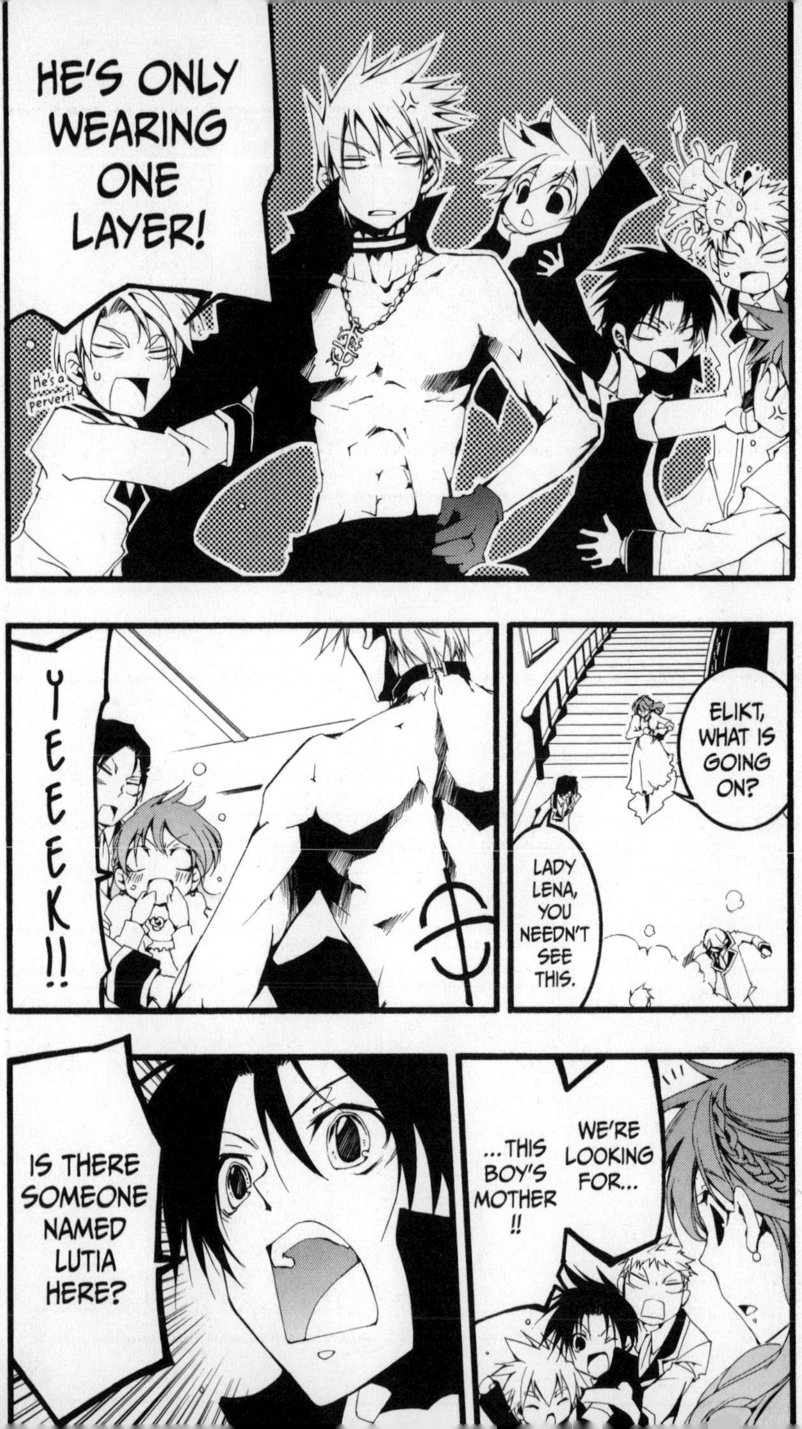
HE'S ONLY WEARING ONE LAYER!
He's a pervert!
ELIKT, WHAT IS GOING ON?
LADY LENA, YOU NEEDN'T SEE THIS.
YEEEEK!!
WE'RE LOOKING FOR...
...THIS BOY'S MOTHER!!
IS THERE SOMEONE NAMED LUTIA HERE?

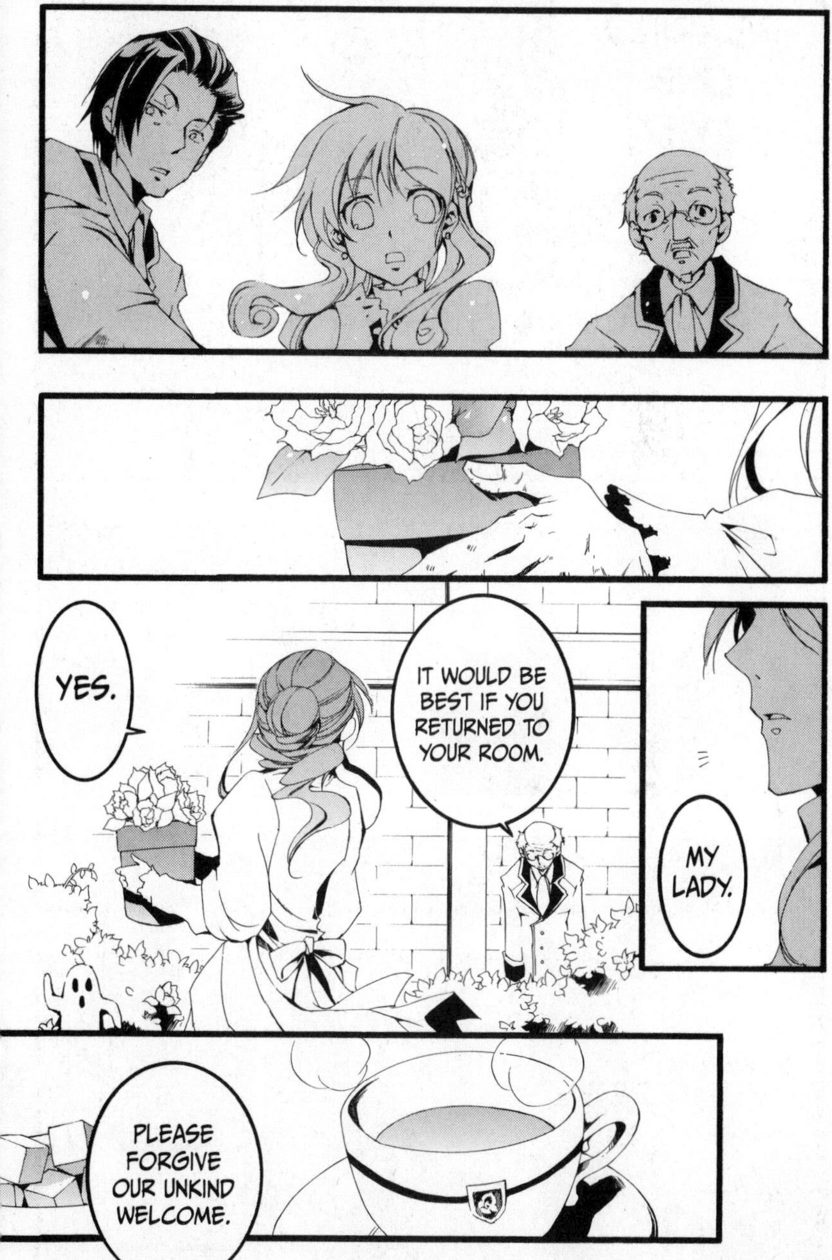
MY LADY.
IT WOULD BE BEST IF YOU RETURNED TO YOUR ROOM.
YES.
PLEASE FORGIVE OUR UNKIND WELCOME.

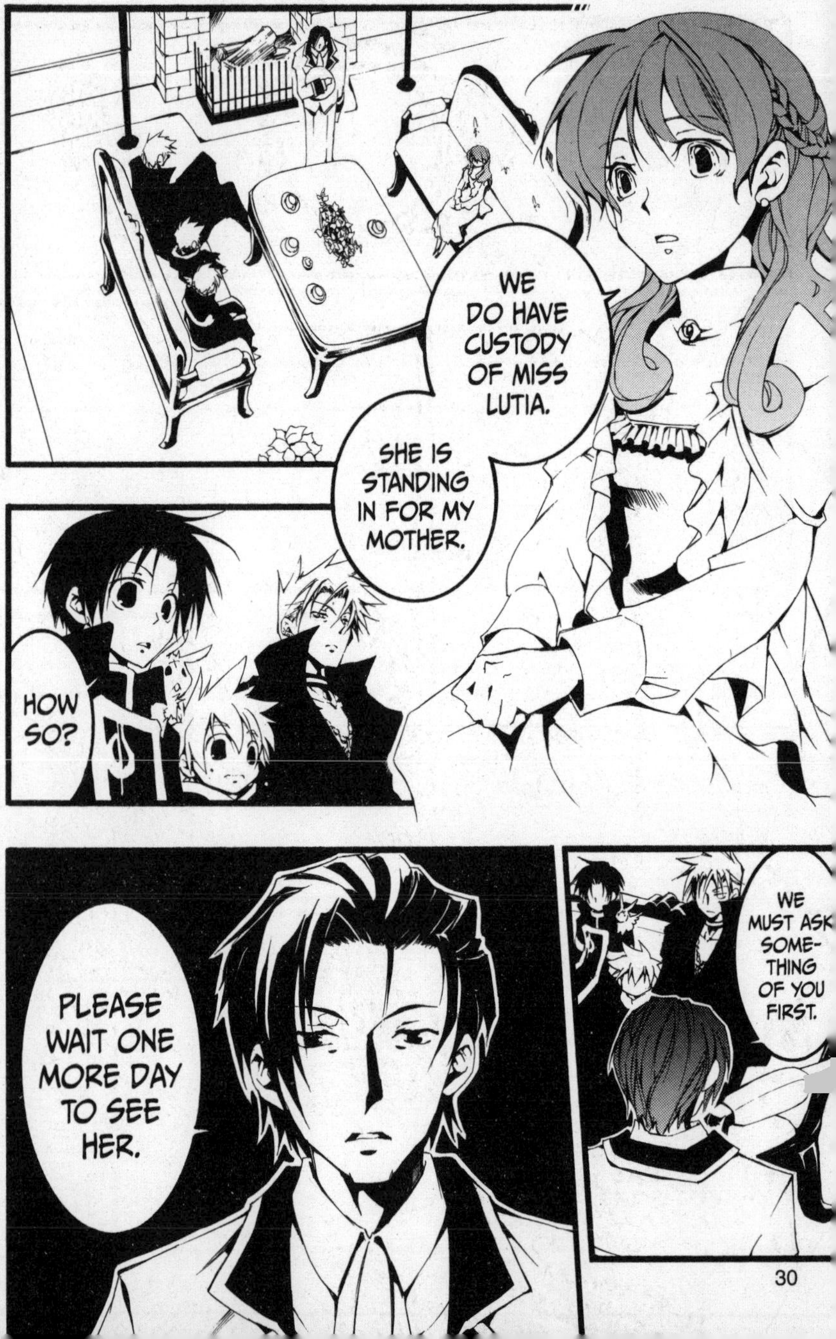
WE DO HAVE CUSTODY OF MISS LUTIA.
SHE IS STANDING IN FOR MY MOTHER.
HOW SO?
WE MUST ASK SOME-THING OF YOU FIRST.
PLEASE WAIT ONE MORE DAY TO SEE HER.

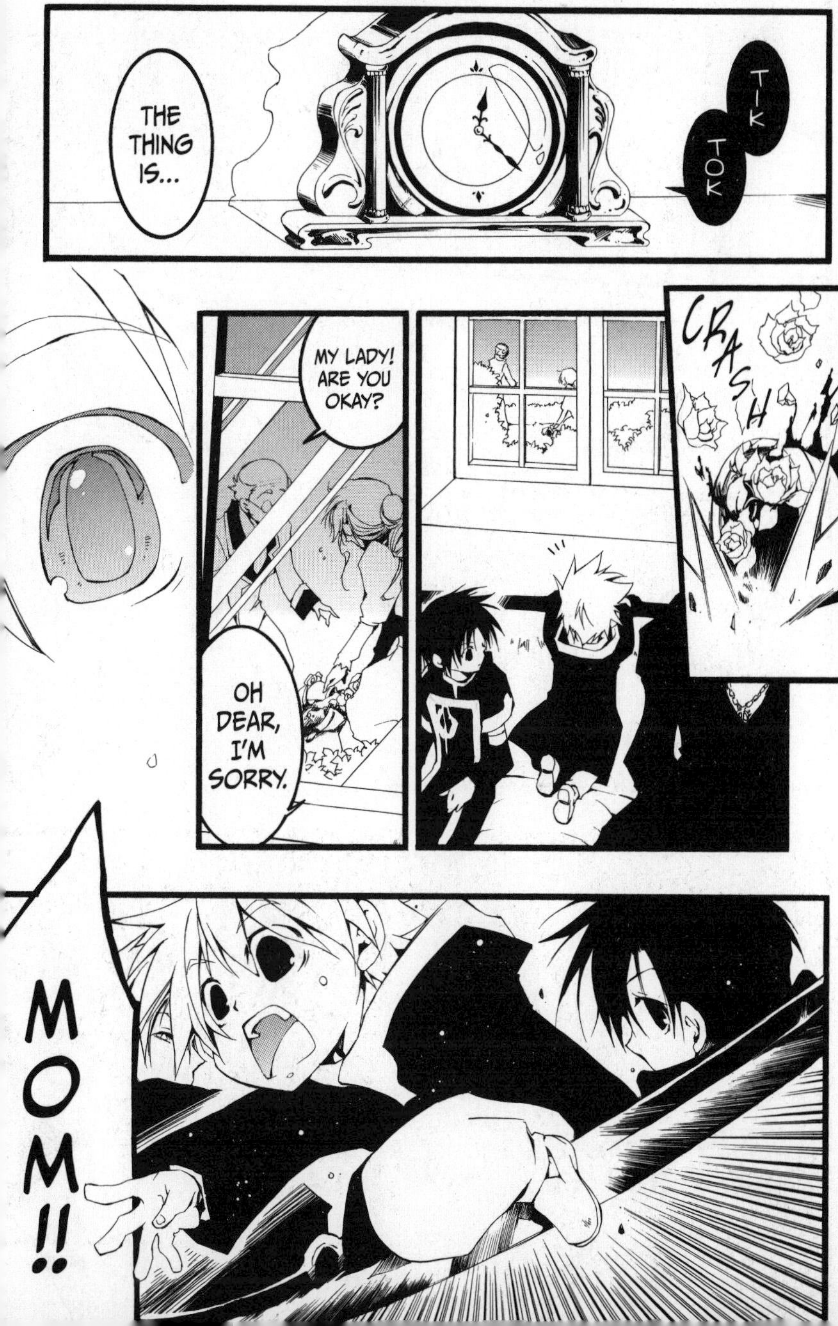
TIK
TOK
THE THING IS...
CRASH
MY LADY! ARE YOU OKAY?
OH DEAR, I'M SORRY.
MOM!!

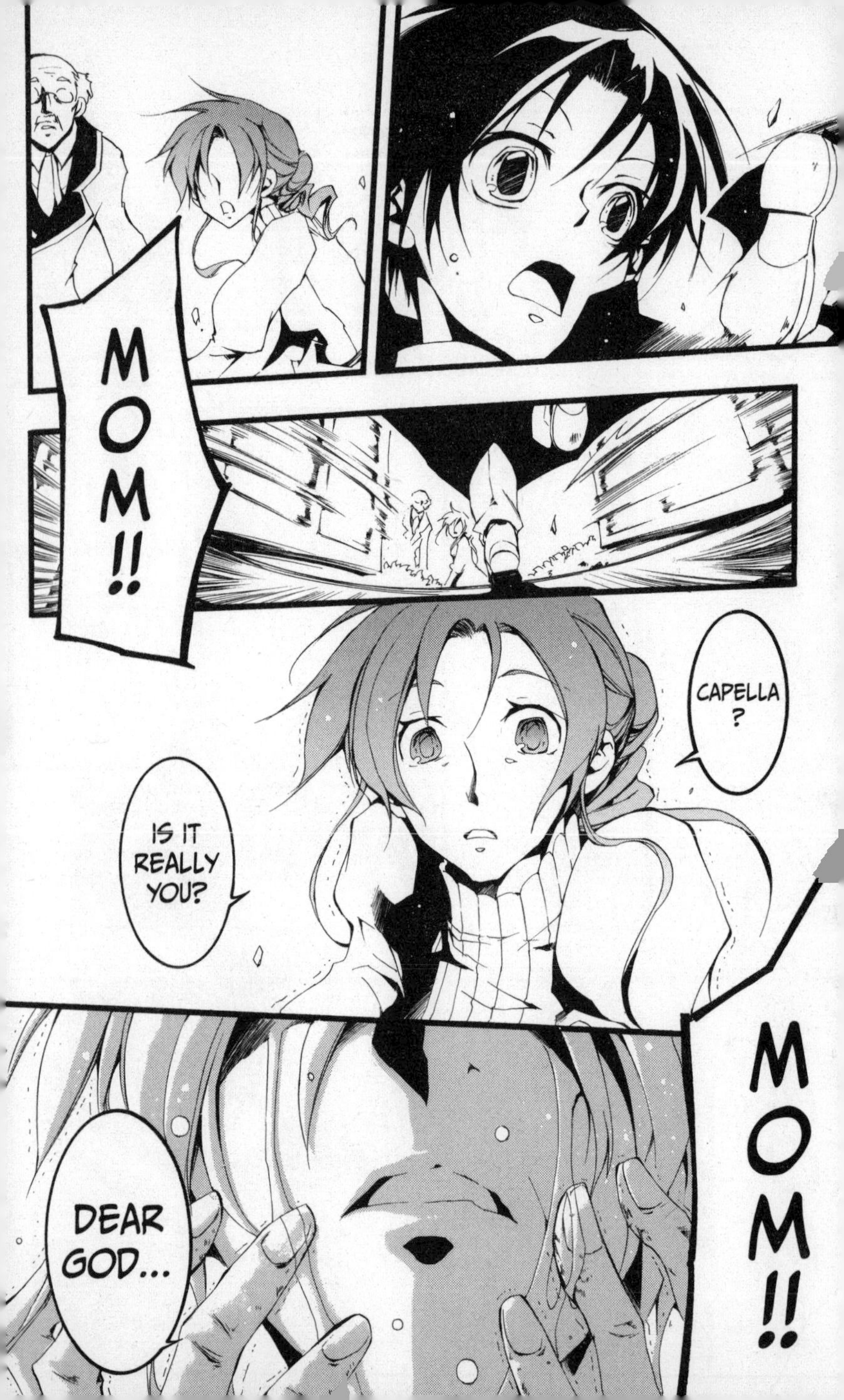
MOM!!
CAPELLA?
IS IT REALLY YOU?
MOM!!
DEAR GOD...

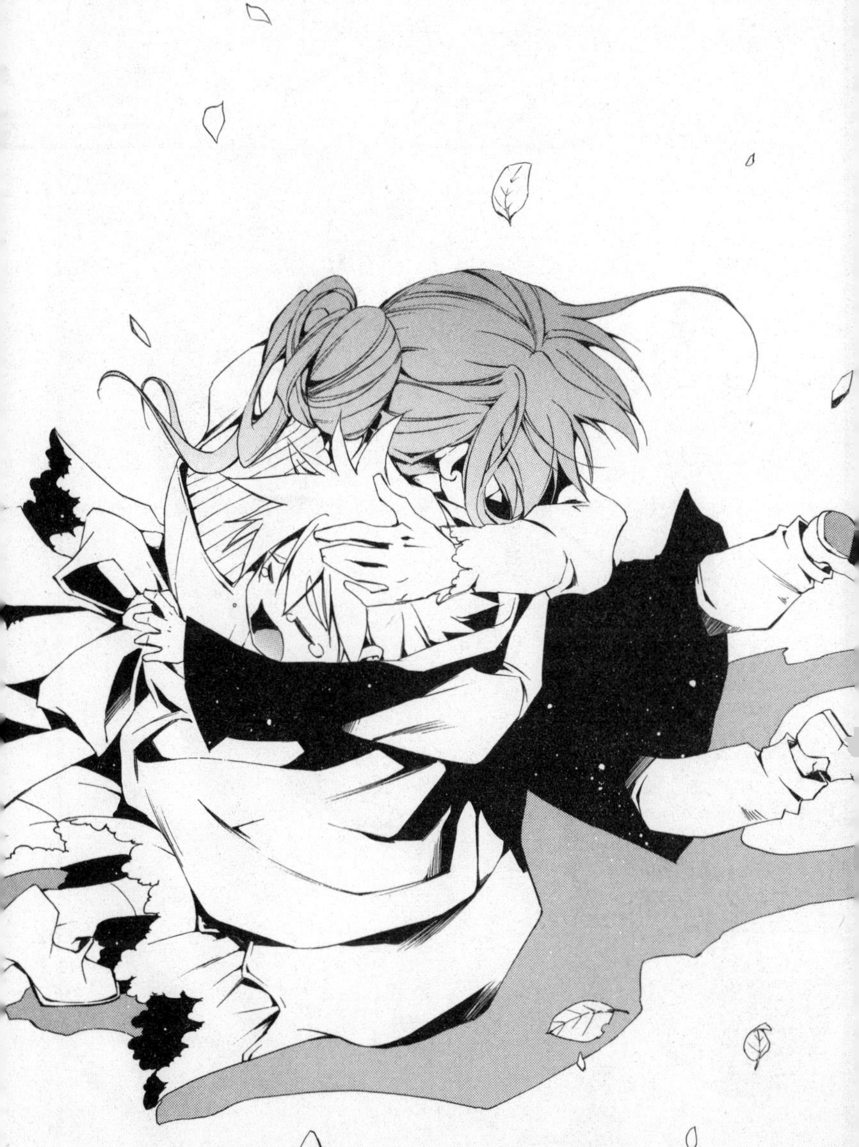

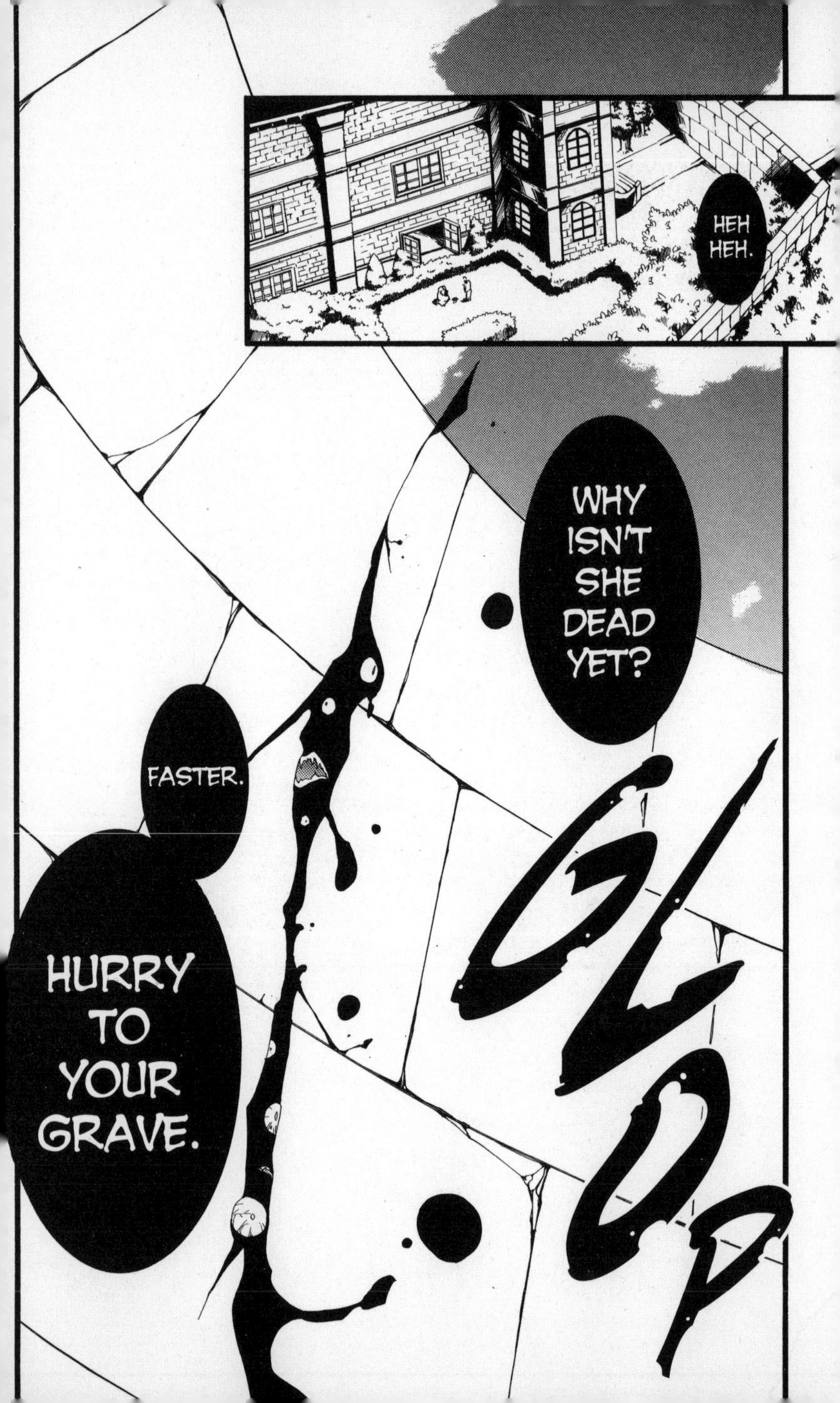
HEH HEH.
WHY ISN'T SHE DEAD YET?
FASTER.
HURRY TO YOUR GRAVE.

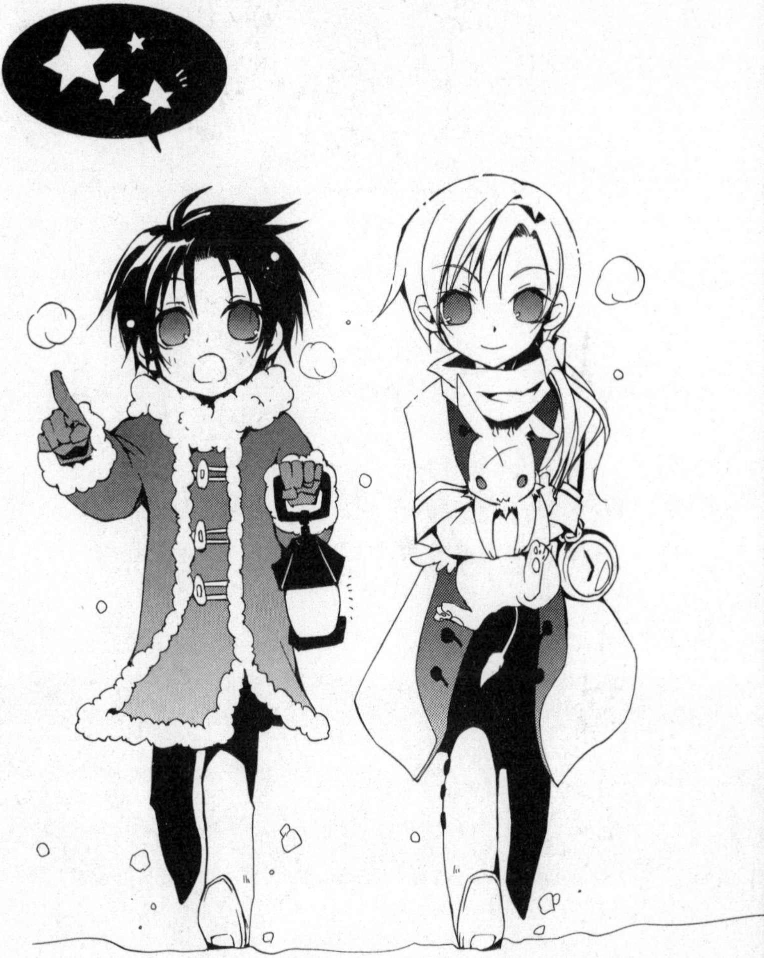

Kapitel.56
“The Day That Never Ends”

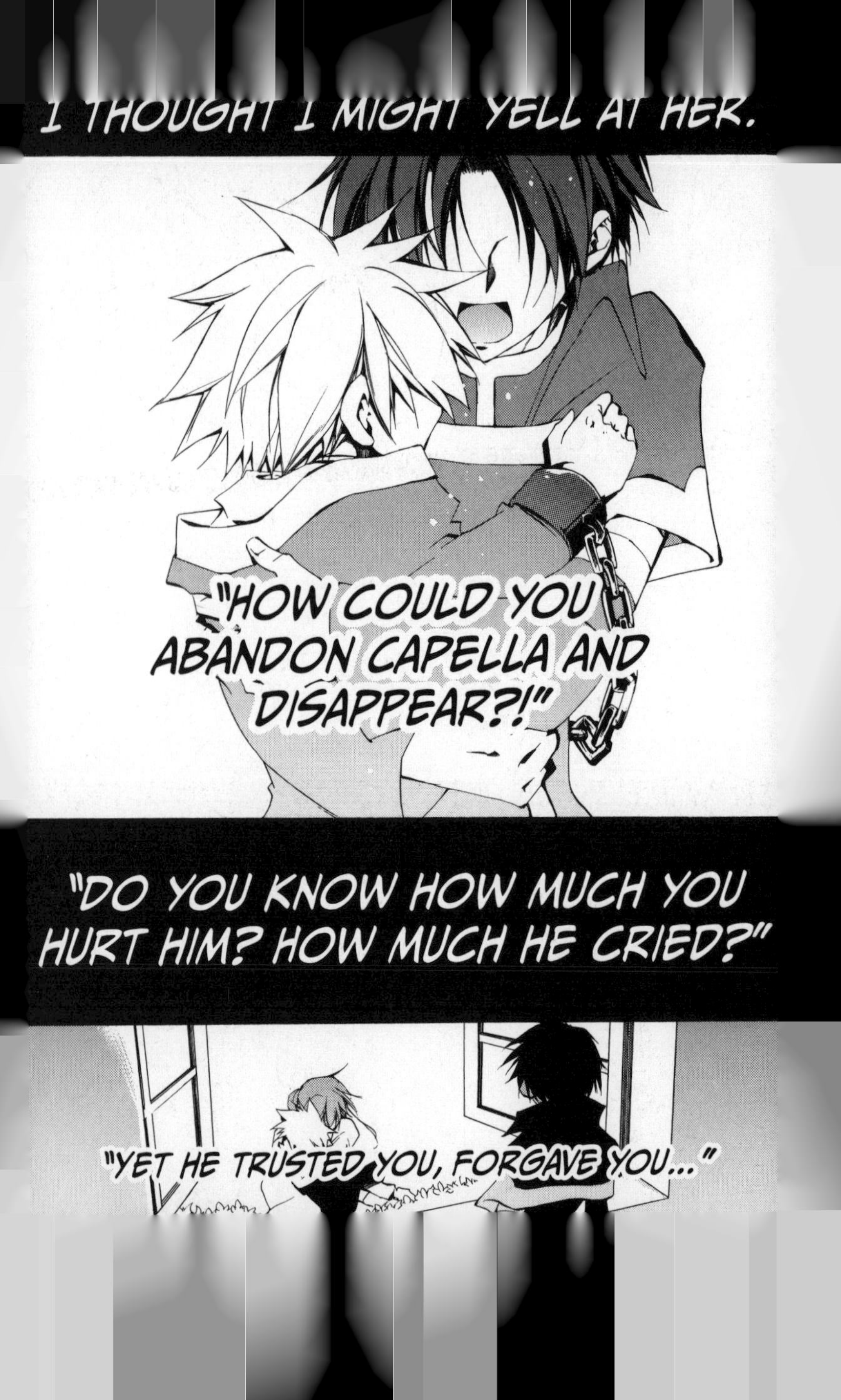
I THOUGHT I MIGHT YELL AT HER.
"HOW COULD YOU ABANDON CAPELLA AND DISAPPEAR?!"
"DO YOU KNOW HOW MUCH YOU HURT HIM? HOW MUCH HE CRIED?"
"YET HE TRUSTED YOU, FORGAVE YOU..."

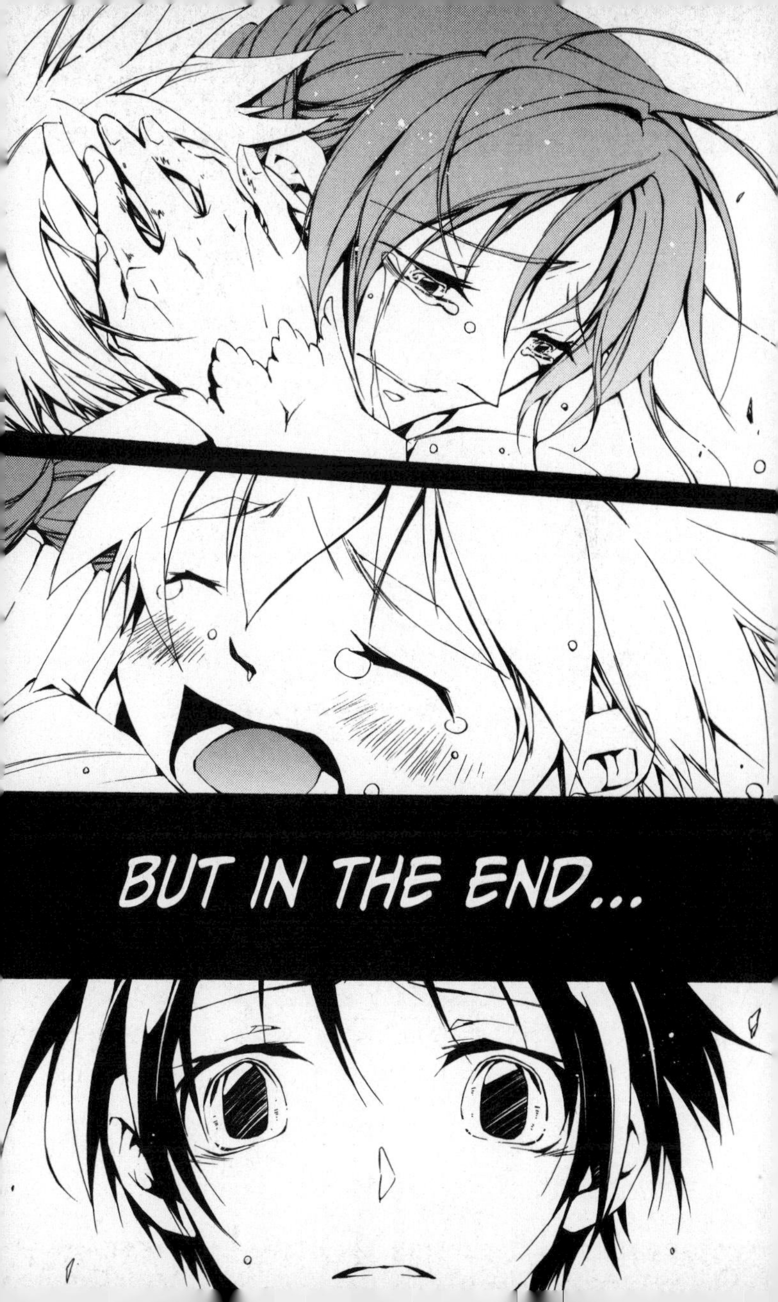
BUT IN THE END...

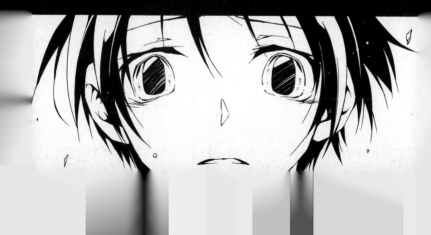

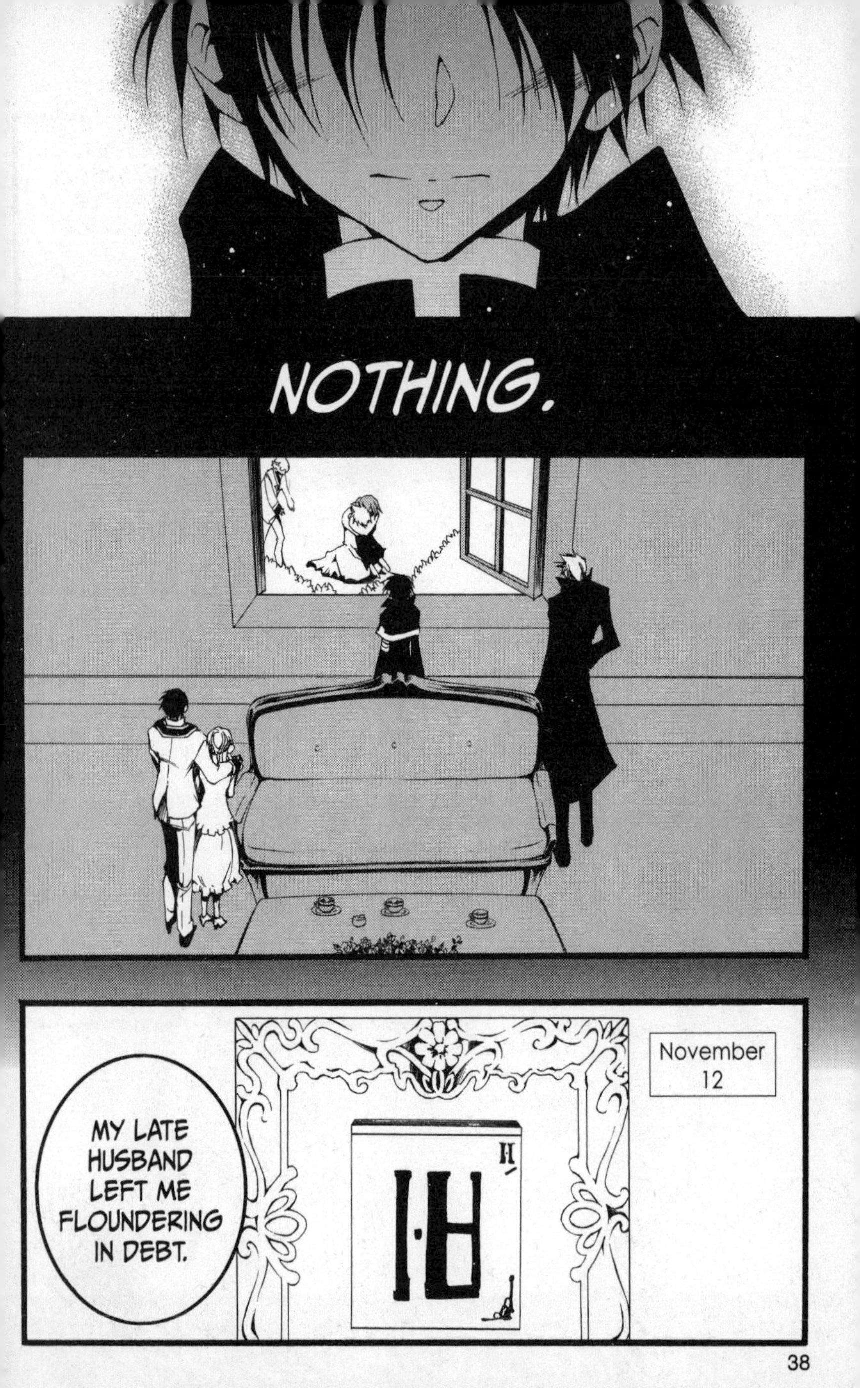
NOTHING.
November 12
MY LATE HUSBAND LEFT ME FLOUNDERING IN DEBT.

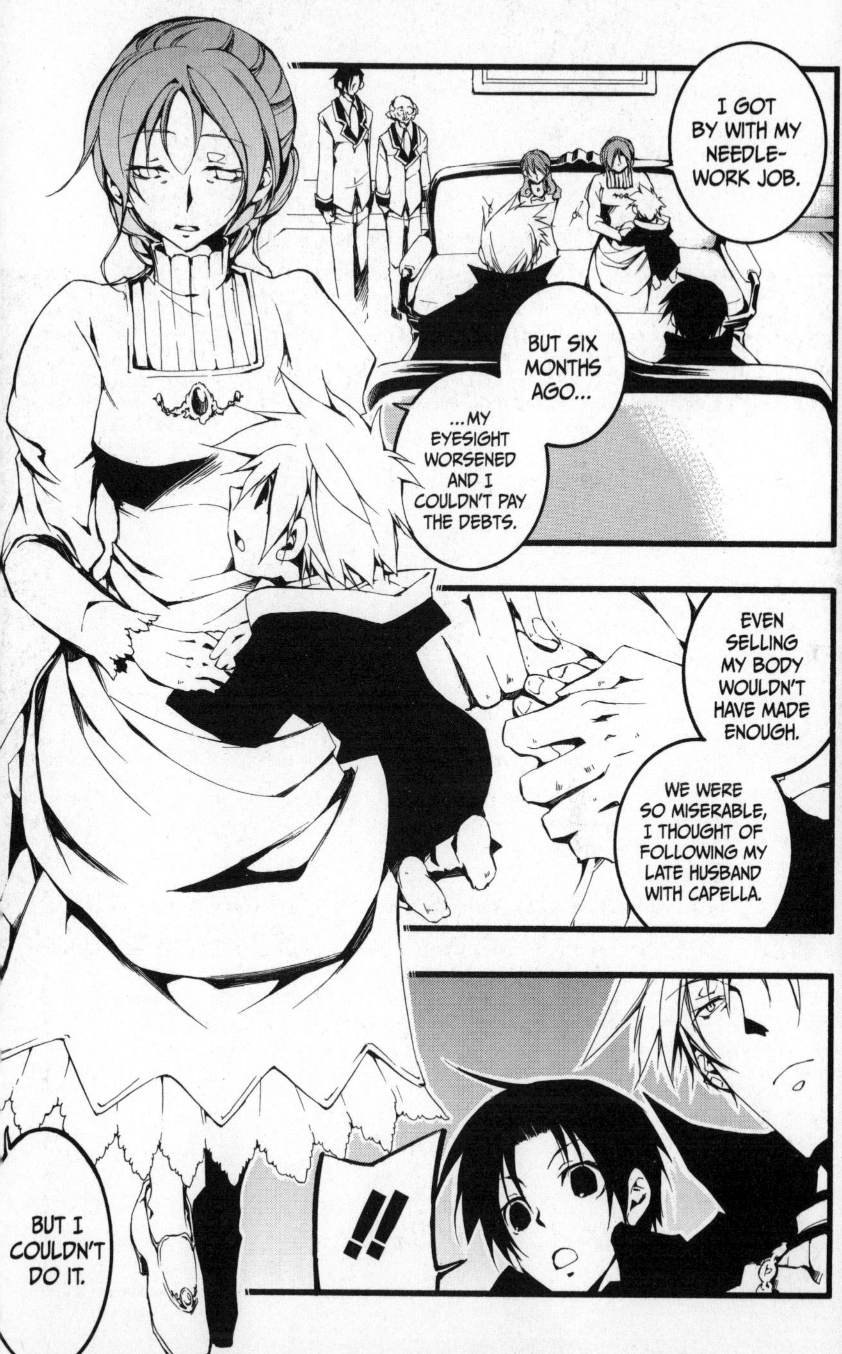
I GOT BY WITH MY NEEDLE-WORK JOB.
BUT SIX MONTHS AGO...
...MY EYESIGHT WORSENED AND I COULDN'T PAY THE DEBTS.
EVEN SELLING MY BODY WOULDN'T HAVE MADE ENOUGH.
WE WERE SO MISERABLE, I THOUGHT OF FOLLOWING MY LATE HUSBAND WITH CAPELLA.
!!
BUT I COULDN'T DO IT.

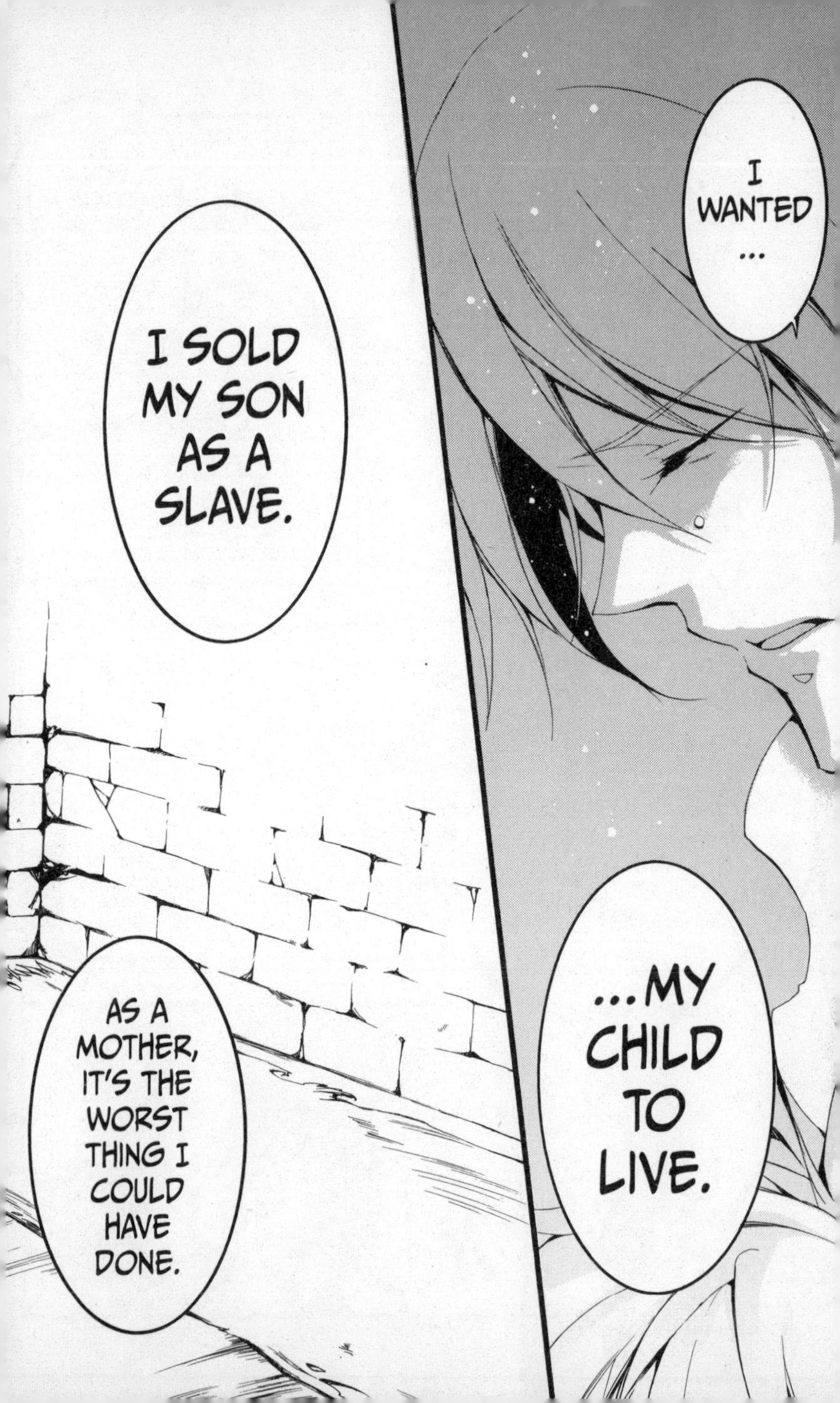
I WANTED ...
...MY CHILD TO LIVE.
I SOLD MY SON AS A SLAVE.
AS A MOTHER, IT'S THE WORST THING I COULD HAVE DONE.

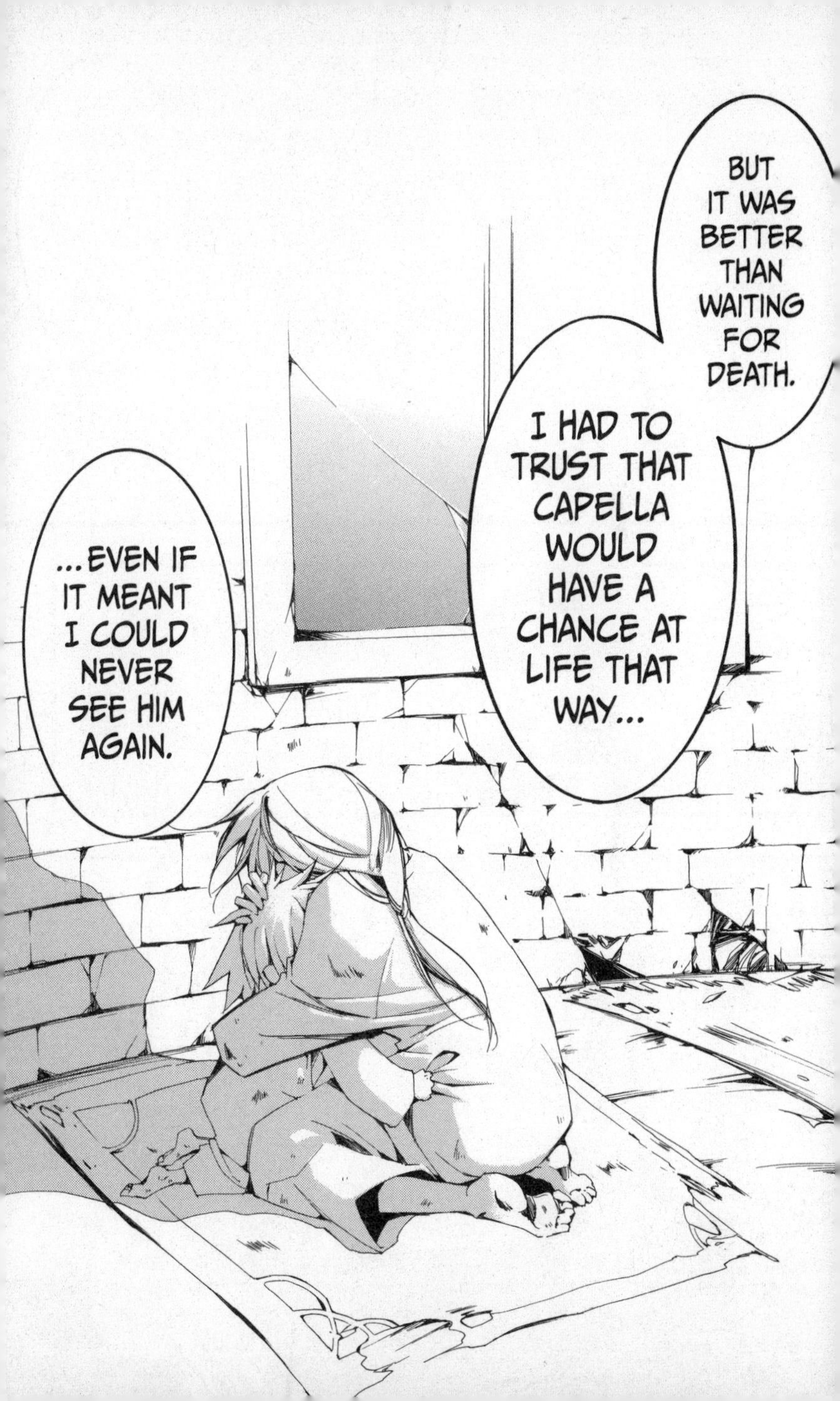
BUT IT WAS BETTER THAN WAITING FOR DEATH.
I HAD TO TRUST THAT CAPELLA WOULD HAVE A CHANCE AT LIFE THAT WAY...
...EVEN IF IT MEANT I COULD NEVER SEE HIM AGAIN.

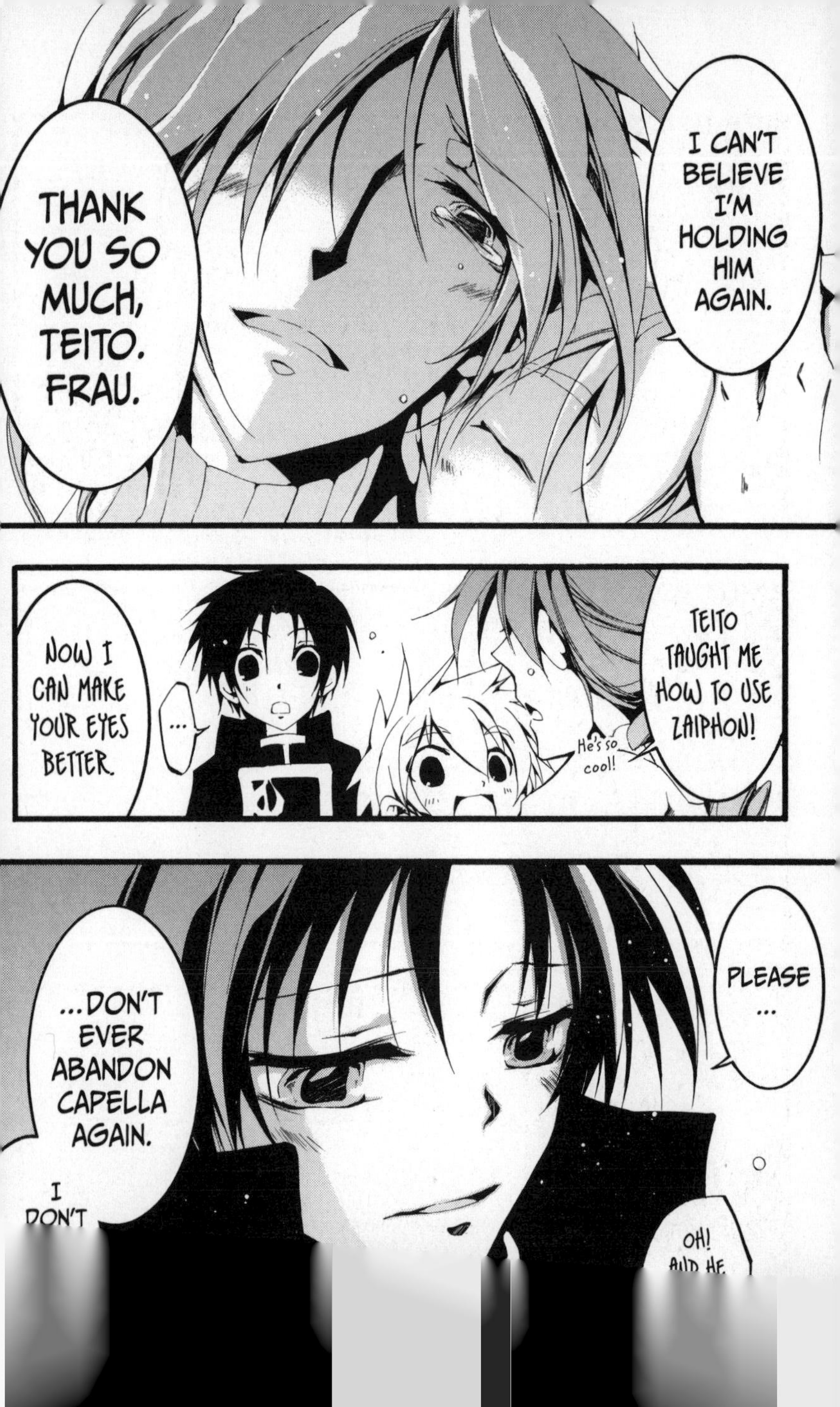
I CAN'T BELIEVE I'M HOLDING HIM AGAIN.
THANK YOU SO MUCH, TEITO. FRAU.
TEITO TAUGHT ME HOW TO USE ZAIPHON!
He's so cool!
NOW I CAN MAKE YOUR EYES BETTER.
...
PLEASE ...
...DON'T EVER ABANDON CAPELLA AGAIN.
OH! AND HE [redacted]
I DON'T [redacted]

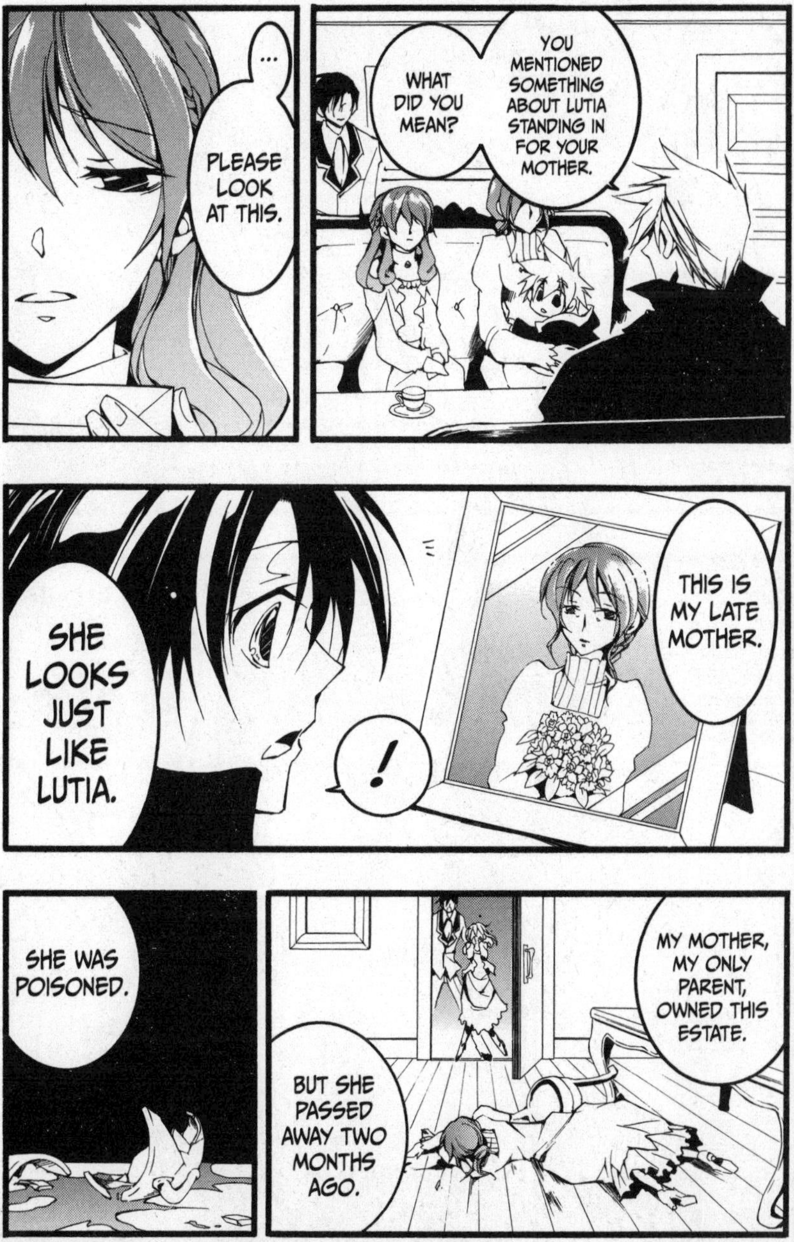
YOU MENTIONED SOMETHING ABOUT LUTIA STANDING IN FOR YOUR MOTHER.
WHAT DID YOU MEAN?
...
PLEASE LOOK AT THIS.
THIS IS MY LATE MOTHER.
!
SHE LOOKS JUST LIKE LUTIA.
MY MOTHER, MY ONLY PARENT, OWNED THIS ESTATE.
BUT SHE PASSED AWAY TWO MONTHS AGO.
SHE WAS POISONED.

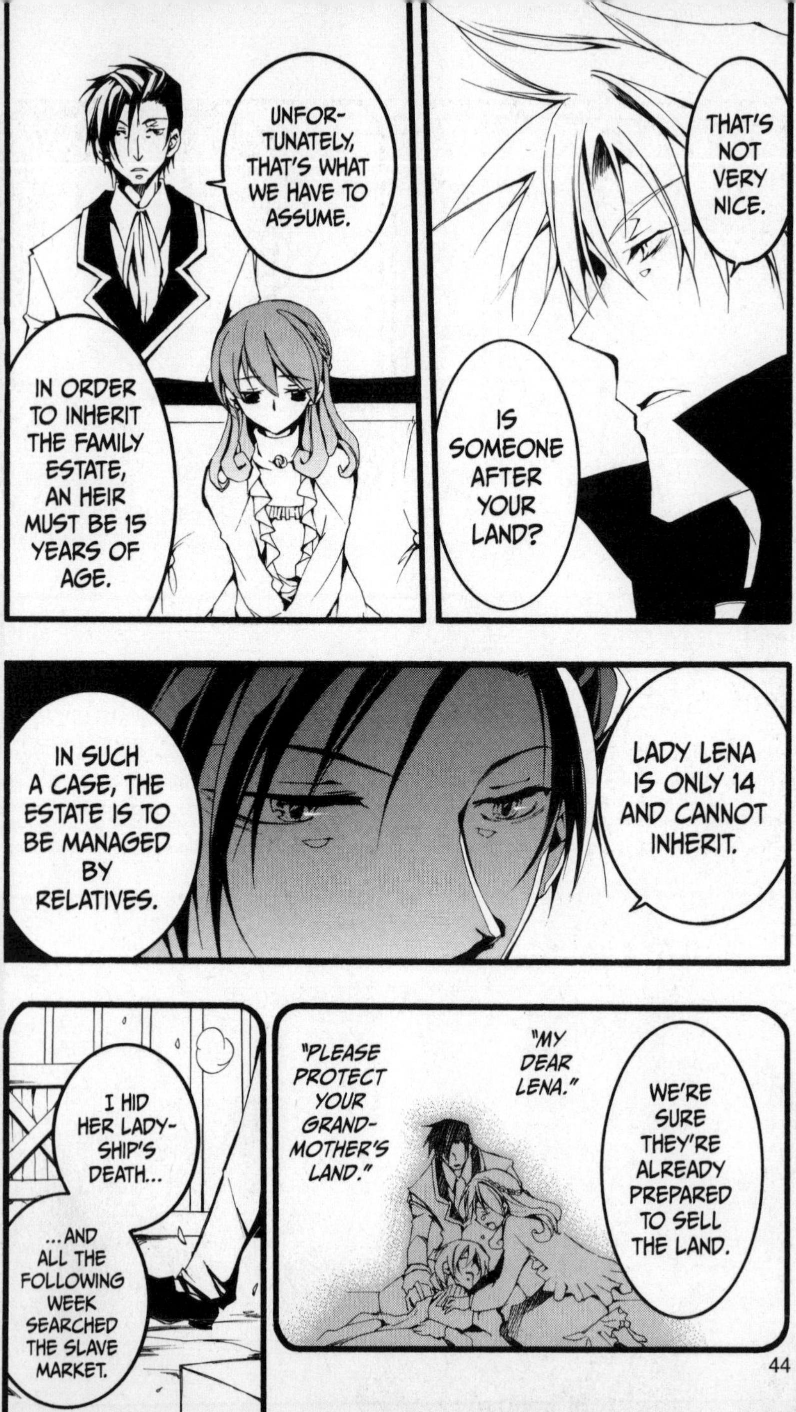

THAT'S NOT VERY NICE.
IS SOMEONE AFTER YOUR LAND?
UNFOR-TUNATELY, THAT'S WHAT WE HAVE TO ASSUME.
IN ORDER TO INHERIT THE FAMILY ESTATE, AN HEIR MUST BE 15 YEARS OF AGE.
LADY LENA IS ONLY 14 AND CANNOT INHERIT.
IN SUCH A CASE, THE ESTATE IS TO BE MANAGED BY RELATIVES.
WE'RE SURE THEY'RE ALREADY PREPARED TO SELL THE LAND.
"MY DEAR LENA."
"PLEASE PROTECT YOUR GRAND-MOTHER'S LAND."
I HID HER LADY-SHIP'S DEATH...
...AND ALL THE FOLLOWING WEEK SEARCHED THE SLAVE MARKET.

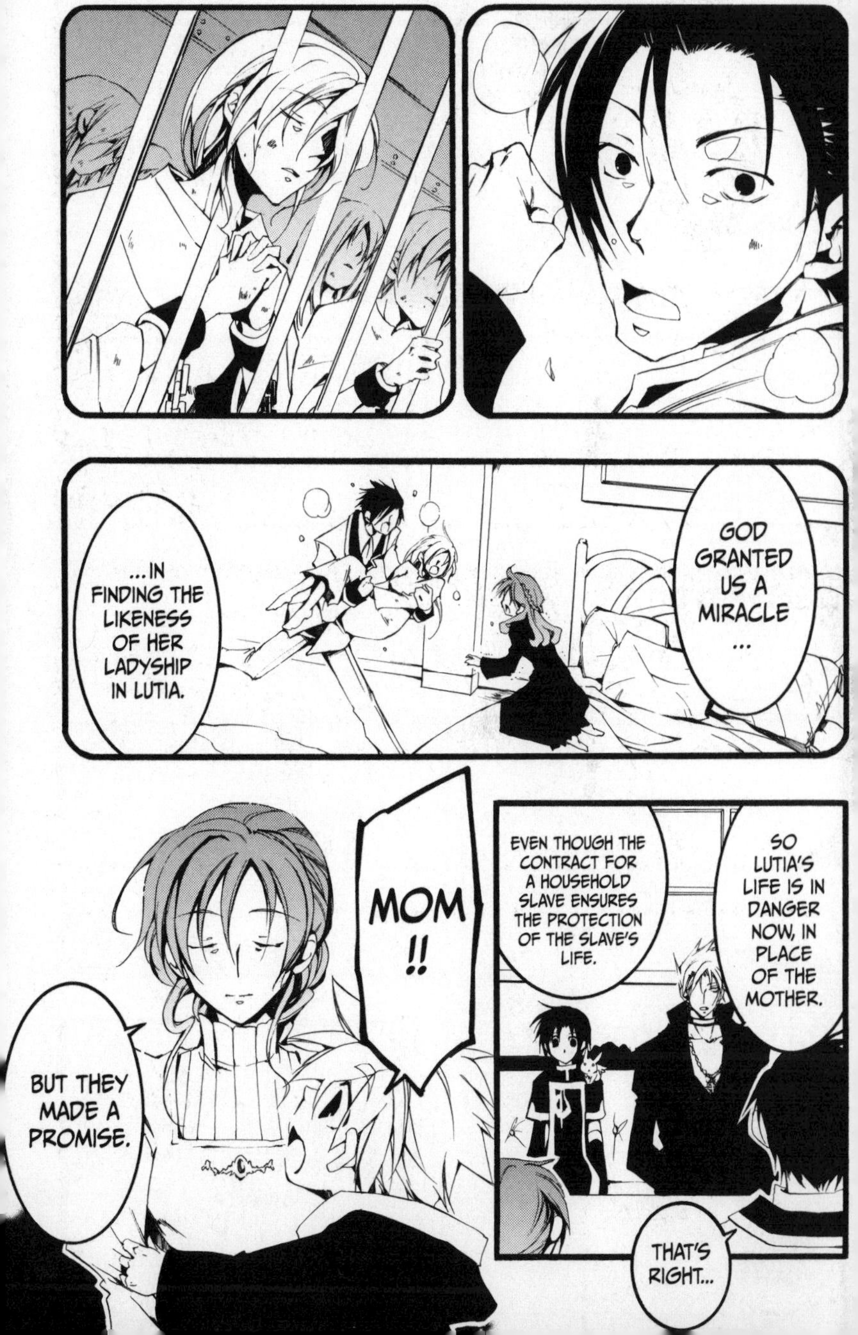
GOD GRANTED US A MIRACLE ...
...IN FINDING THE LIKENESS OF HER LADYSHIP IN LUTIA.
SO LUTIA'S LIFE IS IN DANGER NOW, IN PLACE OF THE MOTHER.
THAT'S RIGHT...
EVEN THOUGH THE CONTRACT FOR A HOUSEHOLD SLAVE ENSURES THE PROTECTION OF THE SLAVE'S LIFE.
MOM !!
BUT THEY MADE A PROMISE.

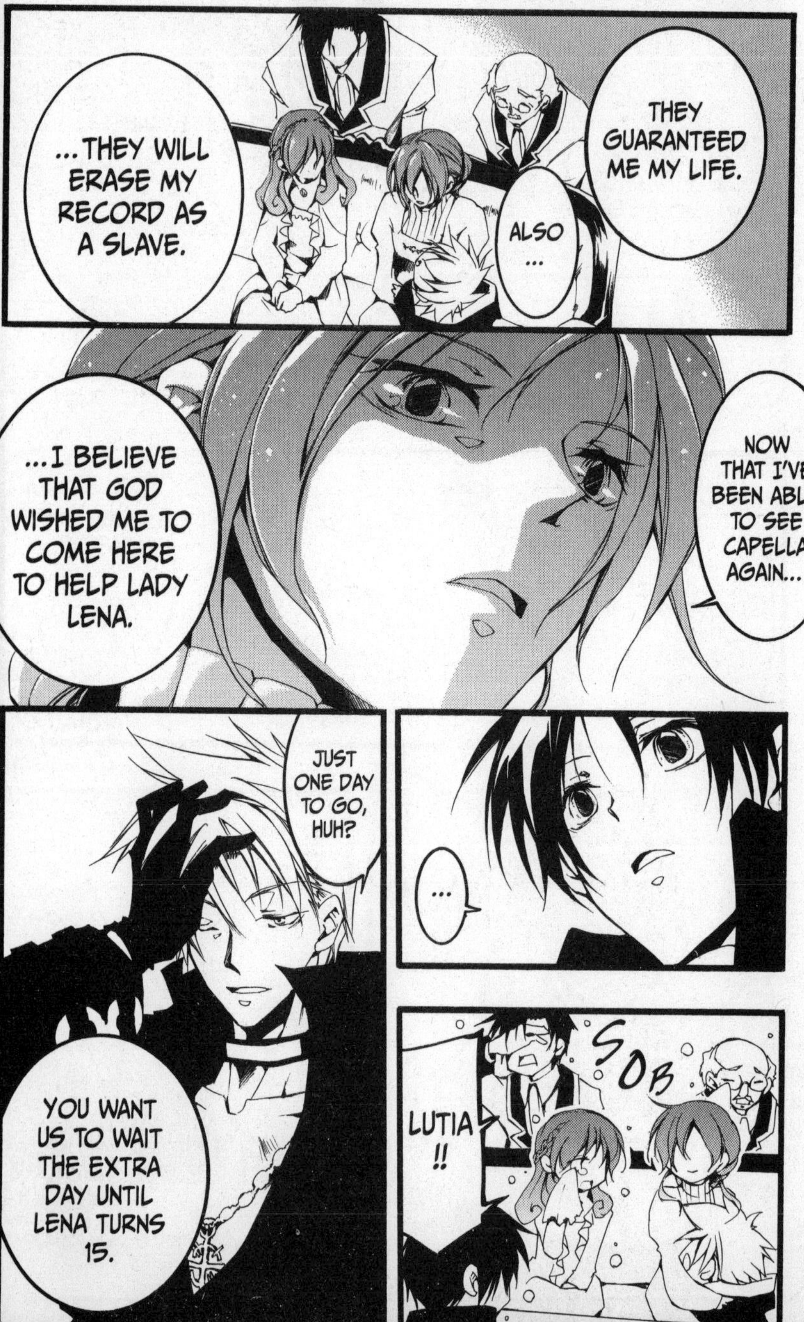

THEY GUARANTEED ME MY LIFE.
ALSO ...
...THEY WILL ERASE MY RECORD AS A SLAVE.
NOW THAT I'VE BEEN ABLE TO SEE CAPELLA AGAIN...
...I BELIEVE THAT GOD WISHED ME TO COME HERE TO HELP LADY LENA.
...
SOB
LUTIA !!
JUST ONE DAY TO GO, HUH?
YOU WANT US TO WAIT THE EXTRA DAY UNTIL LENA TURNS 15.

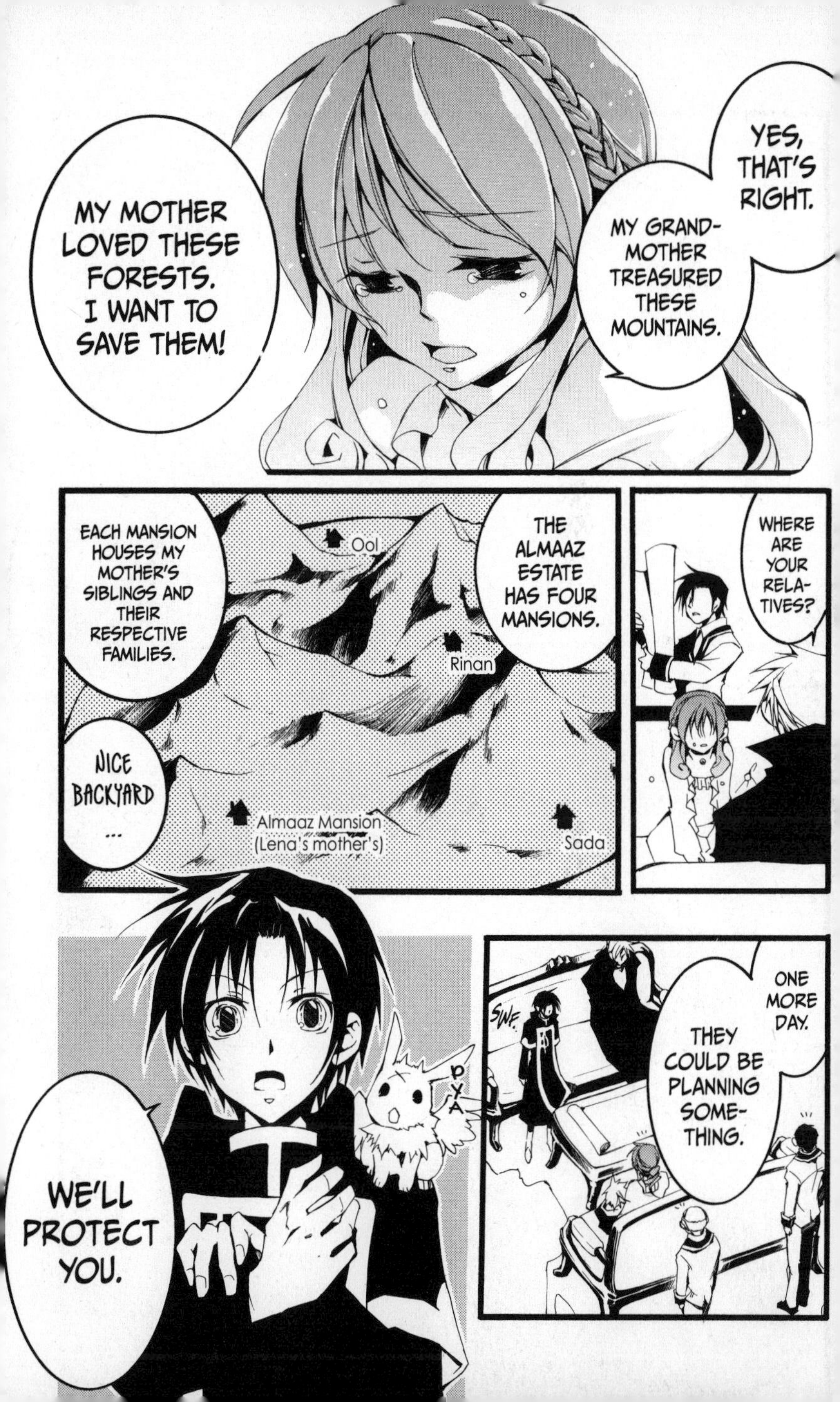
YES, THAT'S RIGHT.
MY GRAND-MOTHER TREASURED THESE MOUNTAINS.
MY MOTHER LOVED THESE FORESTS. I WANT TO SAVE THEM!
WHERE ARE YOUR RELA-TIVES?
THE ALMAAZ ESTATE HAS FOUR MANSIONS.
EACH MANSION HOUSES MY MOTHER'S SIBLINGS AND THEIR RESPECTIVE FAMILIES.
Ool
Rinan
Almaaz Mansion (Lena's mother's)
Sada
NICE BACKYARD ...
ONE MORE DAY.
THEY COULD BE PLANNING SOME-THING.
SWF
PYA
WE'LL PROTECT YOU.

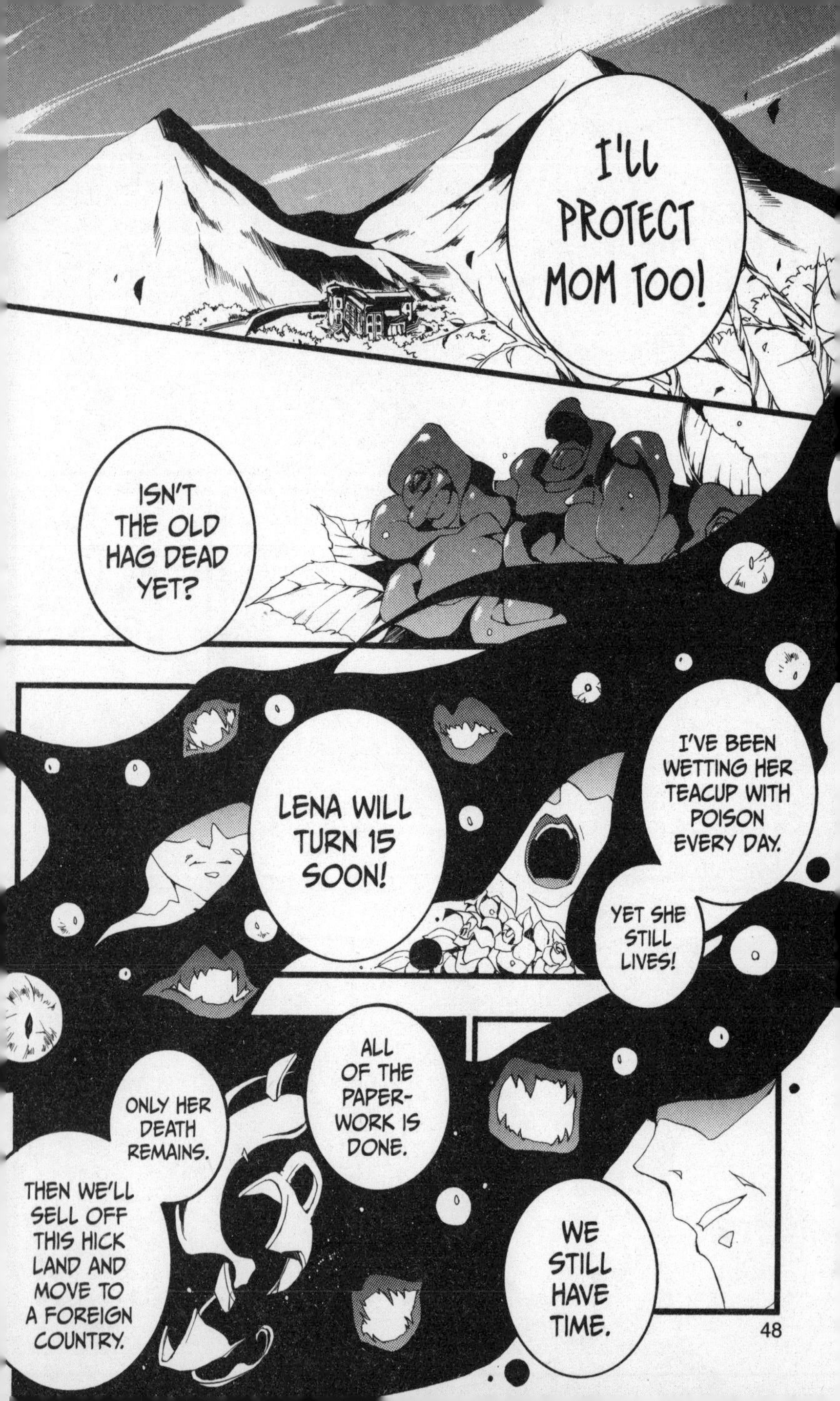
I'LL PROTECT MOM TOO!
ISN'T THE OLD HAG DEAD YET?
I'VE BEEN WETTING HER TEACUP WITH POISON EVERY DAY.
YET SHE STILL LIVES!
LENA WILL TURN 15 SOON!
ALL OF THE PAPER-WORK IS DONE.
ONLY HER DEATH REMAINS.
THEN WE'LL SELL OFF THIS HICK LAND AND MOVE TO A FOREIGN COUNTRY.
WE STILL HAVE TIME.

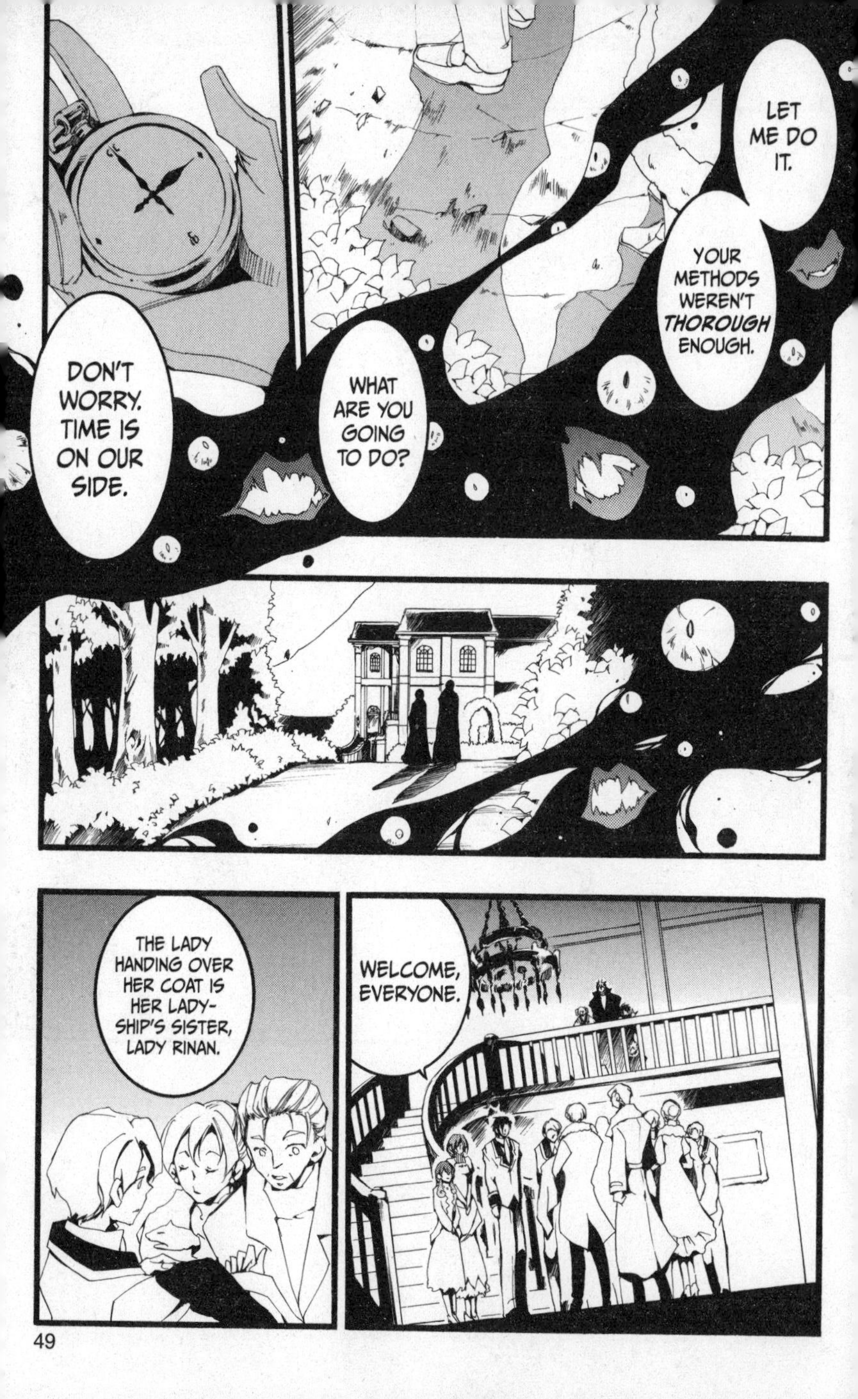
LET ME DO IT.
YOUR METHODS WEREN'T *THOROUGH* ENOUGH.
WHAT ARE YOU GOING TO DO?
DON'T WORRY. TIME IS ON OUR SIDE.
WELCOME, EVERYONE.
THE LADY HANDING OVER HER COAT IS HER LADY-SHIP'S SISTER, LADY RINAN.

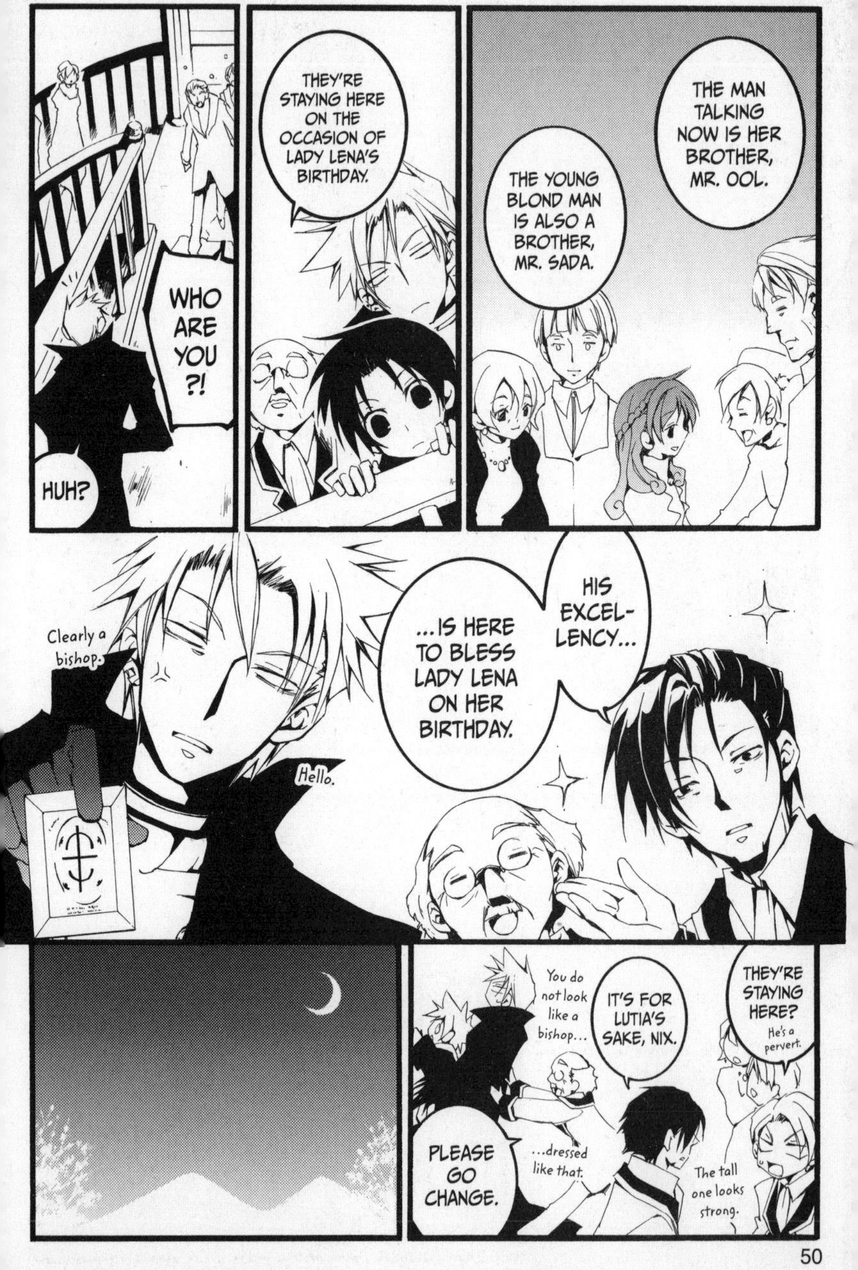
THE MAN TALKING NOW IS HER BROTHER, MR. OOL.
THE YOUNG BLOND MAN IS ALSO A BROTHER, MR. SADA.
THEY'RE STAYING HERE ON THE OCCASION OF LADY LENA'S BIRTHDAY.
WHO ARE YOU ?!
HUH?
HIS EXCEL-LENCY...
...IS HERE TO BLESS LADY LENA ON HER BIRTHDAY.
Hello.
Clearly a bishop.
THEY'RE STAYING HERE?
He's a pervert.
IT'S FOR LUTIA'S SAKE, NIX.
You do not look like a bishop...
...dressed like that.
The tall one looks strong.
PLEASE GO CHANGE.

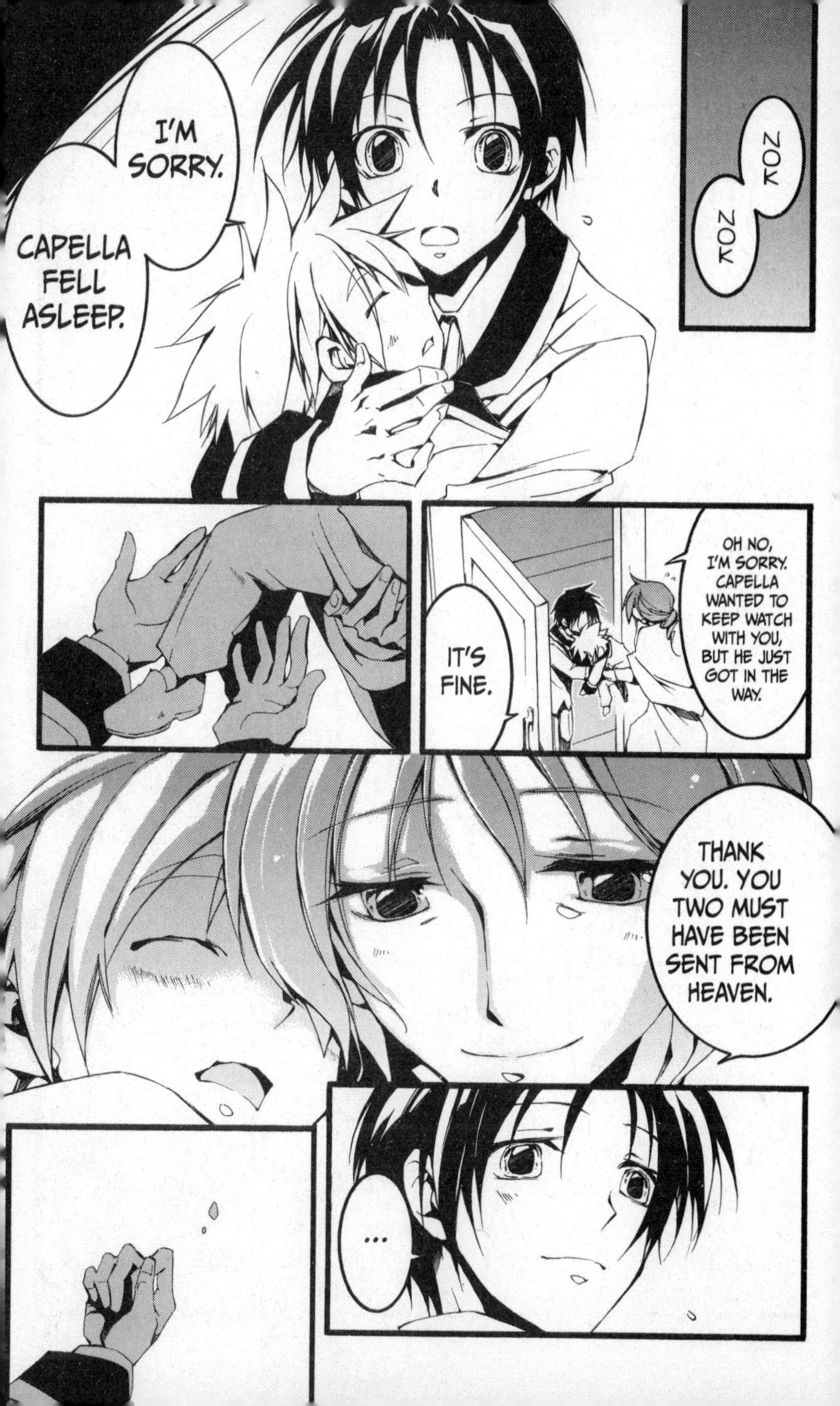
NOK NOK
I'M SORRY.
CAPELLA FELL ASLEEP.
OH NO, I'M SORRY. CAPELLA WANTED TO KEEP WATCH WITH YOU, BUT HE JUST GOT IN THE WAY.
IT'S FINE.
THANK YOU. YOU TWO MUST HAVE BEEN SENT FROM HEAVEN.
...

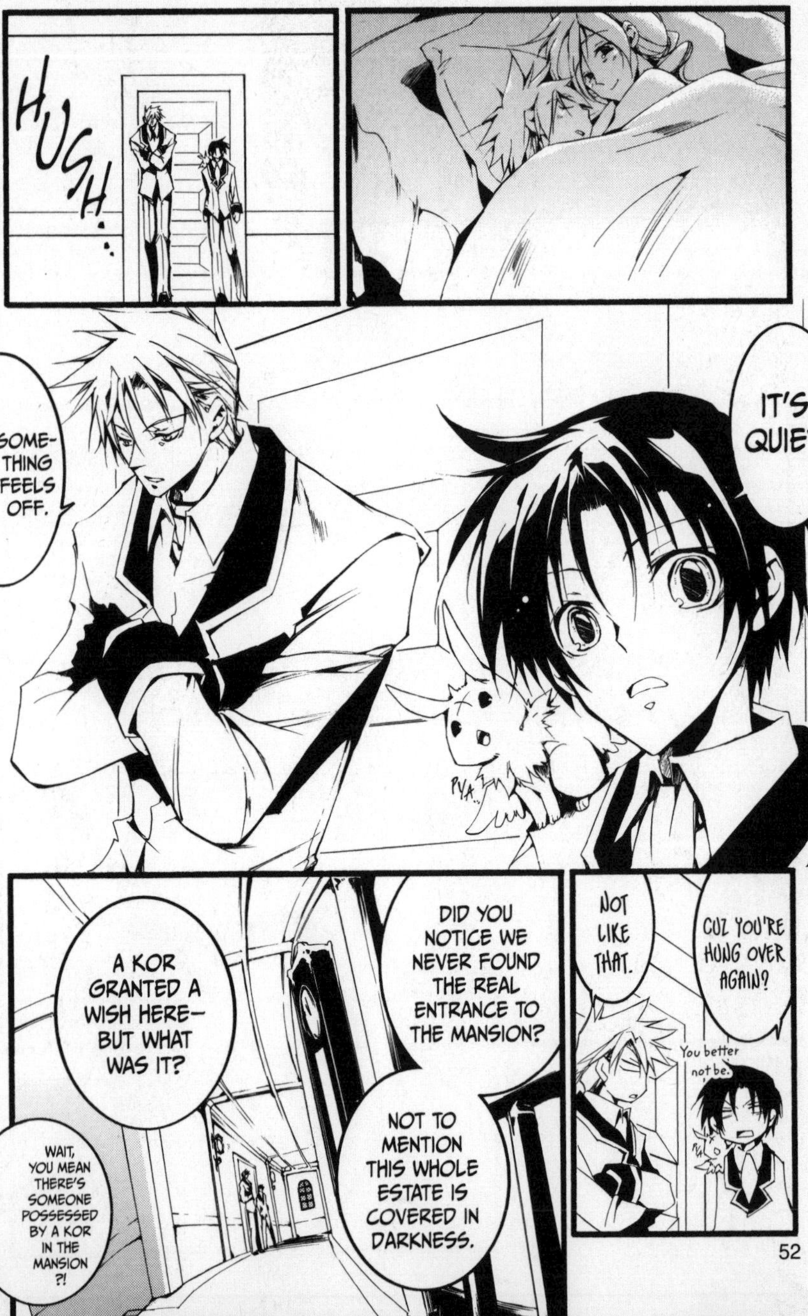
HUSH..
IT'S QUIET.
SOME-THING FEELS OFF.
PYA..
CUZ YOU'RE HUNG OVER AGAIN?
NOT LIKE THAT.
You better not be.
PYA
DID YOU NOTICE WE NEVER FOUND THE REAL ENTRANCE TO THE MANSION?
A KOR GRANTED A WISH HERE— BUT WHAT WAS IT?
NOT TO MENTION THIS WHOLE ESTATE IS COVERED IN DARKNESS.
WAIT, YOU MEAN THERE'S SOMEONE POSSESSED BY A KOR IN THE MANSION?!

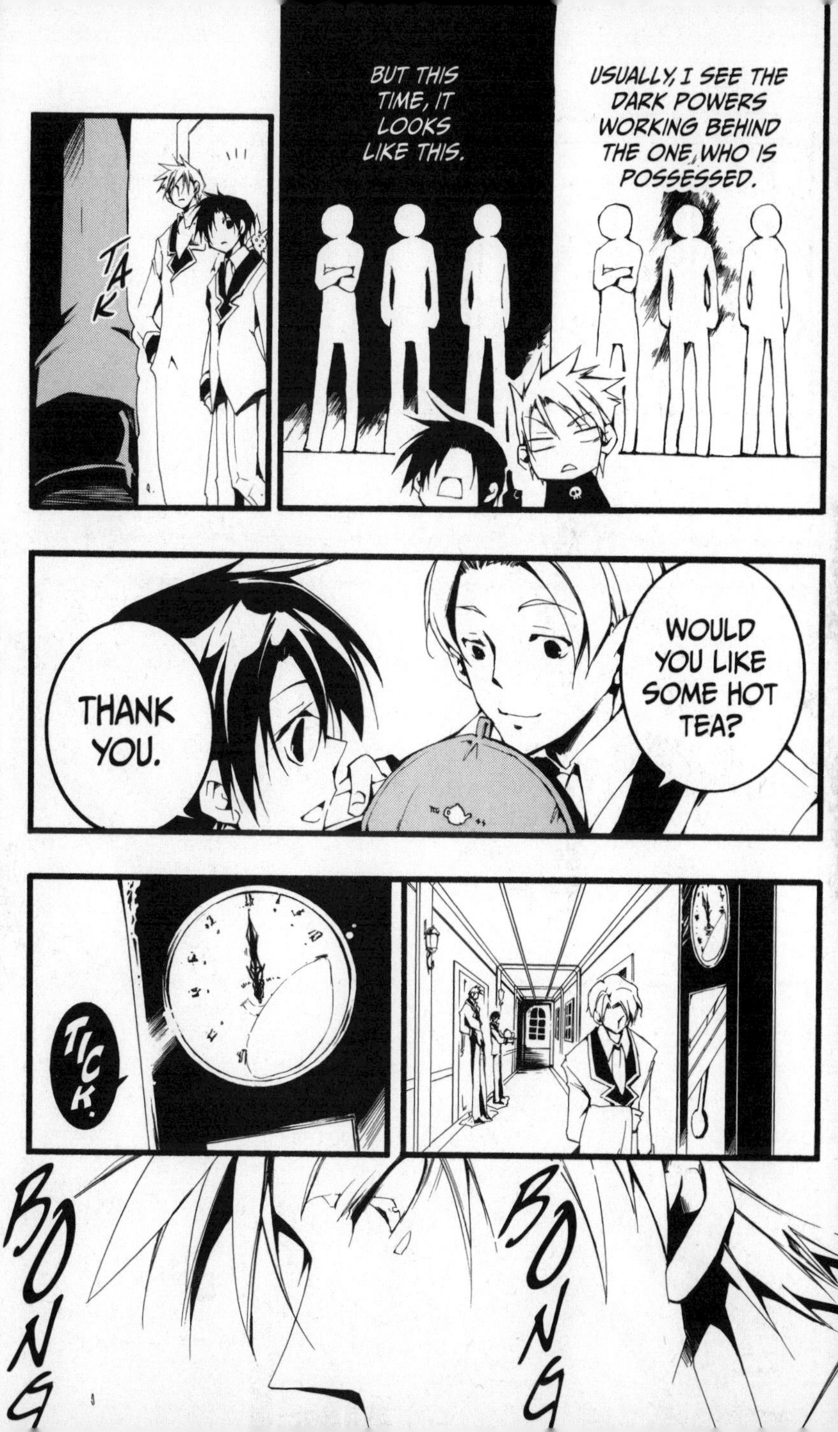
USUALLY, I SEE THE DARK POWERS WORKING BEHIND THE ONE WHO IS POSSESSED.
BUT THIS TIME, IT LOOKS LIKE THIS.
TAK
WOULD YOU LIKE SOME HOT TEA?
THANK YOU.
TICK.
BONG
BONG

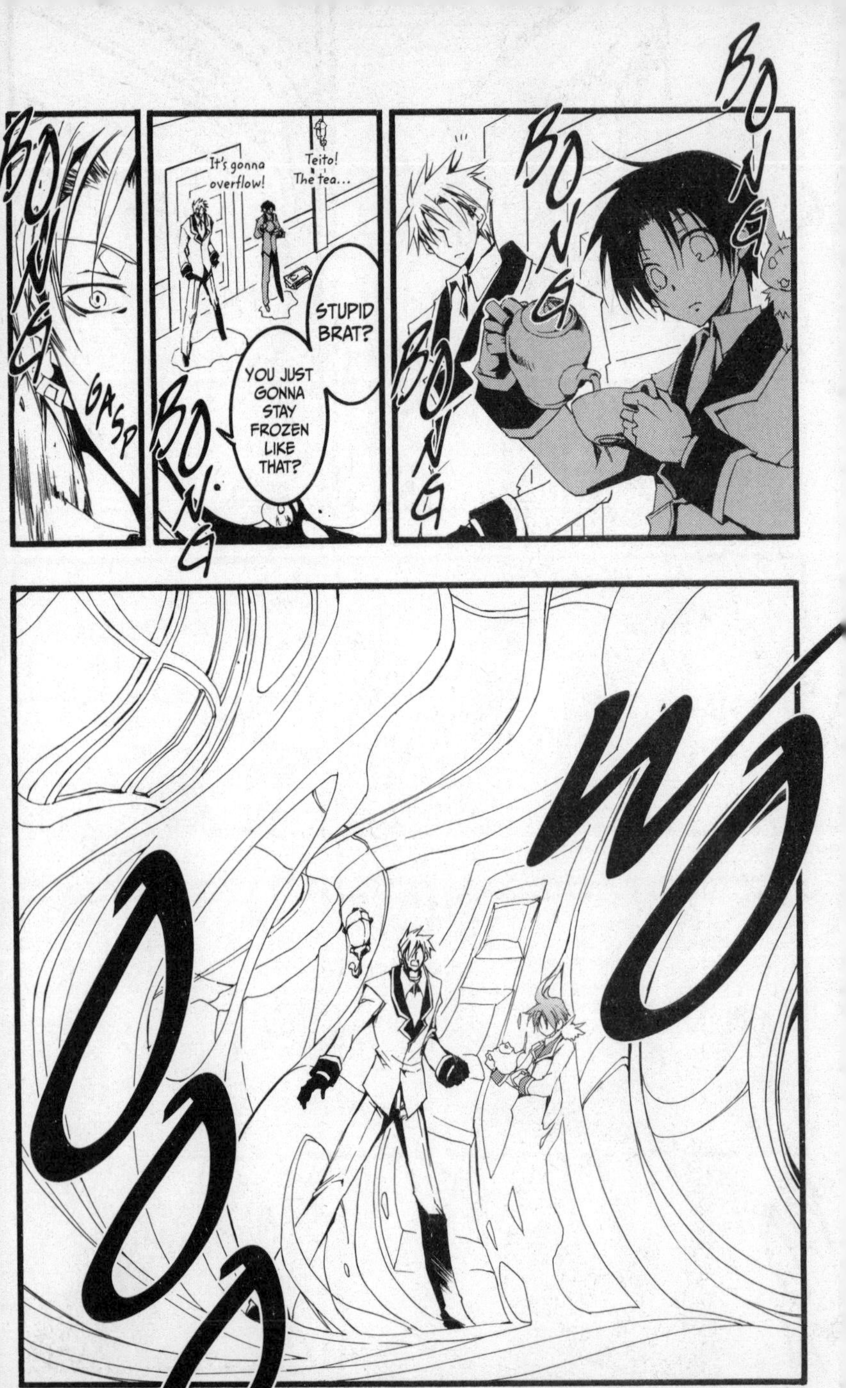
BONG
BONG
BONG
BONG
Teito! The tea...
It's gonna overflow!
STUPID BRAT?
YOU JUST GONNA STAY FROZEN LIKE THAT?
BONG
BONG
GASP

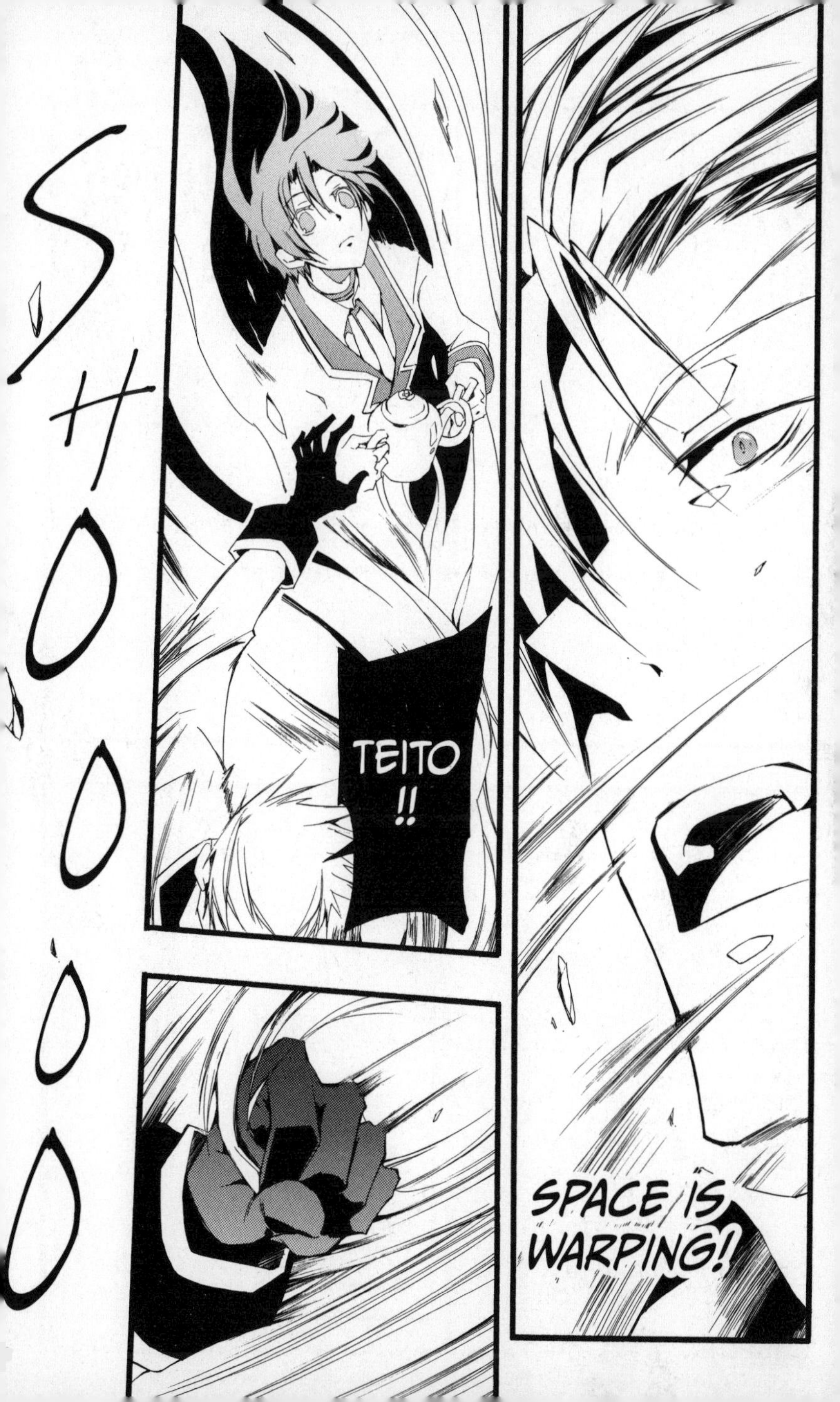
SPACE IS WARPING!
TEITO !!
SHOOOO

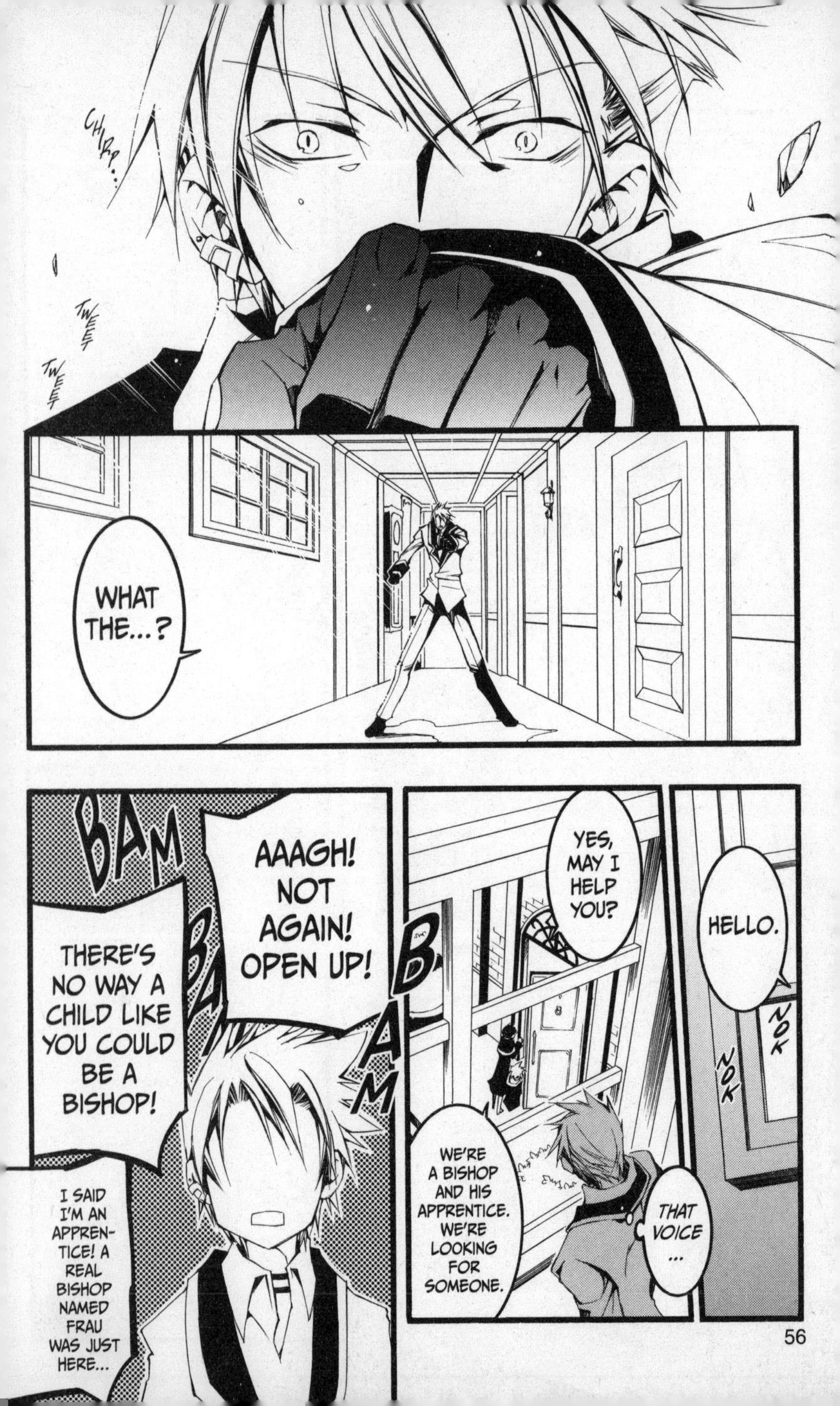
CHIRP...
TWEET
TWEET
WHAT THE...?
HELLO.
NOK
NOK
THAT VOICE...
YES, MAY I HELP YOU?
WE'RE A BISHOP AND HIS APPRENTICE. WE'RE LOOKING FOR SOMEONE.
BAM
BAM
BAM
AAAGH! NOT AGAIN! OPEN UP!
THERE'S NO WAY A CHILD LIKE YOU COULD BE A BISHOP!
I SAID I'M AN APPREN-TICE! A REAL BISHOP NAMED FRAU WAS JUST HERE...

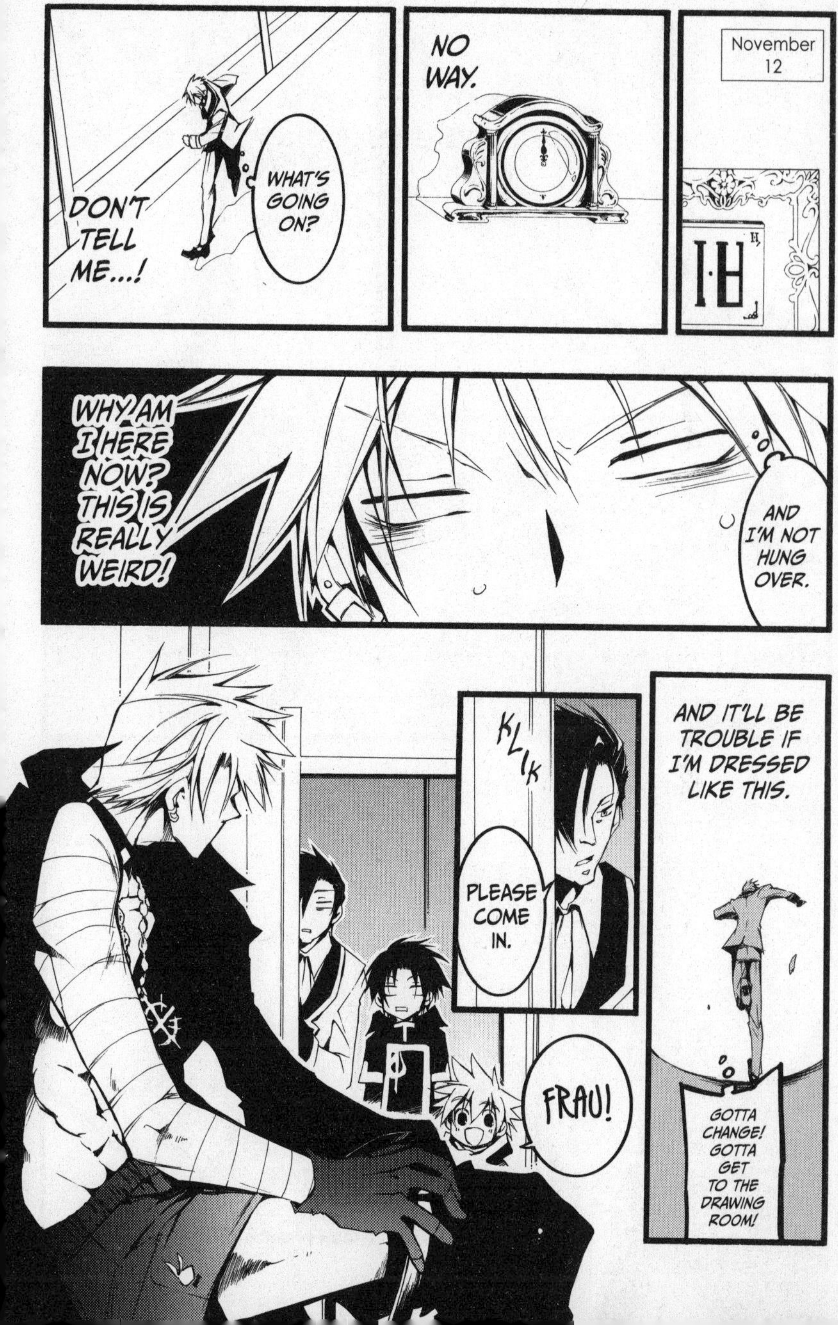
November 12
NO WAY.
WHAT'S GOING ON?
DON'T TELL ME...!
AND I'M NOT HUNG OVER.
WHY AM I HERE NOW? THIS IS REALLY WEIRD!
AND IT'LL BE TROUBLE IF I'M DRESSED LIKE THIS.
GOTTA CHANGE! GOTTA GET TO THE DRAWING ROOM!
KLIK
PLEASE COME IN.
FRAU!

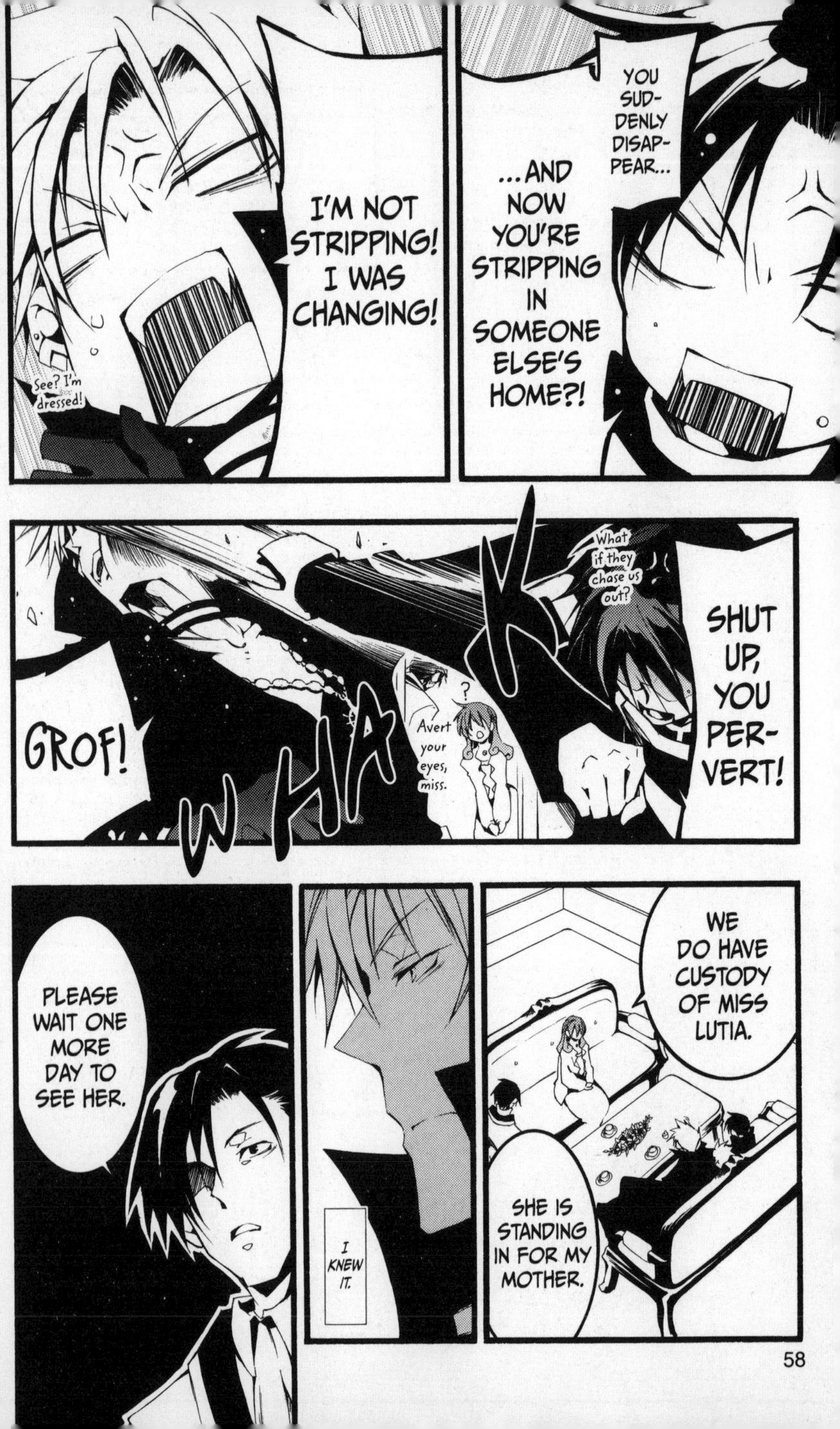
YOU SUDDENLY DISAPPEAR...
...AND NOW YOU'RE STRIPPING IN SOMEONE ELSE'S HOME?!
I'M NOT STRIPPING! I WAS CHANGING!
See? I'm dressed!
What if they chase us out?
SHUT UP, YOU PERVERT!
WHAK
?
Avert your eyes, miss.
GROF!
WE DO HAVE CUSTODY OF MISS LUTIA.
SHE IS STANDING IN FOR MY MOTHER.
I KNEW IT.
PLEASE WAIT ONE MORE DAY TO SEE HER.

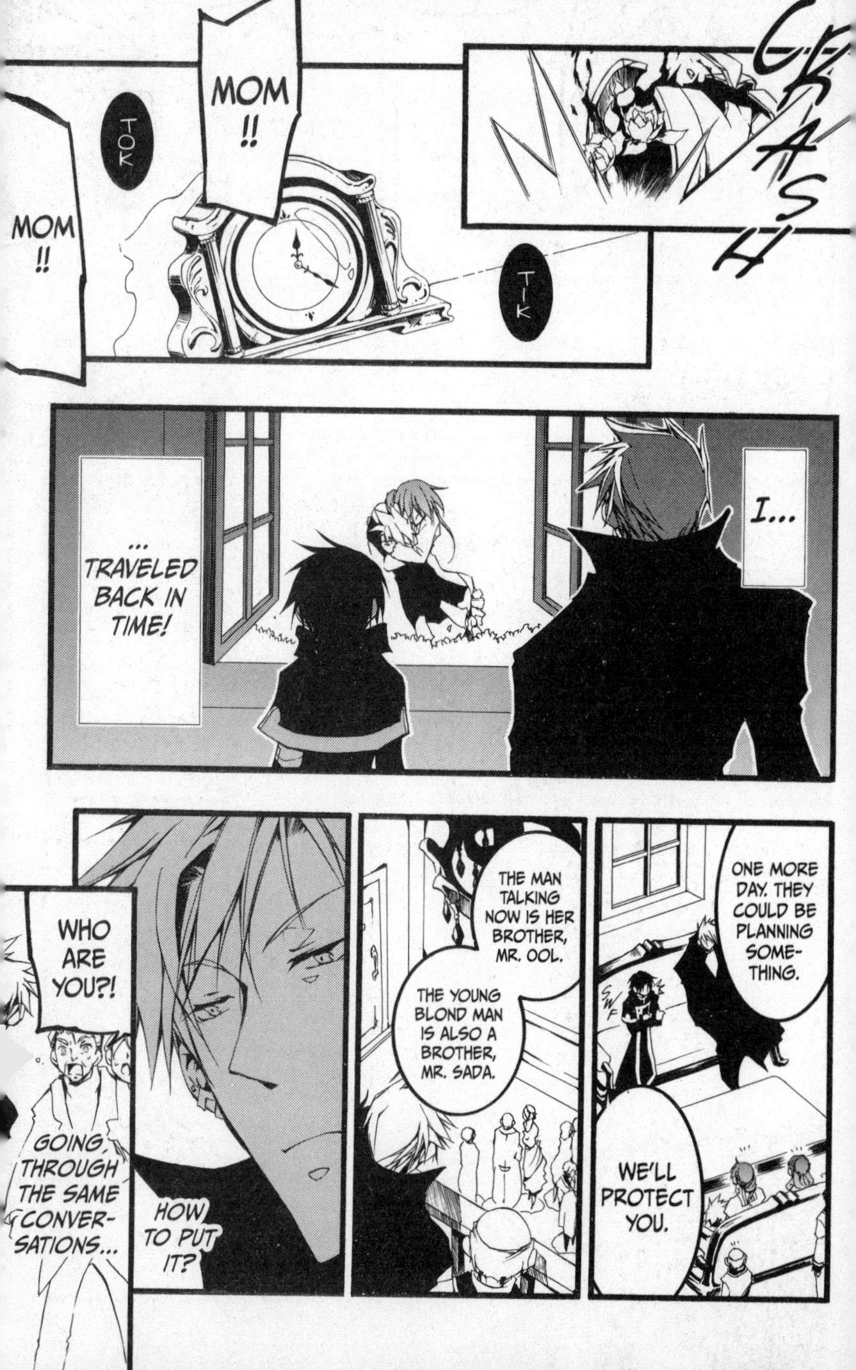
GKRASH
MOM !!
TOK
MOM !!
TIK
I...
... TRAVELED BACK IN TIME!
ONE MORE DAY. THEY COULD BE PLANNING SOME-THING.
SWF
WE'LL PROTECT YOU.
THE MAN TALKING NOW IS HER BROTHER, MR. OOL.
THE YOUNG BLOND MAN IS ALSO A BROTHER, MR. SADA.
WHO ARE YOU?!
GOING THROUGH THE SAME CONVER-SATIONS...
HOW TO PUT IT?

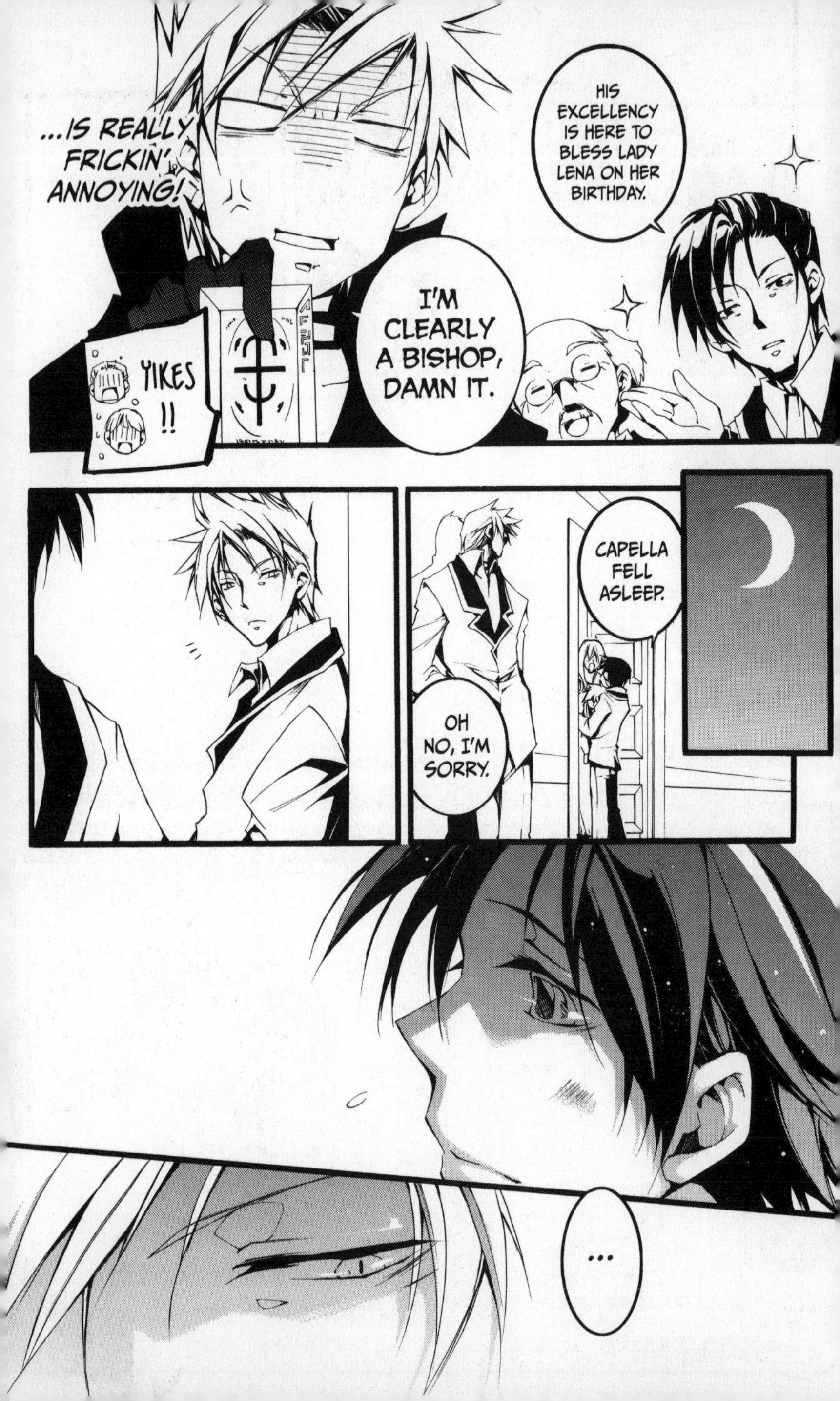
HIS EXCELLENCY IS HERE TO BLESS LADY LENA ON HER BIRTHDAY.
...IS REALLY FRICKIN' ANNOYING!
I'M CLEARLY A BISHOP, DAMN IT.
YIKES !!
CAPELLA FELL ASLEEP.
OH NO, I'M SORRY.
...

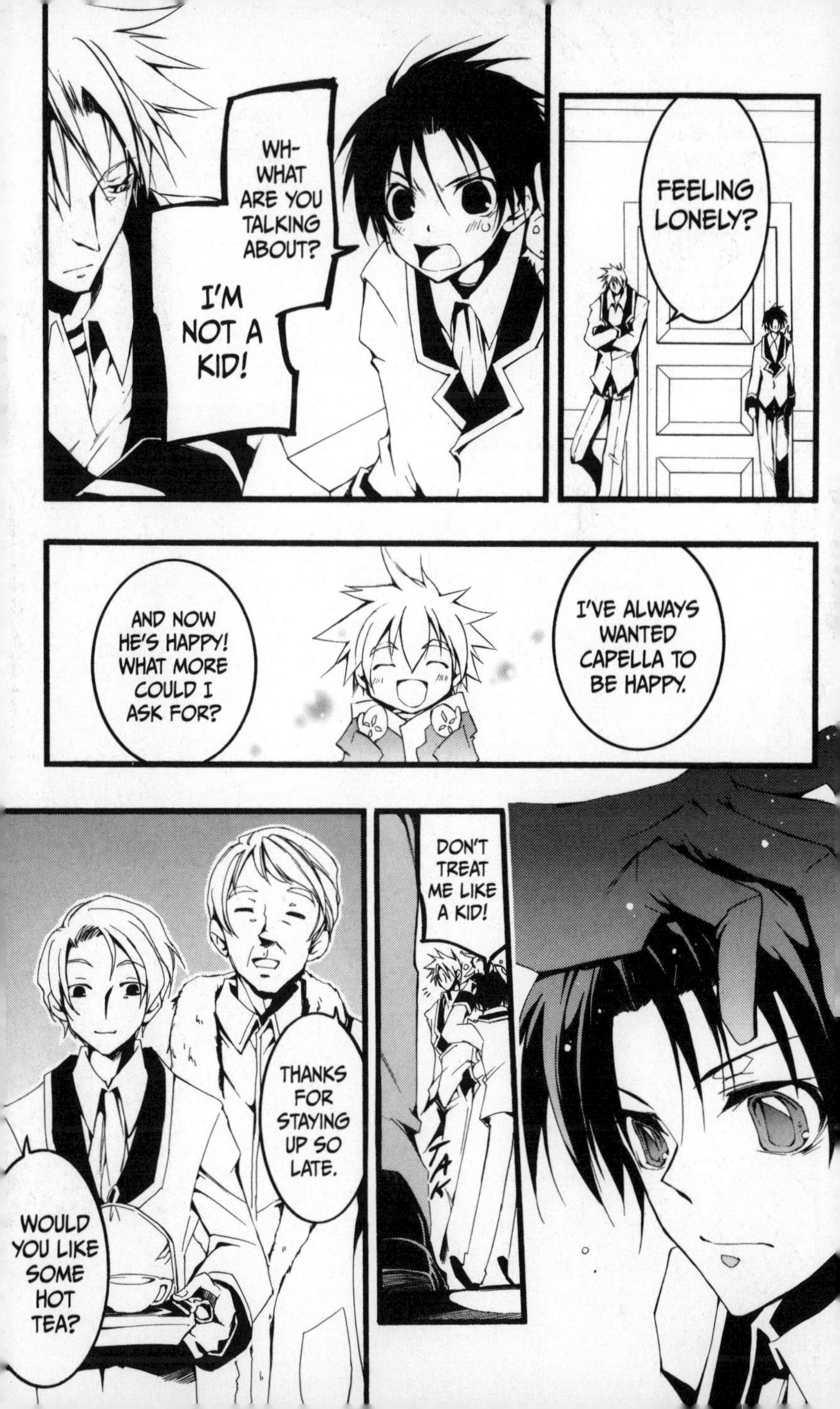
FEELING LONELY?
WH- WHAT ARE YOU TALKING ABOUT?
I'M NOT A KID!
I'VE ALWAYS WANTED CAPELLA TO BE HAPPY.
AND NOW HE'S HAPPY! WHAT MORE COULD I ASK FOR?
DON'T TREAT ME LIKE A KID!
TAK
THANKS FOR STAYING UP SO LATE.
WOULD YOU LIKE SOME HOT TEA?

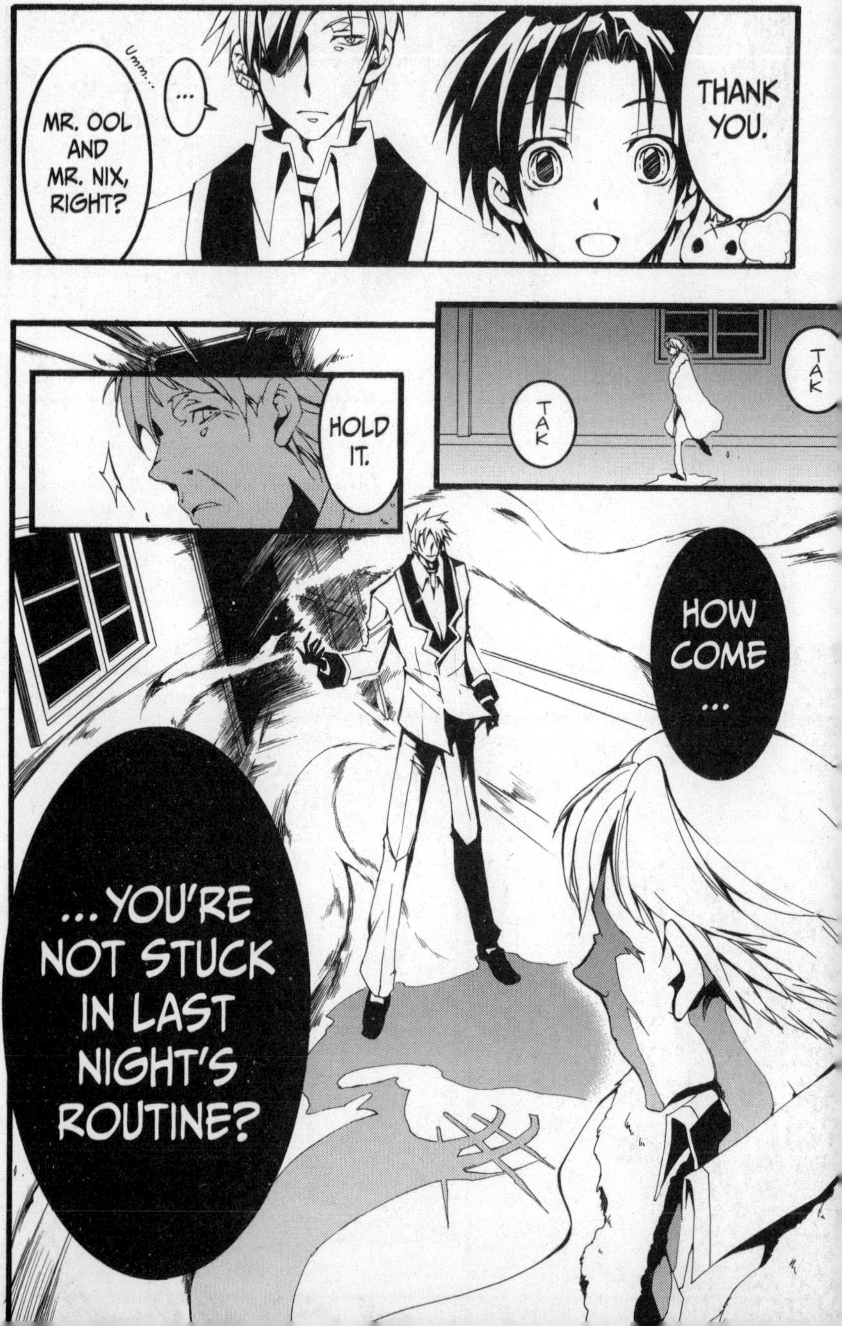
THANK YOU.
...
Umm...
MR. OOL AND MR. NIX, RIGHT?
TAK
TAK
HOLD IT.
HOW COME ...
...YOU'RE NOT STUCK IN LAST NIGHT'S ROUTINE?

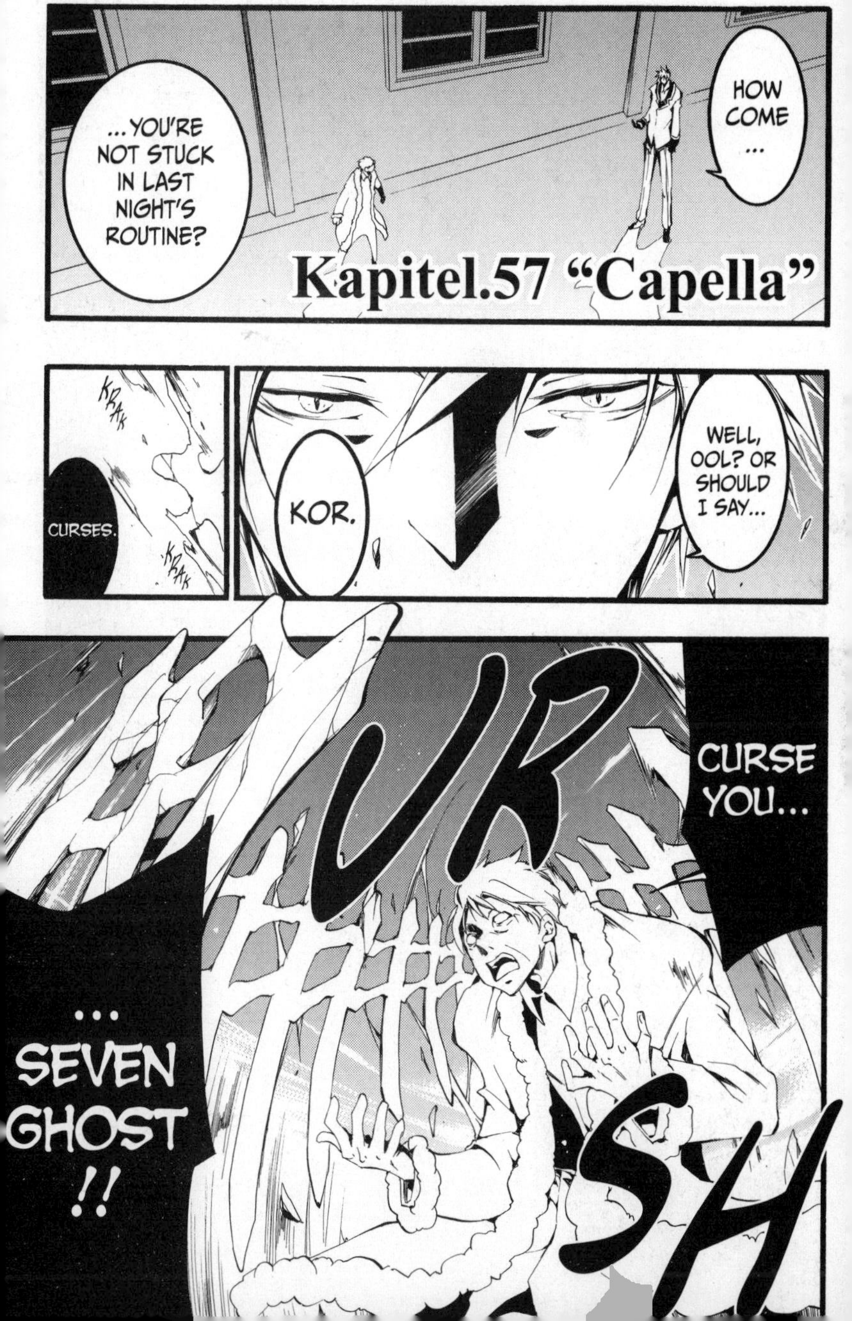
HOW COME ...
...YOU'RE NOT STUCK IN LAST NIGHT'S ROUTINE?
Kapitel.57 "Capella"
WELL, OOL? OR SHOULD I SAY...
KOR.
KRAK
CURSES.
KRAK
VR
CURSE YOU...
... ...SEVEN GHOST !!
SH

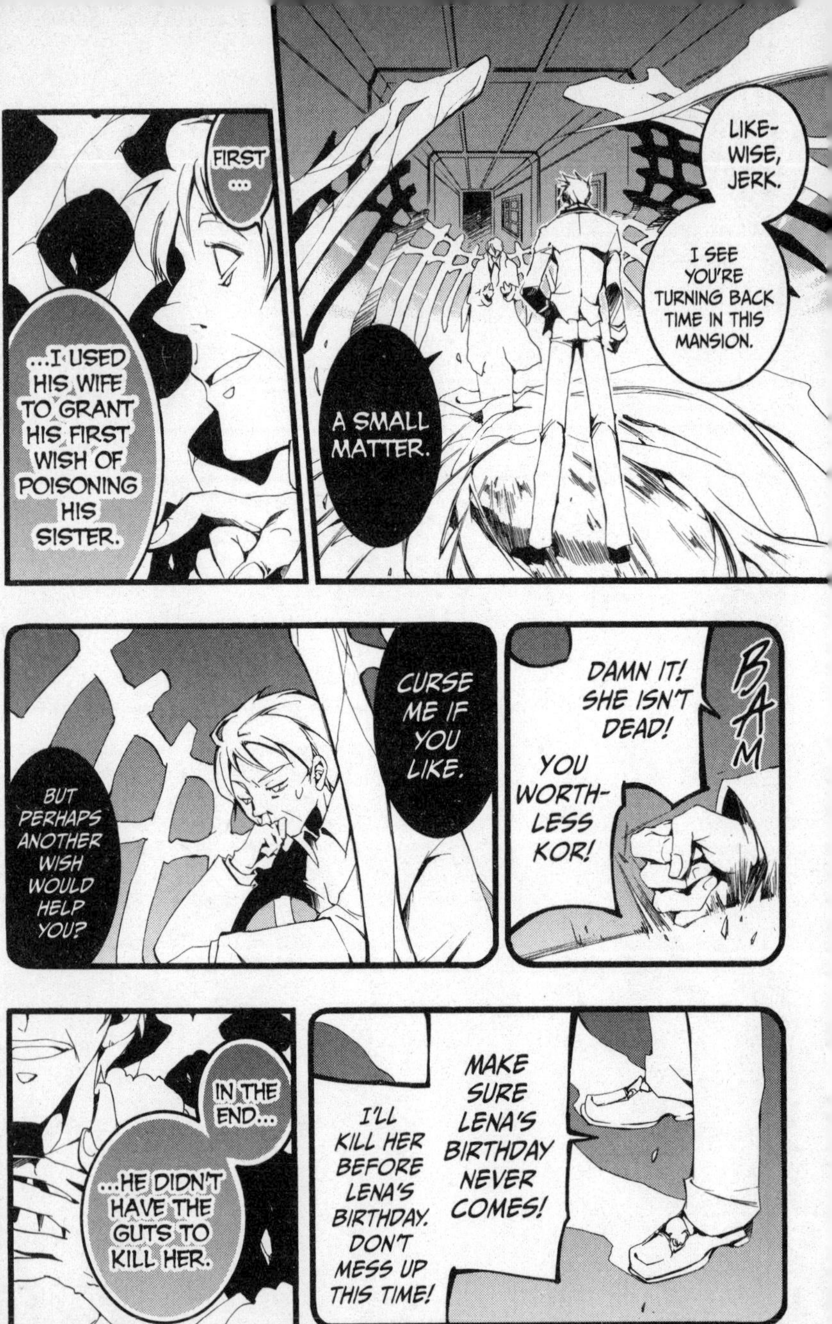
LIKE-WISE, JERK.
I SEE YOU'RE TURNING BACK TIME IN THIS MANSION.
A SMALL MATTER.
FIRST...
...I USED HIS WIFE TO GRANT HIS FIRST WISH OF POISONING HIS SISTER.
BAM
DAMN IT! SHE ISN'T DEAD!
YOU WORTH-LESS KOR!
CURSE ME IF YOU LIKE.
BUT PERHAPS ANOTHER WISH WOULD HELP YOU?
MAKE SURE LENA'S BIRTHDAY NEVER COMES!
I'LL KILL HER BEFORE LENA'S BIRTHDAY. DON'T MESS UP THIS TIME!
IN THE END...
...HE DIDN'T HAVE THE GUTS TO KILL HER.

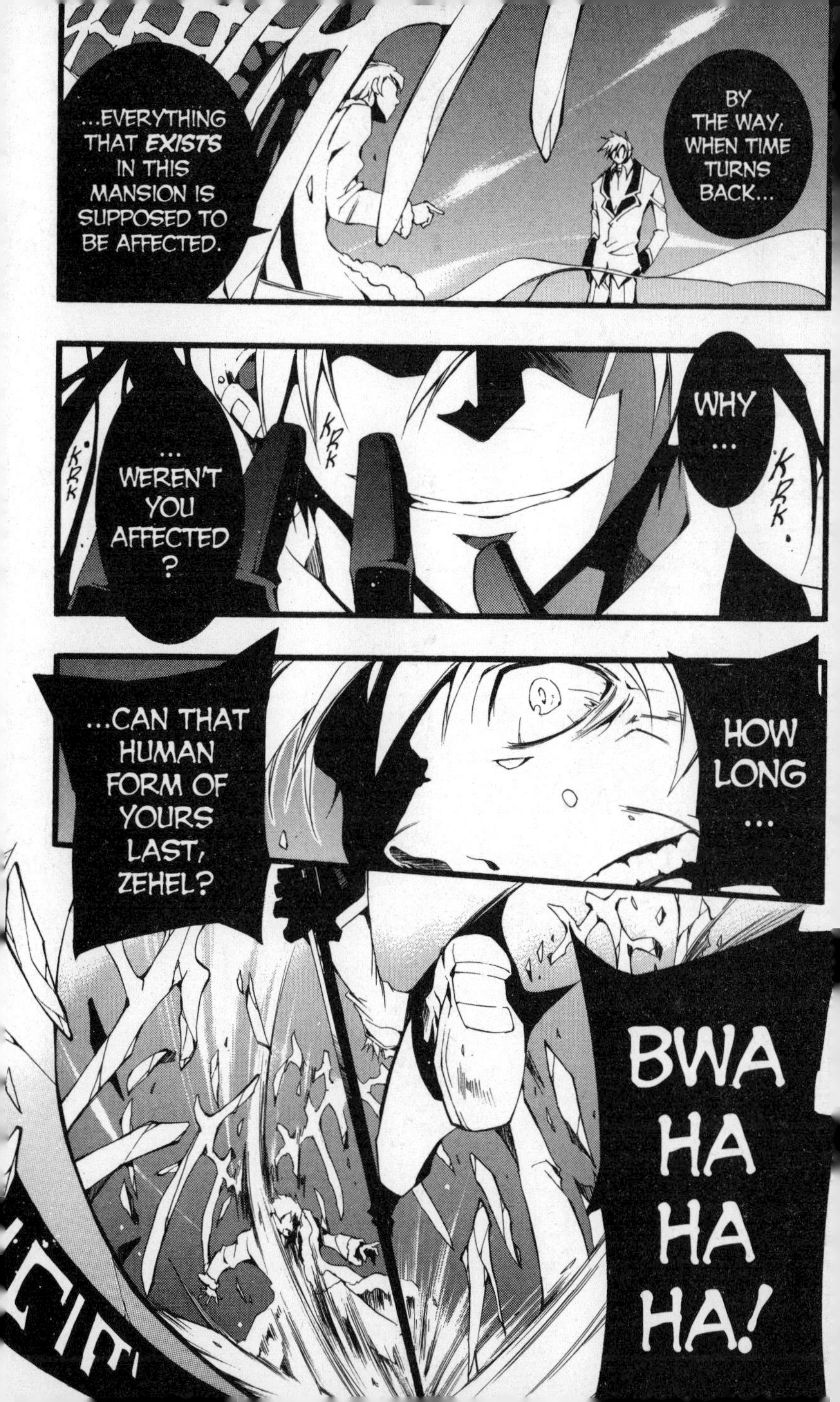
BY THE WAY, WHEN TIME TURNS BACK...
...EVERYTHING THAT EXISTS IN THIS MANSION IS SUPPOSED TO BE AFFECTED.
WHY ...
KRK
KRK
... WEREN'T YOU AFFECTED ?
KRK
HOW LONG ...
...CAN THAT HUMAN FORM OF YOURS LAST, ZEHEL?
BWA HA HA HA!

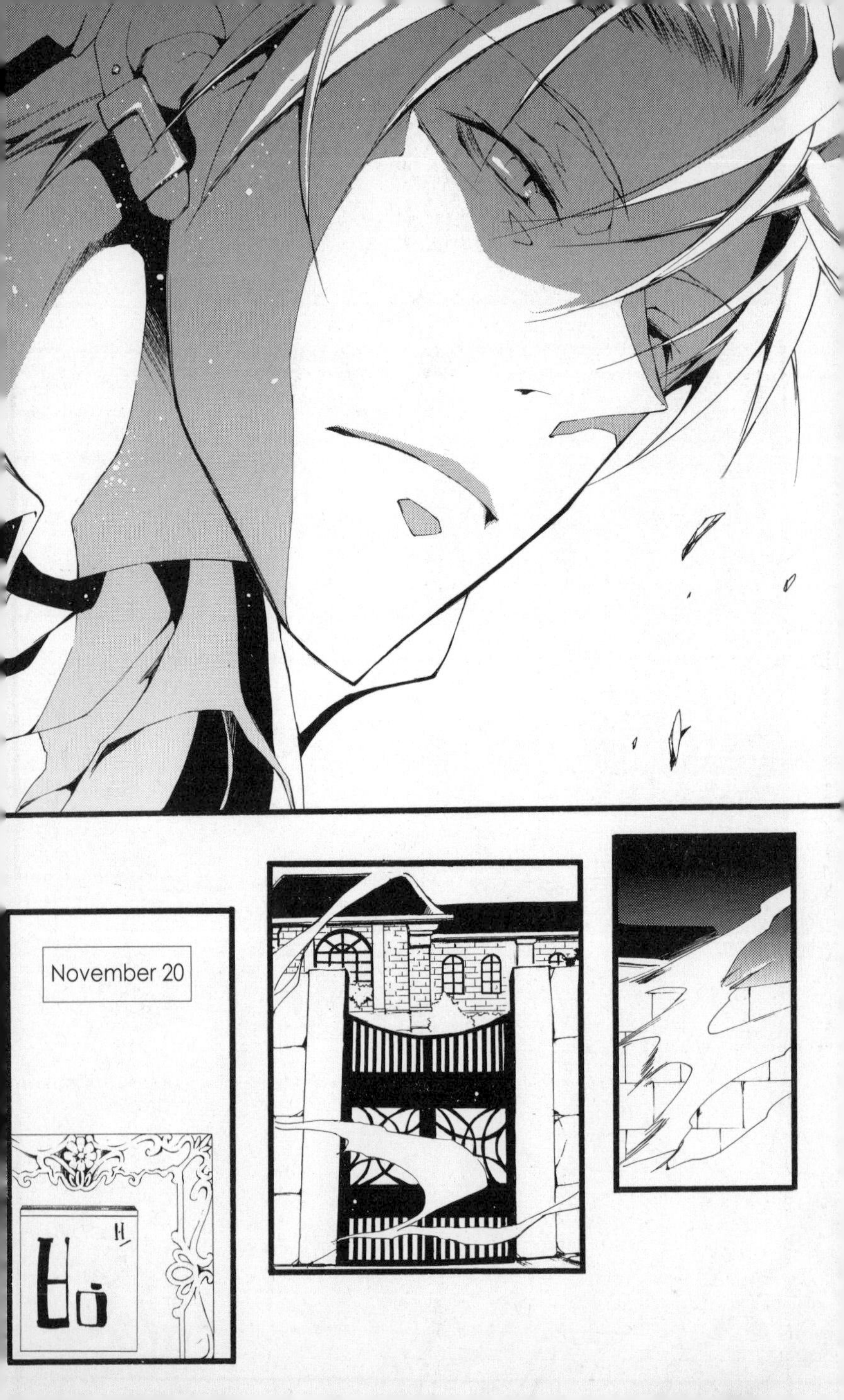
November 20

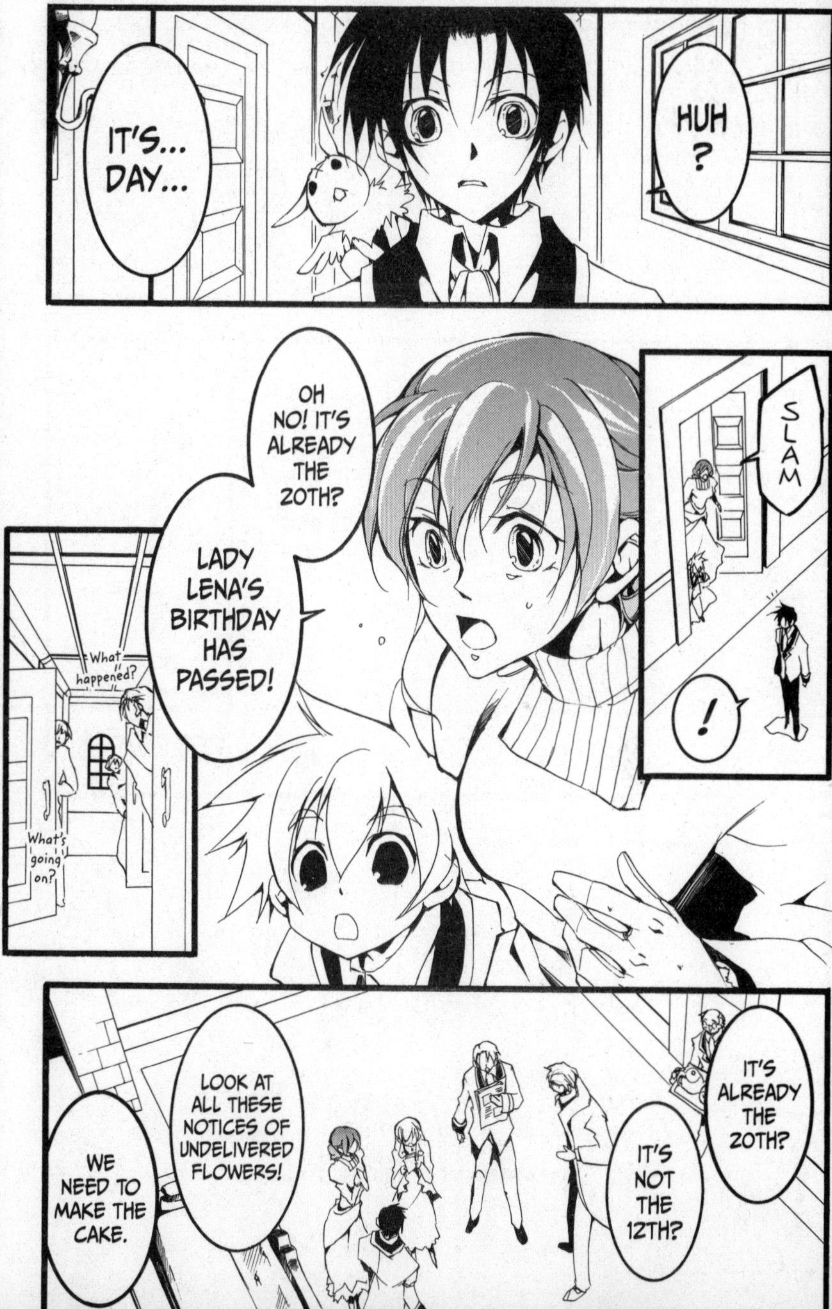
HUH?
IT'S... DAY...
SLAM
!
OH NO! IT'S ALREADY THE 20TH?
LADY LENA'S BIRTHDAY HAS PASSED!
What happened?
What's going on?
IT'S ALREADY THE 20TH?
IT'S NOT THE 12TH?
LOOK AT ALL THESE NOTICES OF UNDELIVERED FLOWERS!
WE NEED TO MAKE THE CAKE.

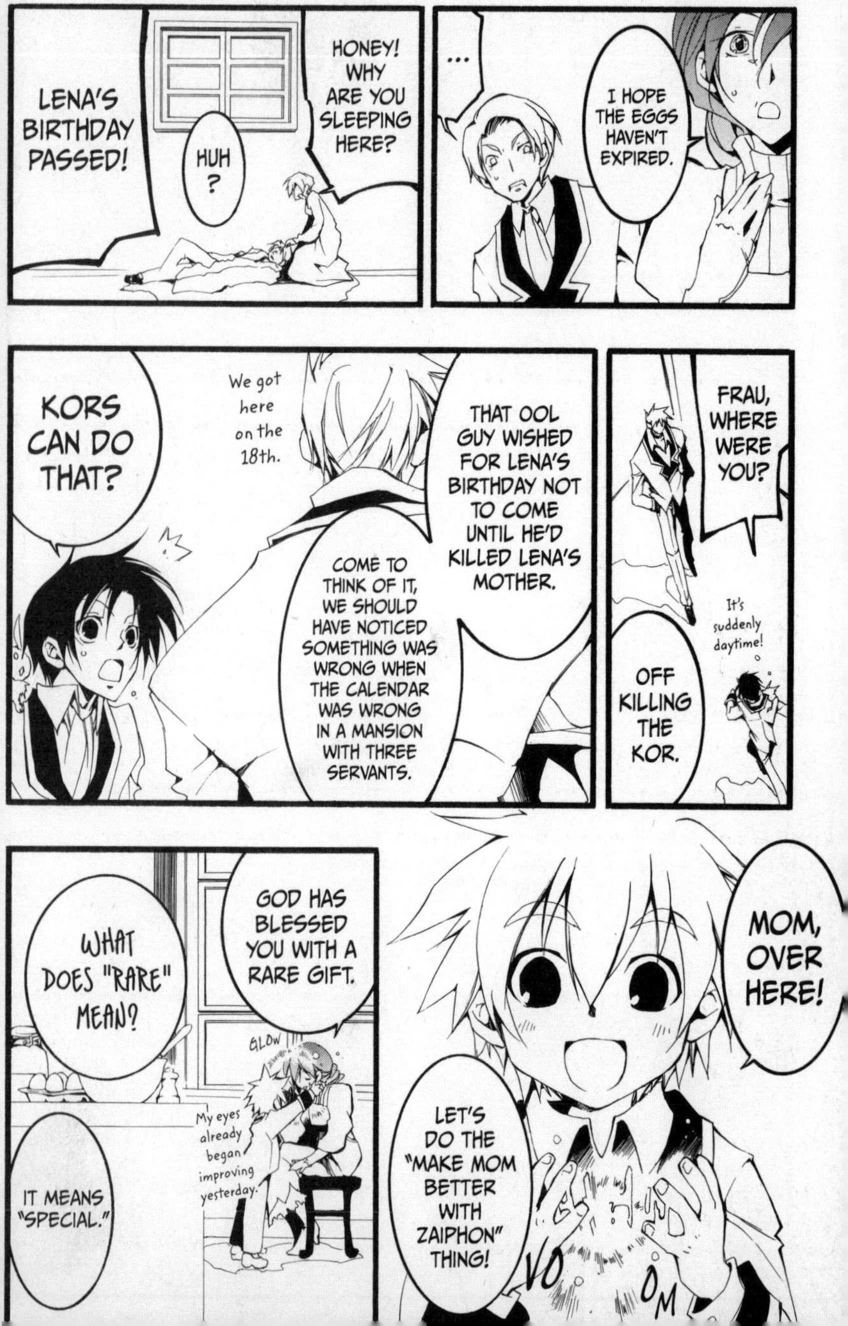
...
I HOPE THE EGGS HAVEN'T EXPIRED.
HONEY! WHY ARE YOU SLEEPING HERE?
HUH?
LENA'S BIRTHDAY PASSED!
FRAU, WHERE WERE YOU?
OFF KILLING THE KOR.
It's suddenly daytime!
THAT OOL GUY WISHED FOR LENA'S BIRTHDAY NOT TO COME UNTIL HE'D KILLED LENA'S MOTHER.
We got here on the 18th.
KORS CAN DO THAT?
COME TO THINK OF IT, WE SHOULD HAVE NOTICED SOMETHING WAS WRONG WHEN THE CALENDAR WAS WRONG IN A MANSION WITH THREE SERVANTS.
MOM, OVER HERE!
LET'S DO THE "MAKE MOM BETTER WITH ZAIPHON" THING!
VO
OM
GOD HAS BLESSED YOU WITH A RARE GIFT.
WHAT DOES "RARE" MEAN?
GLOW
My eyes already began improving yesterday.
IT MEANS "SPECIAL."

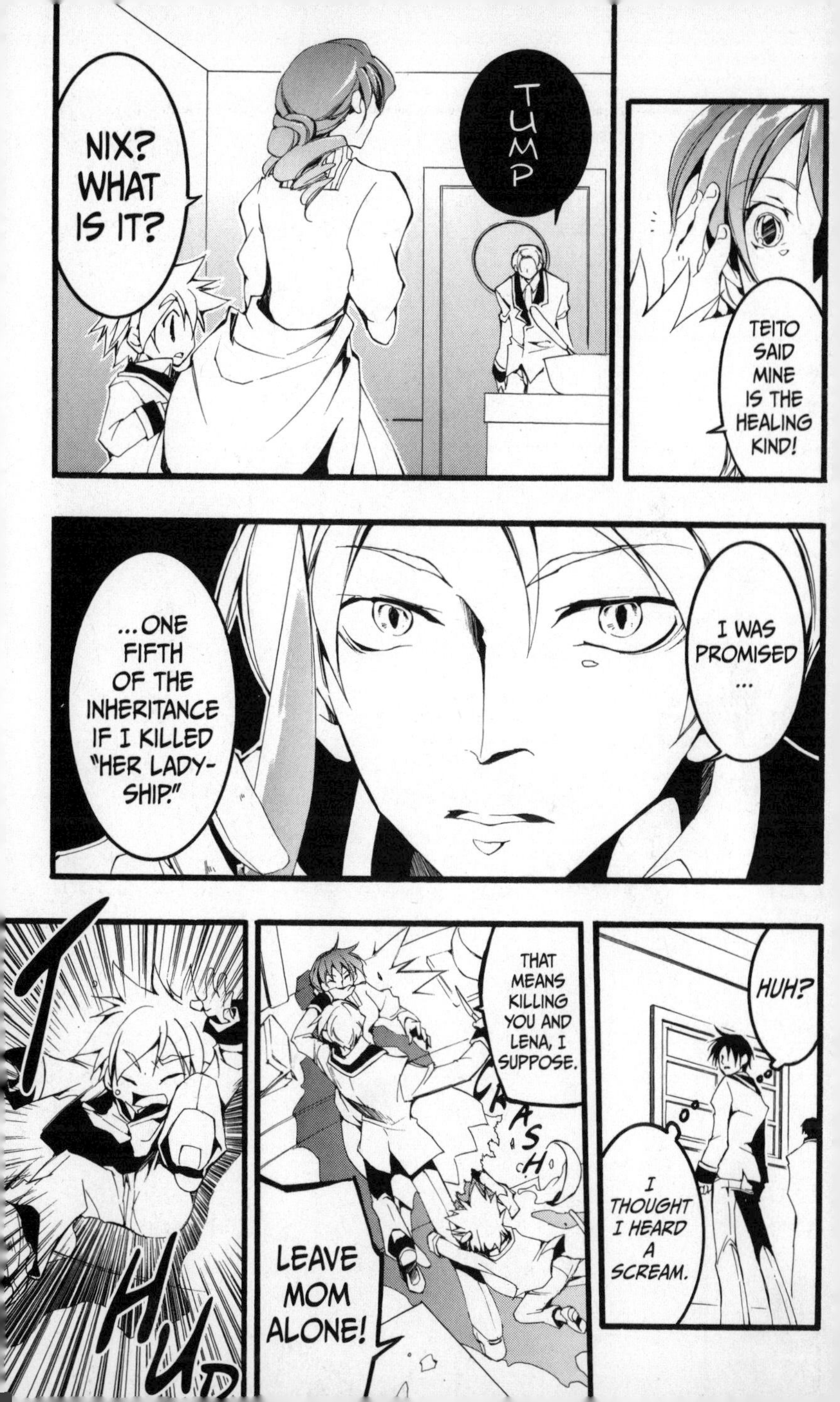
TEITO SAID MINE IS THE HEALING KIND!
TUMP
NIX? WHAT IS IT?
I WAS PROMISED ...
...ONE FIFTH OF THE INHERITANCE IF I KILLED "HER LADYSHIP."
HUH?
I THOUGHT I HEARD A SCREAM.
THAT MEANS KILLING YOU AND LENA, I SUPPOSE.
CRASH
LEAVE MOM ALONE!
THUD

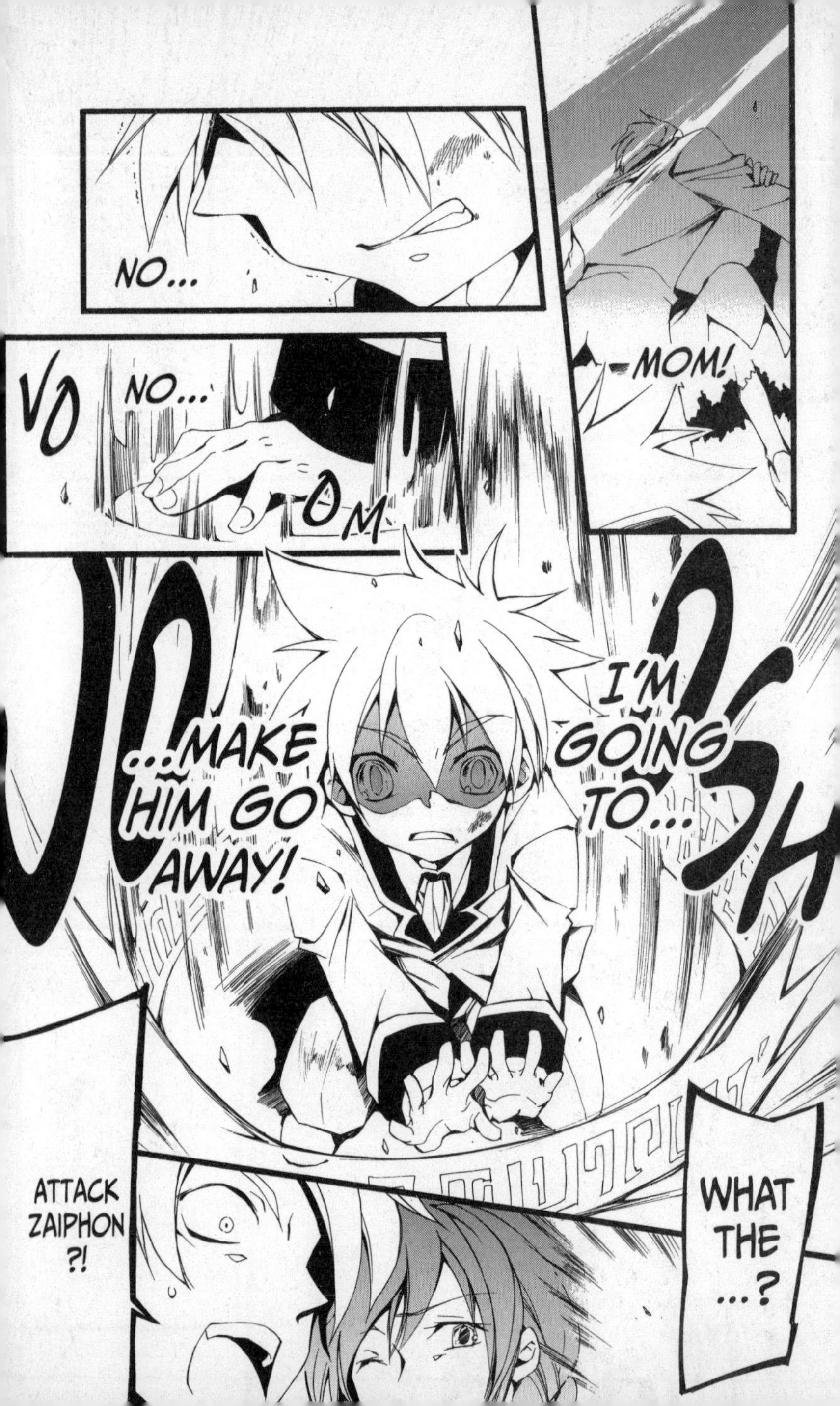

MOM!
NO...
NO...
VO
OM
I'M GOING TO...
...MAKE HIM GO AWAY!
WHAT THE ...?
ATTACK ZAIPHON ?!

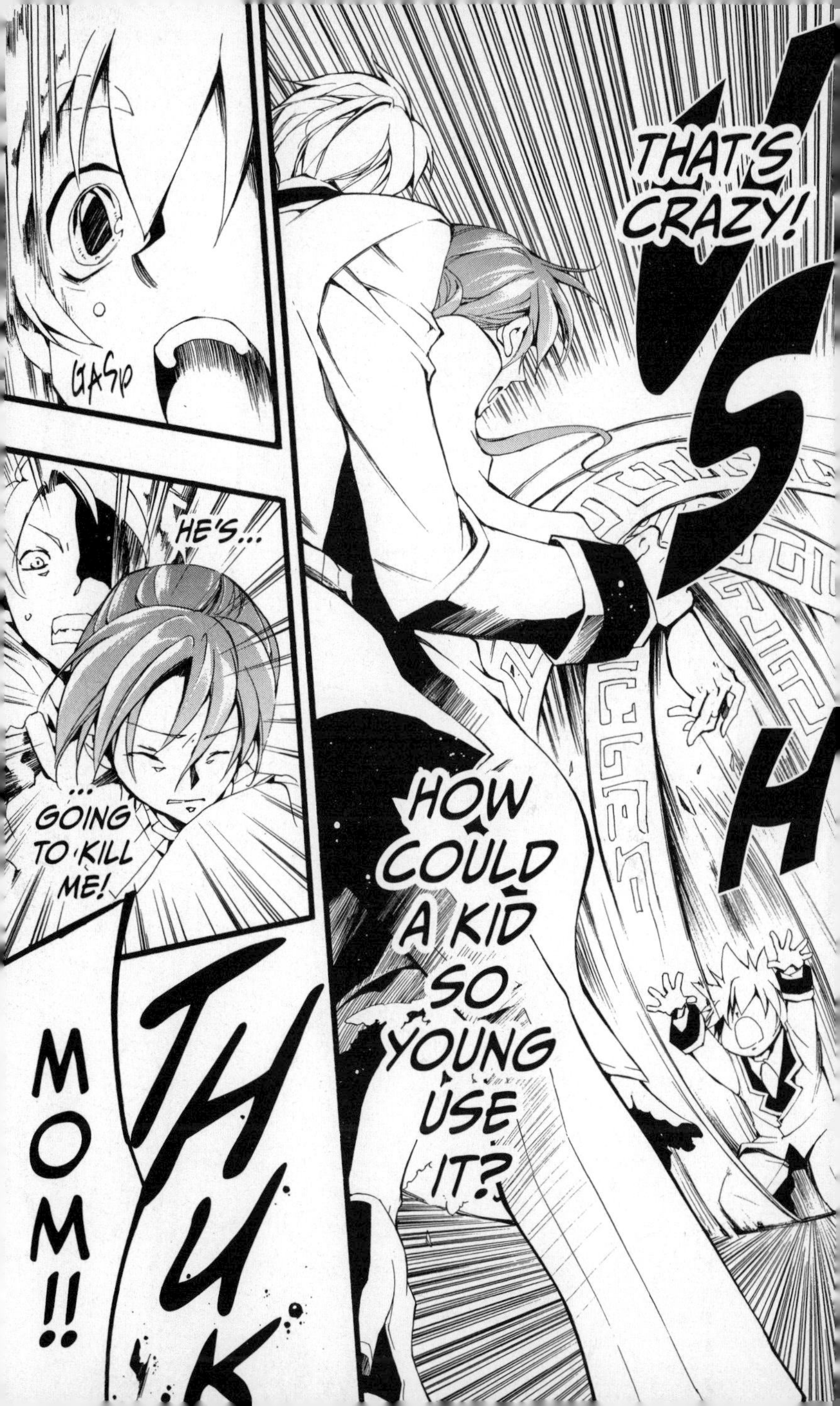
THAT'S CRAZY!
HOW COULD A KID SO YOUNG USE IT?
GASP
HE'S...
...GOING TO KILL ME!
THUK
MOM!!

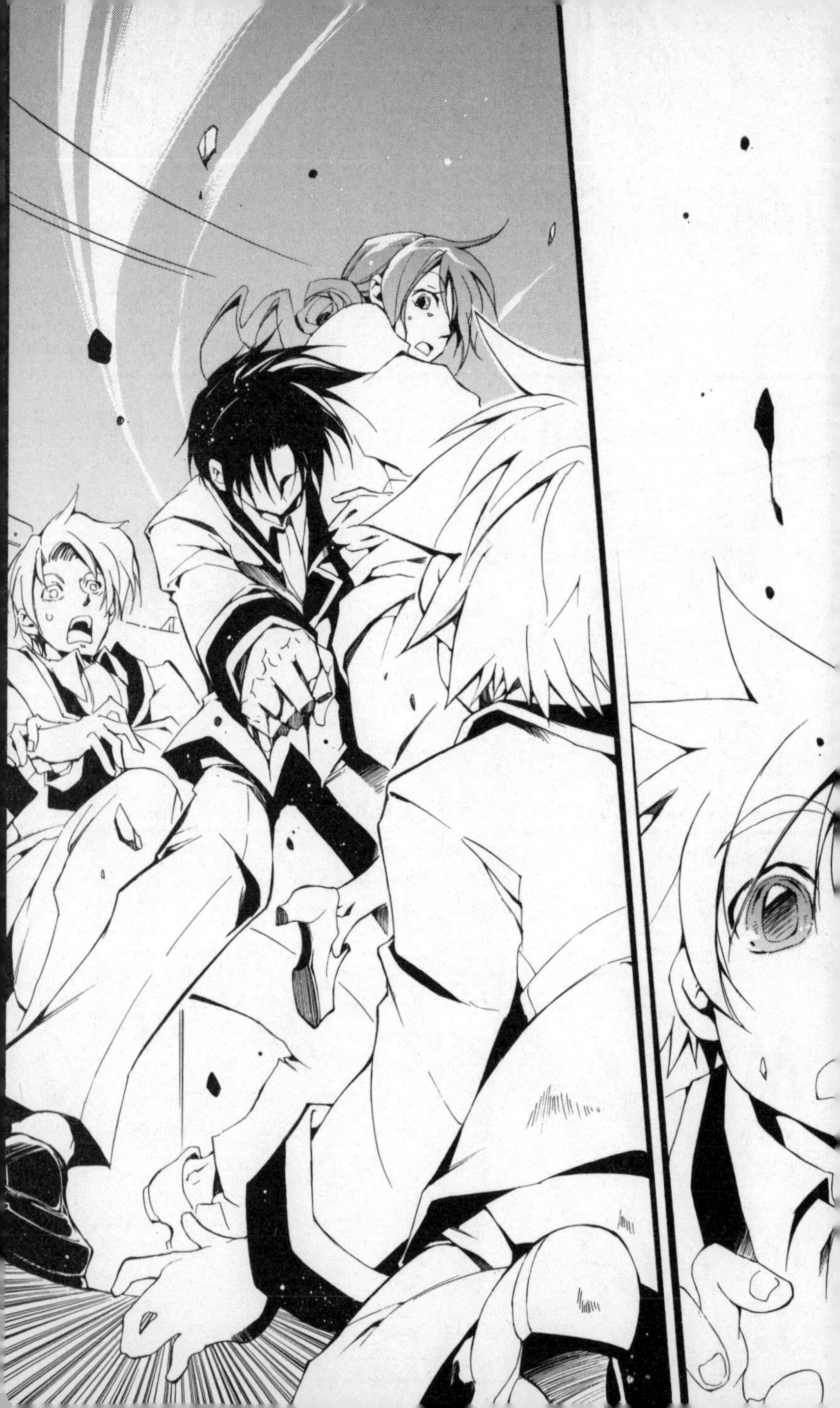

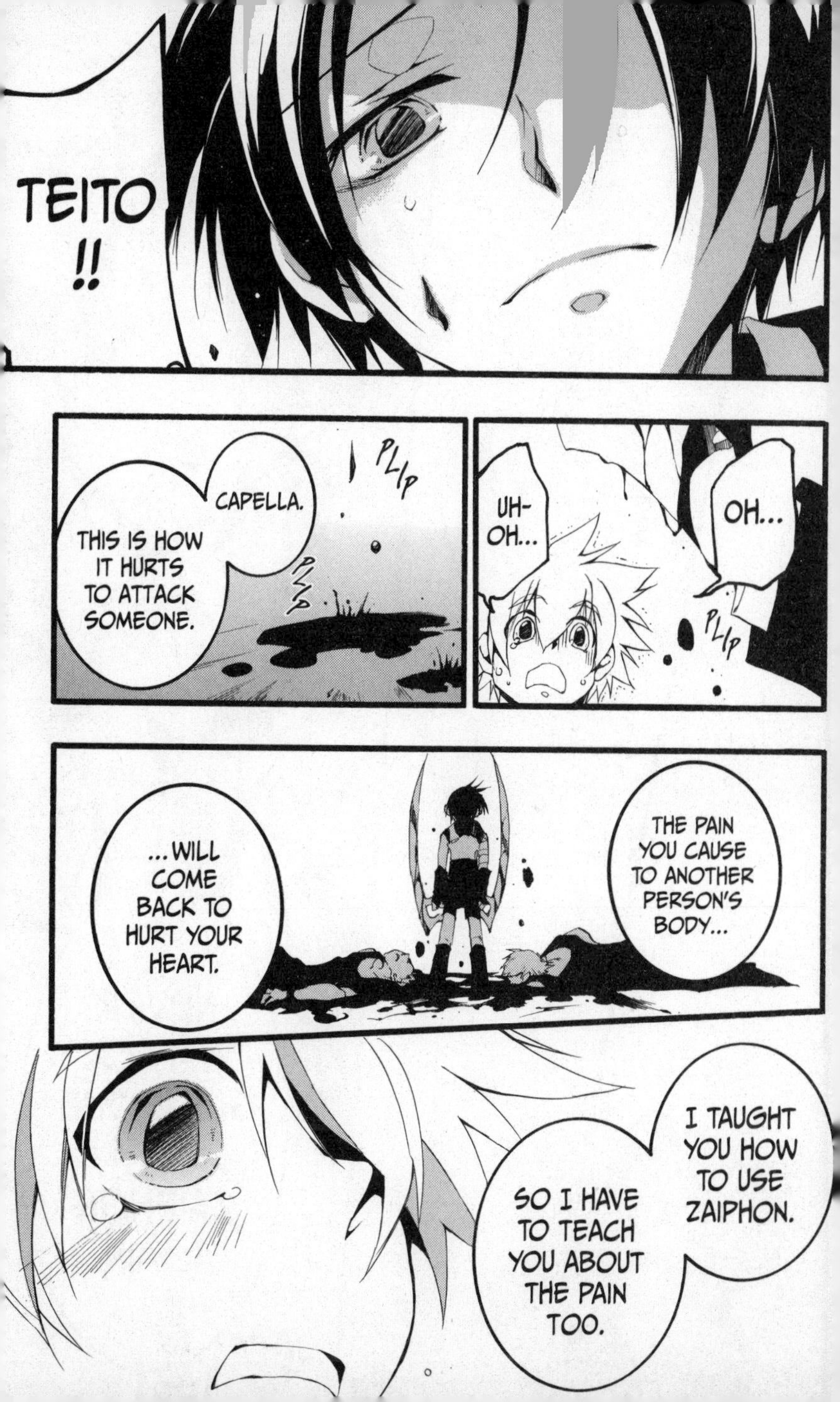

TEITO!!
OH...
UH-OH...
PLIP
PLIP
CAPELLA.
THIS IS HOW IT HURTS TO ATTACK SOMEONE.
PLIP
THE PAIN YOU CAUSE TO ANOTHER PERSON'S BODY...
...WILL COME BACK TO HURT YOUR HEART.
I TAUGHT YOU HOW TO USE ZAIPHON.
SO I HAVE TO TEACH YOU ABOUT THE PAIN TOO.

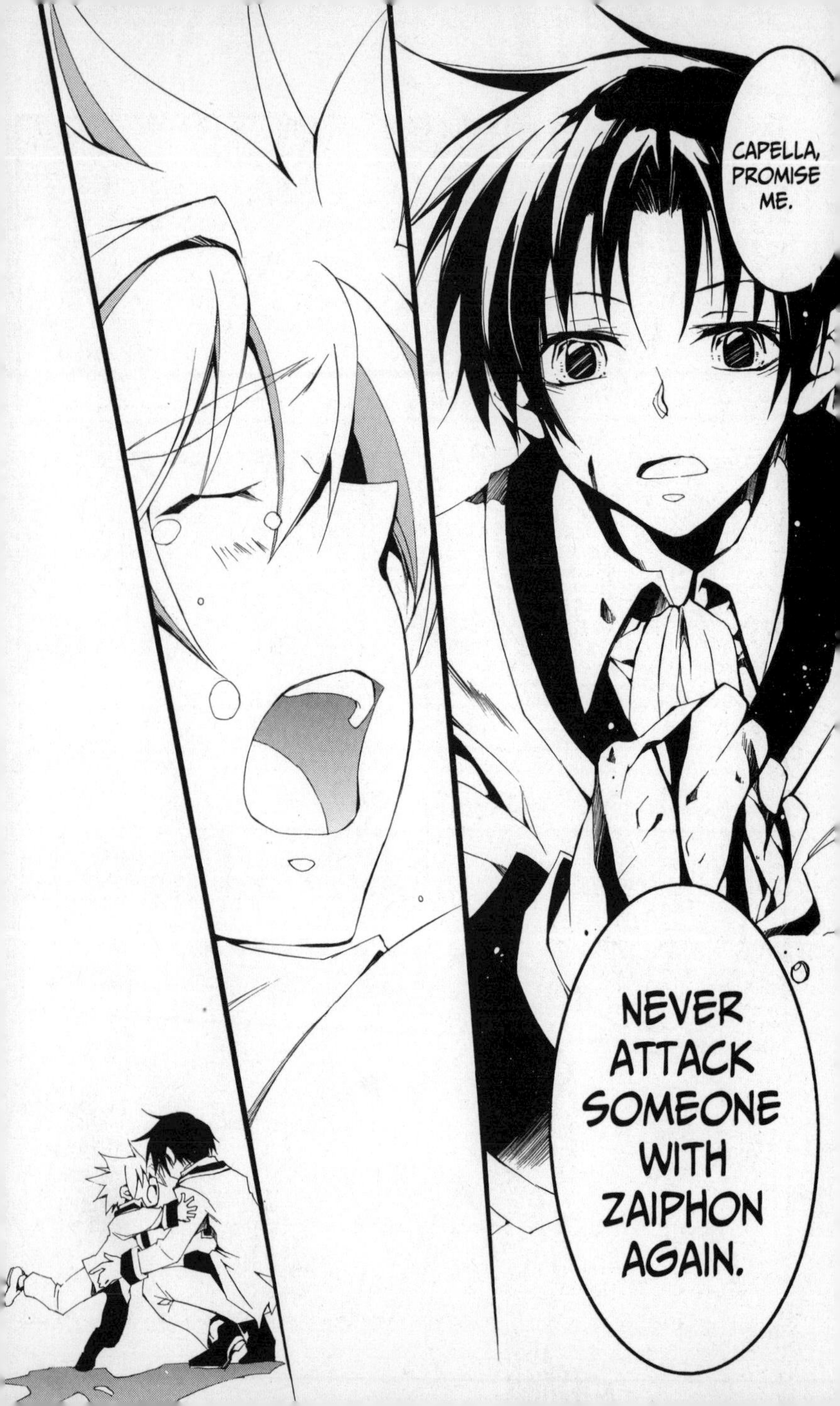
CAPELLA, PROMISE ME.
NEVER ATTACK SOMEONE WITH ZAIPHON AGAIN.

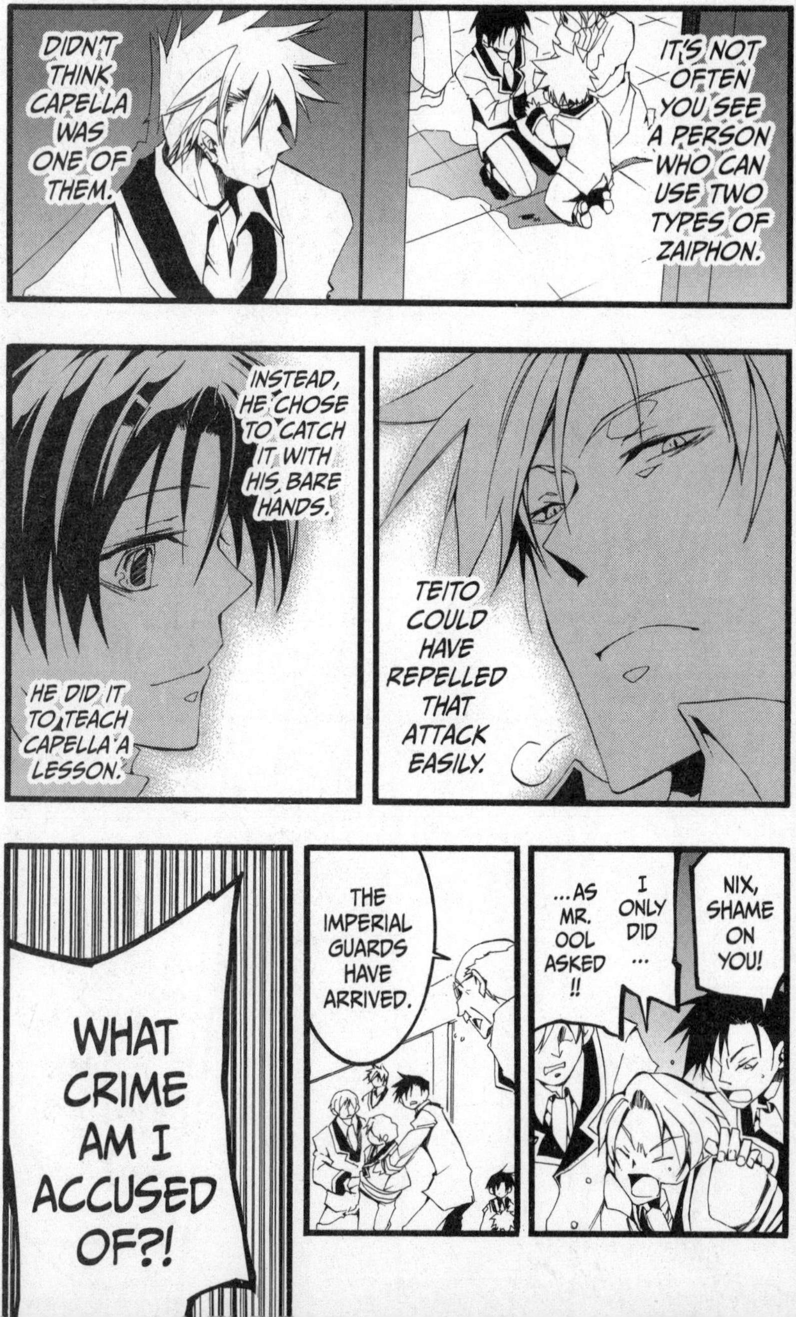
IT'S NOT OFTEN YOU SEE A PERSON WHO CAN USE TWO TYPES OF ZAIPHON.
DIDN'T THINK CAPELLA WAS ONE OF THEM.
TEITO COULD HAVE REPELLED THAT ATTACK EASILY.
INSTEAD, HE CHOSE TO CATCH IT WITH HIS BARE HANDS.
HE DID IT TO TEACH CAPELLA A LESSON.
NIX, SHAME ON YOU!
I ONLY DID ...
...AS MR. OOL ASKED !!
THE IMPERIAL GUARDS HAVE ARRIVED.
WHAT CRIME AM I ACCUSED OF?!

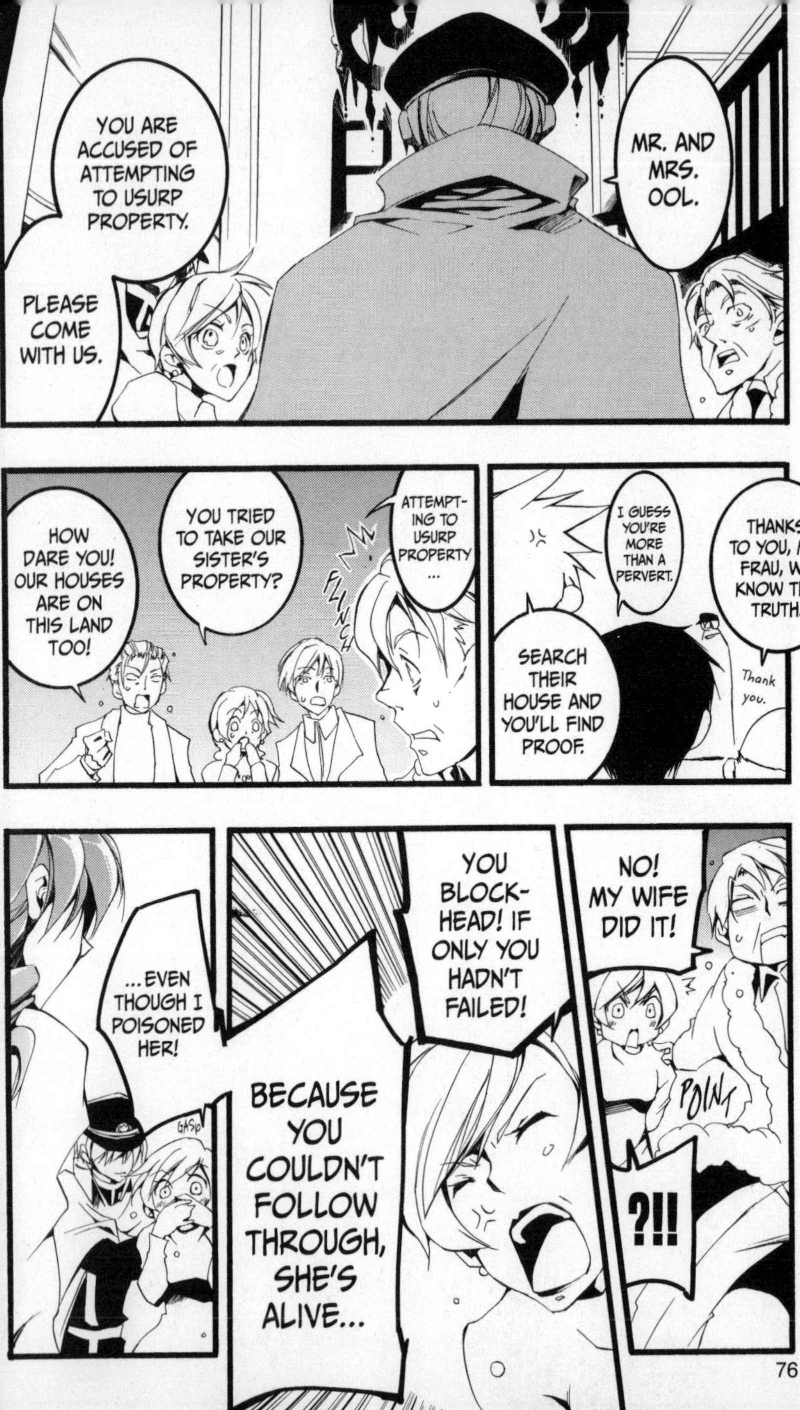
MR. AND MRS. OOL.
YOU ARE ACCUSED OF ATTEMPTING TO USURP PROPERTY.
PLEASE COME WITH US.
THANKS TO YOU, MR. FRAU, WE KNOW THE TRUTH.
Thank you.
I GUESS YOU'RE MORE THAN A PERVERT.
SEARCH THEIR HOUSE AND YOU'LL FIND PROOF.
ATTEMPTING TO USURP PROPERTY...
FLINCH
YOU TRIED TO TAKE OUR SISTER'S PROPERTY?
HOW DARE YOU! OUR HOUSES ARE ON THIS LAND TOO!
NO! MY WIFE DID IT!
POINT
?!!
YOU BLOCKHEAD! IF ONLY YOU HADN'T FAILED!
BECAUSE YOU COULDN'T FOLLOW THROUGH, SHE'S ALIVE...
...EVEN THOUGH I POISONED HER!
GASP

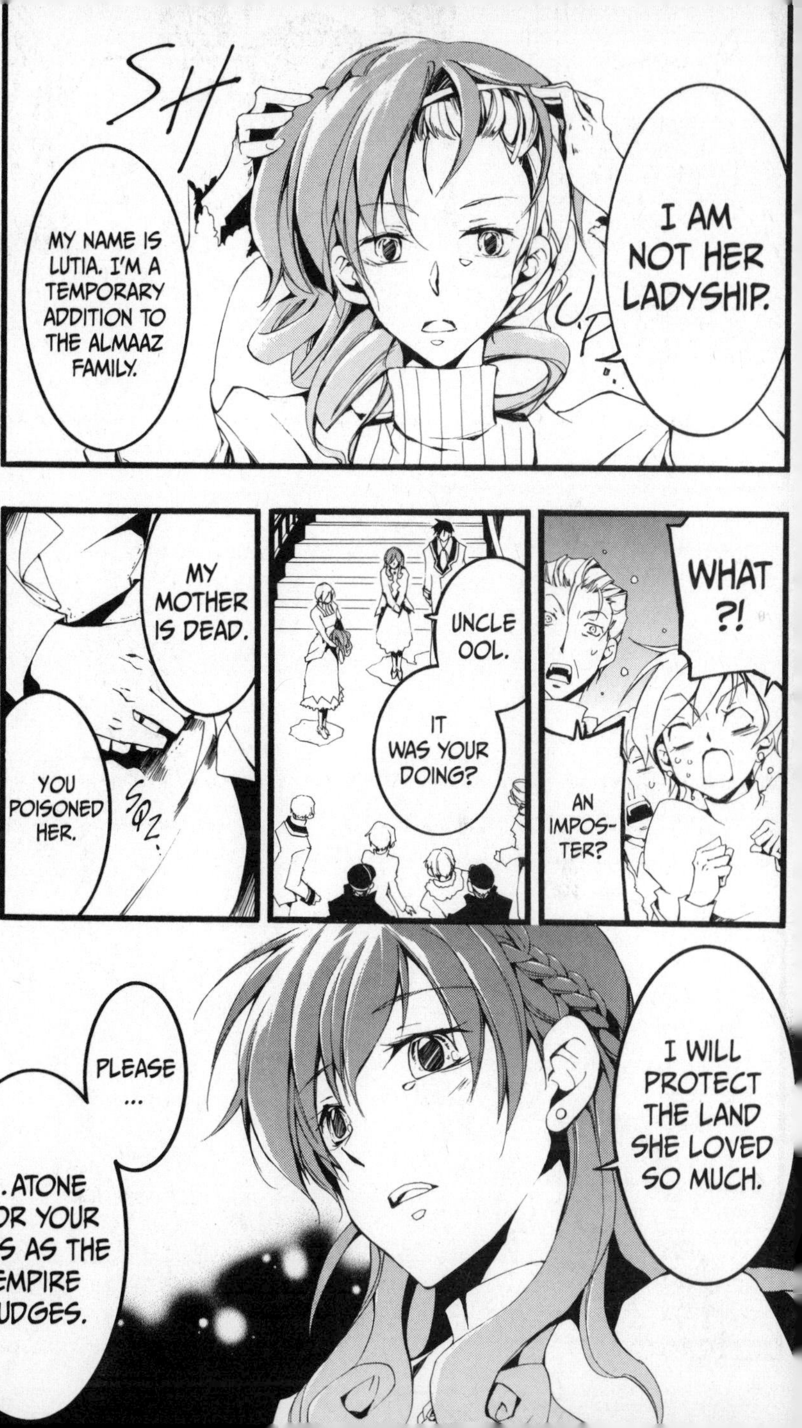
I AM NOT HER LADYSHIP.
SH
MY NAME IS LUTIA. I'M A TEMPORARY ADDITION TO THE ALMAAZ FAMILY.
WHAT?!
AN IMPOS-TER?
UNCLE OOL.
IT WAS YOUR DOING?
MY MOTHER IS DEAD.
YOU POISONED HER.
SQZ
I WILL PROTECT THE LAND SHE LOVED SO MUCH.
PLEASE...
...ATONE FOR YOUR SINS AS THE EMPIRE JUDGES.

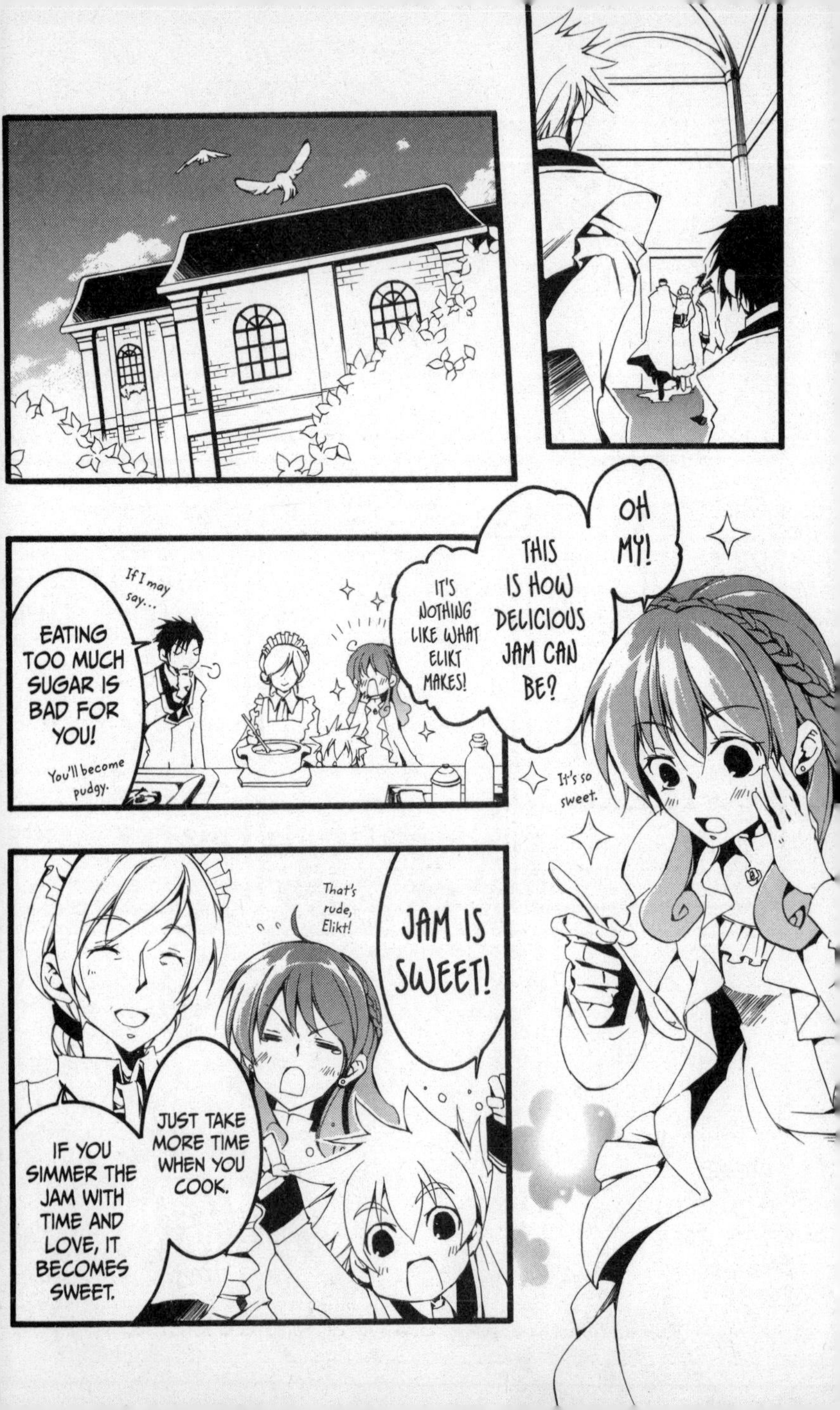
OH MY!
THIS IS HOW DELICIOUS JAM CAN BE?
IT'S NOTHING LIKE WHAT ELIKT MAKES!
It's so sweet.
If I may say...
EATING TOO MUCH SUGAR IS BAD FOR YOU!
You'll become pudgy.
JAM IS SWEET!
That's rude, Elikt!
JUST TAKE MORE TIME WHEN YOU COOK.
IF YOU SIMMER THE JAM WITH TIME AND LOVE, IT BECOMES SWEET.

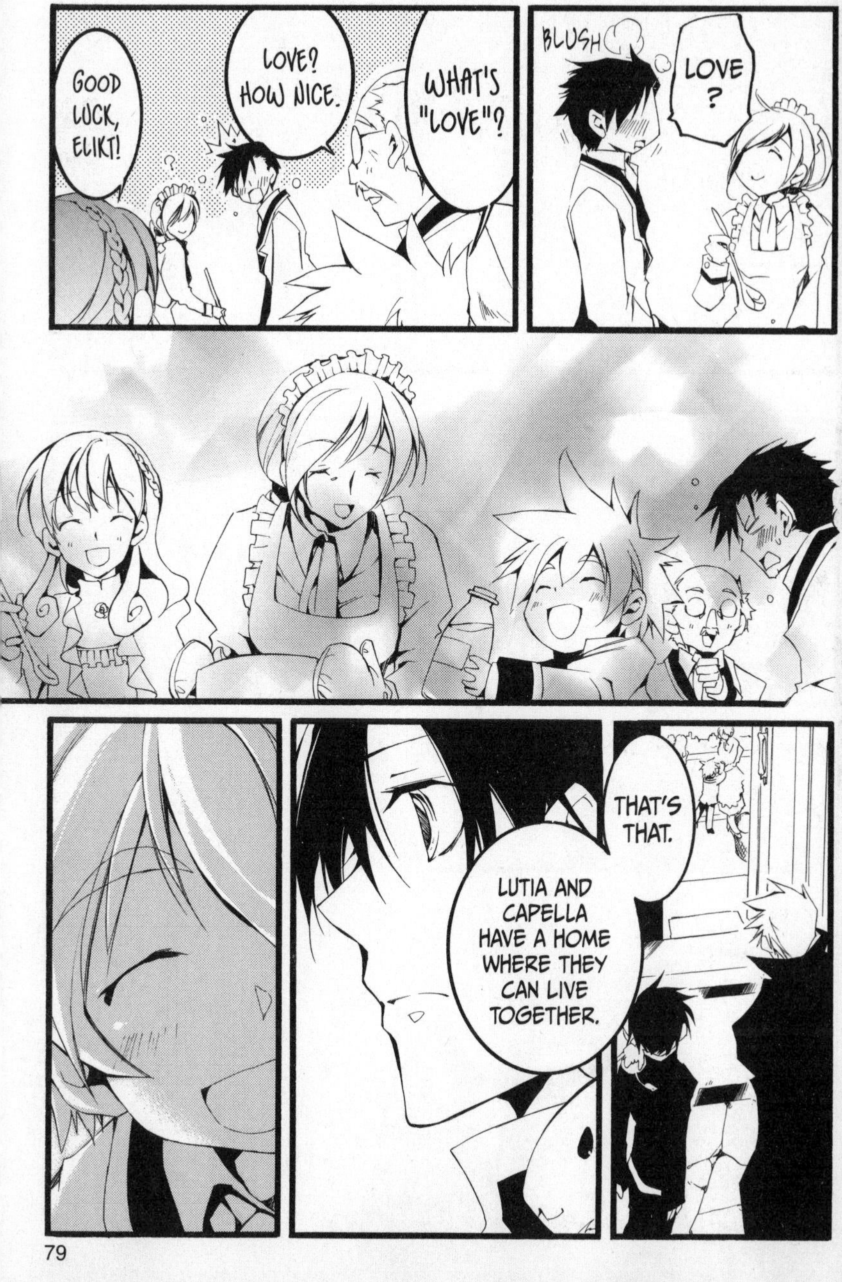
BLUSH
LOVE ?
WHAT'S "LOVE"?
LOVE? HOW NICE.
GOOD LUCK, ELIKT!
THAT'S THAT.
LUTIA AND CAPELLA HAVE A HOME WHERE THEY CAN LIVE TOGETHER.

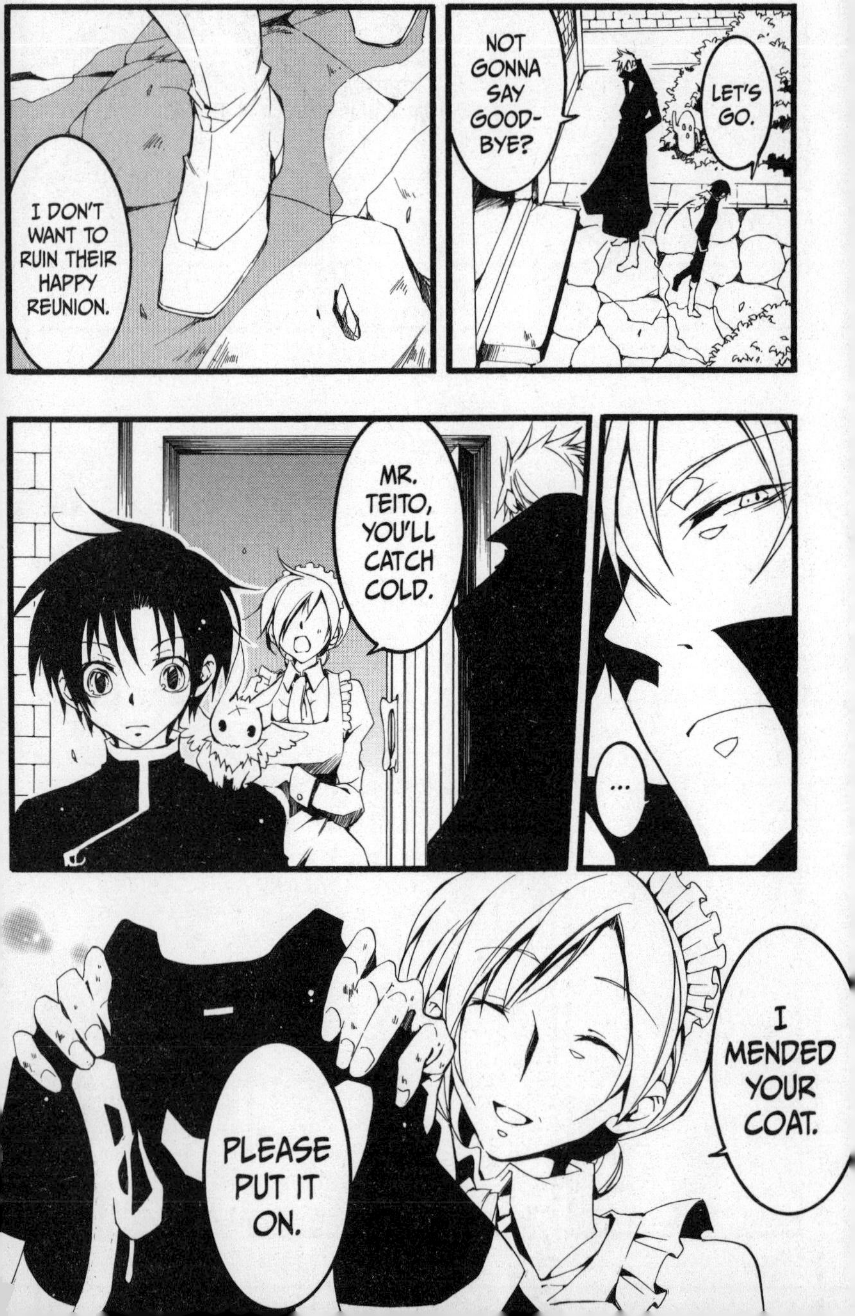
LET'S GO.
NOT GONNA SAY GOOD-BYE?
I DON'T WANT TO RUIN THEIR HAPPY REUNION.
...
MR. TEITO, YOU'LL CATCH COLD.
I MENDED YOUR COAT.
PLEASE PUT IT ON.

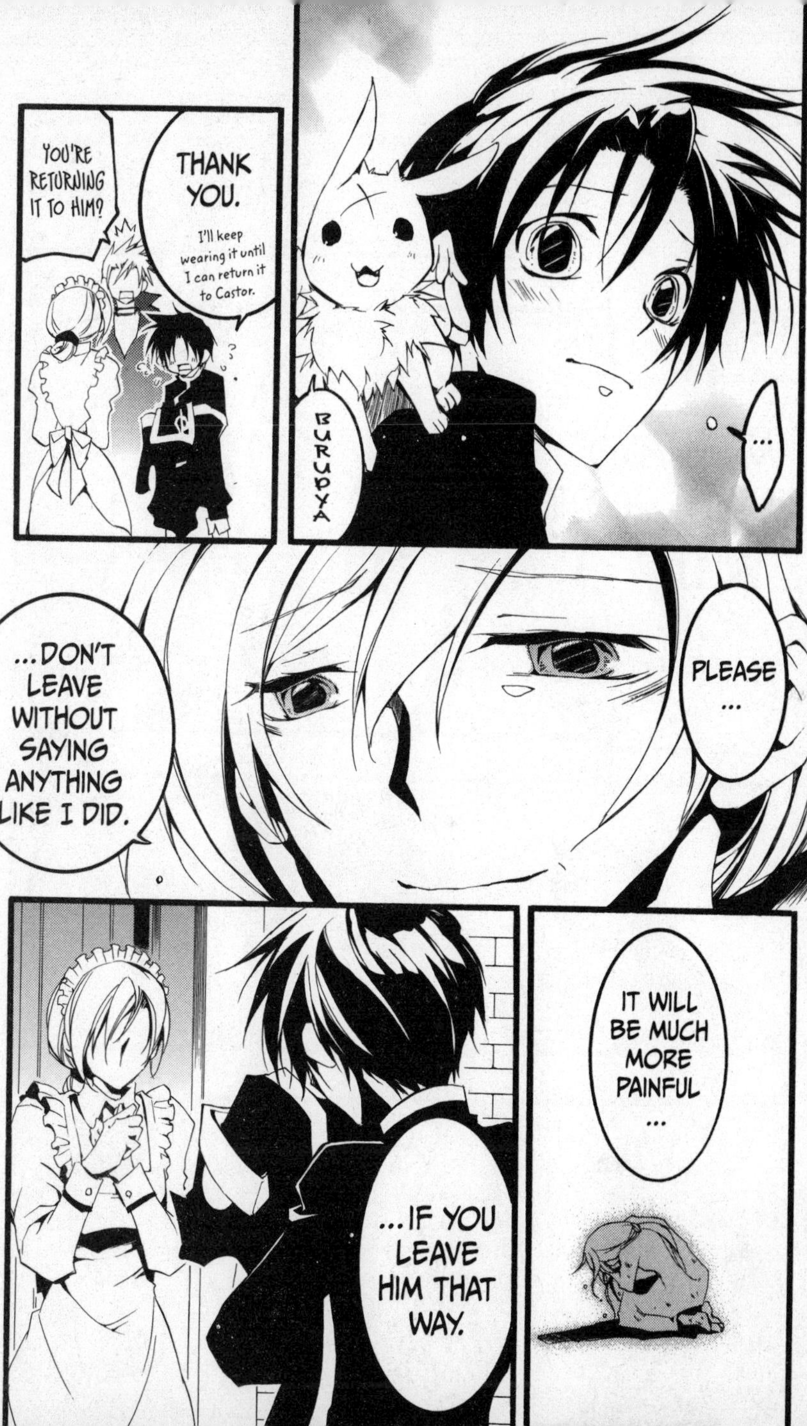
...
BURUPYA
THANK YOU.
I'll keep wearing it until I can return it to Castor.
YOU'RE RETURNING IT TO HIM?
PLEASE...
...DON'T LEAVE WITHOUT SAYING ANYTHING LIKE I DID.
IT WILL BE MUCH MORE PAINFUL...
...IF YOU LEAVE HIM THAT WAY.

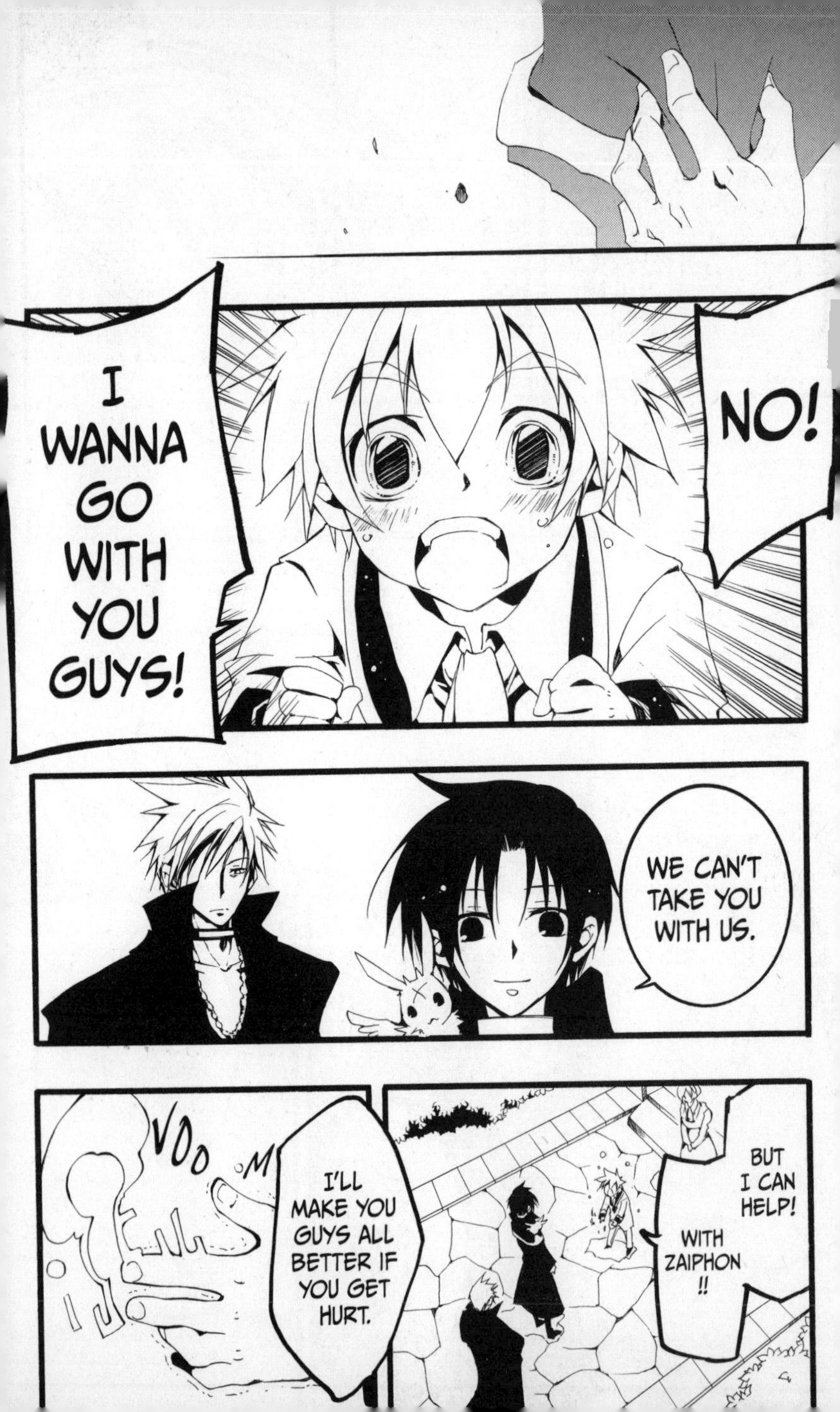
NO!
I WANNA GO WITH YOU GUYS!
WE CAN'T TAKE YOU WITH US.
BUT I CAN HELP!
WITH ZAIPHON !!
I'LL MAKE YOU GUYS ALL BETTER IF YOU GET HURT.
VOOM

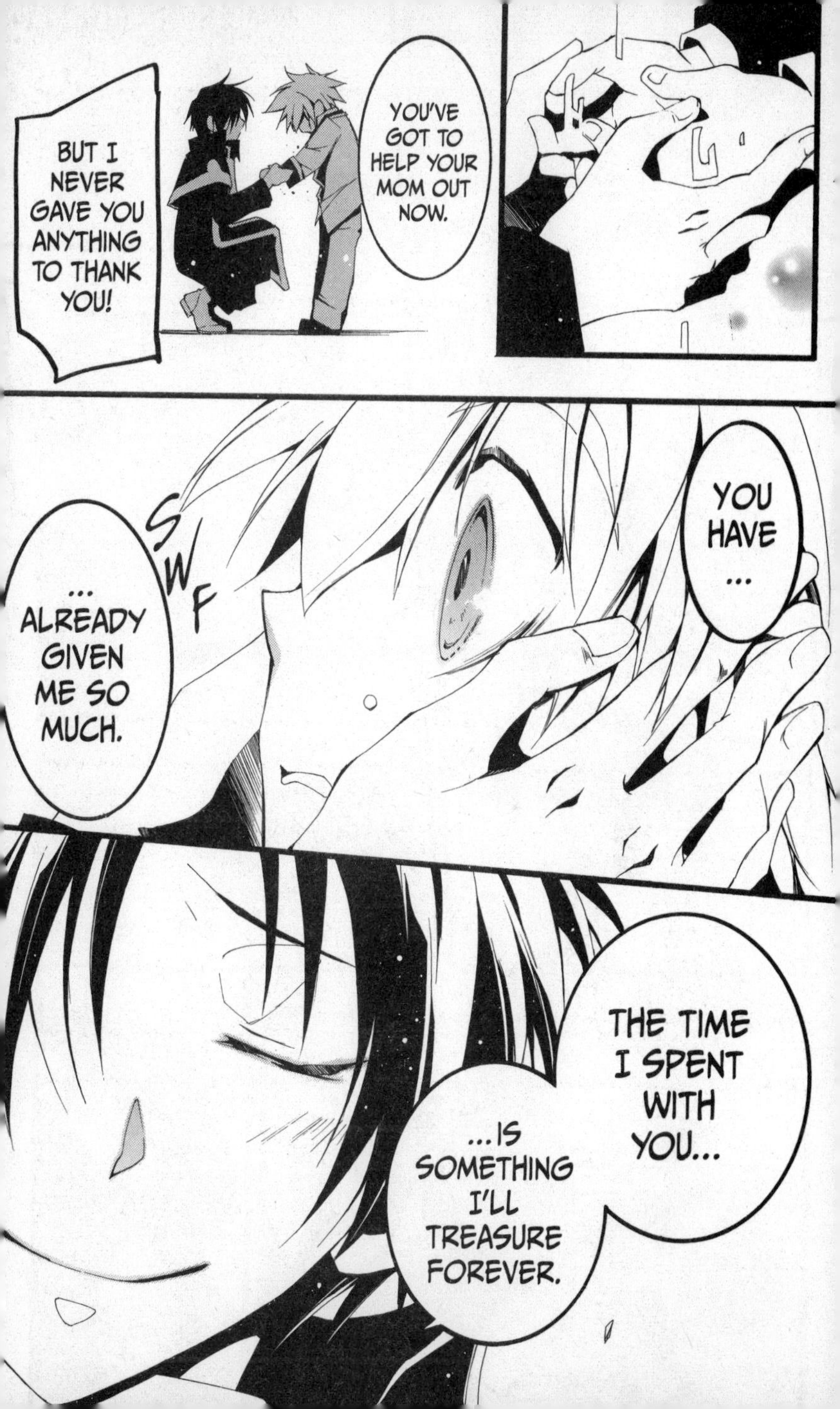
YOU'VE GOT TO HELP YOUR MOM OUT NOW.
BUT I NEVER GAVE YOU ANYTHING TO THANK YOU!
YOU HAVE ...
SWF
... ALREADY GIVEN ME SO MUCH.
THE TIME I SPENT WITH YOU...
...IS SOMETHING I'LL TREASURE FOREVER.

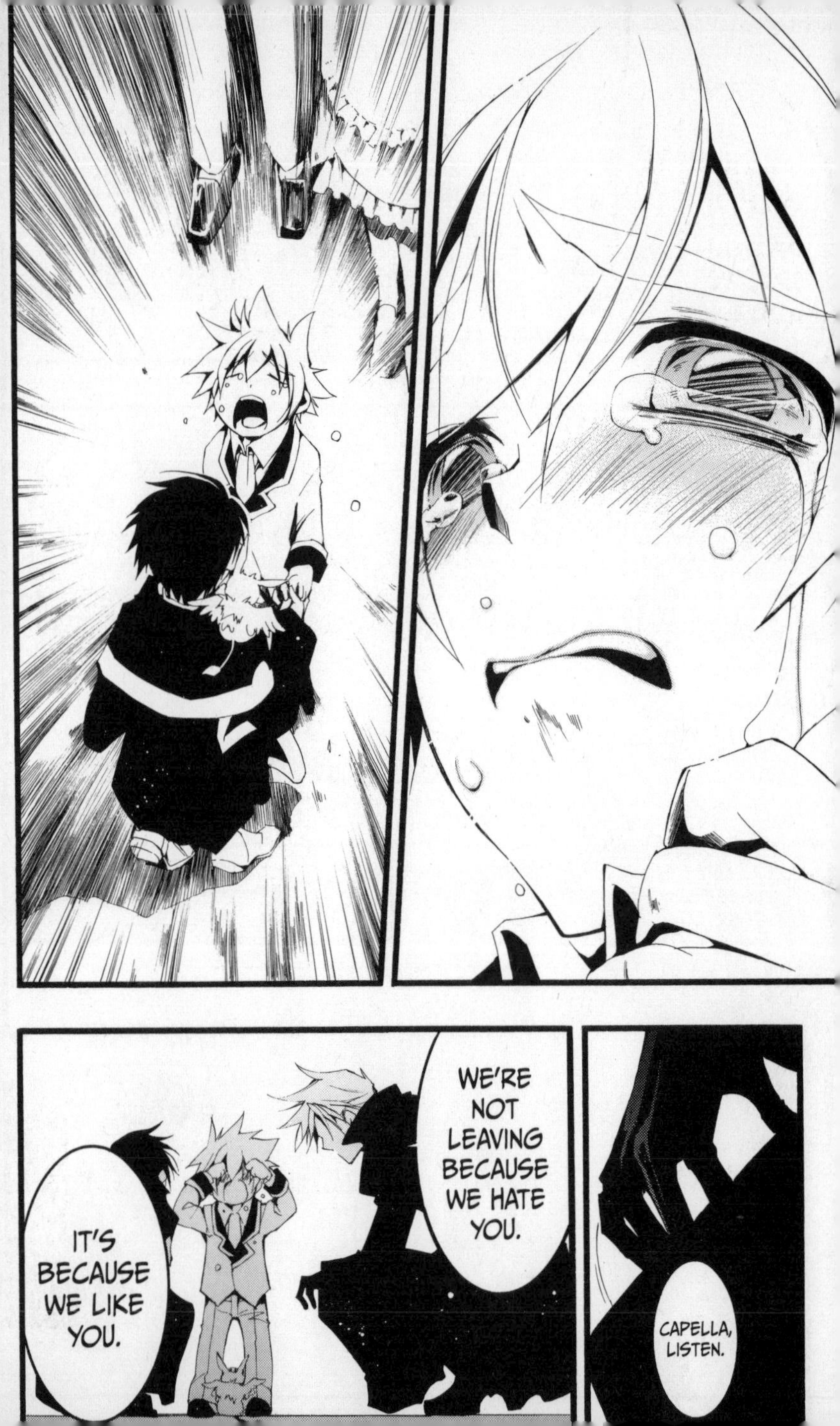
CAPELLA, LISTEN.
WE'RE NOT LEAVING BECAUSE WE HATE YOU.
IT'S BECAUSE WE LIKE YOU.

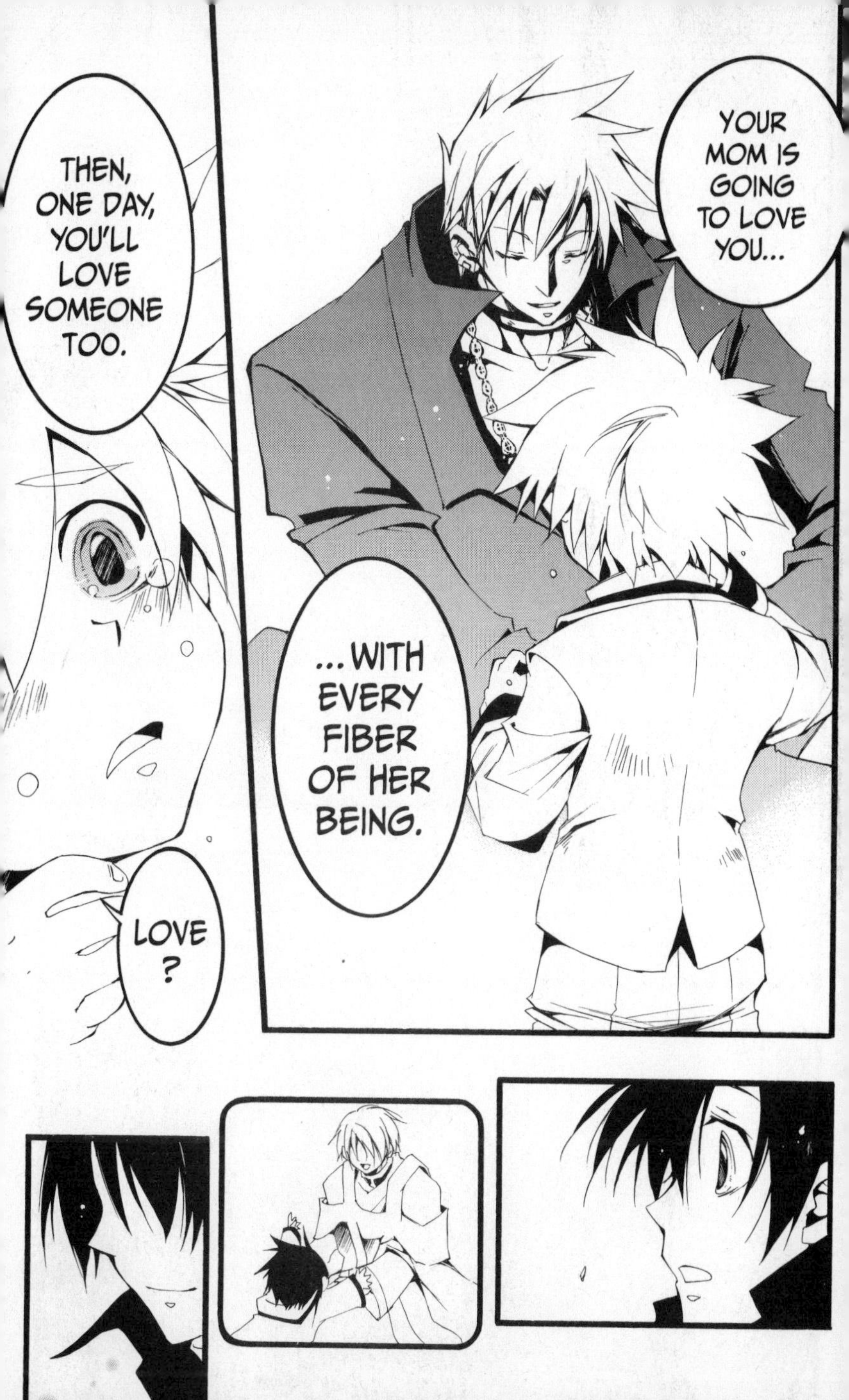

YOUR MOM IS GOING TO LOVE YOU...
...WITH EVERY FIBER OF HER BEING.
THEN, ONE DAY, YOU'LL LOVE SOMEONE TOO.
LOVE?

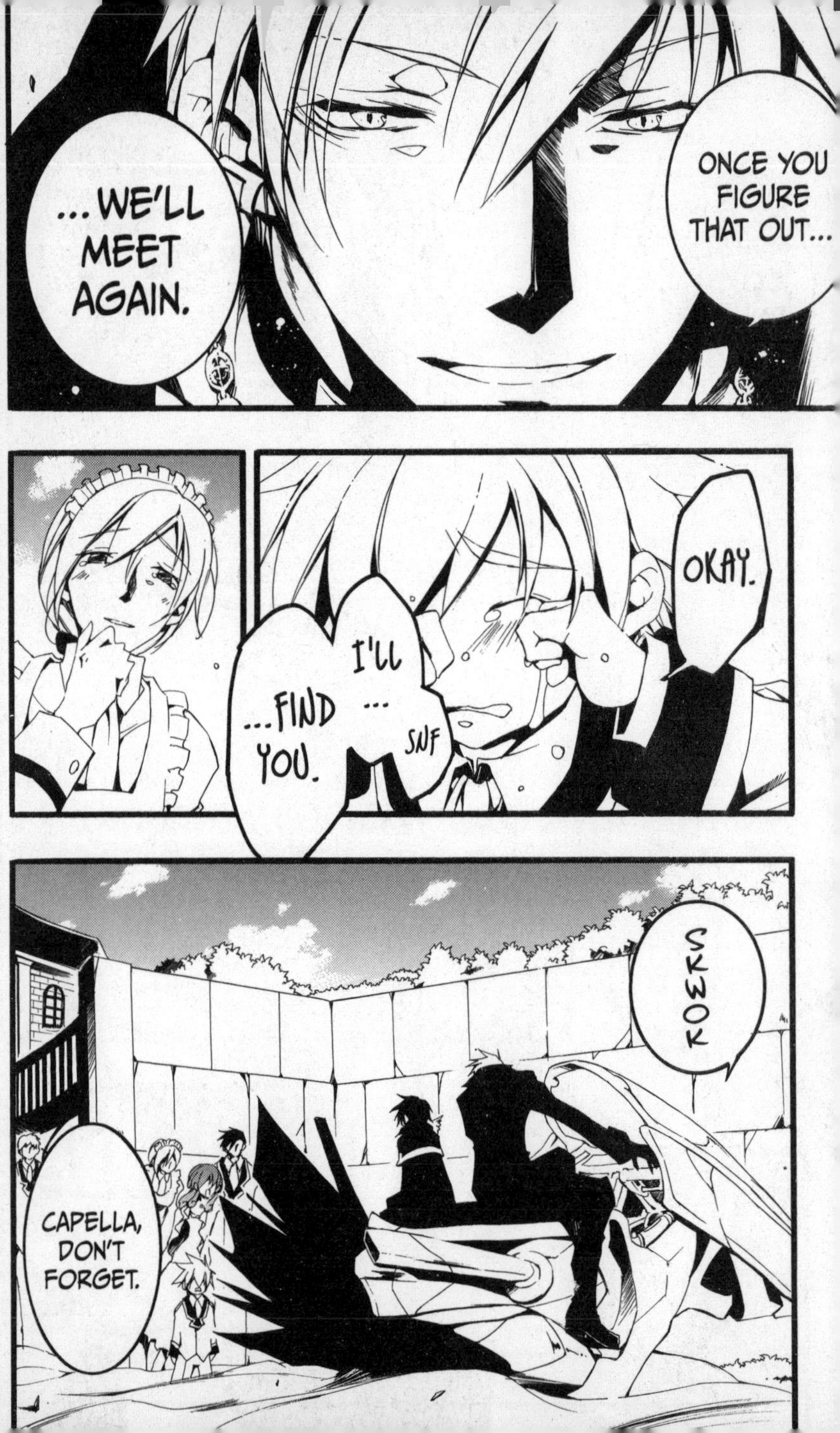
ONCE YOU FIGURE THAT OUT...
...WE'LL MEET AGAIN.
OKAY.
I'LL ... ...FIND YOU.
SNF
SKWOK
CAPELLA, DON'T FORGET.

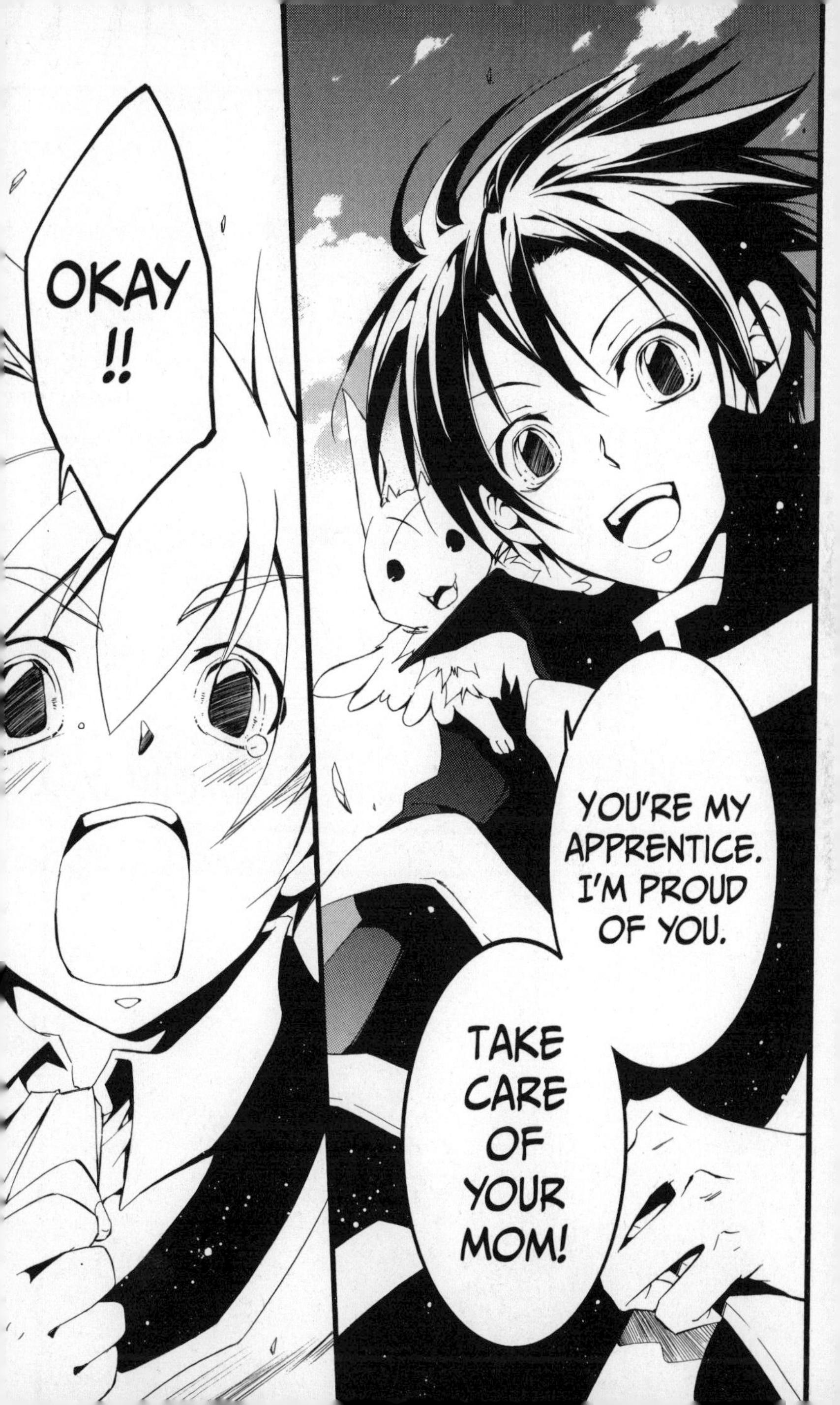
YOU'RE MY APPRENTICE. I'M PROUD OF YOU.
TAKE CARE OF YOUR MOM!
OKAY !!

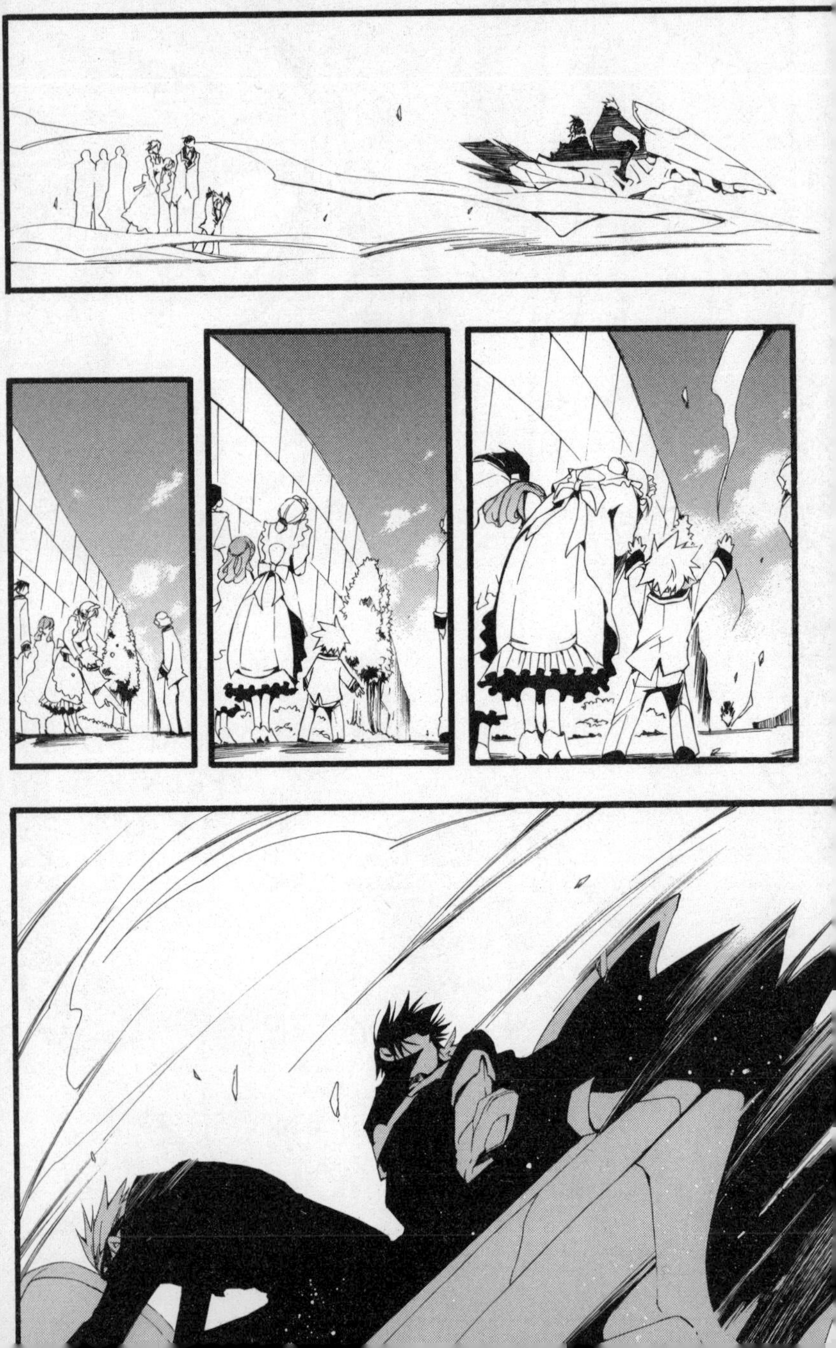

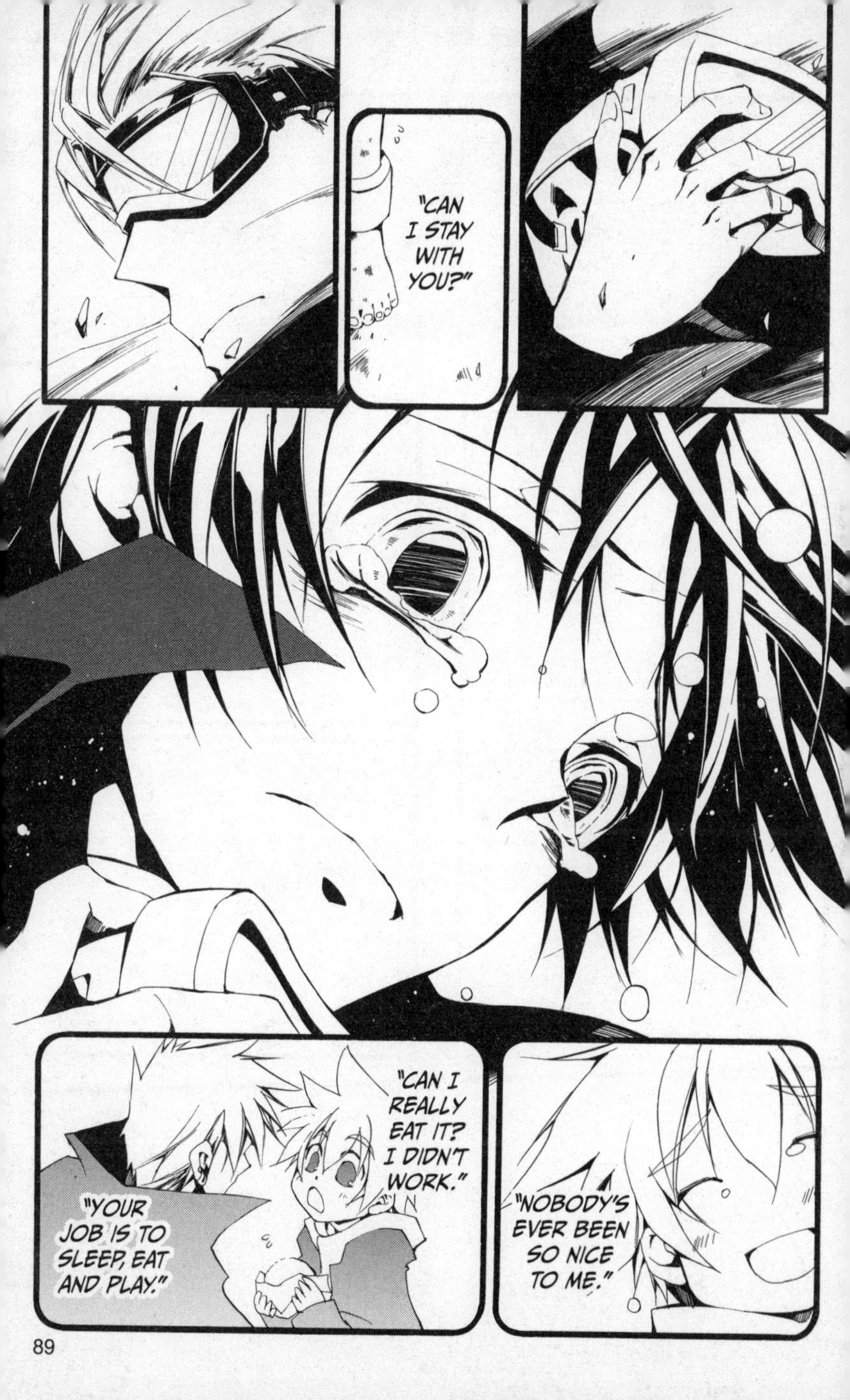
"CAN I STAY WITH YOU?"
"NOBODY'S EVER BEEN SO NICE TO ME."
"CAN I REALLY EAT IT? I DIDN'T WORK."
"YOUR JOB IS TO SLEEP, EAT AND PLAY."

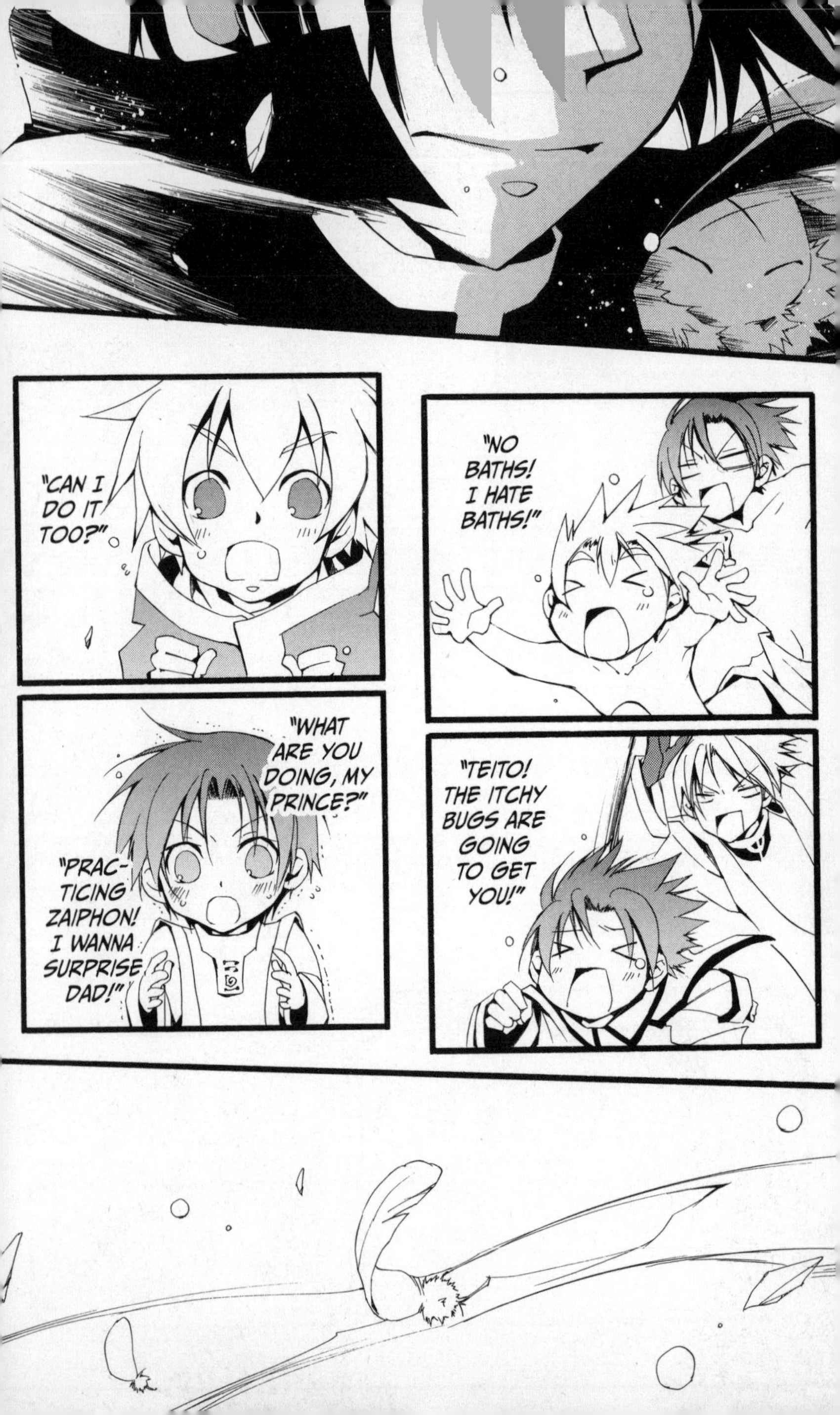
"NO BATHS! I HATE BATHS!"
"CAN I DO IT TOO?"
"TEITO! THE ITCHY BUGS ARE GOING TO GET YOU!"
"WHAT ARE YOU DOING, MY PRINCE?"
"PRAC-TICING ZAIPHON! I WANNA SURPRISE DAD!"

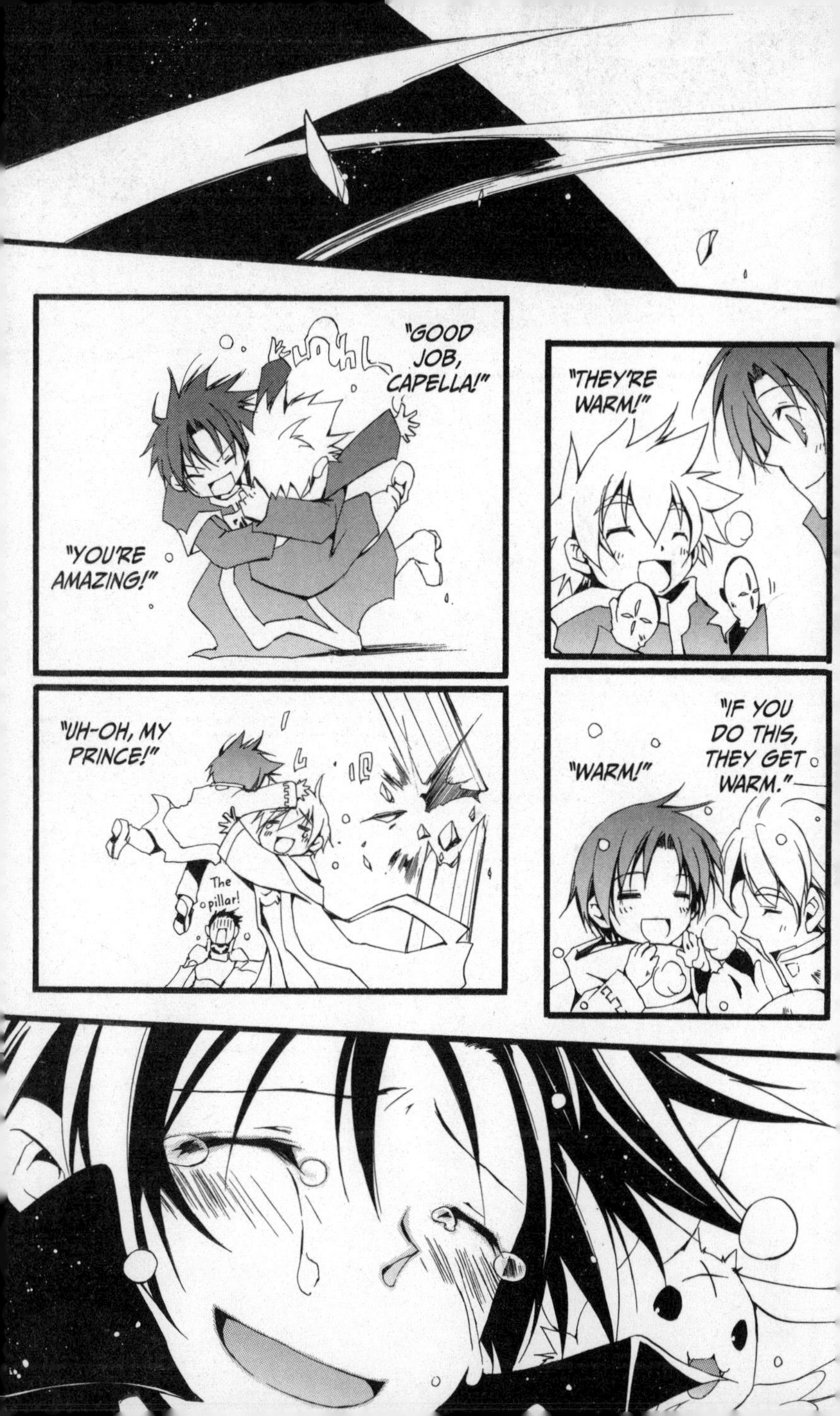
"THEY'RE WARM!"
"GOOD JOB, CAPELLA!"
"YOU'RE AMAZING!"
"IF YOU DO THIS, THEY GET WARM."
"WARM!"
"UH-OH, MY PRINCE!"
The pillar!

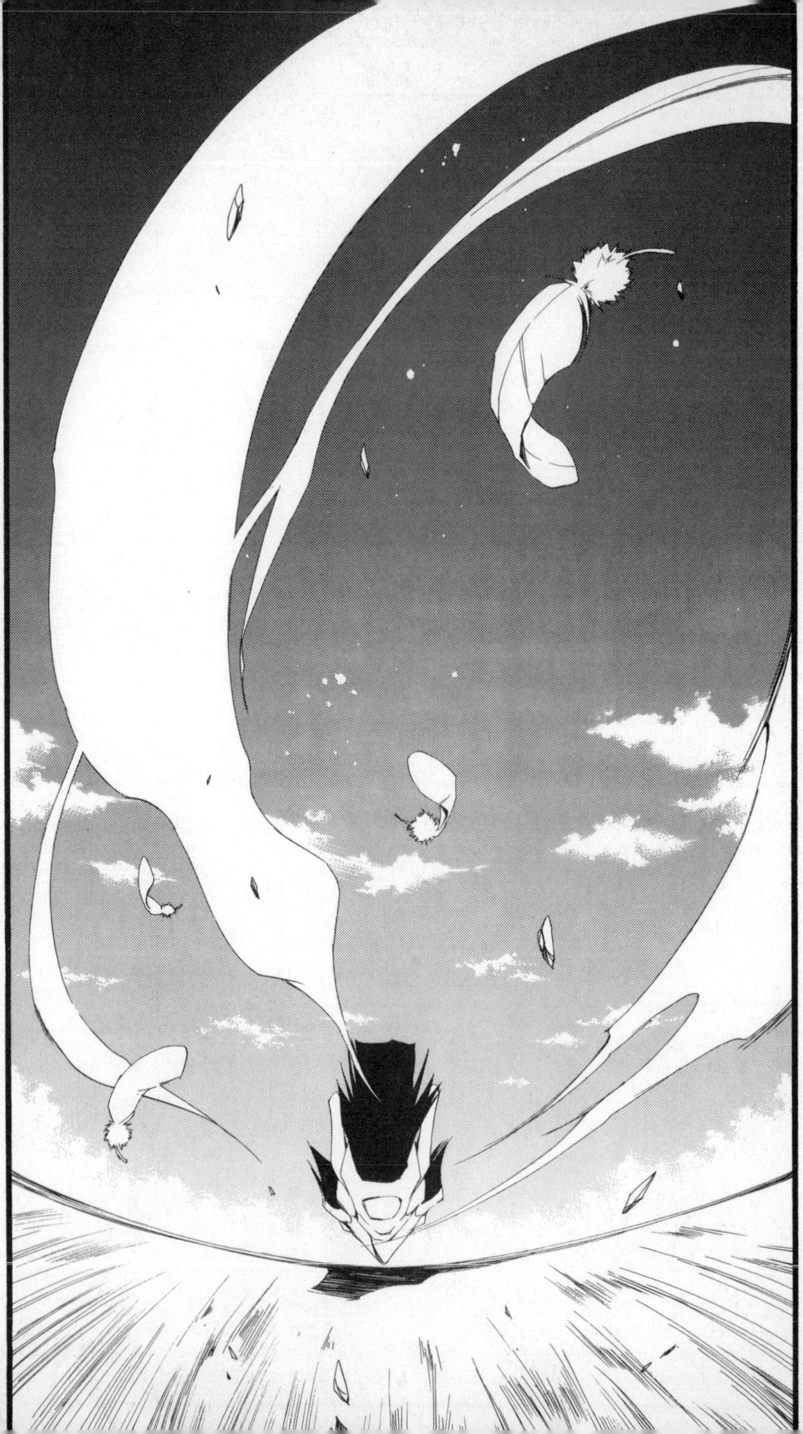

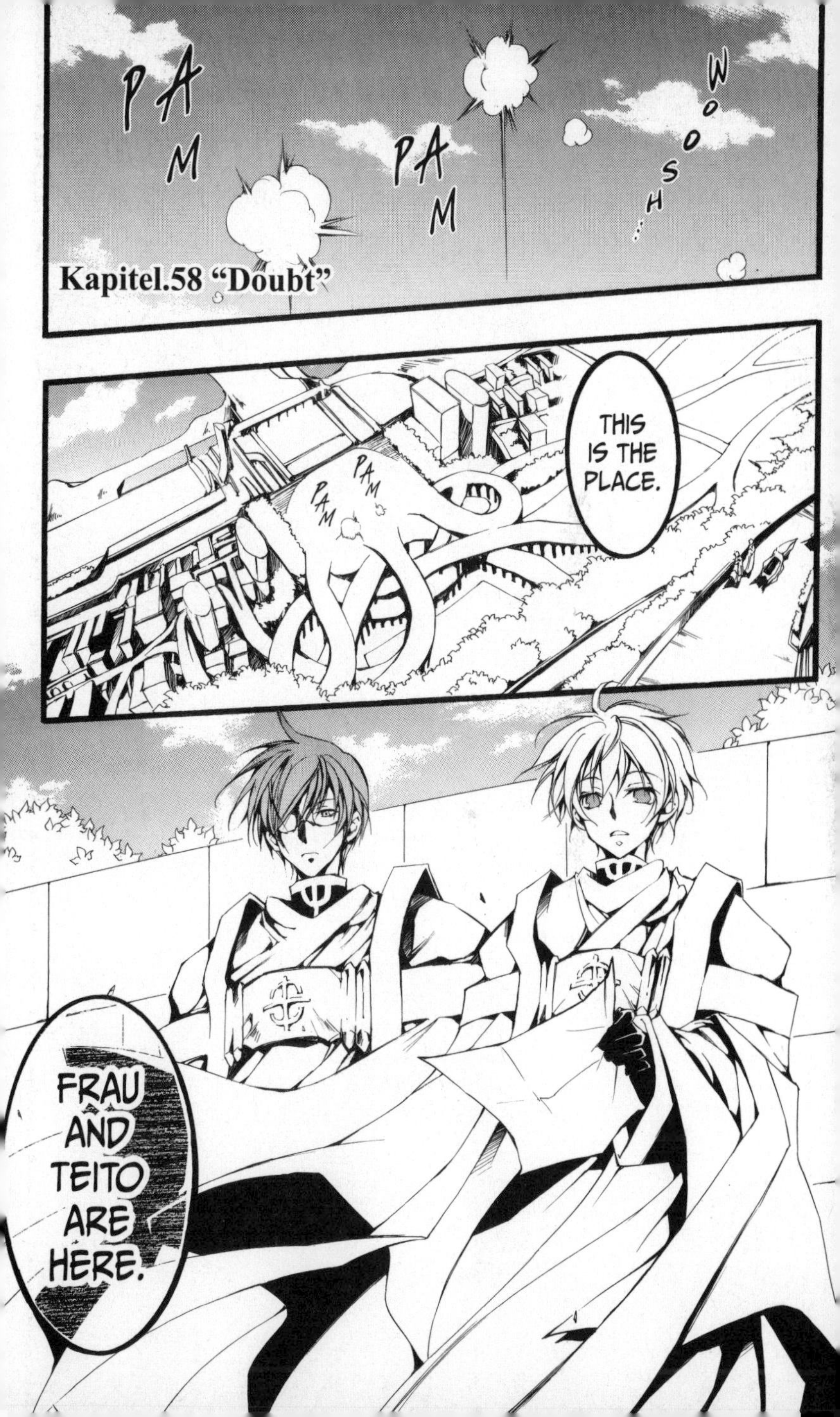

WOOSH...
PAM
PAM
Kapitel.58 "Doubt"
PAM
PAM
THIS IS THE PLACE.
FRAU AND TEITO ARE HERE.

Kapitel.58 "Doubt"

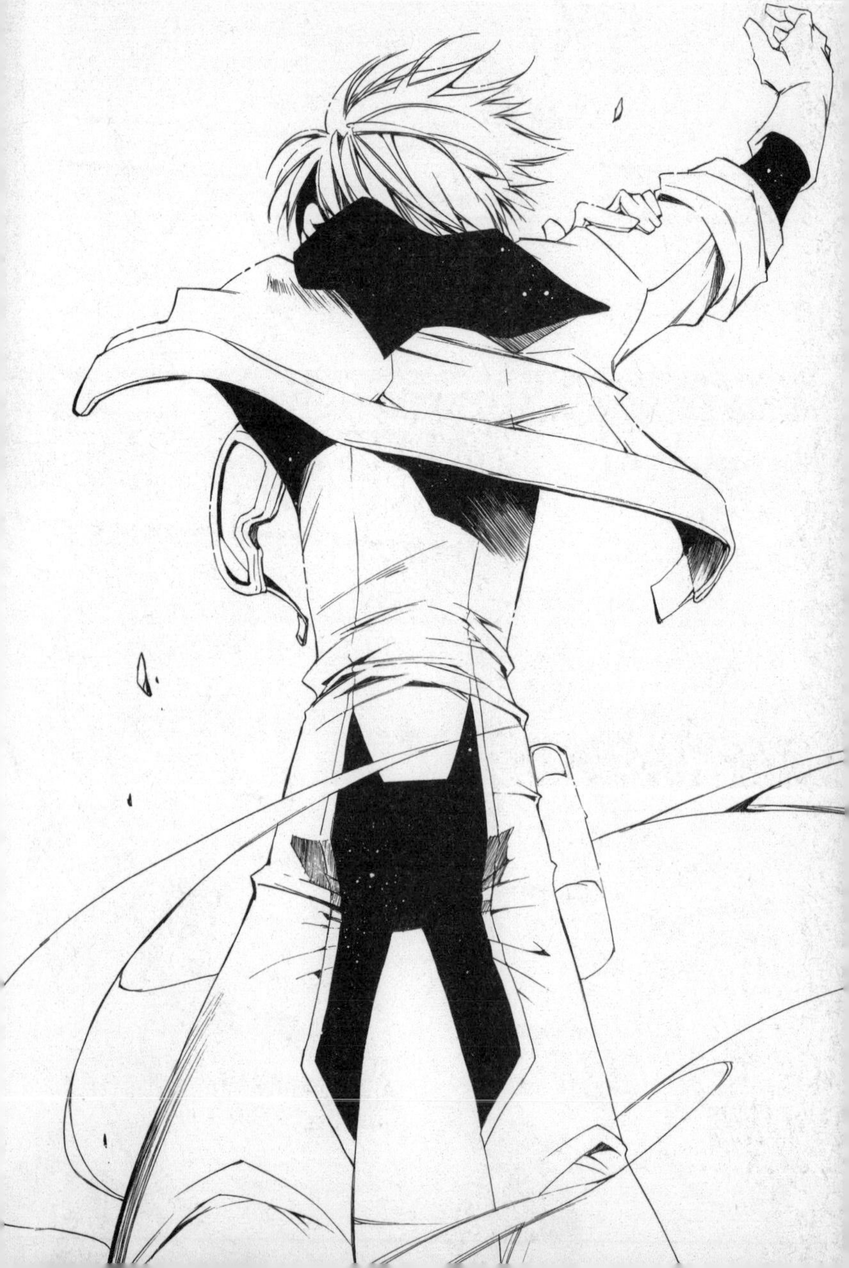

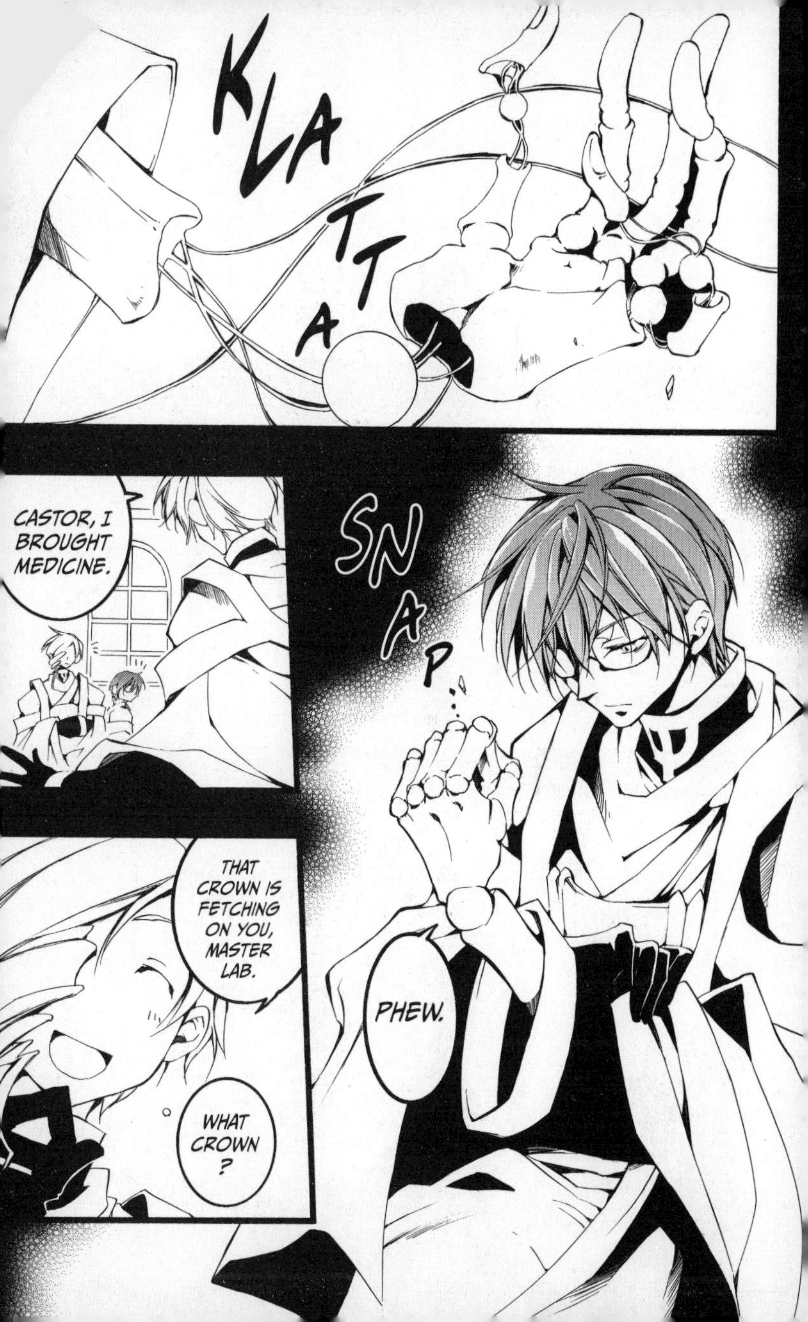
KLATTA
SNAP
PHEW.
CASTOR, I BROUGHT MEDICINE.
THAT CROWN IS FETCHING ON YOU, MASTER LAB.
WHAT CROWN?

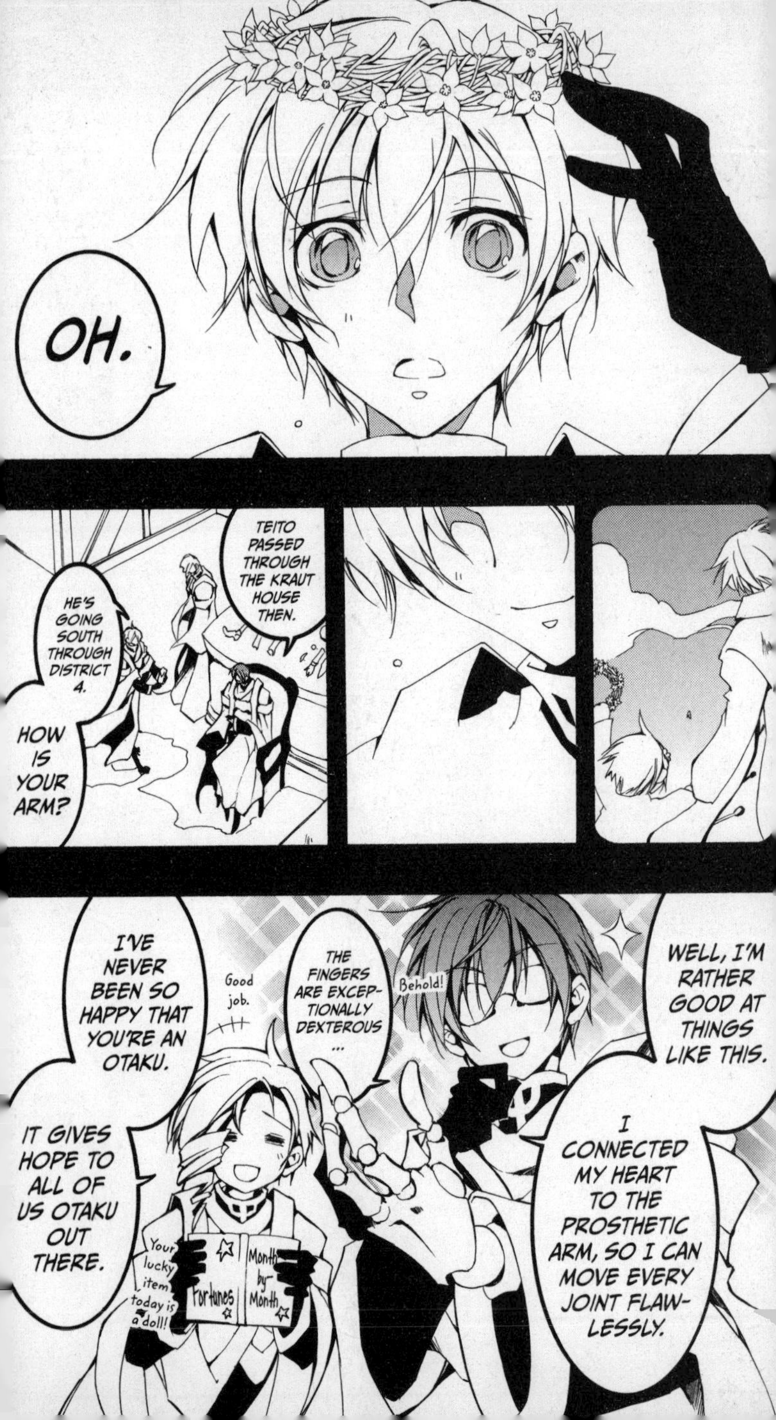
OH.
TEITO PASSED THROUGH THE KRAUT HOUSE THEN.
HE'S GOING SOUTH THROUGH DISTRICT 4.
HOW IS YOUR ARM?
WELL, I'M RATHER GOOD AT THINGS LIKE THIS.
Behold!
I CONNECTED MY HEART TO THE PROSTHETIC ARM, SO I CAN MOVE EVERY JOINT FLAWLESSLY.
THE FINGERS ARE EXCEPTIONALLY DEXTEROUS...
Good job.
I'VE NEVER BEEN SO HAPPY THAT YOU'RE AN OTAKU.
IT GIVES HOPE TO ALL OF US OTAKU OUT THERE.
Your lucky item today is a doll!
Month by Month Fortunes

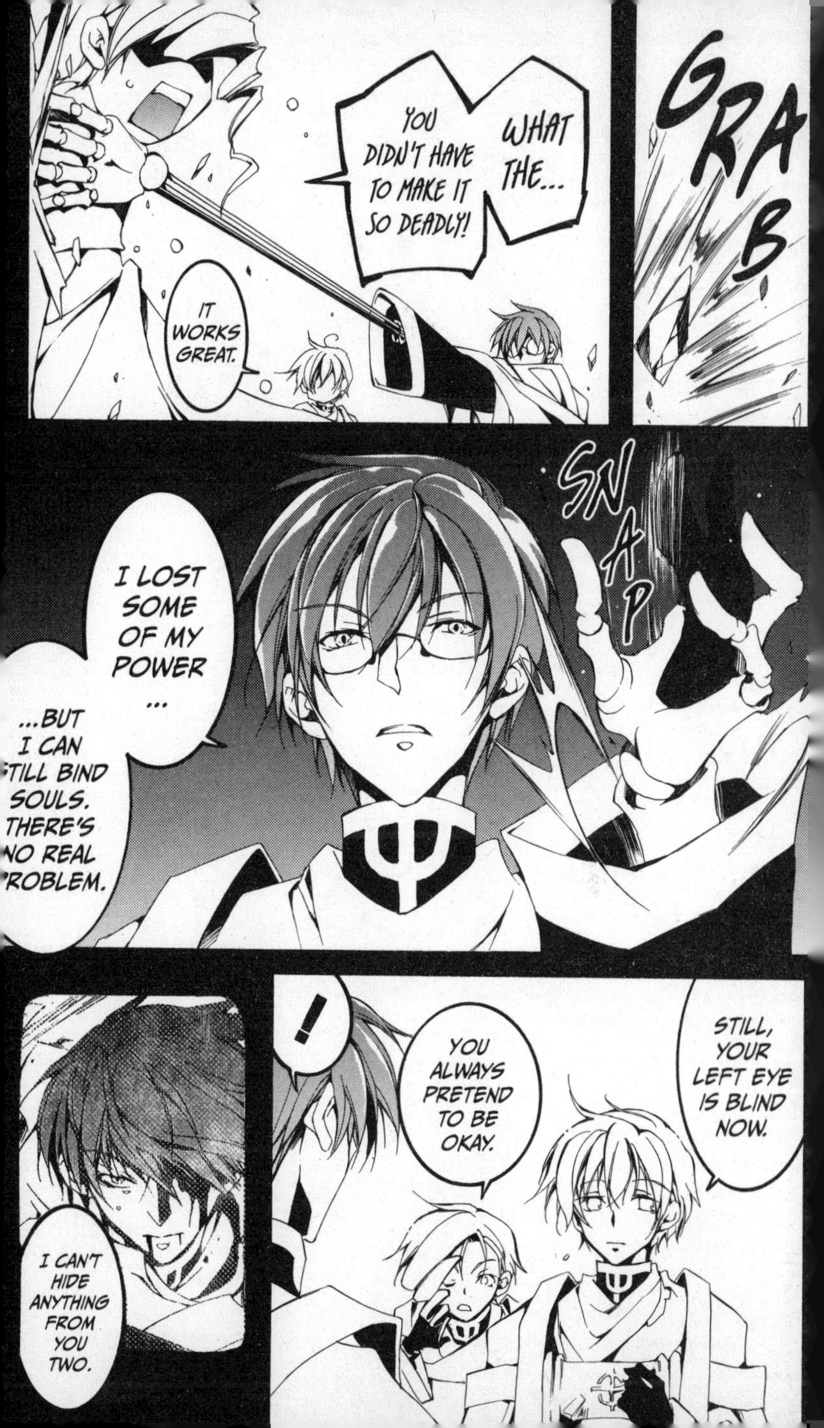
GRAB
WHAT THE...
YOU DIDN'T HAVE TO MAKE IT SO DEADLY!
IT WORKS GREAT.
SNAP
I LOST SOME OF MY POWER ...
...BUT I CAN STILL BIND SOULS. THERE'S NO REAL PROBLEM.
STILL, YOUR LEFT EYE IS BLIND NOW.
YOU ALWAYS PRETEND TO BE OKAY.
!
I CAN'T HIDE ANYTHING FROM YOU TWO.

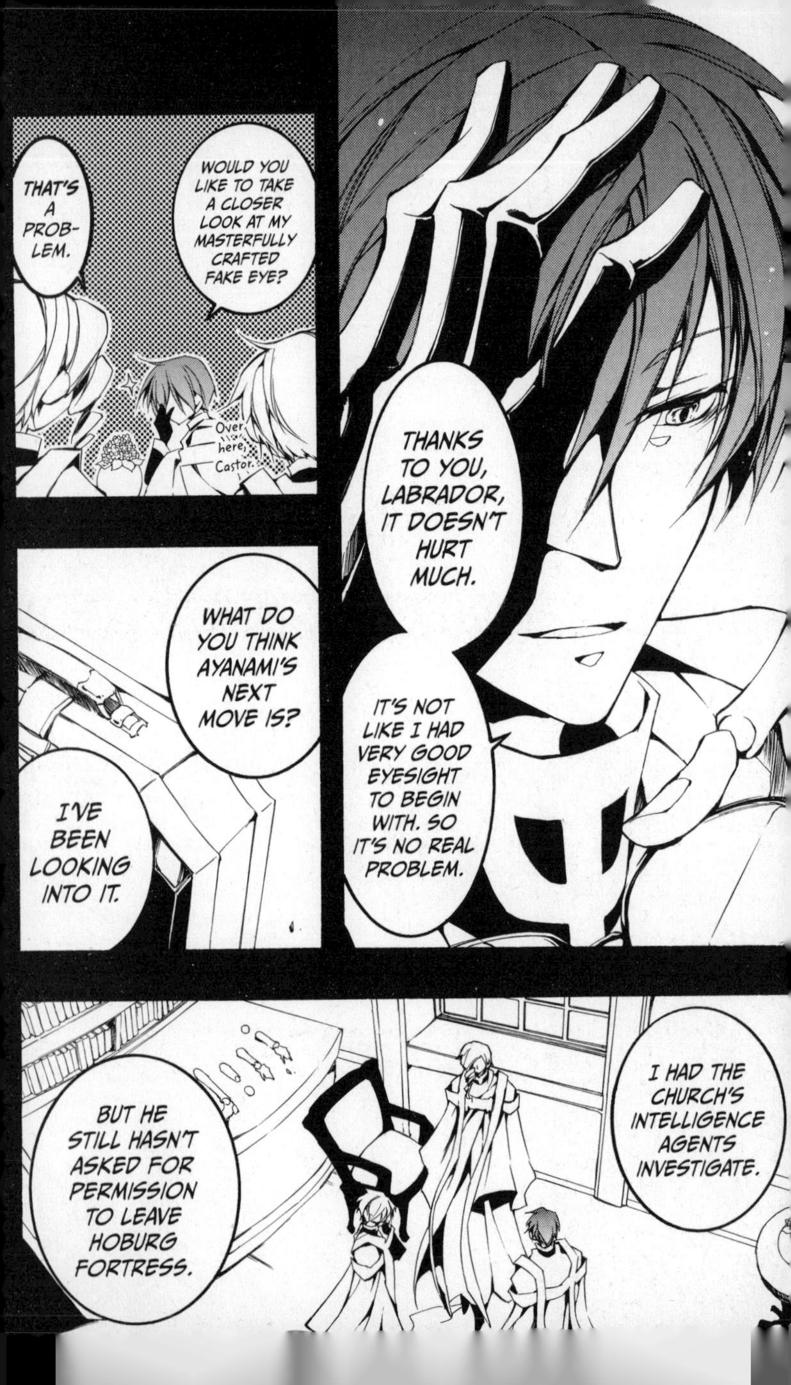
THANKS TO YOU, LABRADOR, IT DOESN'T HURT MUCH.
IT'S NOT LIKE I HAD VERY GOOD EYESIGHT TO BEGIN WITH. SO IT'S NO REAL PROBLEM.
WOULD YOU LIKE TO TAKE A CLOSER LOOK AT MY MASTERFULLY CRAFTED FAKE EYE?
THAT'S A PROB-LEM.
Over here, Castor.
WHAT DO YOU THINK AYANAMI'S NEXT MOVE IS?
I'VE BEEN LOOKING INTO IT.
I HAD THE CHURCH'S INTELLIGENCE AGENTS INVESTIGATE.
BUT HE STILL HASN'T ASKED FOR PERMISSION TO LEAVE HOBURG FORTRESS.

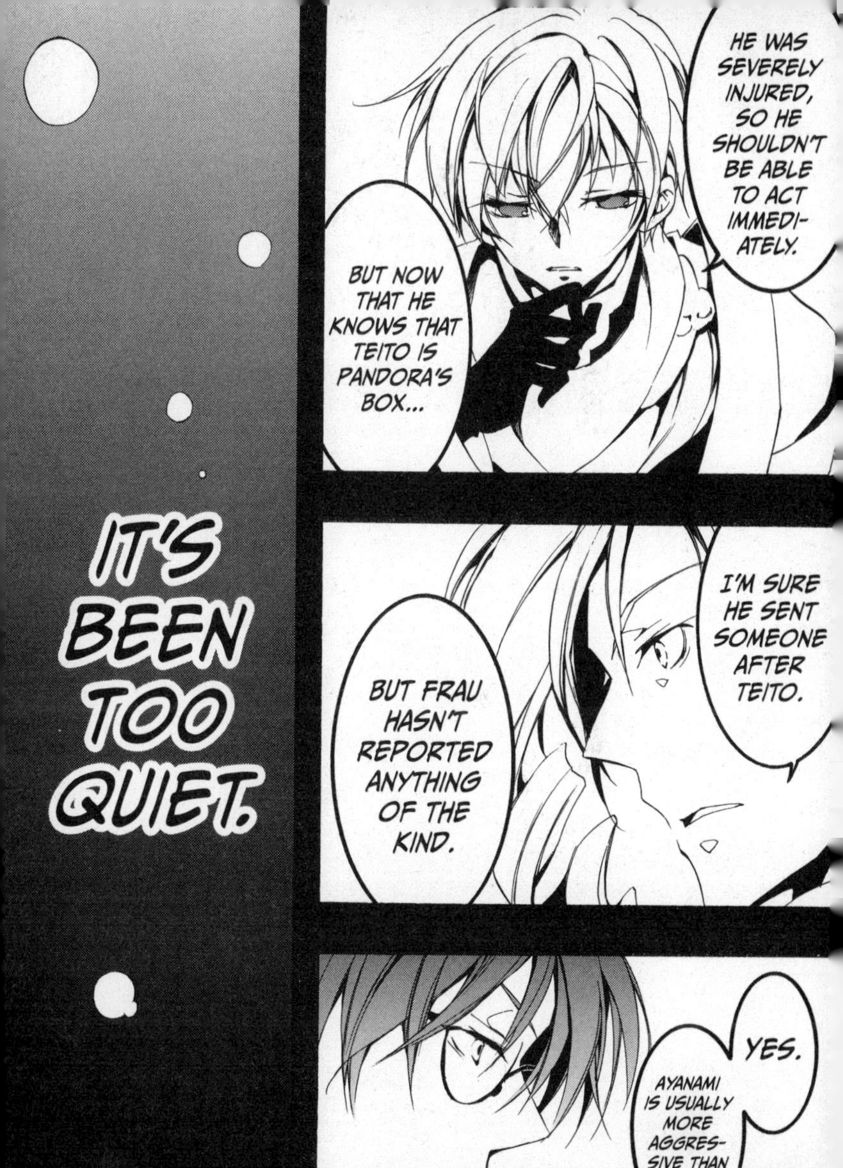
HE WAS SEVERELY INJURED, SO HE SHOULDN'T BE ABLE TO ACT IMMEDI-ATELY.
BUT NOW THAT HE KNOWS THAT TEITO IS PANDORA'S BOX...
I'M SURE HE SENT SOMEONE AFTER TEITO.
BUT FRAU HASN'T REPORTED ANYTHING OF THE KIND.
YES.
AYANAMI IS USUALLY MORE AGGRES-SIVE THAN THIS.
IT'S BEEN TOO QUIET.

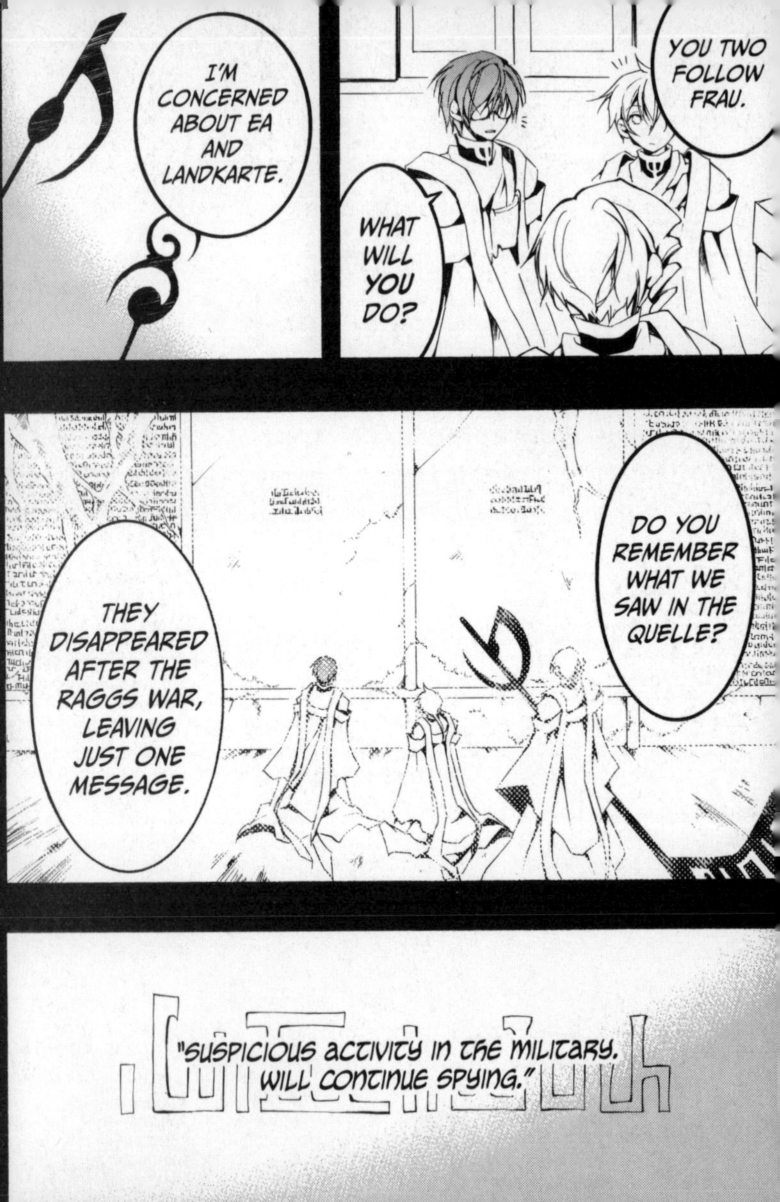
YOU TWO FOLLOW FRAU.
WHAT WILL YOU DO?
I'M CONCERNED ABOUT EA AND LANDKARTE.
DO YOU REMEMBER WHAT WE SAW IN THE QUELLE?
THEY DISAPPEARED AFTER THE RAGGS WAR, LEAVING JUST ONE MESSAGE.
"SUSPICIOUS ACTIVITY IN THE MILITARY. WILL CONTINUE SPYING."

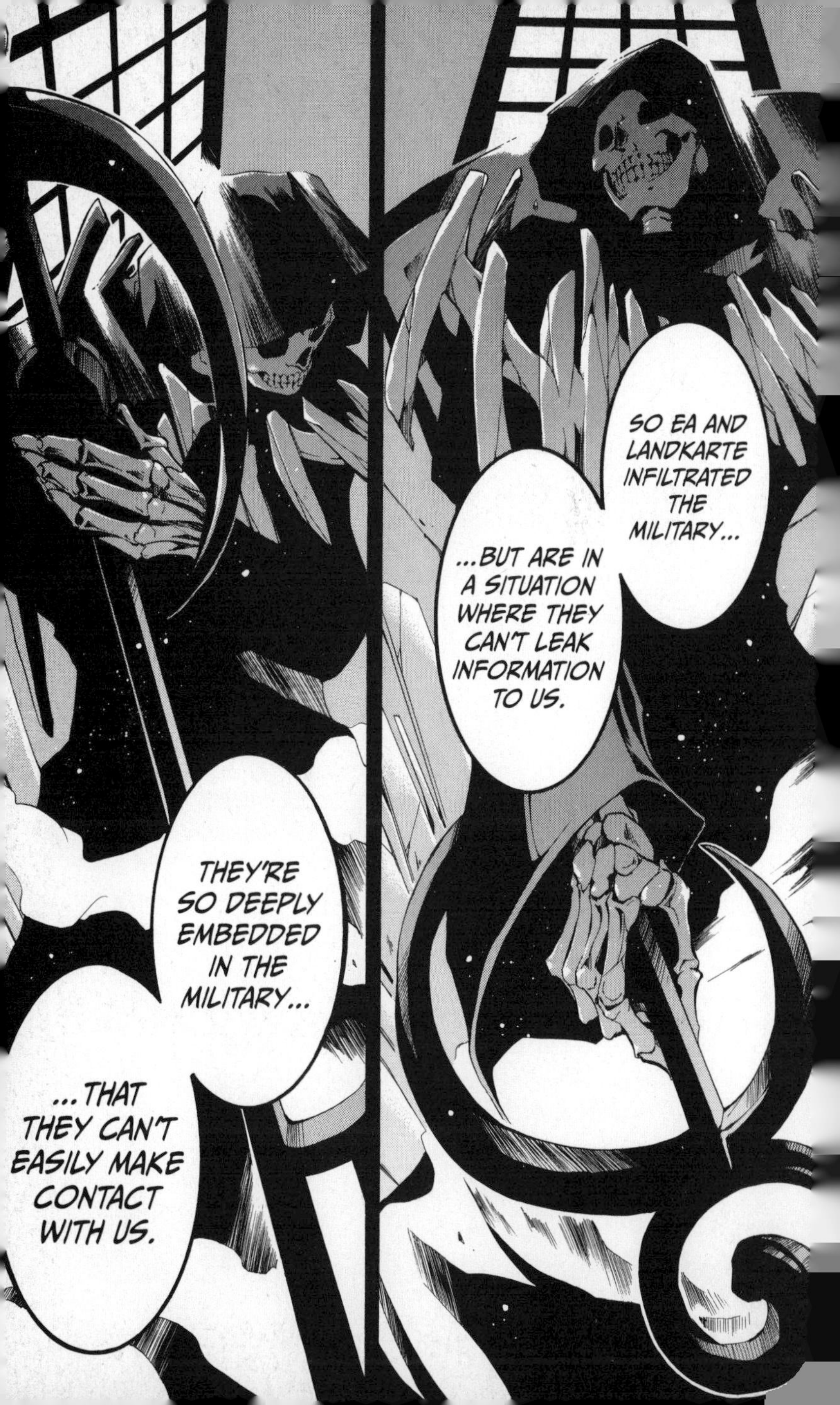

SO EA AND LANDKARTE INFILTRATED THE MILITARY...
...BUT ARE IN A SITUATION WHERE THEY CAN'T LEAK INFORMATION TO US.
THEY'RE SO DEEPLY EMBEDDED IN THE MILITARY...
...THAT THEY CAN'T EASILY MAKE CONTACT WITH US.

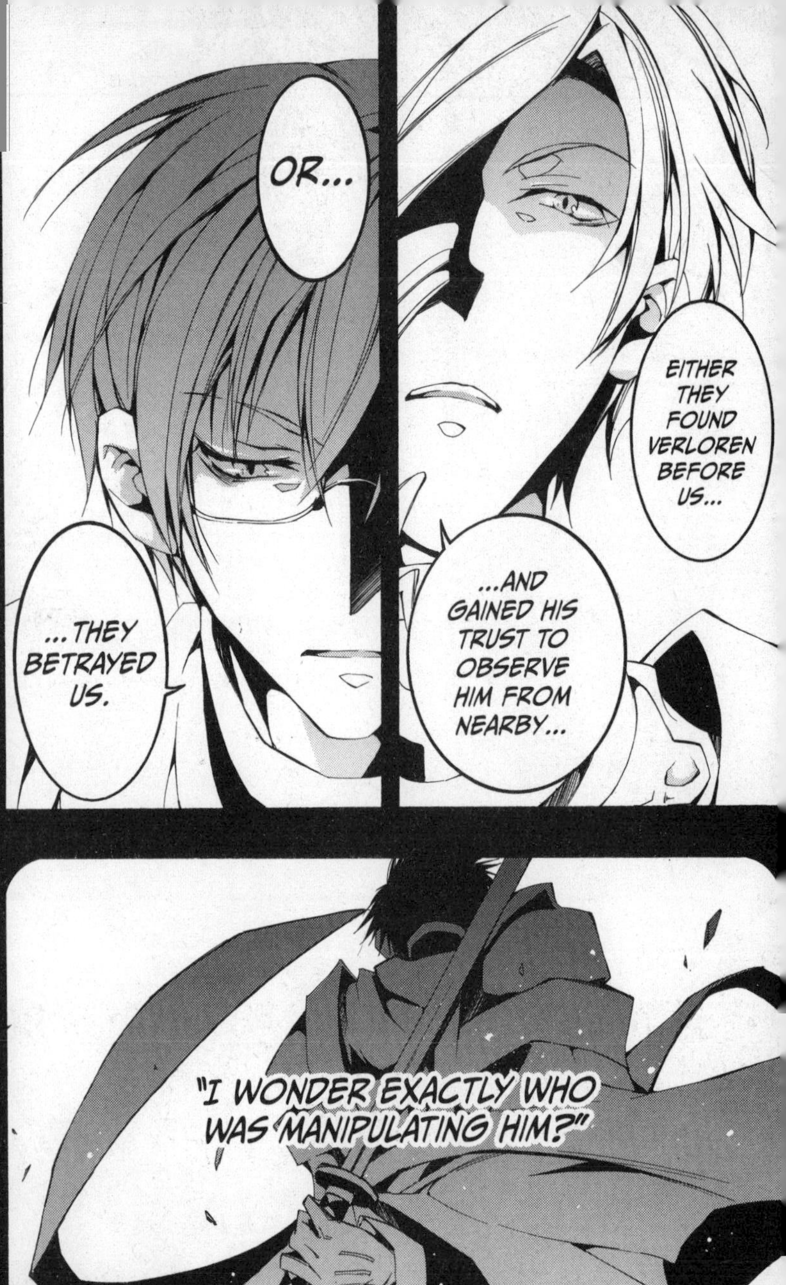
EITHER THEY FOUND VERLOREN BEFORE US...
...AND GAINED HIS TRUST TO OBSERVE HIM FROM NEARBY...
OR...
...THEY BETRAYED US.
"I WONDER EXACTLY WHO WAS MANIPULATING HIM?"

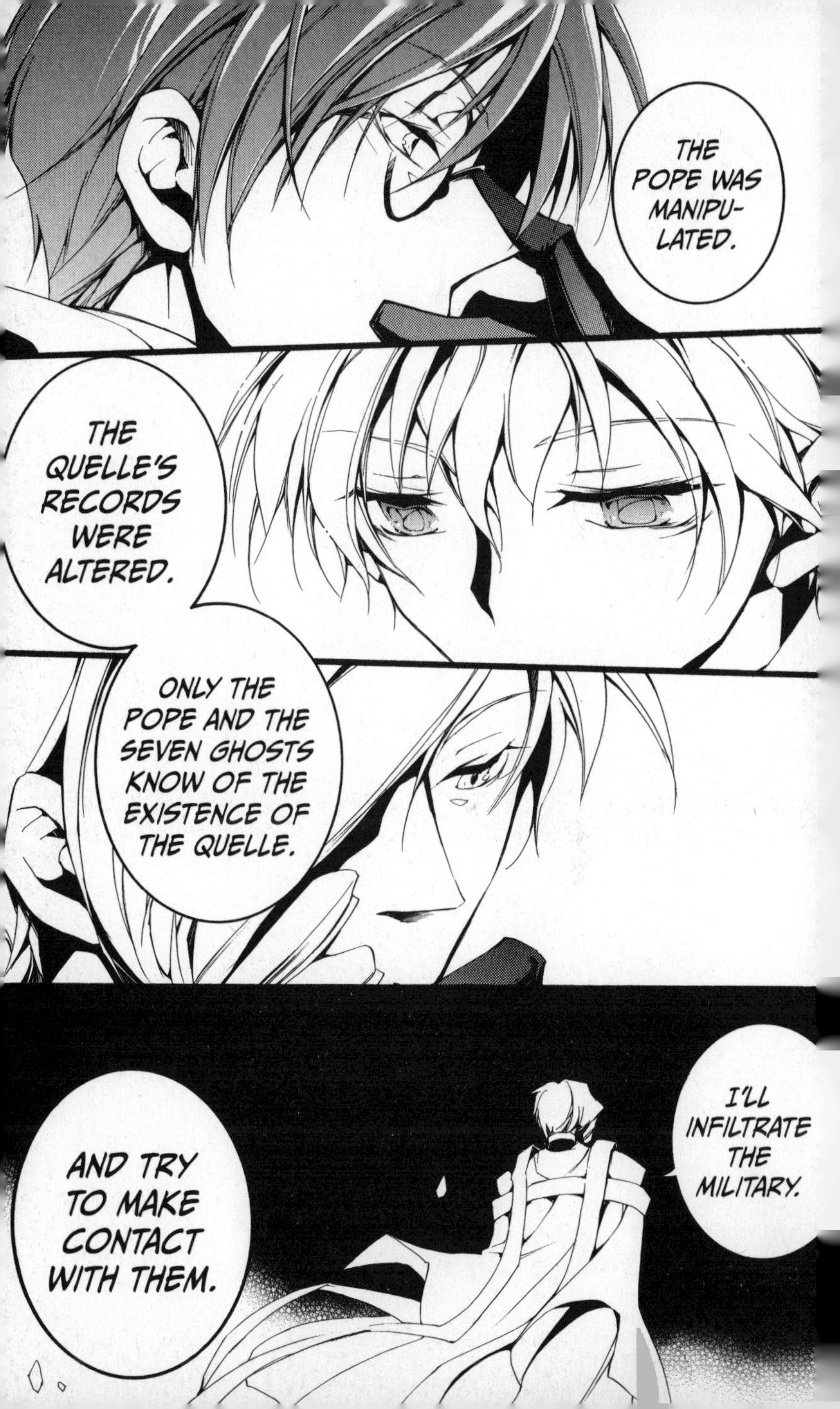
THE POPE WAS MANIPU-LATED.
THE QUELLE'S RECORDS WERE ALTERED.
ONLY THE POPE AND THE SEVEN GHOSTS KNOW OF THE EXISTENCE OF THE QUELLE.
I'LL INFILTRATE THE MILITARY.
AND TRY TO MAKE CONTACT WITH THEM.

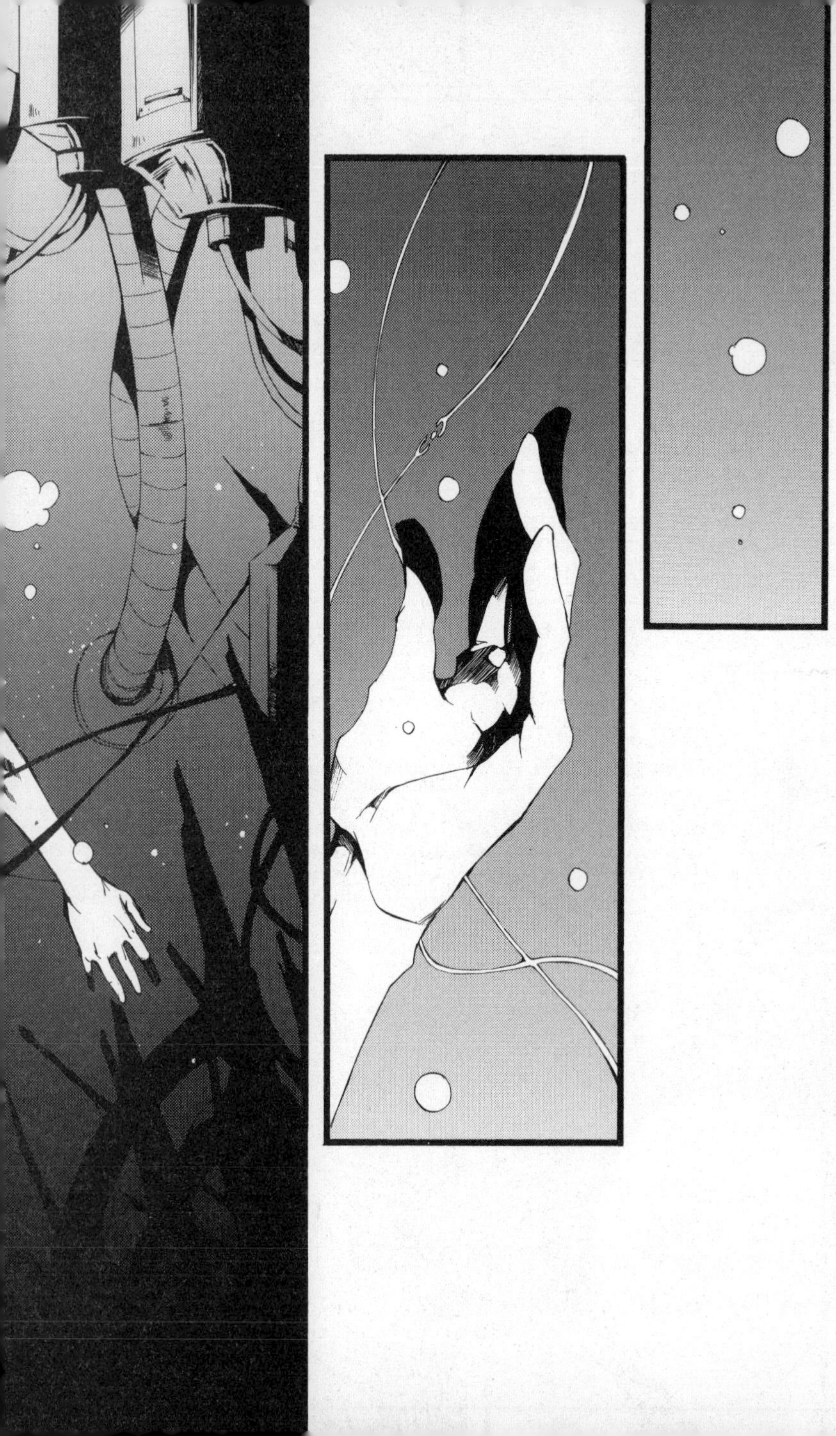

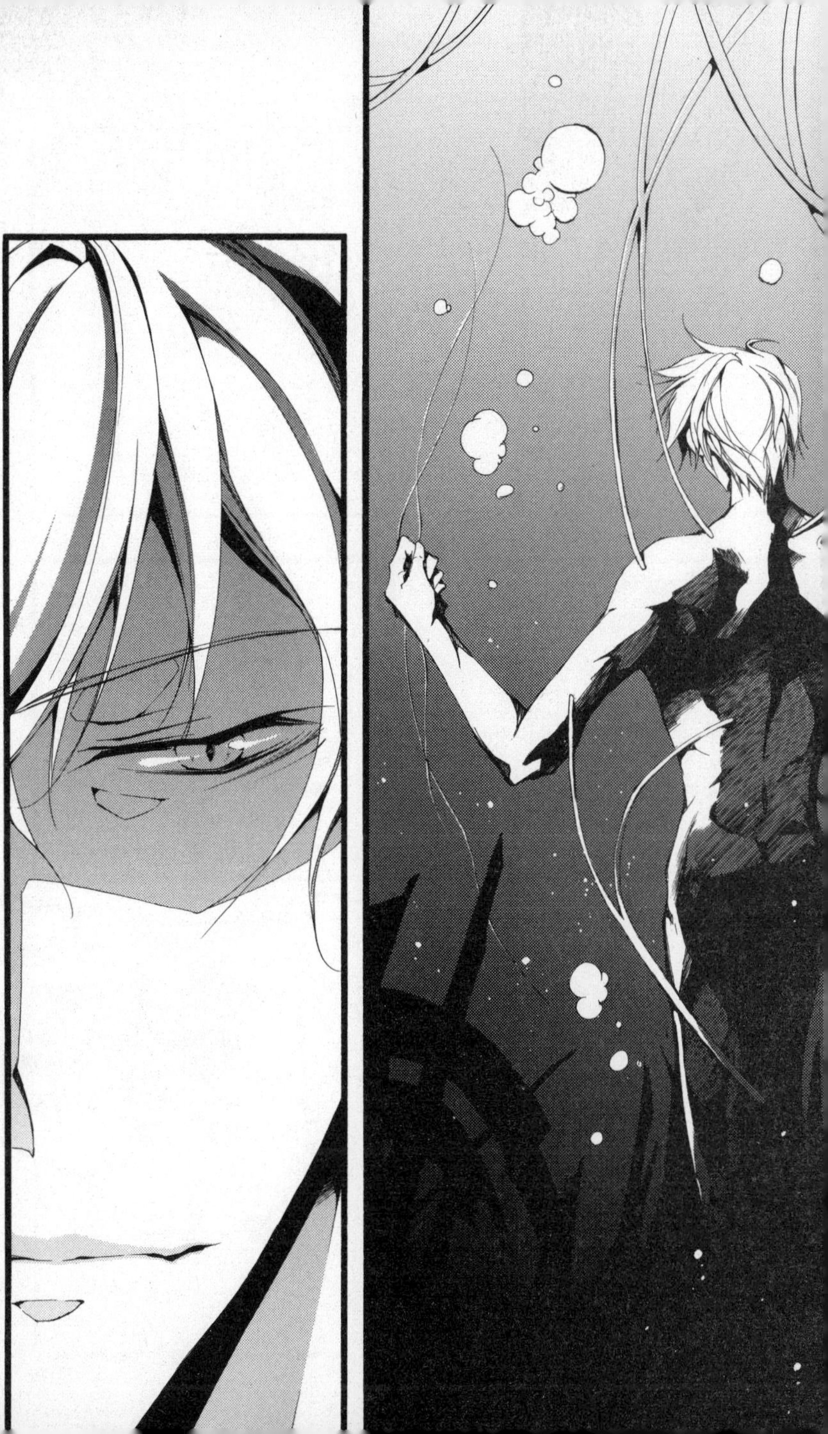

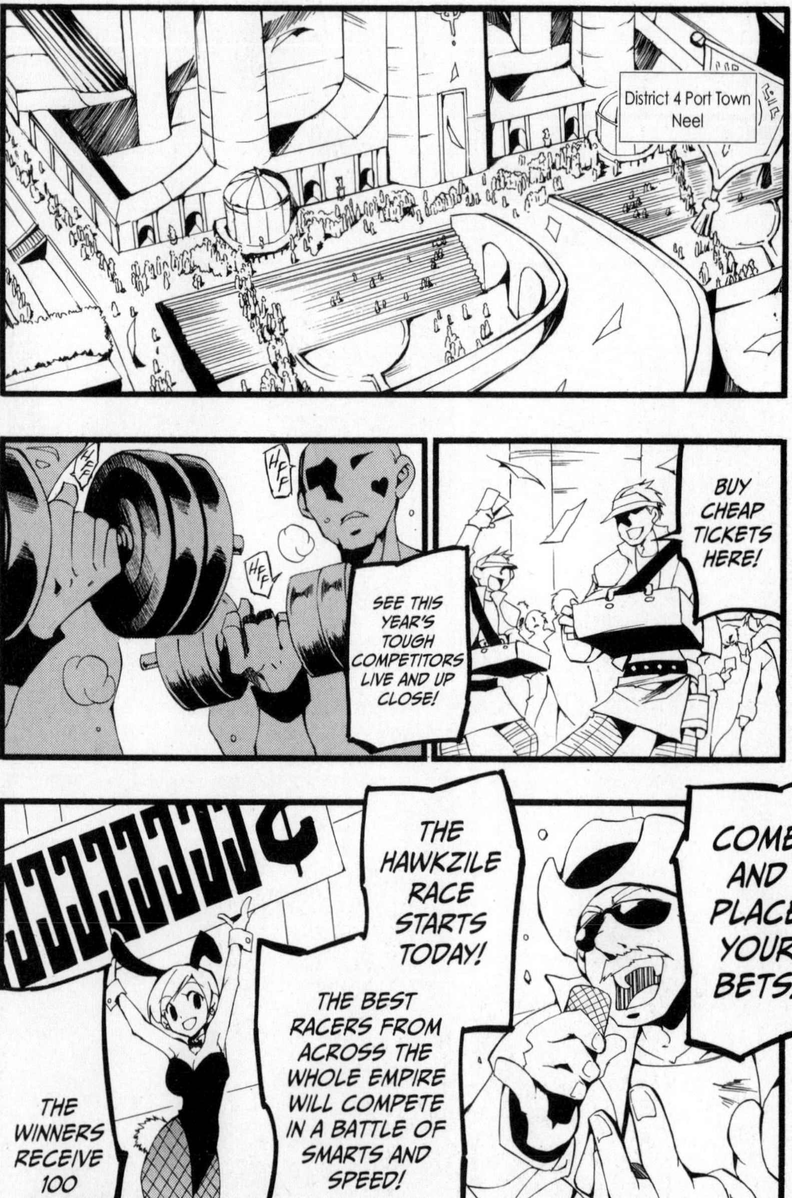
District 4 Port Town Neel
BUY CHEAP TICKETS HERE!
HFF
HFF
SEE THIS YEAR'S TOUGH COMPETITORS LIVE AND UP CLOSE!
COME AND PLACE YOUR BETS!
THE HAWKZILE RACE STARTS TODAY!
THE BEST RACERS FROM ACROSS THE WHOLE EMPIRE WILL COMPETE IN A BATTLE OF SMARTS AND SPEED!
THE WINNERS RECEIVE 100 MILLION YUS!

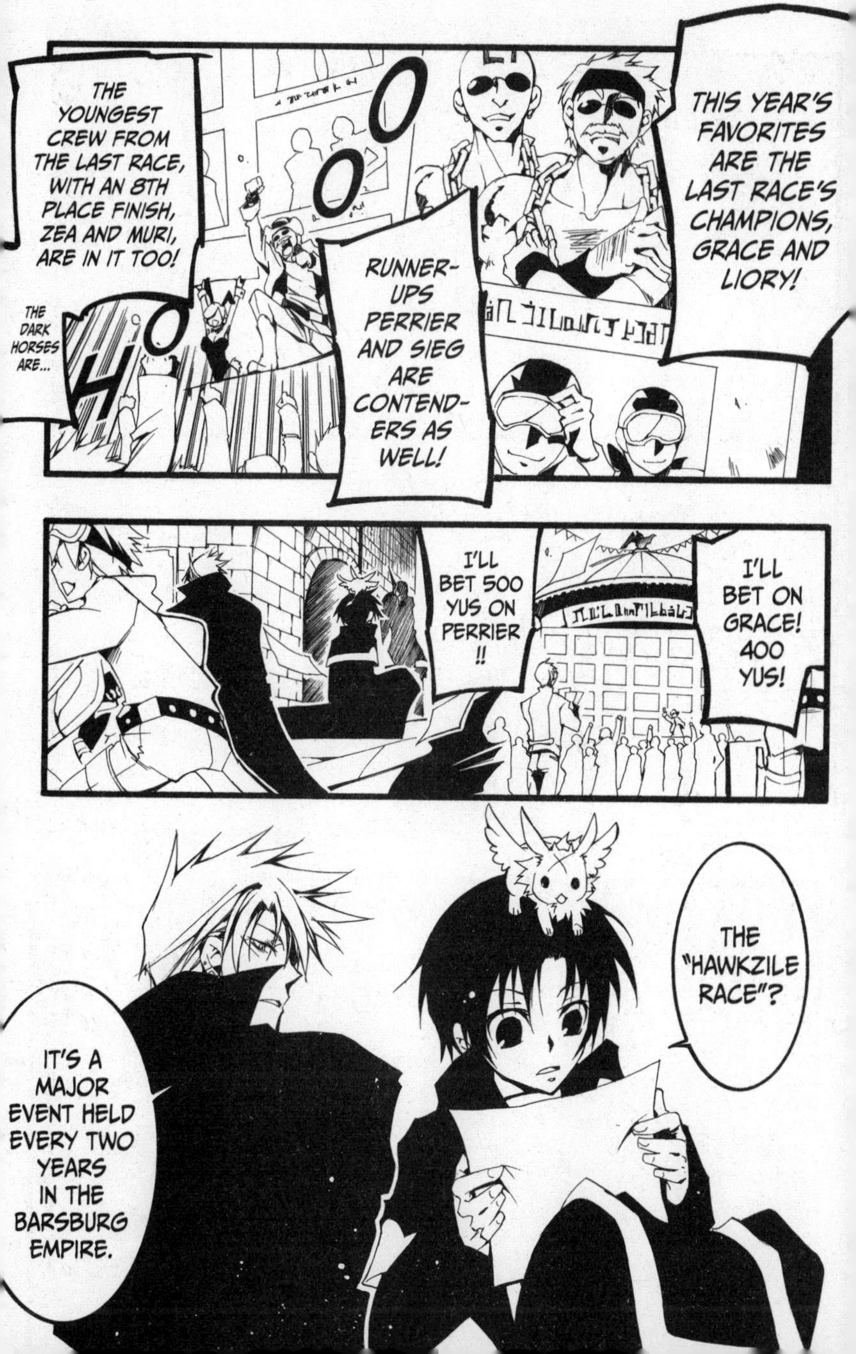
THIS YEAR'S FAVORITES ARE THE LAST RACE'S CHAMPIONS, GRACE AND LIORY!
RUNNER-UPS PERRIER AND SIEG ARE CONTENDERS AS WELL!
THE YOUNGEST CREW FROM THE LAST RACE, WITH AN 8TH PLACE FINISH, ZEA AND MURI, ARE IN IT TOO!
THE DARK HORSES ARE...
I'LL BET ON GRACE! 400 YUS!
I'LL BET 500 YUS ON PERRIER!!
THE "HAWKZILE RACE"?
IT'S A MAJOR EVENT HELD EVERY TWO YEARS IN THE BARSBURG EMPIRE.

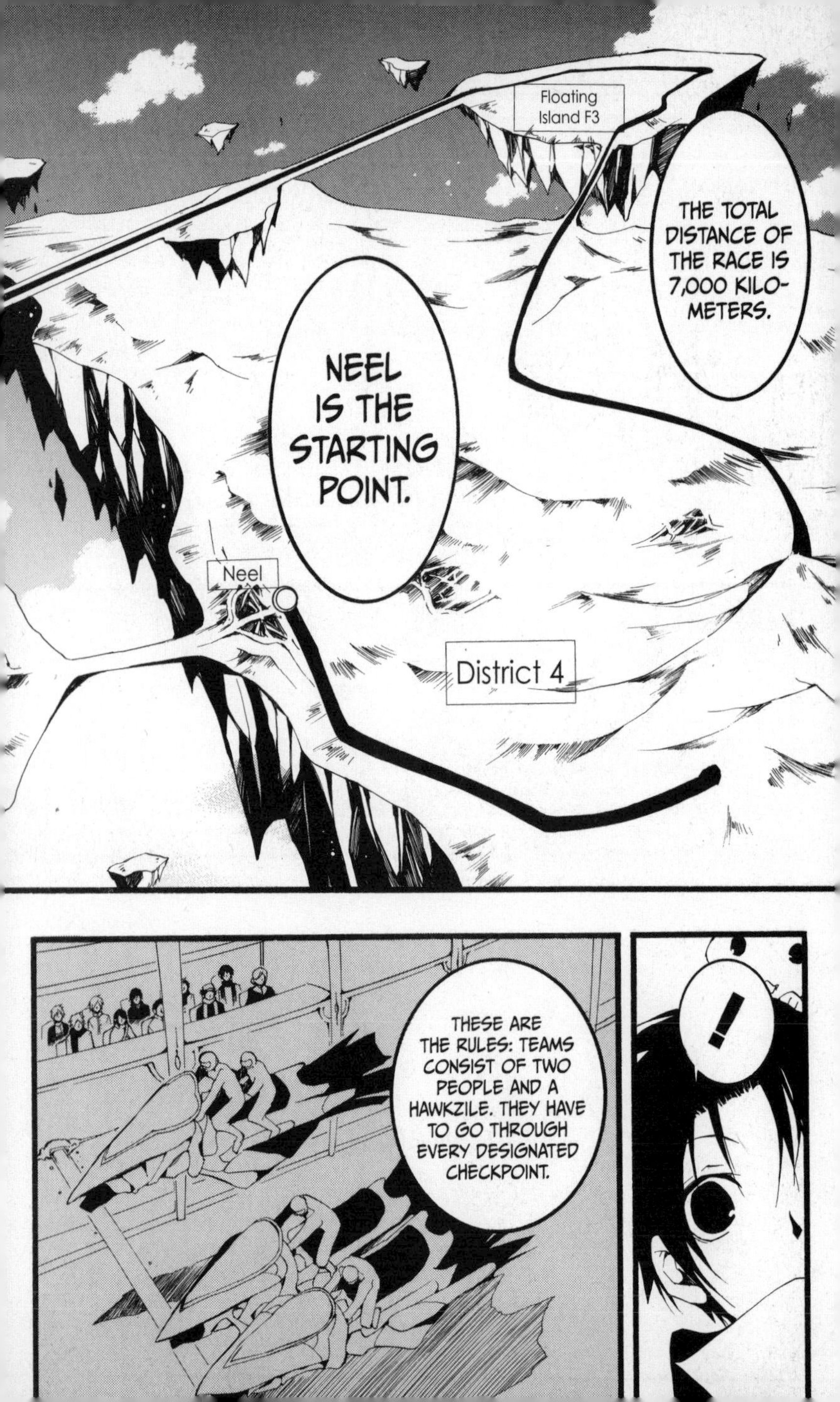
Floating Island F3
THE TOTAL DISTANCE OF THE RACE IS 7,000 KILO-METERS.
NEEL IS THE STARTING POINT.
Neel
District 4
!
THESE ARE THE RULES: TEAMS CONSIST OF TWO PEOPLE AND A HAWKZILE. THEY HAVE TO GO THROUGH EVERY DESIGNATED CHECKPOINT.

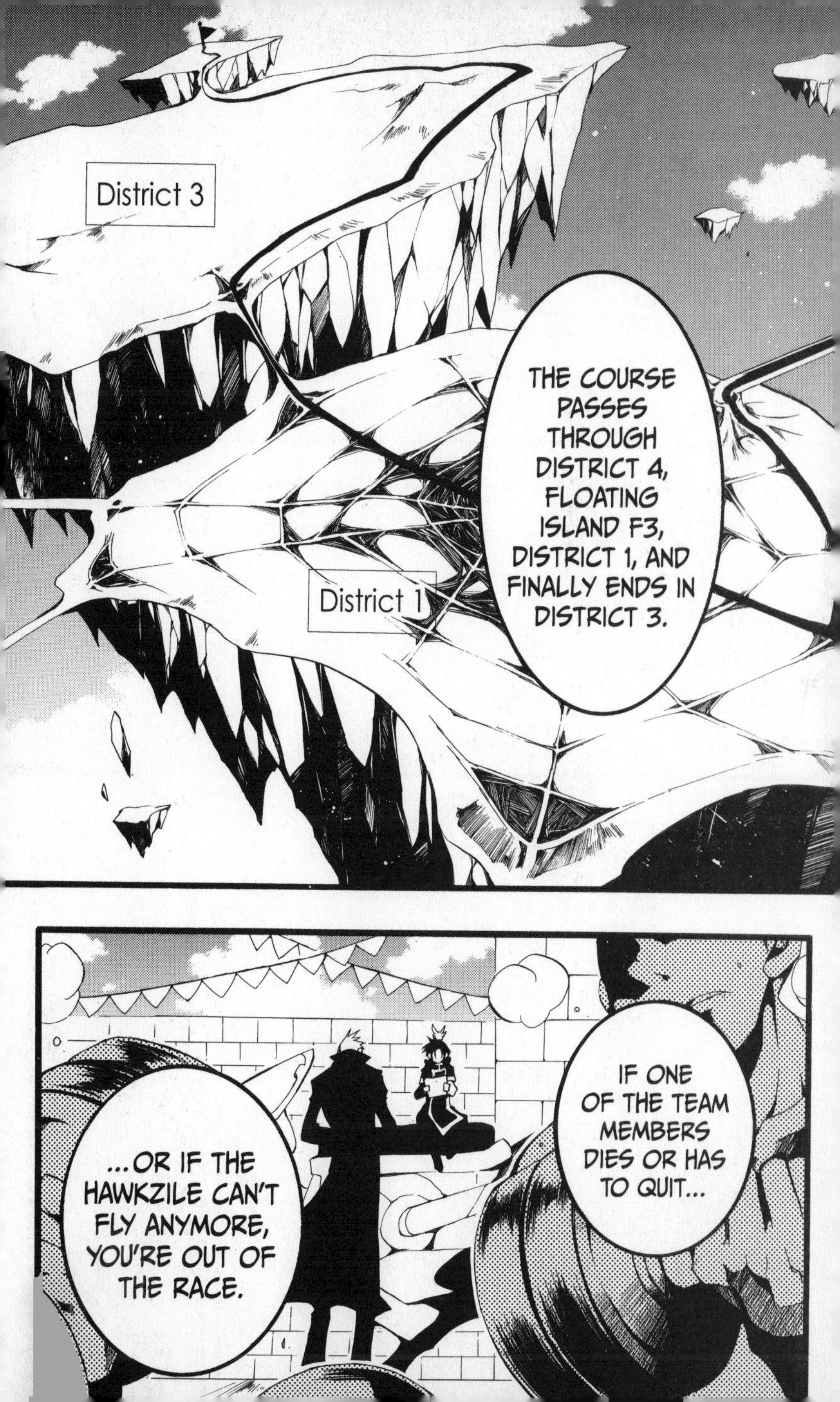
District 3
THE COURSE PASSES THROUGH DISTRICT 4, FLOATING ISLAND F3, DISTRICT 1, AND FINALLY ENDS IN DISTRICT 3.
District 1
IF ONE OF THE TEAM MEMBERS DIES OR HAS TO QUIT...
...OR IF THE HAWKZILE CAN'T FLY ANYMORE, YOU'RE OUT OF THE RACE.

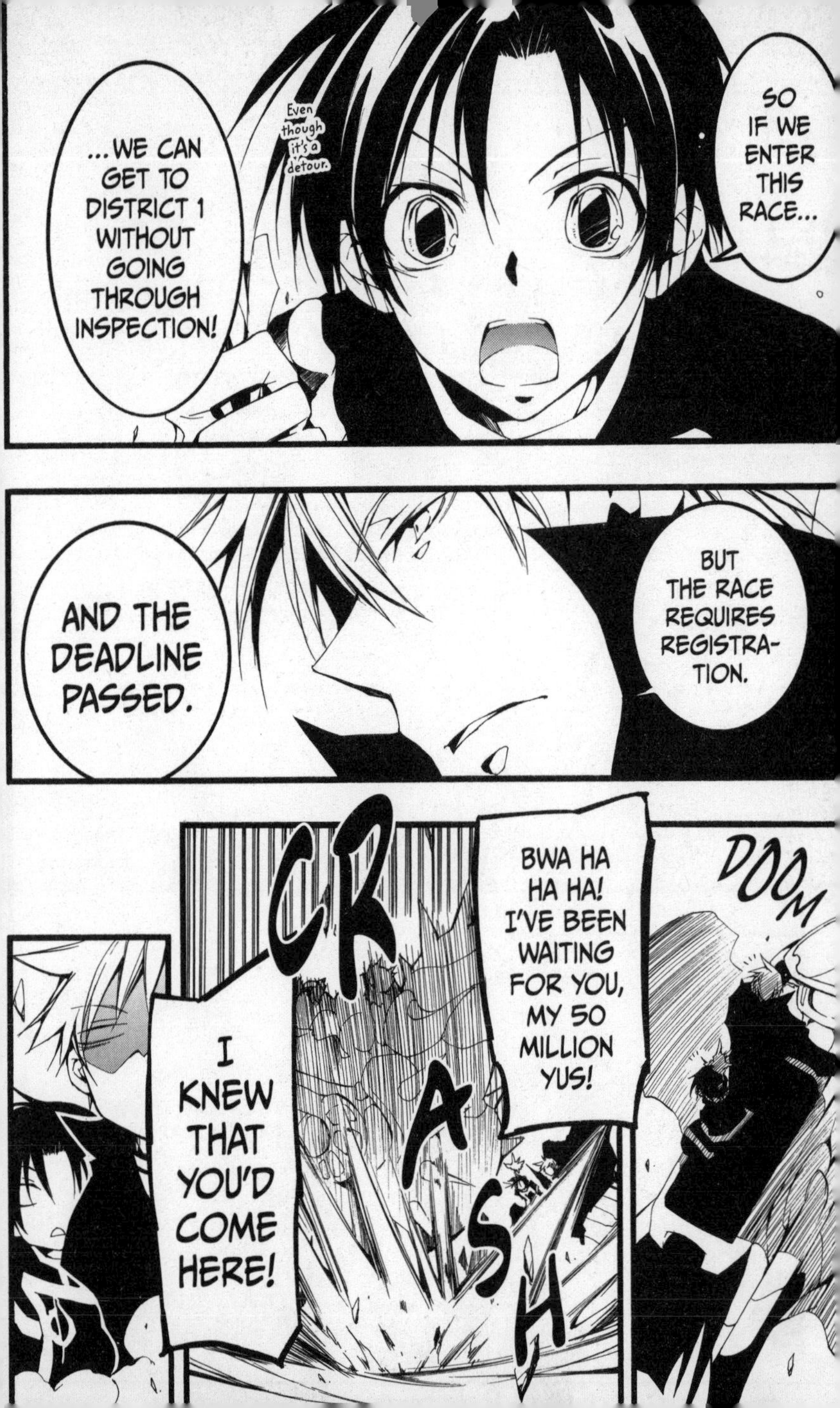
SO IF WE ENTER THIS RACE...
...WE CAN GET TO DISTRICT 1 WITHOUT GOING THROUGH INSPECTION!
Even though it's a detour.
BUT THE RACE REQUIRES REGISTRATION.
AND THE DEADLINE PASSED.
DOOM
BWA HA HA HA! I'VE BEEN WAITING FOR YOU, MY 50 MILLION YUS!
CRASH
I KNEW THAT YOU'D COME HERE!

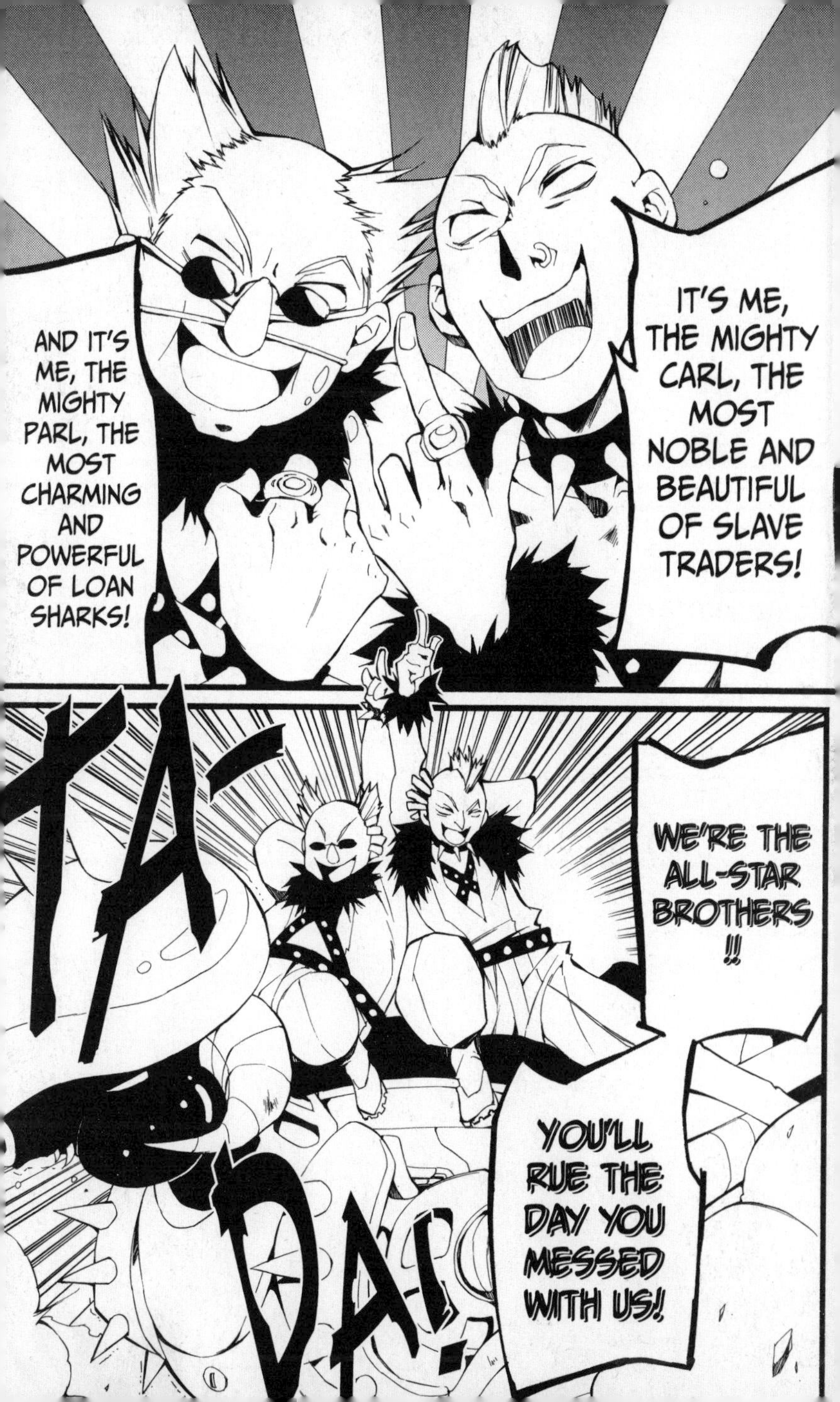
IT'S ME, THE MIGHTY CARL, THE MOST NOBLE AND BEAUTIFUL OF SLAVE TRADERS!
AND IT'S ME, THE MIGHTY PARL, THE MOST CHARMING AND POWERFUL OF LOAN SHARKS!
WE'RE THE ALL-STAR BROTHERS!!
TA-
YOU'LL RUE THE DAY YOU MESSED WITH US!
DA!

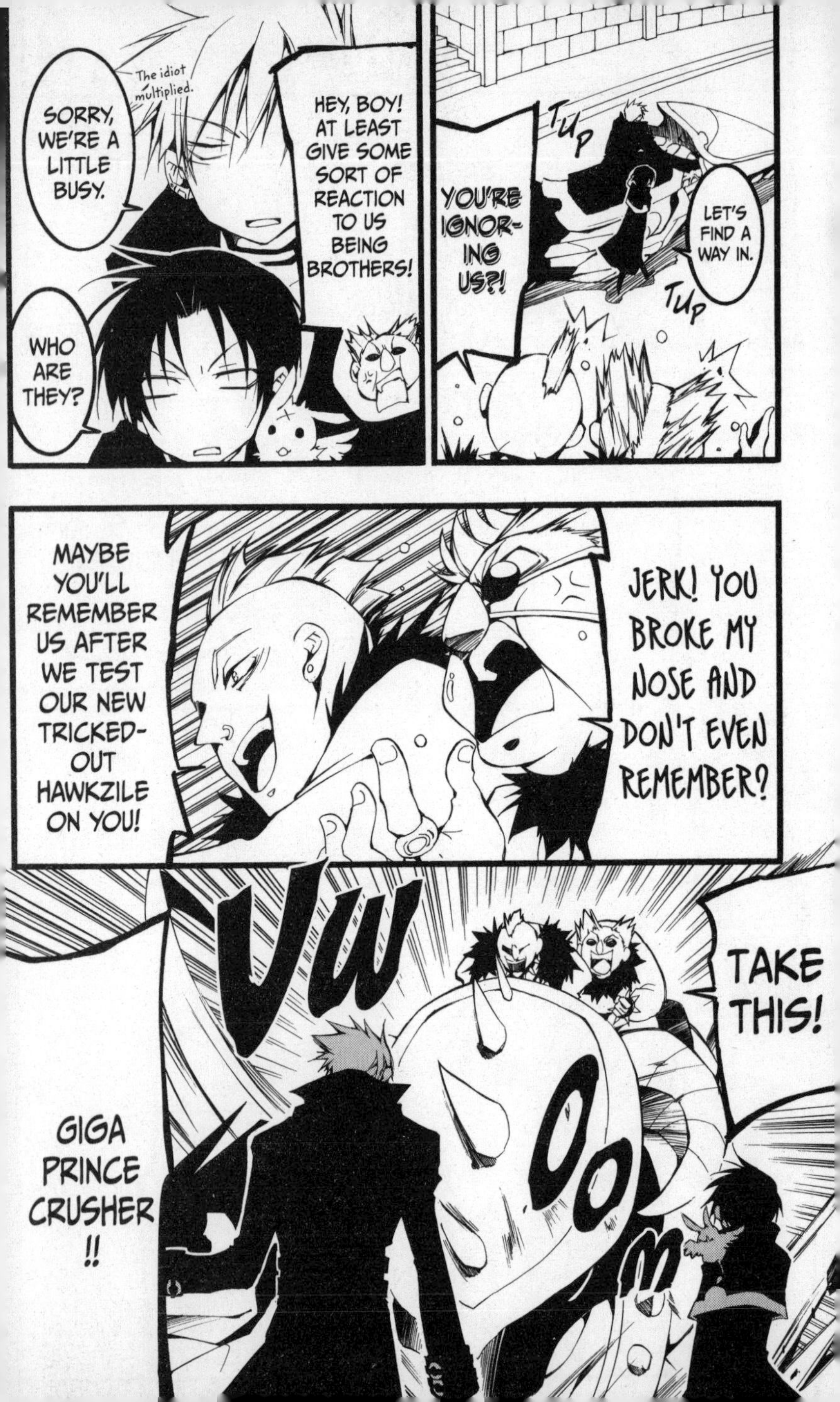
TUP
LET'S FIND A WAY IN.
TUP
YOU'RE IGNOR-ING US?!
HEY, BOY! AT LEAST GIVE SOME SORT OF REACTION TO US BEING BROTHERS!
The idiot multiplied.
SORRY, WE'RE A LITTLE BUSY.
WHO ARE THEY?
JERK! YOU BROKE MY NOSE AND DON'T EVEN REMEMBER?
MAYBE YOU'LL REMEMBER US AFTER WE TEST OUR NEW TRICKED-OUT HAWKZILE ON YOU!
TAKE THIS!
VW
GIGA PRINCE CRUSHER!!

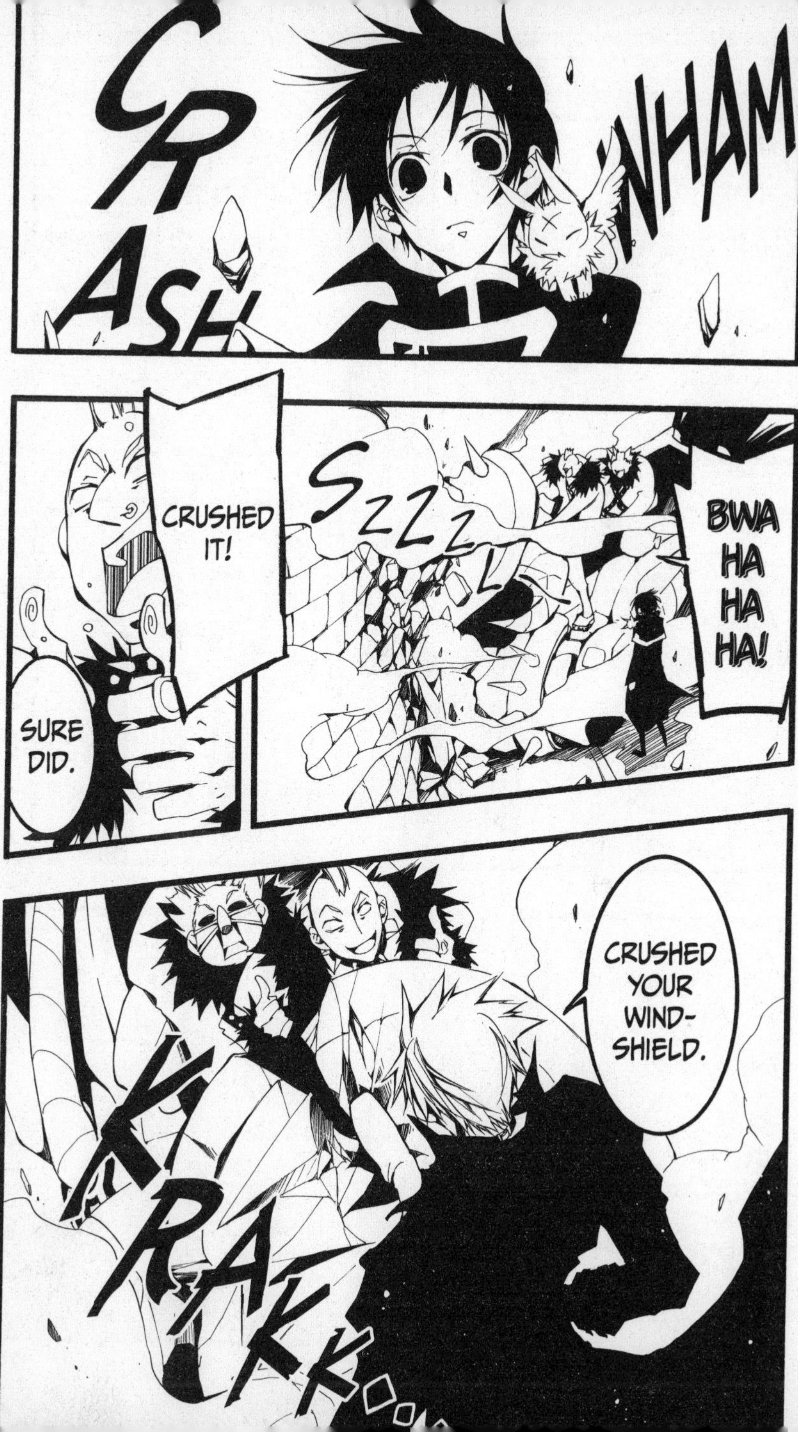
CRASH
WHAM
BWA HA HA HA!
SZZZZ
CRUSHED IT!
SURE DID.
CRUSHED YOUR WIND-SHIELD.
KRAKKOOO

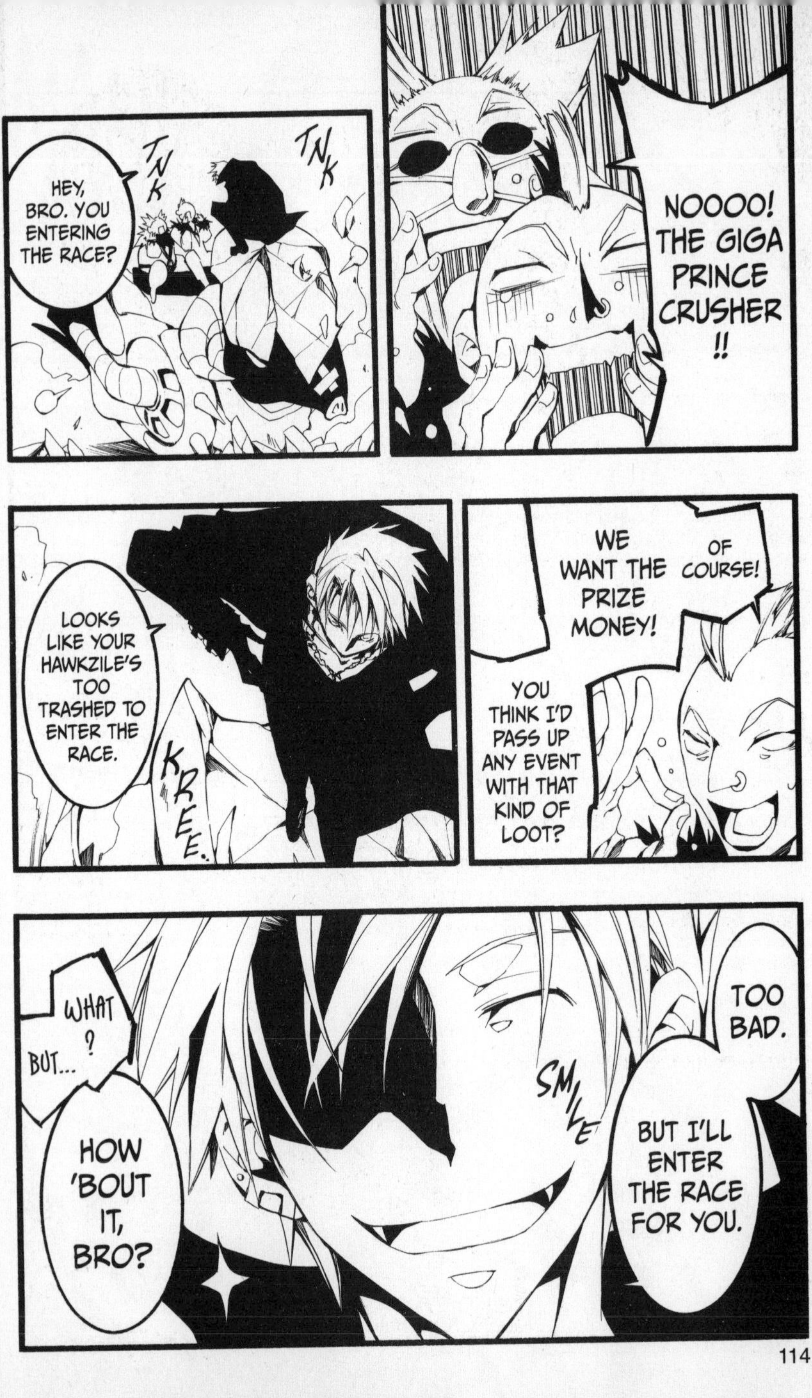

NOOOO! THE GIGA PRINCE CRUSHER !!
TNK
TNK
HEY, BRO. YOU ENTERING THE RACE?
OF COURSE!
WE WANT THE PRIZE MONEY!
YOU THINK I'D PASS UP ANY EVENT WITH THAT KIND OF LOOT?
LOOKS LIKE YOUR HAWKZILE'S TOO TRASHED TO ENTER THE RACE.
KREEE...
TOO BAD.
BUT I'LL ENTER THE RACE FOR YOU.
SMIVE
WHAT ?
BUT...
HOW 'BOUT IT, BRO?

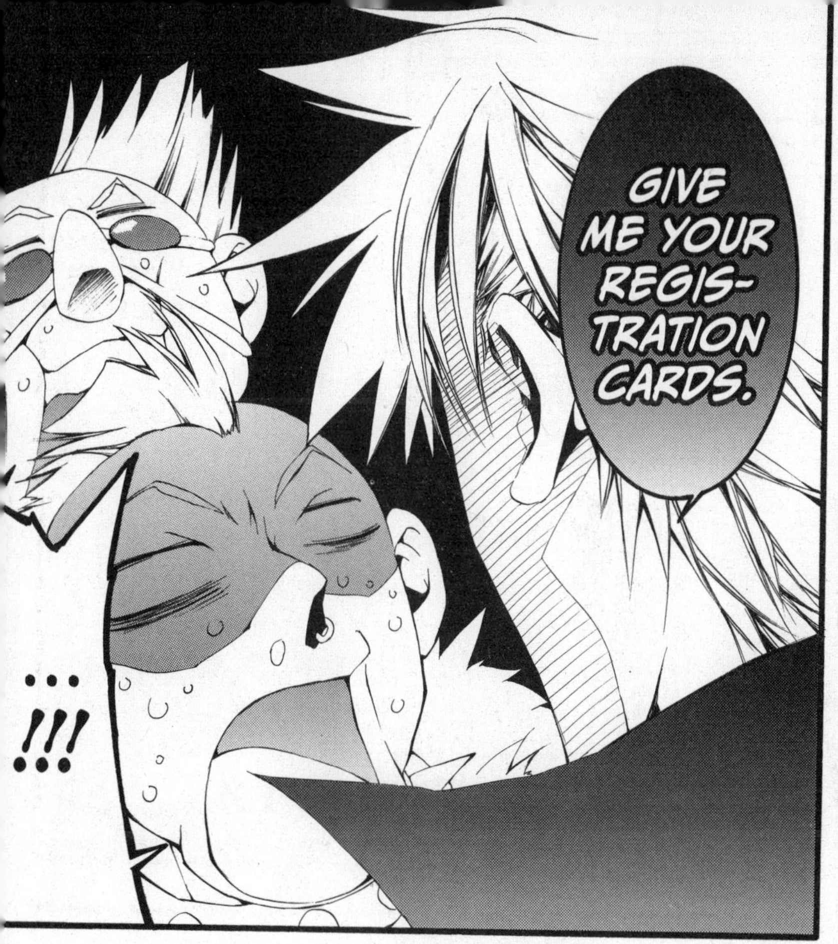
GIVE ME YOUR REGIS-TRATION CARDS.
...!!!

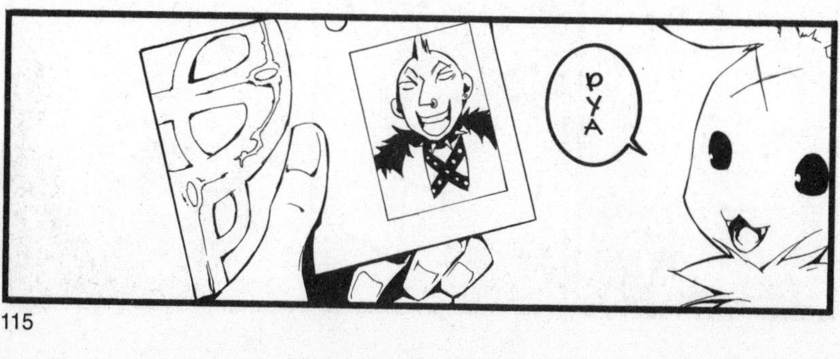
PYA

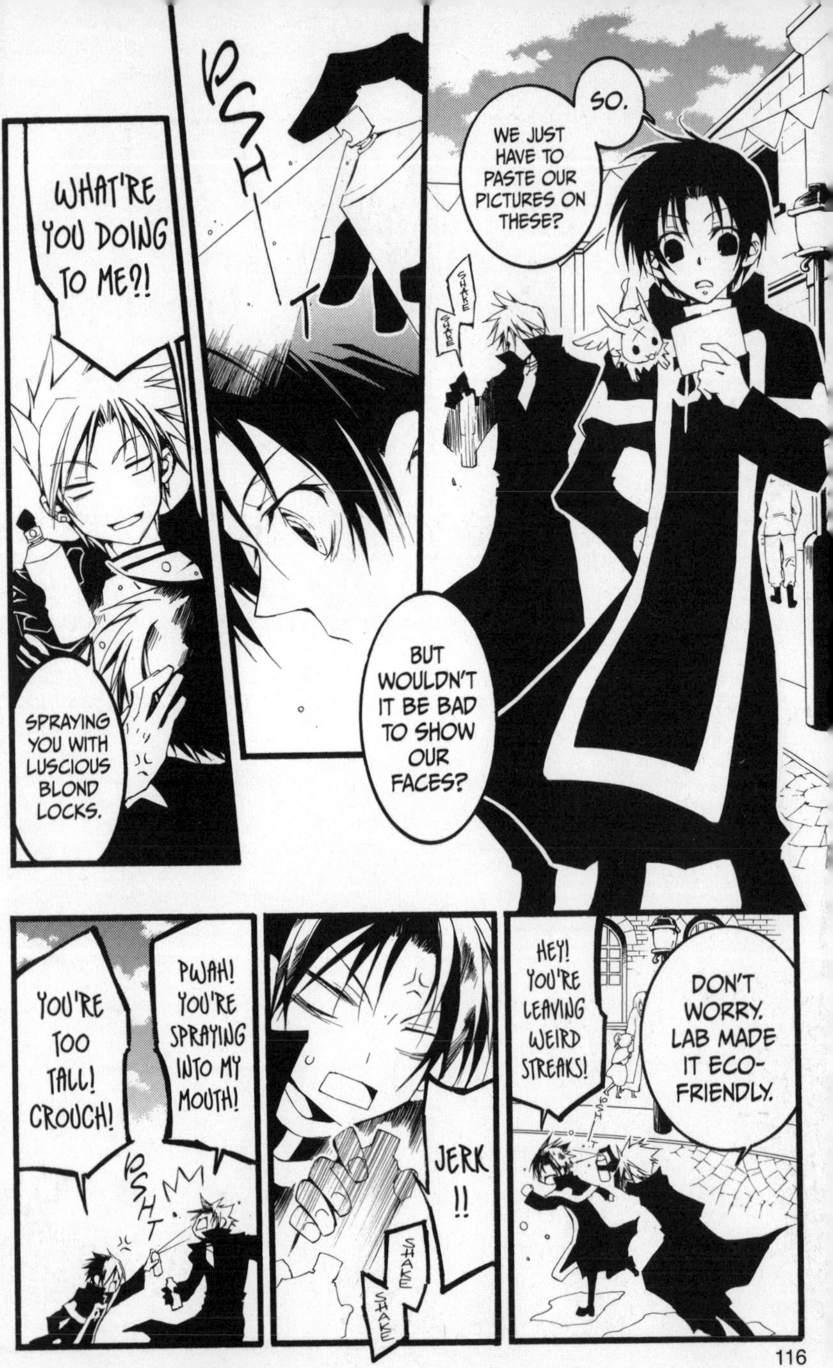
SO.
WE JUST HAVE TO PASTE OUR PICTURES ON THESE?
SHAKE
SHAKE
BUT WOULDN'T IT BE BAD TO SHOW OUR FACES?
PSHT
WHAT'RE YOU DOING TO ME?!
SPRAYING YOU WITH LUSCIOUS BLOND LOCKS.
DON'T WORRY. LAB MADE IT ECO-FRIENDLY.
HEY! YOU'RE LEAVING WEIRD STREAKS!
JERK!!
SHAKE
SHAKE
PWAH! YOU'RE SPRAYING INTO MY MOUTH!
YOU'RE TOO TALL! CROUCH!
PSHT

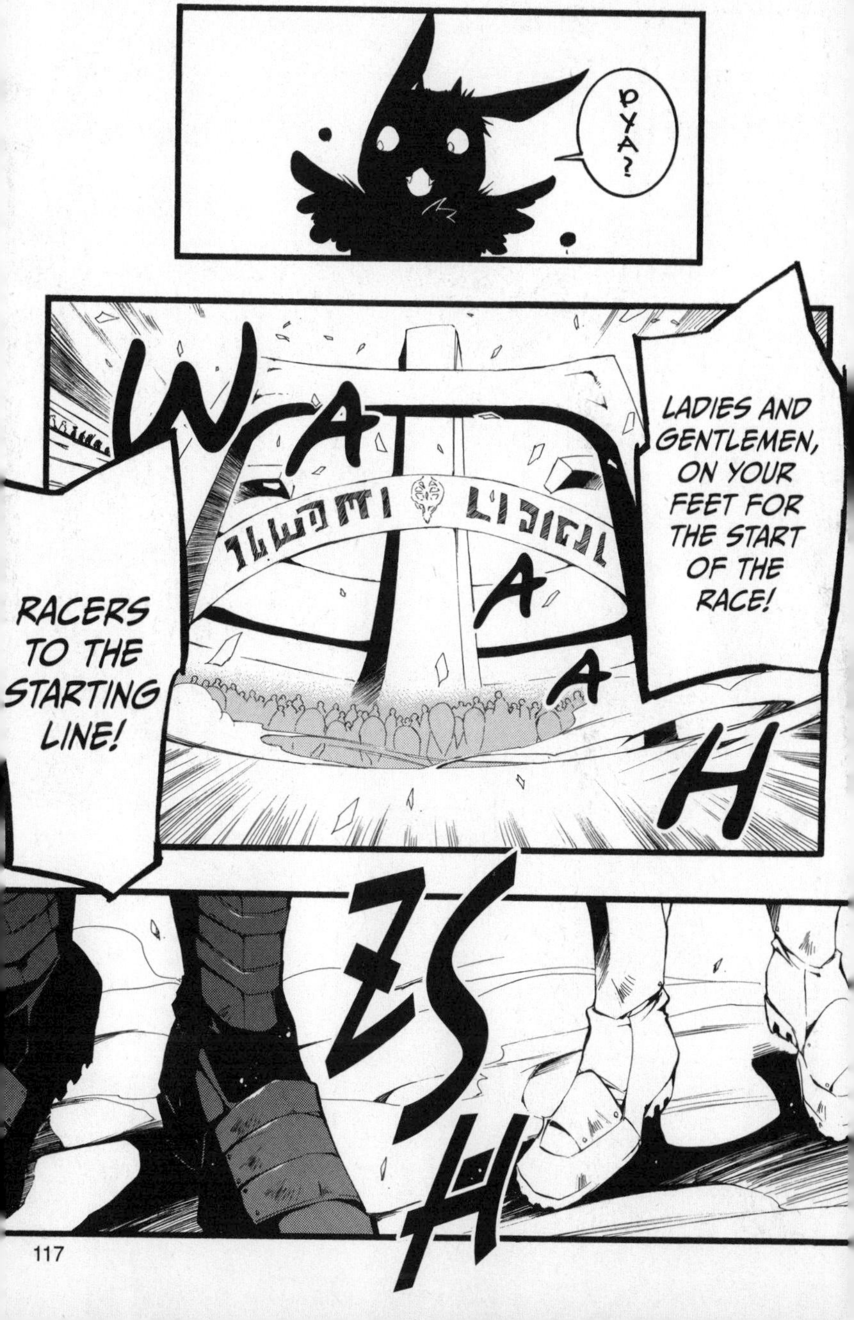
PYA?
LADIES AND GENTLEMEN, ON YOUR FEET FOR THE START OF THE RACE!
WAAAH
RACERS TO THE STARTING LINE!
ZSH

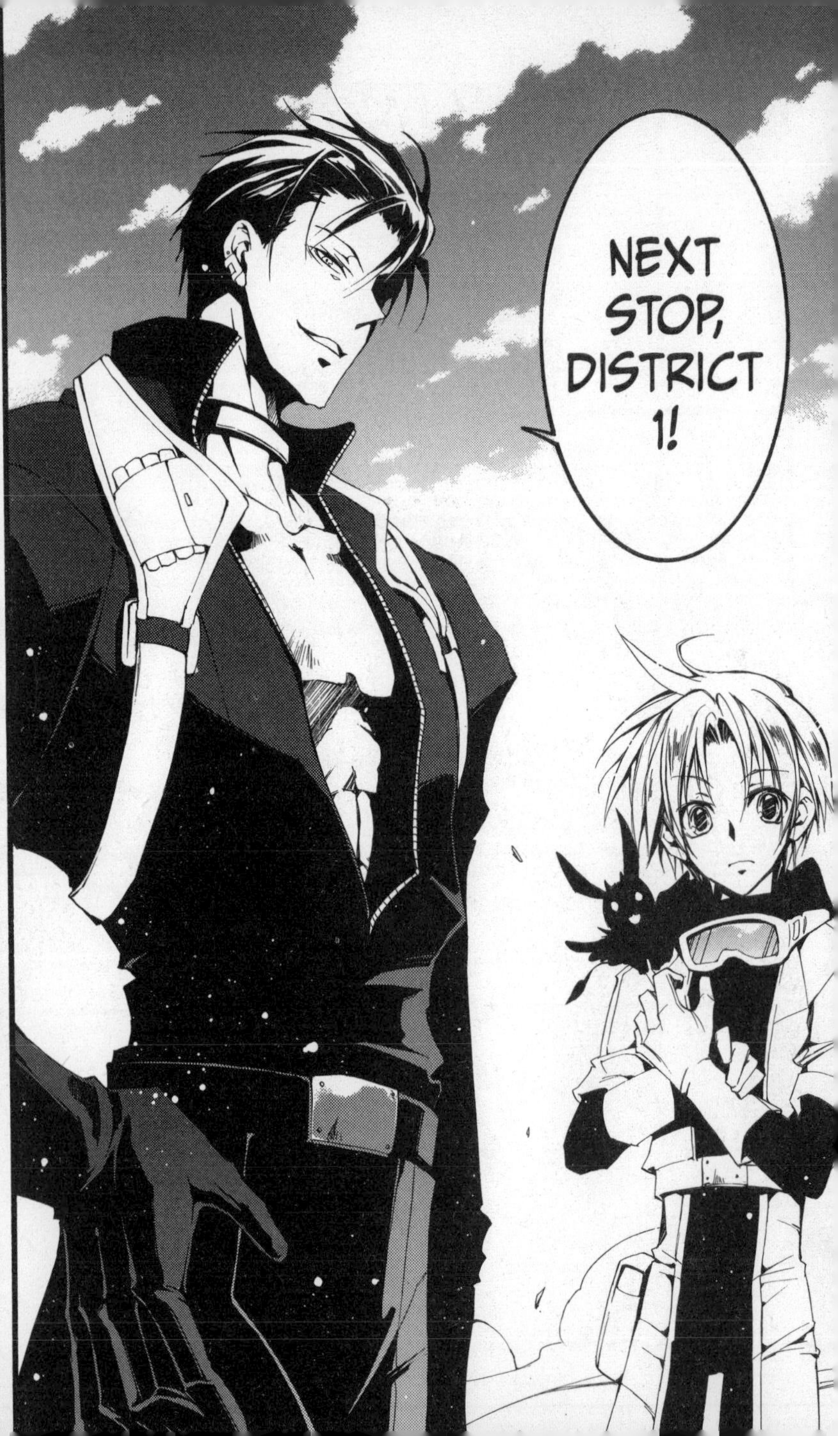
NEXT STOP, DISTRICT 1!

Kapitel.59 "Hawkzile Race"

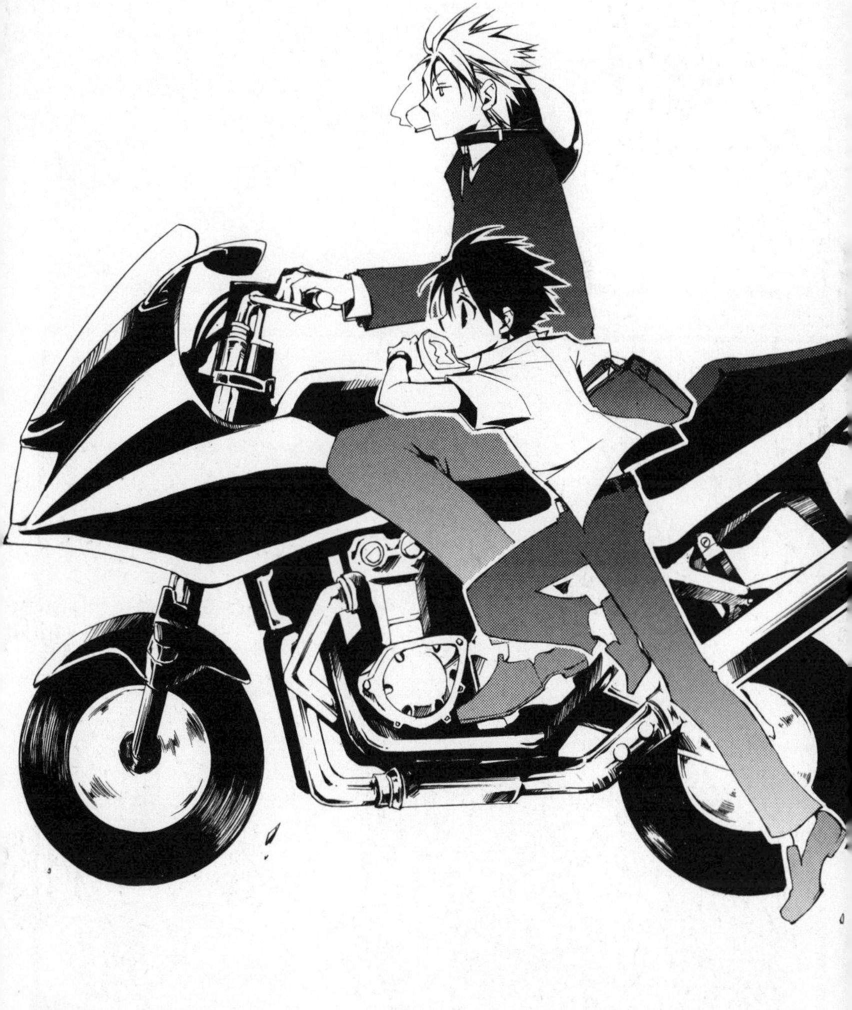

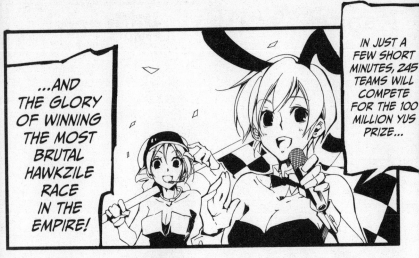

IN JUST A FEW SHORT MINUTES, 245 TEAMS WILL COMPETE FOR THE 100 MILLION YUS PRIZE...
...AND THE GLORY OF WINNING THE MOST BRUTAL HAWKZILE RACE IN THE EMPIRE!
IF WE COMPLETE THIS WHOLE RACE...
...WE'LL PASS THROUGH FLOATING ISLAND F3...
F3
Goal
District 3
District 4
District 1
Start
Hoburg Fortress
...THEN DISTRICT 1, AND END IN DISTRICT 3.

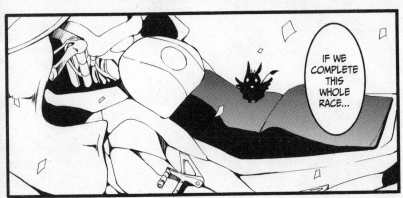

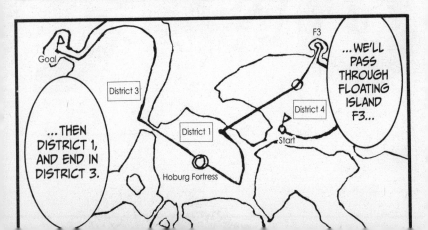

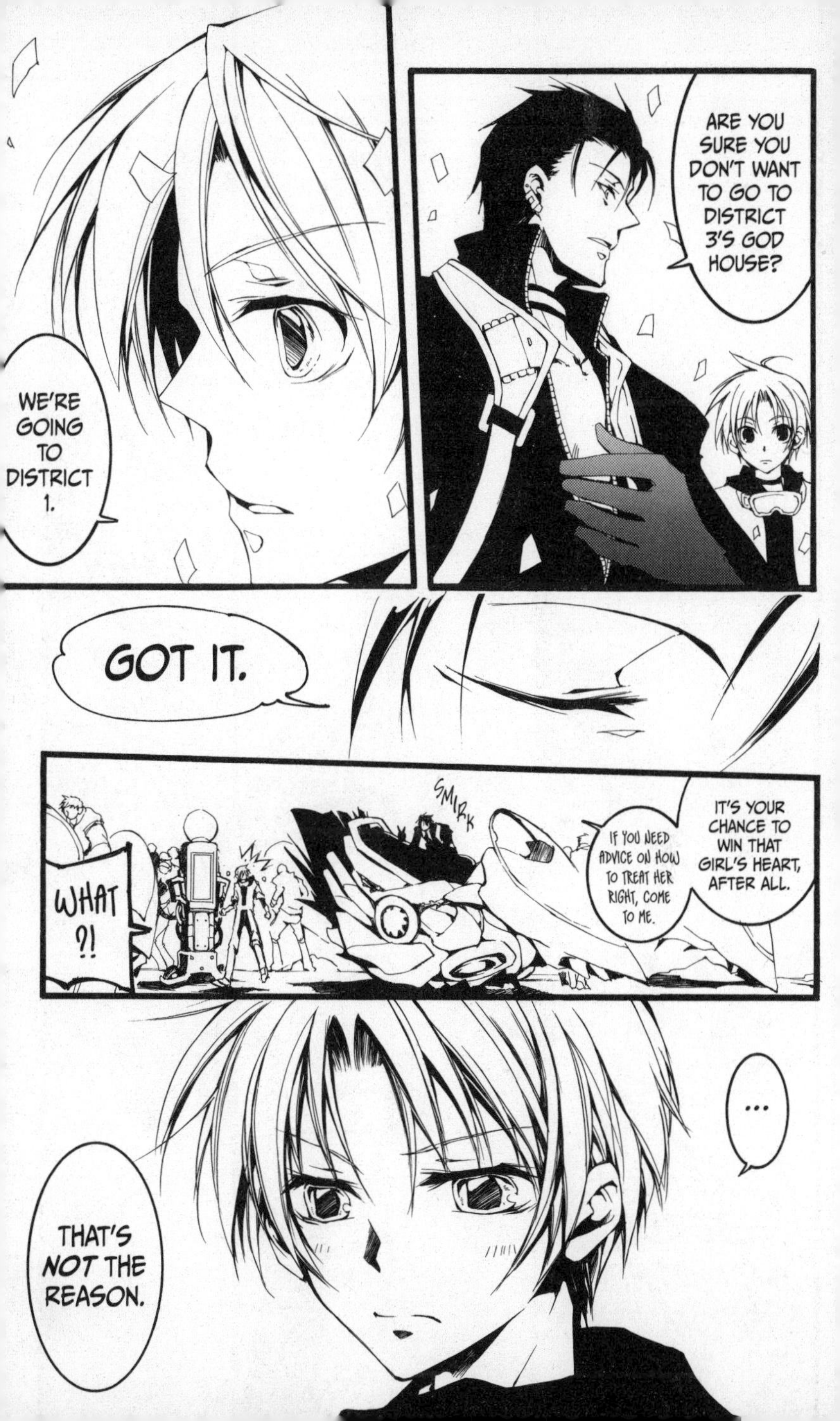
ARE YOU SURE YOU DON'T WANT TO GO TO DISTRICT 3'S GOD HOUSE?
WE'RE GOING TO DISTRICT 1.
GOT IT.
IT'S YOUR CHANCE TO WIN THAT GIRL'S HEART, AFTER ALL.
IF YOU NEED ADVICE ON HOW TO TREAT HER RIGHT, COME TO ME.
SMIRK
WHAT?!
...
THAT'S *NOT* THE REASON.

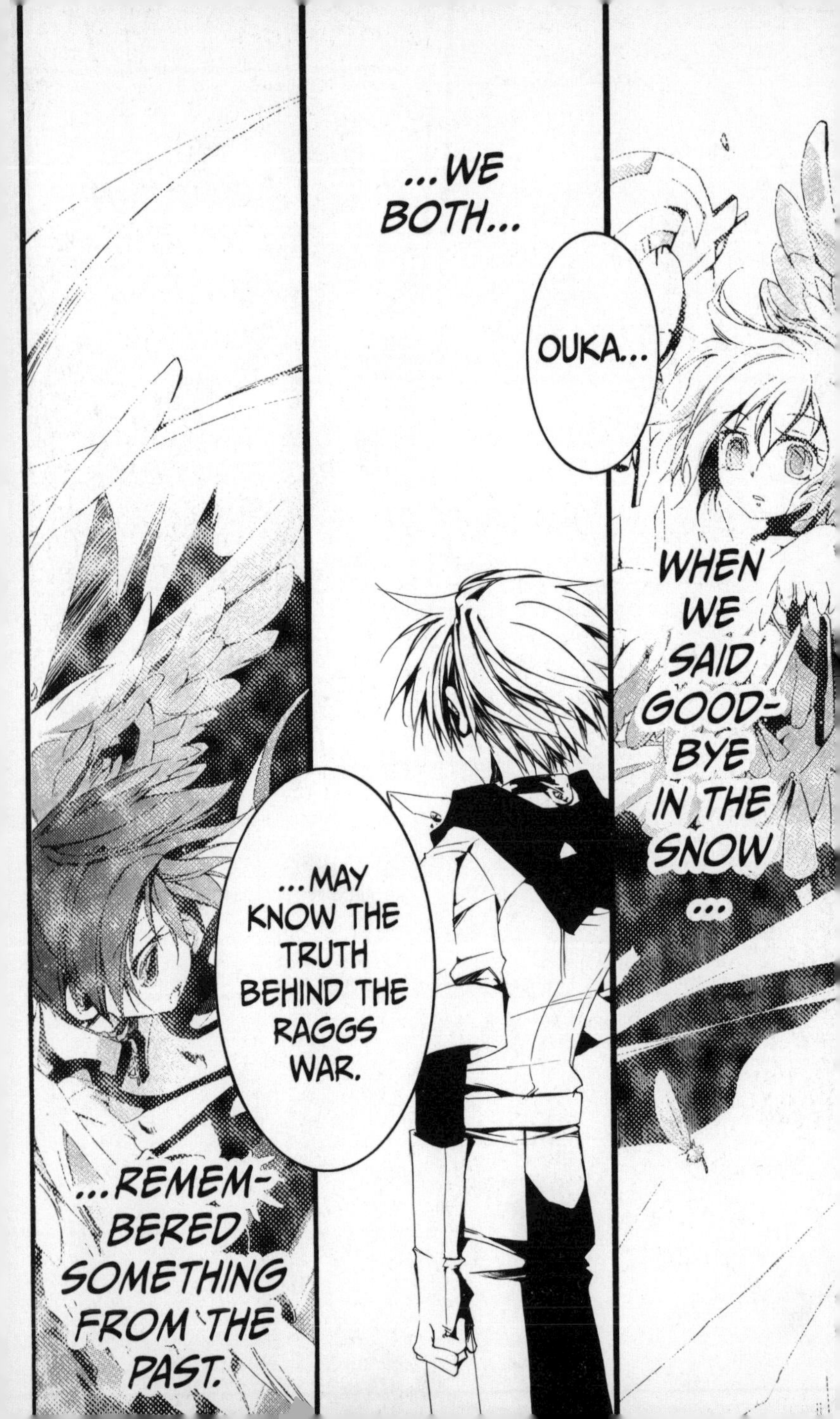
OUKA...
WHEN WE SAID GOOD-BYE IN THE SNOW...
...WE BOTH...
...MAY KNOW THE TRUTH BEHIND THE RAGGS WAR.
...REMEM-BERED SOMETHING FROM THE PAST.

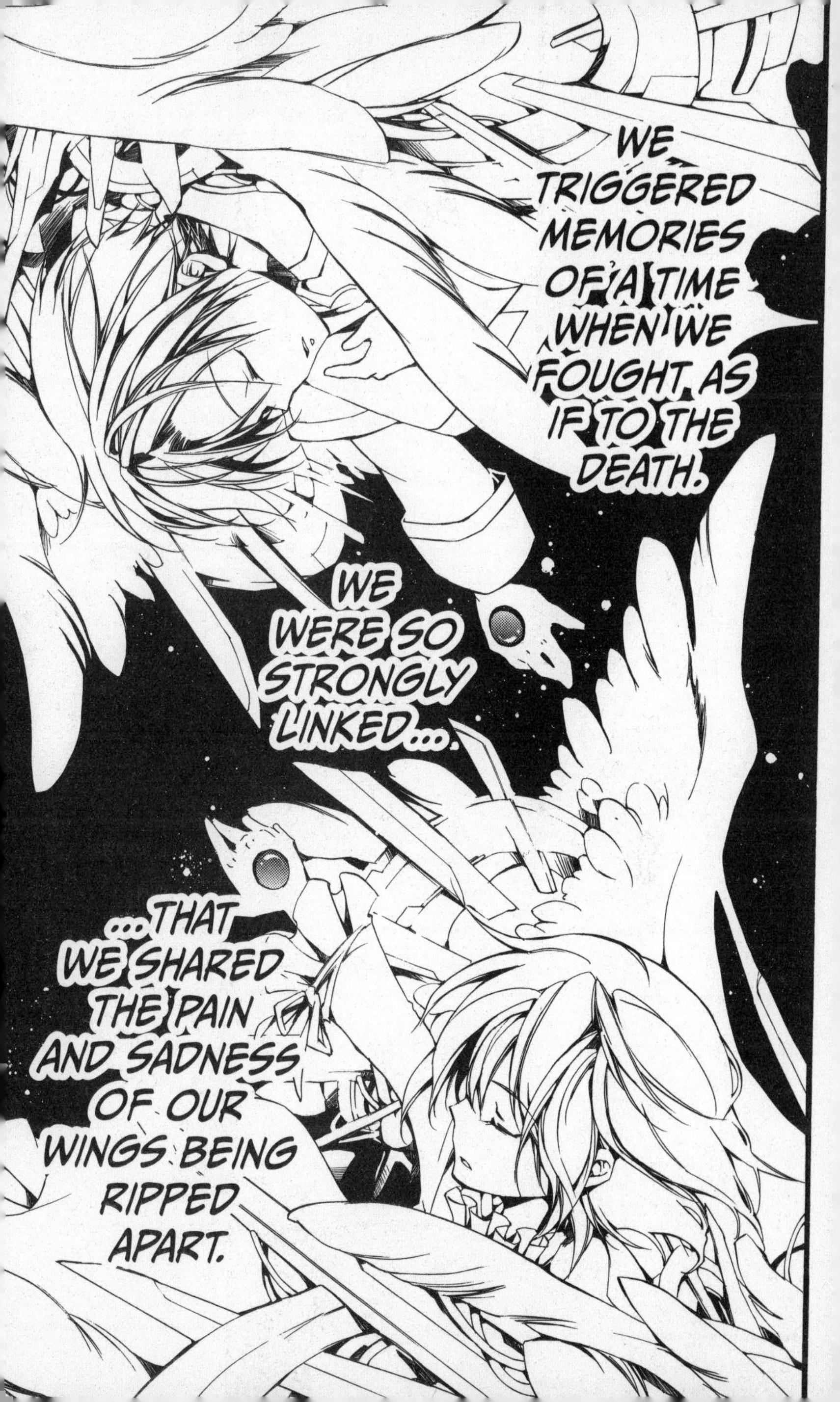
WE TRIGGERED MEMORIES OF A TIME WHEN WE FOUGHT AS IF TO THE DEATH.
WE WERE SO STRONGLY LINKED...
...THAT WE SHARED THE PAIN AND SADNESS OF OUR WINGS BEING RIPPED APART.

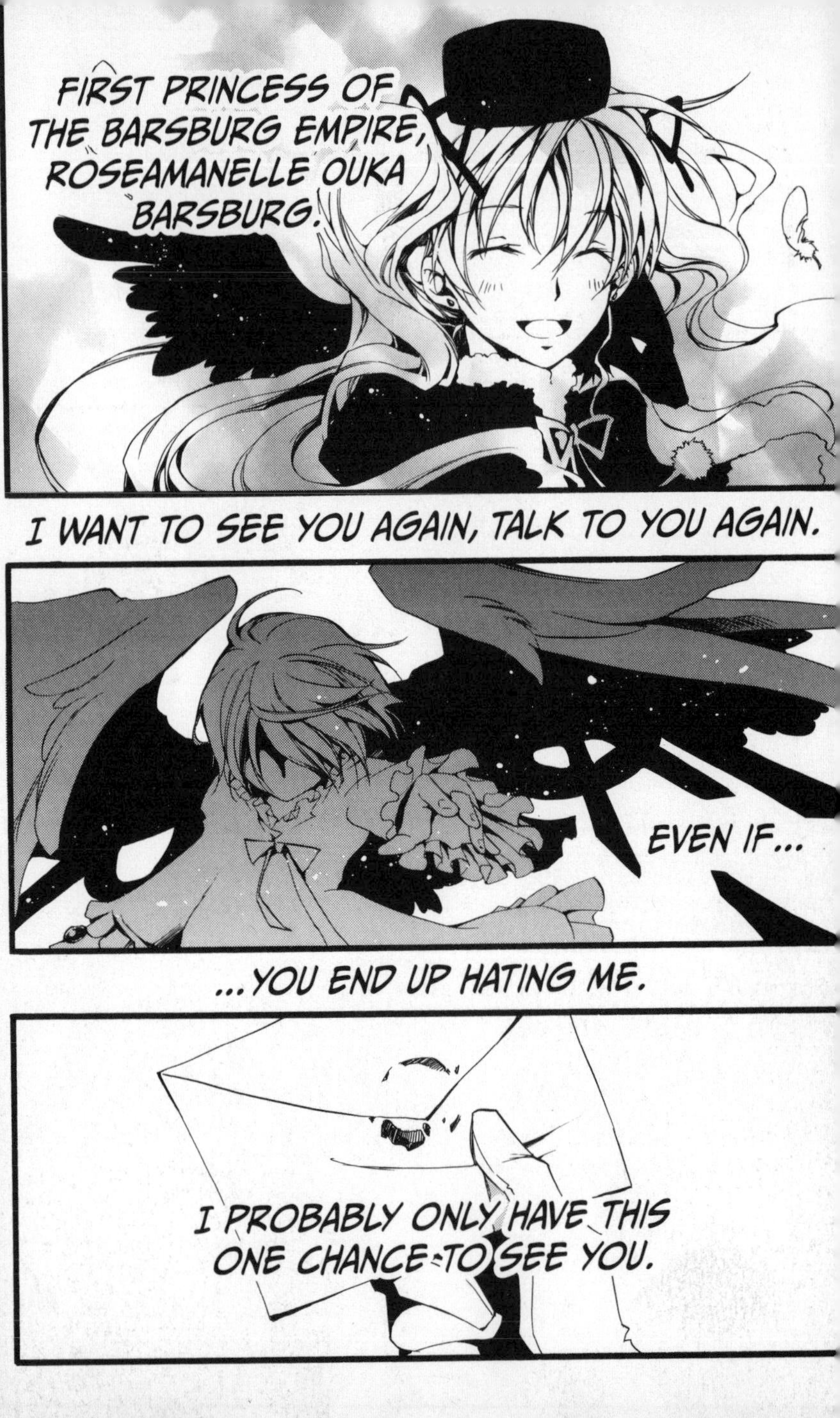
FIRST PRINCESS OF THE BARSBURG EMPIRE, ROSEAMANELLE OUKA BARSBURG.
I WANT TO SEE YOU AGAIN, TALK TO YOU AGAIN.
EVEN IF...
...YOU END UP HATING ME.
I PROBABLY ONLY HAVE THIS ONE CHANCE TO SEE YOU.

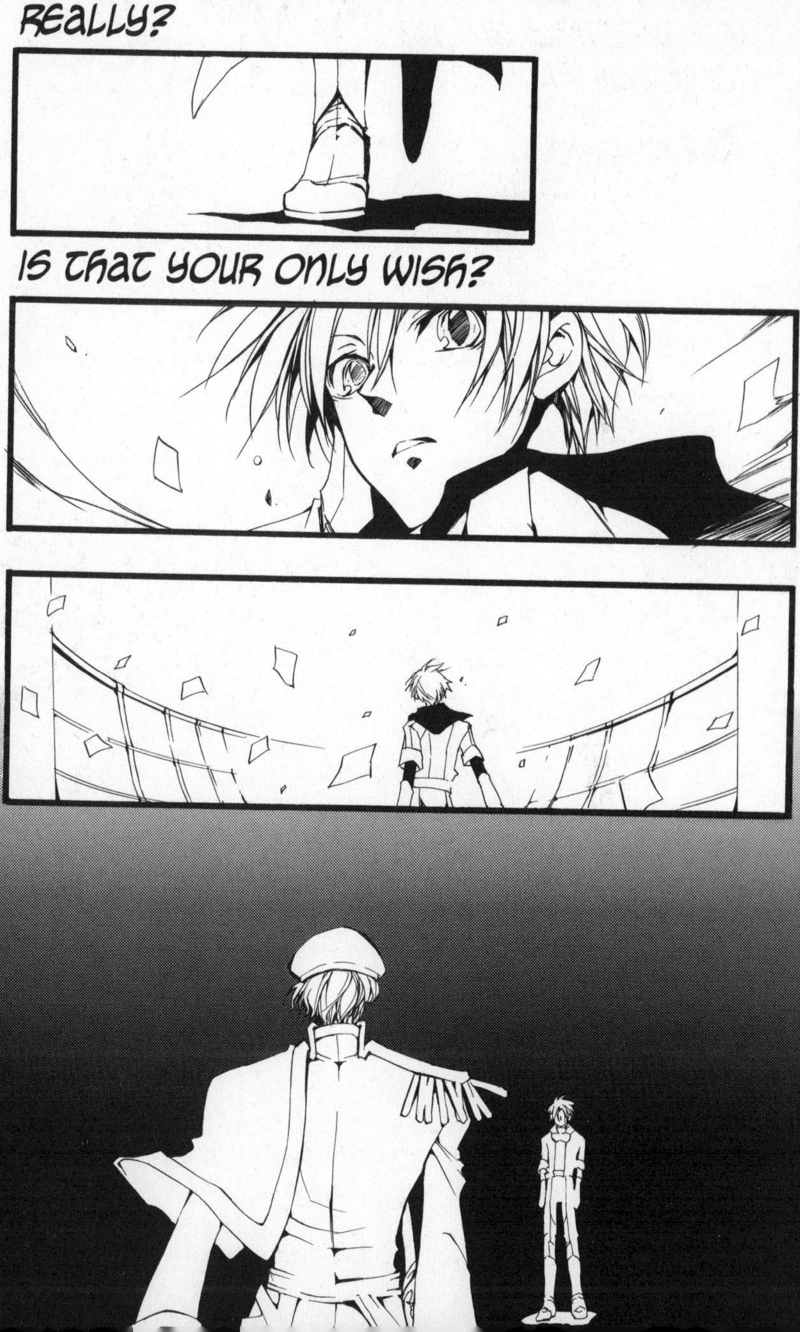
REALLY?
IS THAT YOUR ONLY WISH?

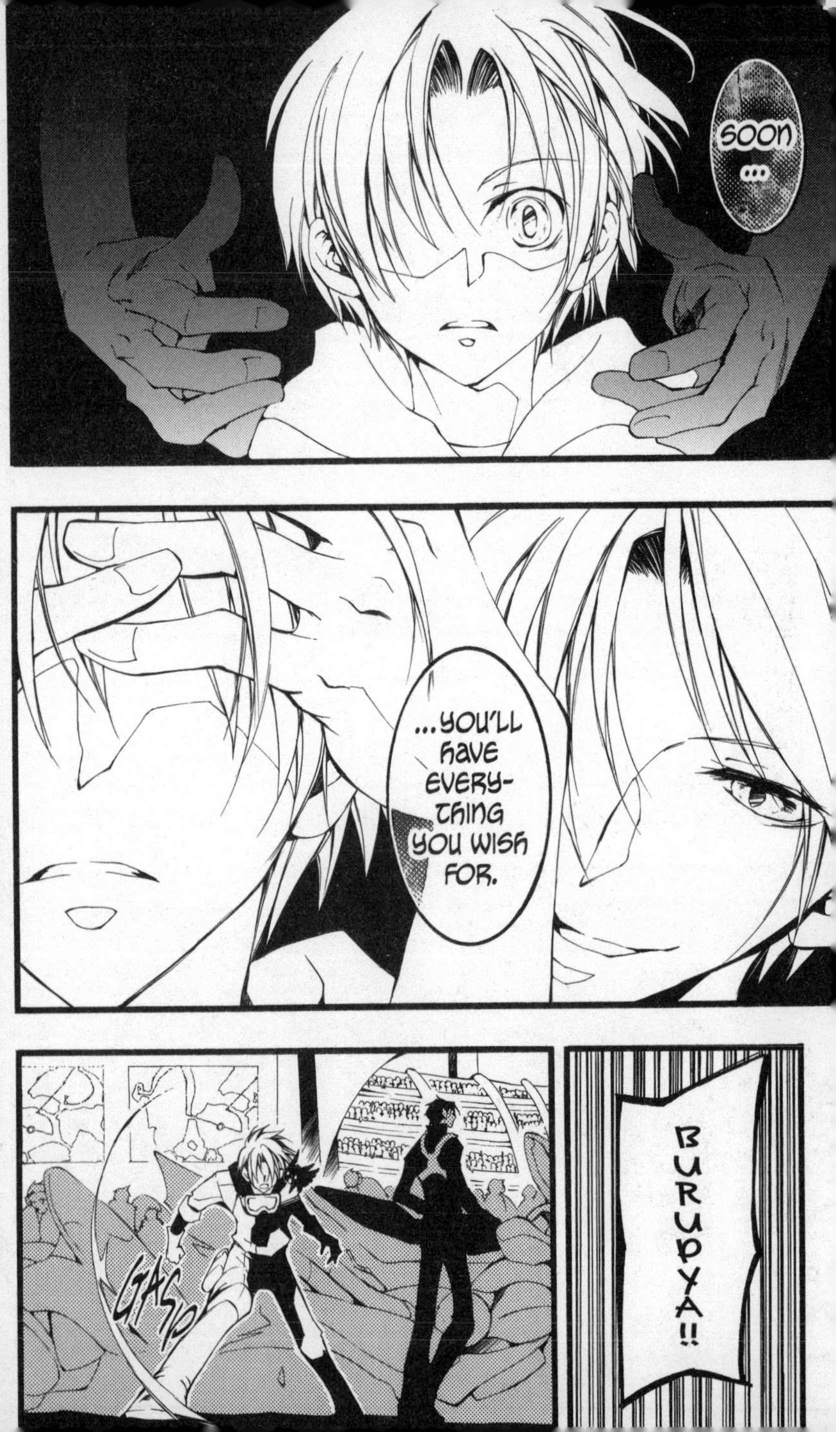
SOON ...
...YOU'LL HAVE EVERY-THING YOU WISH FOR.
BURUPYA!!
GASP

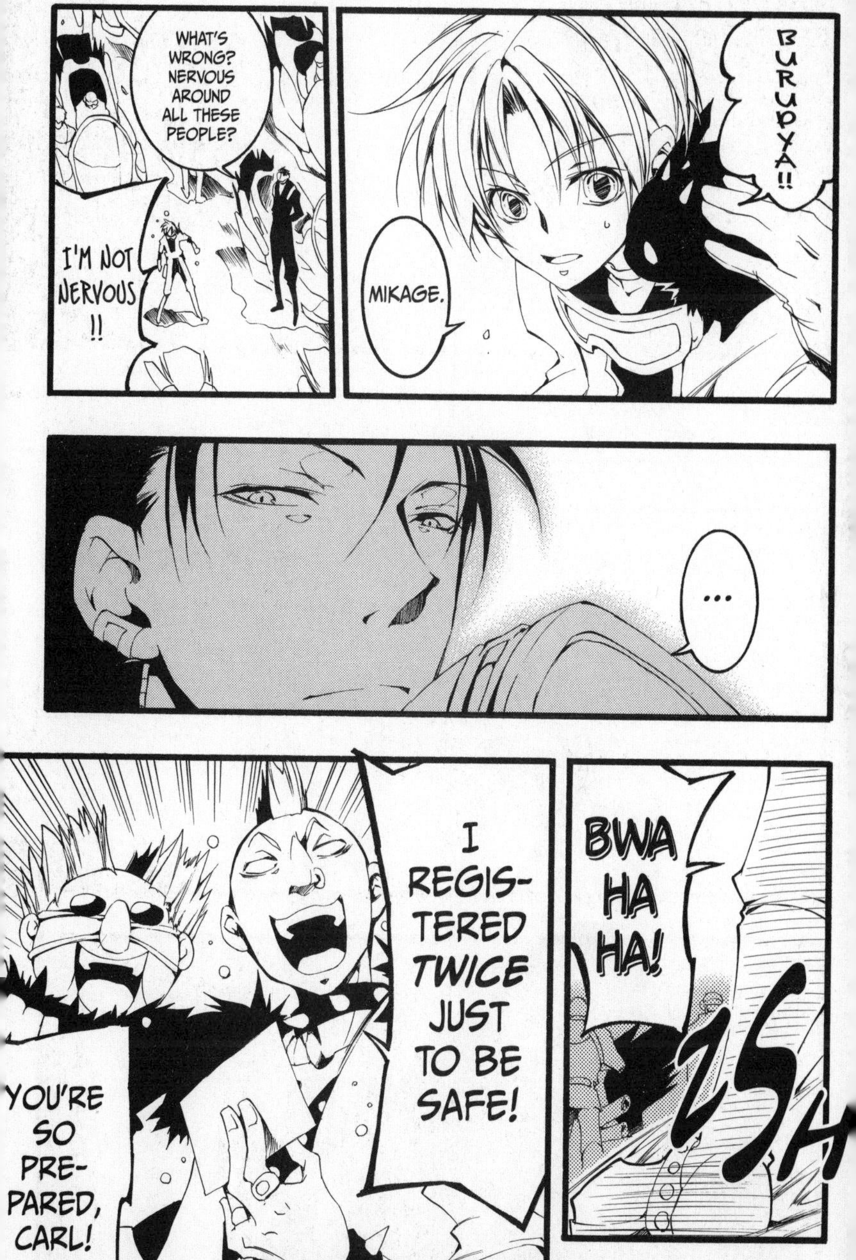
BURUPYA!!
MIKAGE.
WHAT'S WRONG? NERVOUS AROUND ALL THESE PEOPLE?
I'M NOT NERVOUS!!
...
BWA HA HA!
ZSH
I REGIS-TERED TWICE JUST TO BE SAFE!
YOU'RE SO PRE-PARED, CARL!

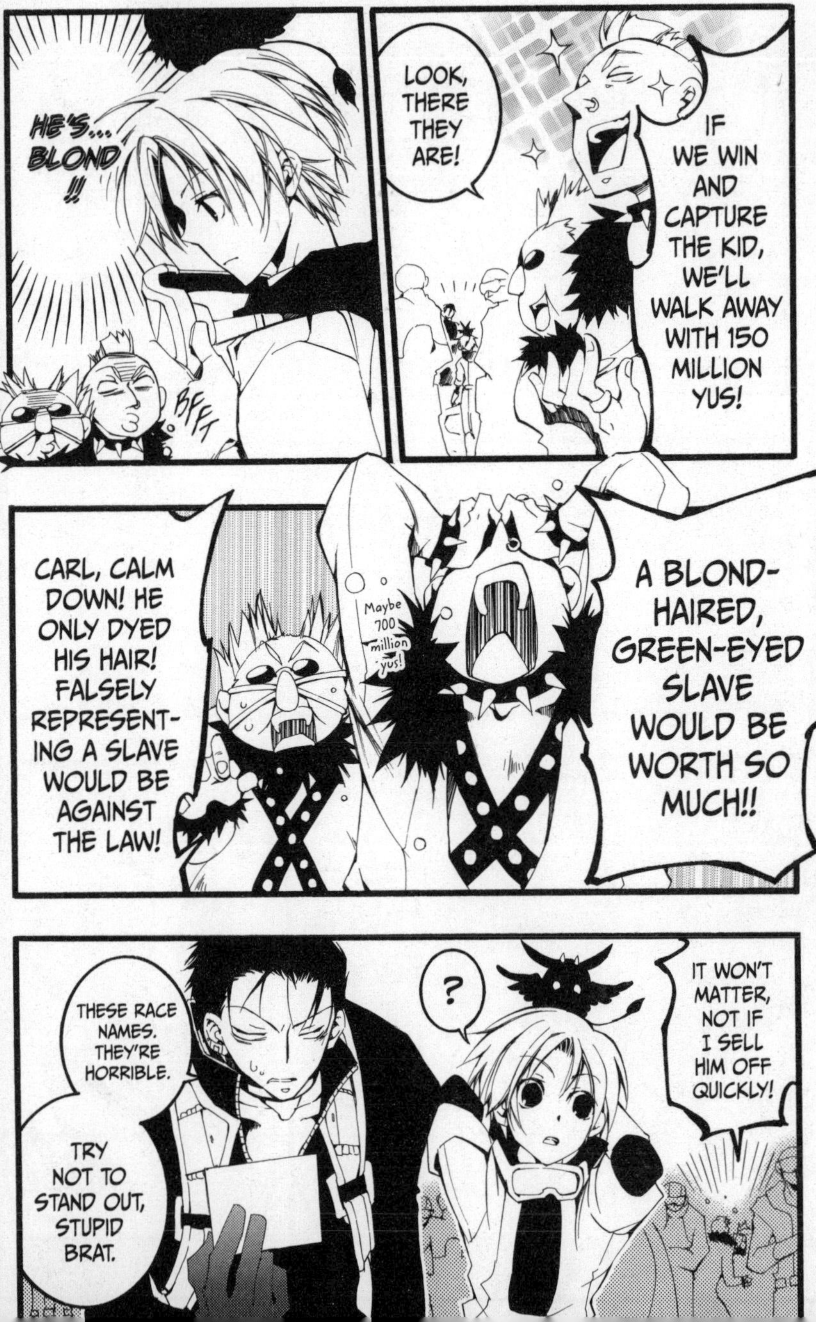
LOOK, THERE THEY ARE!
IF WE WIN AND CAPTURE THE KID, WE'LL WALK AWAY WITH 150 MILLION YUS!
HE'S... BLOND !!
BFFT
A BLOND-HAIRED, GREEN-EYED SLAVE WOULD BE WORTH SO MUCH!!
Maybe 700 million yus!
CARL, CALM DOWN! HE ONLY DYED HIS HAIR! FALSELY REPRESENTING A SLAVE WOULD BE AGAINST THE LAW!
IT WON'T MATTER, NOT IF I SELL HIM OFF QUICKLY!
?
THESE RACE NAMES. THEY'RE HORRIBLE.
TRY NOT TO STAND OUT, STUPID BRAT.

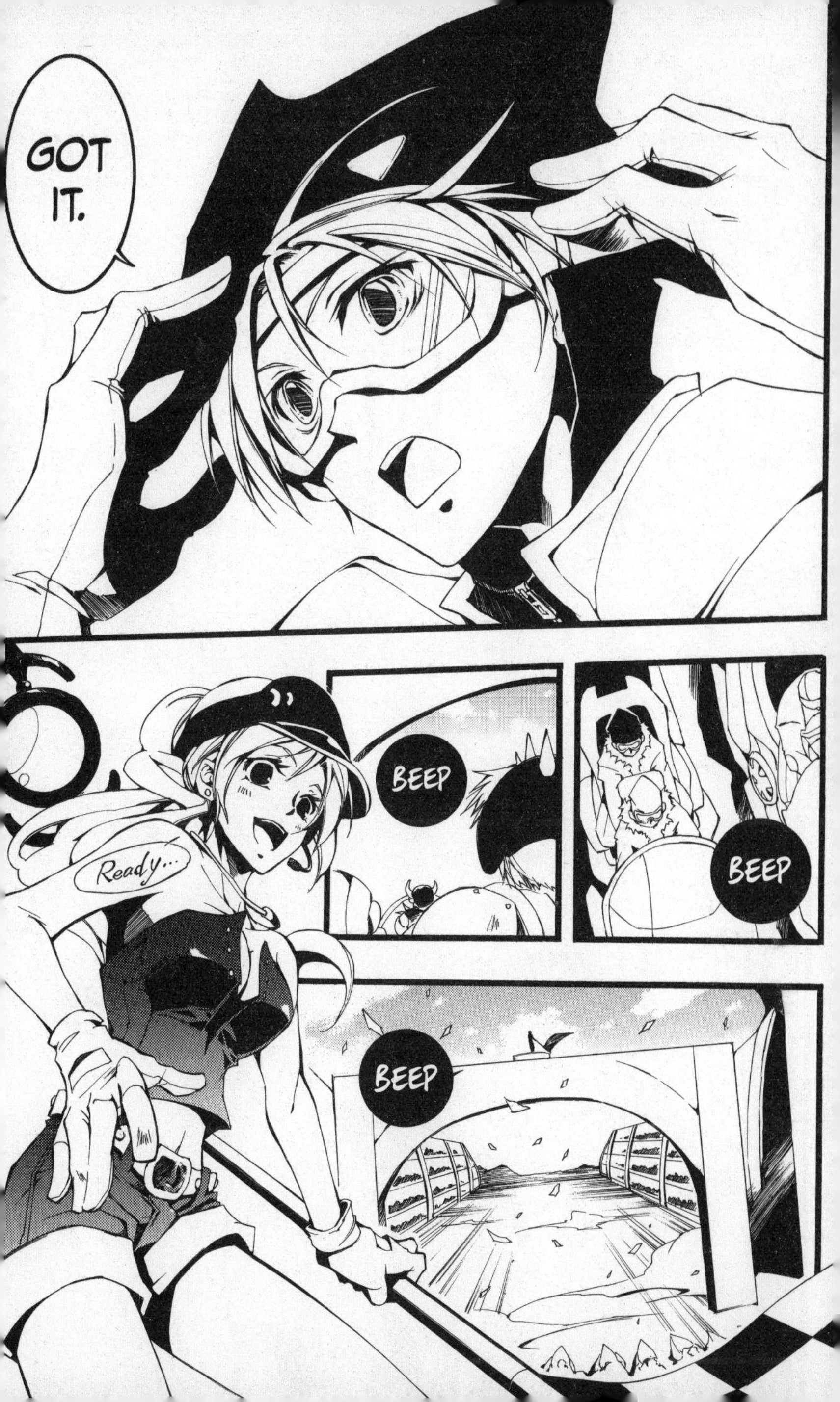
GOT IT.
BEEP
BEEP
BEEP
Ready...

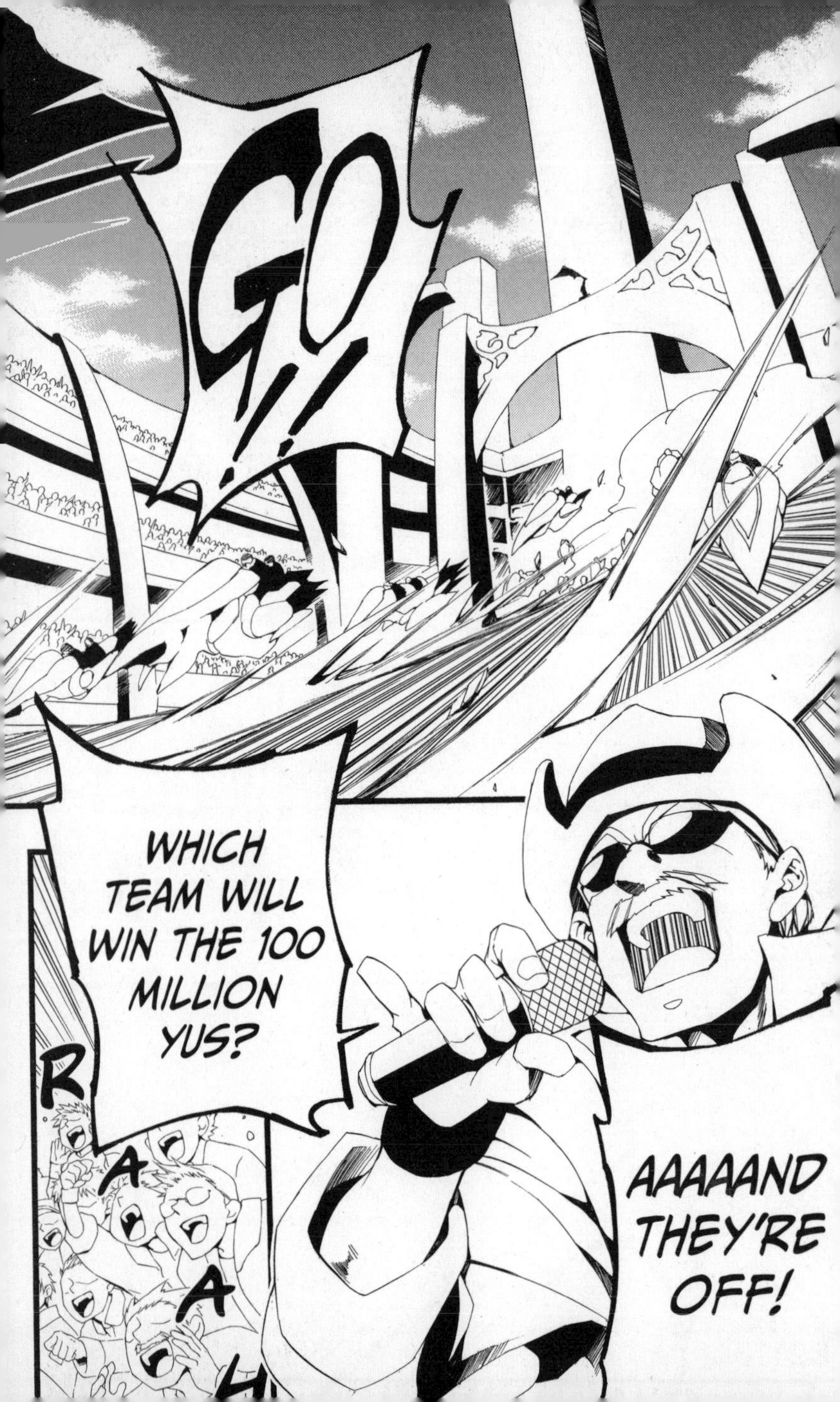
GO!!
AAAAAND THEY'RE OFF!
WHICH TEAM WILL WIN THE 100 MILLION YUS?
RAAH

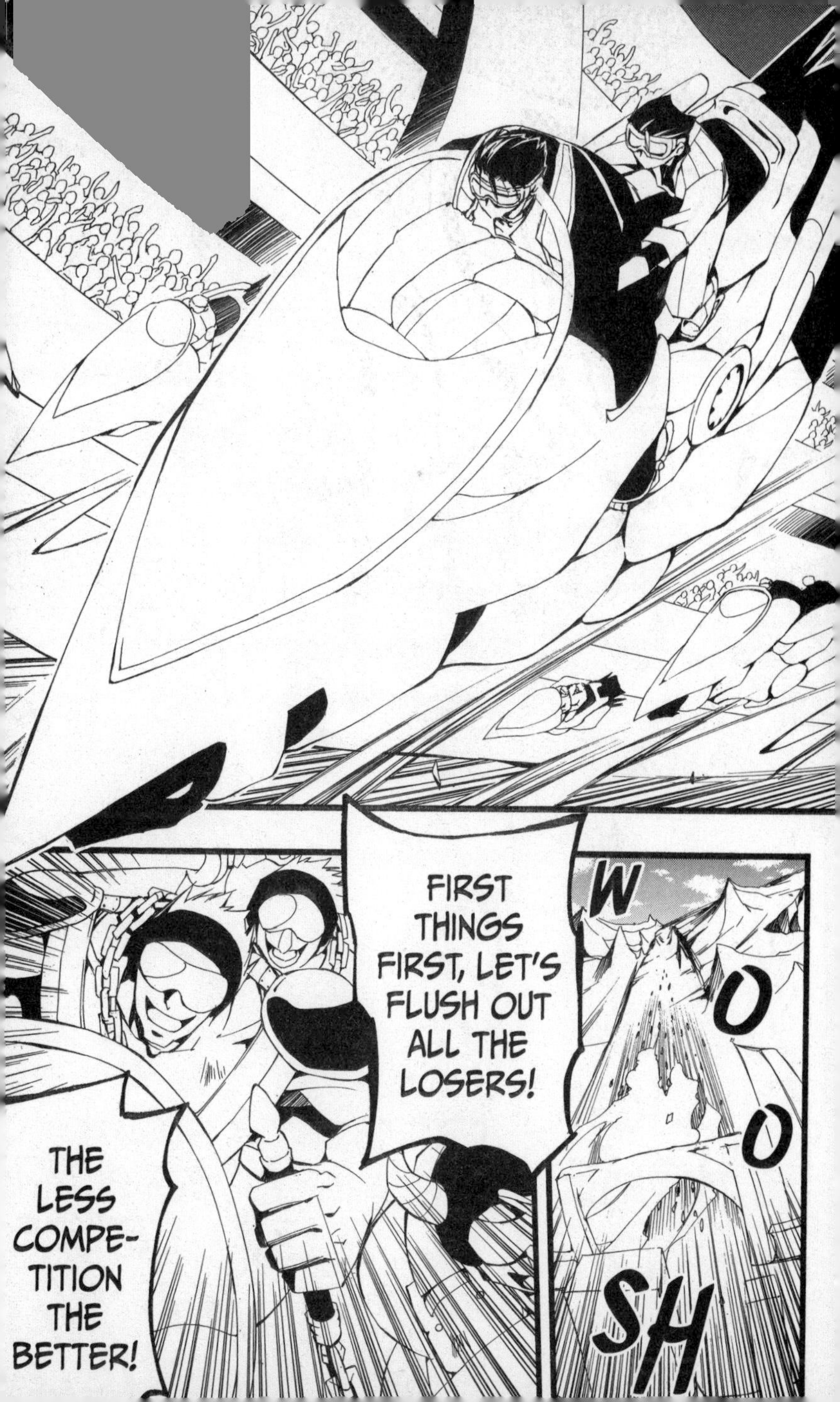
WOOOSH
FIRST THINGS FIRST, LET'S FLUSH OUT ALL THE LOSERS!
THE LESS COMPETITION THE BETTER!

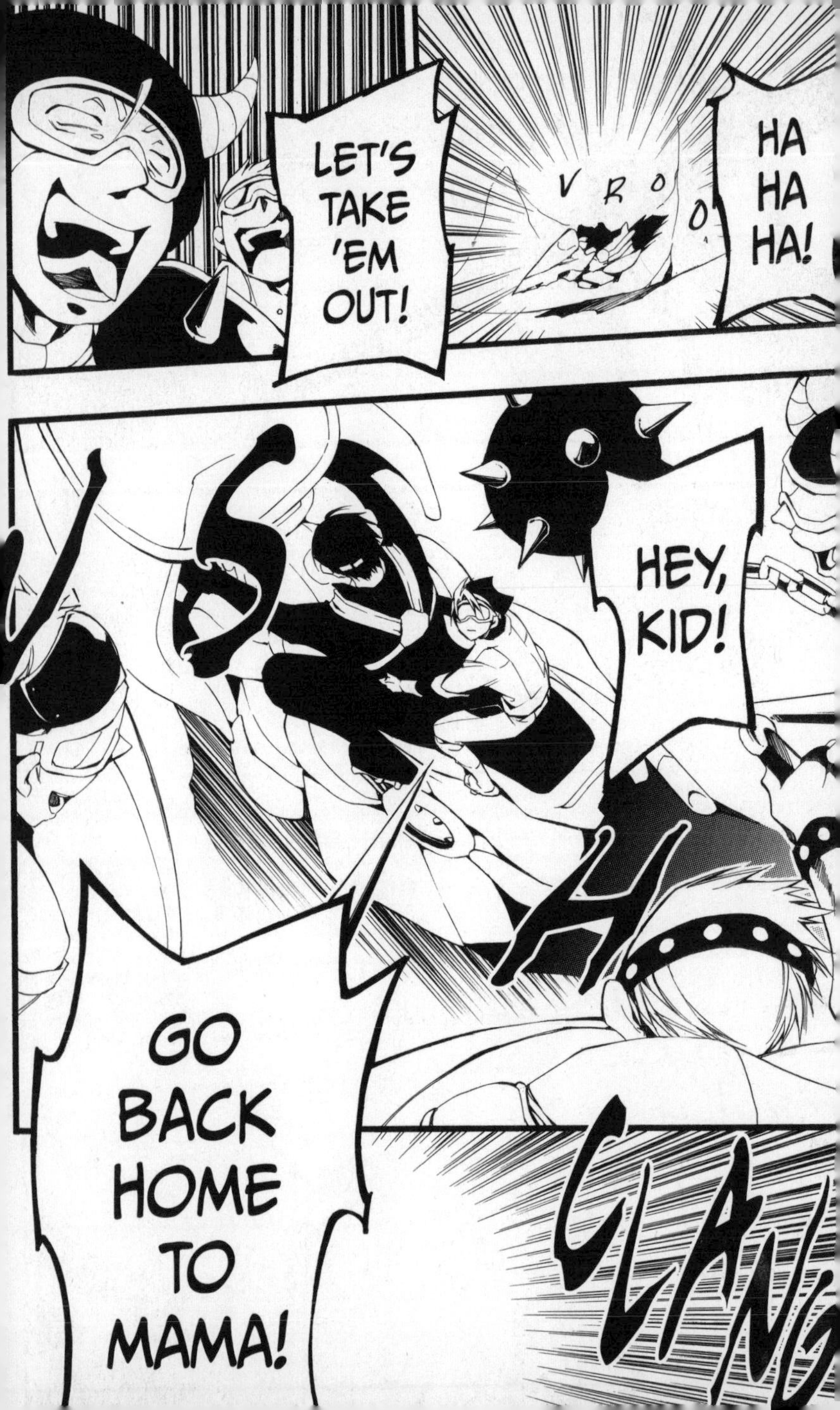
HA HA HA!
VROO
LET'S TAKE 'EM OUT!
HEY, KID!
GO BACK HOME TO MAMA!
CLANG

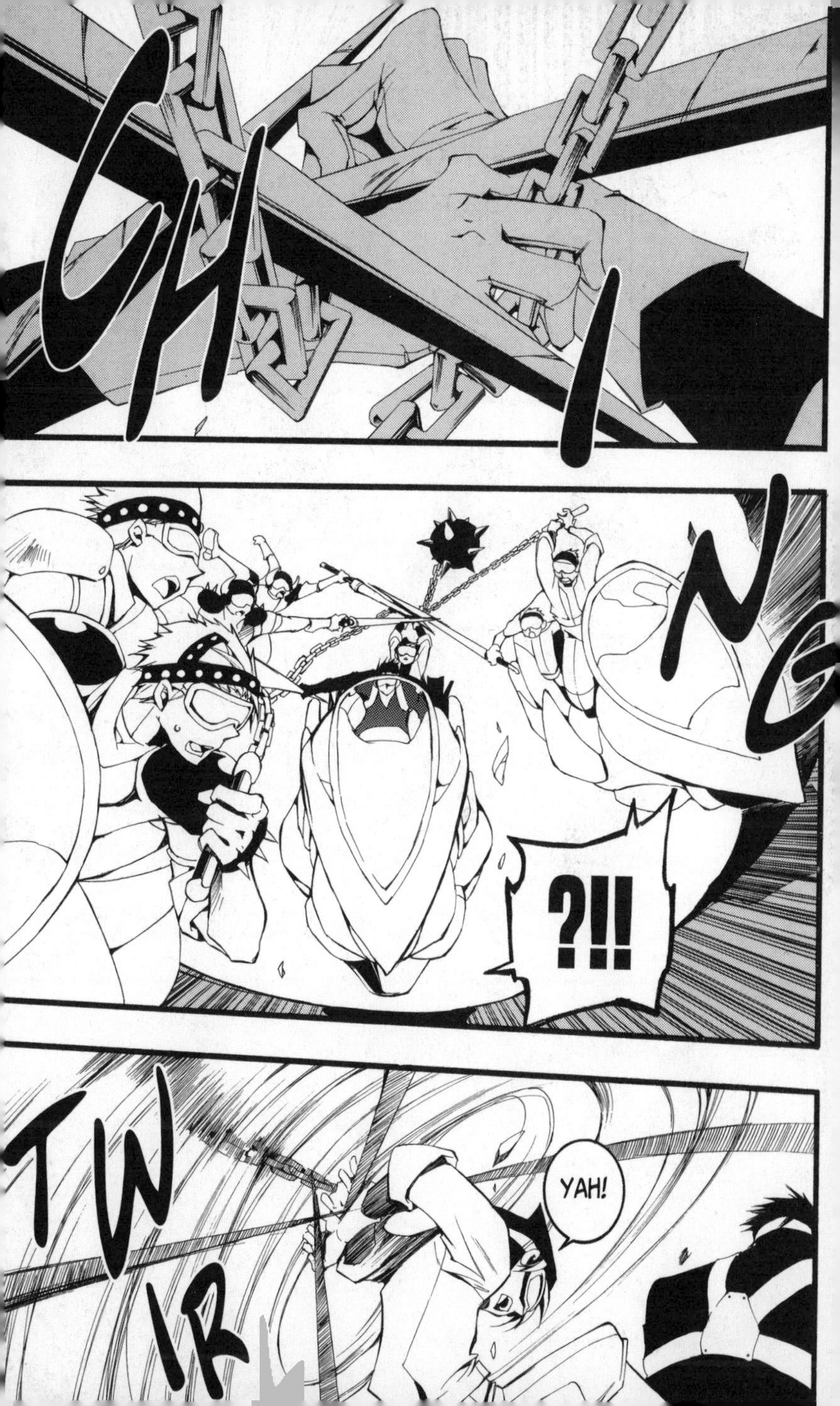
CHI
NG
?!!
YAH!
TWIR

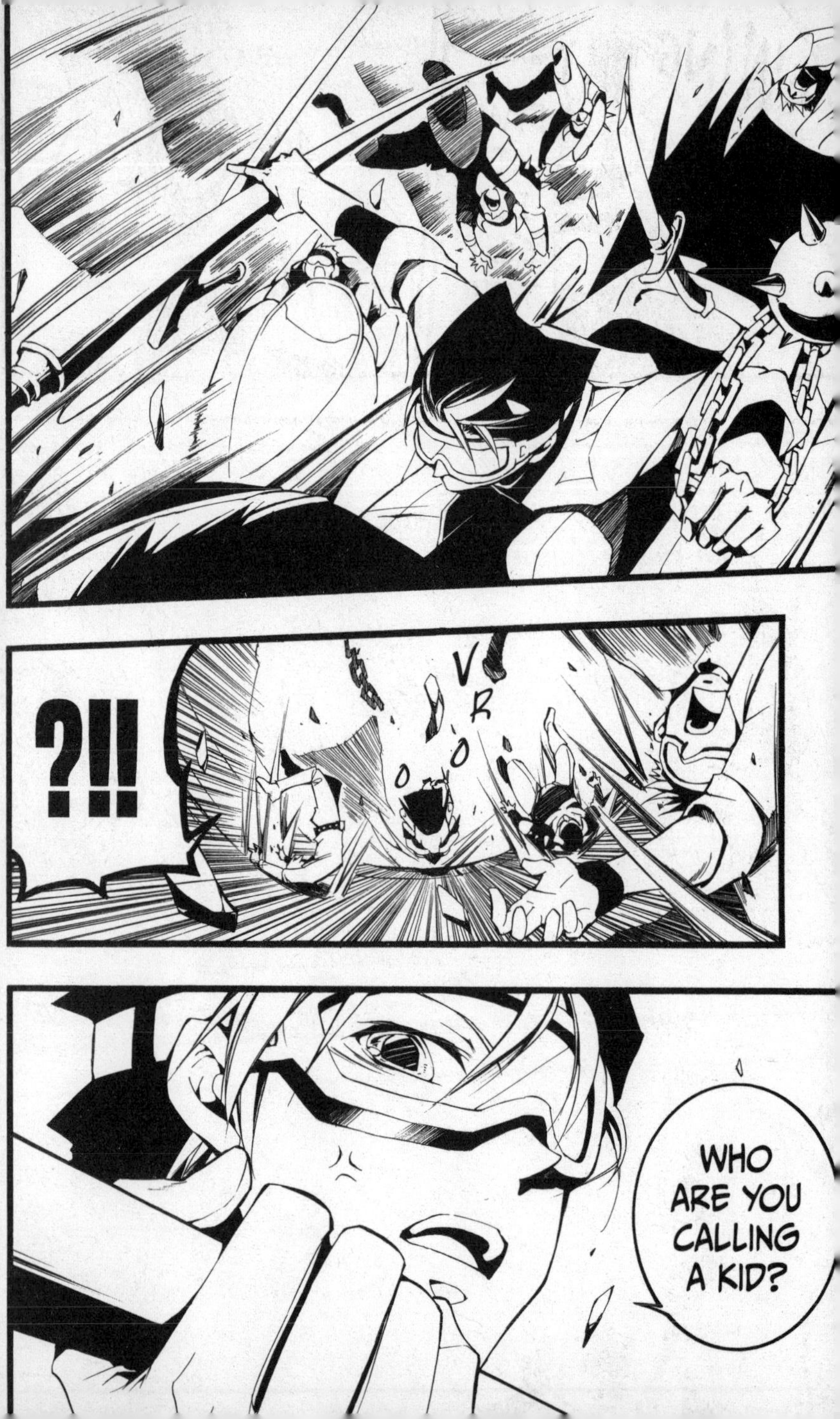
?!!
VROOO
WHO ARE YOU CALLING A KID?

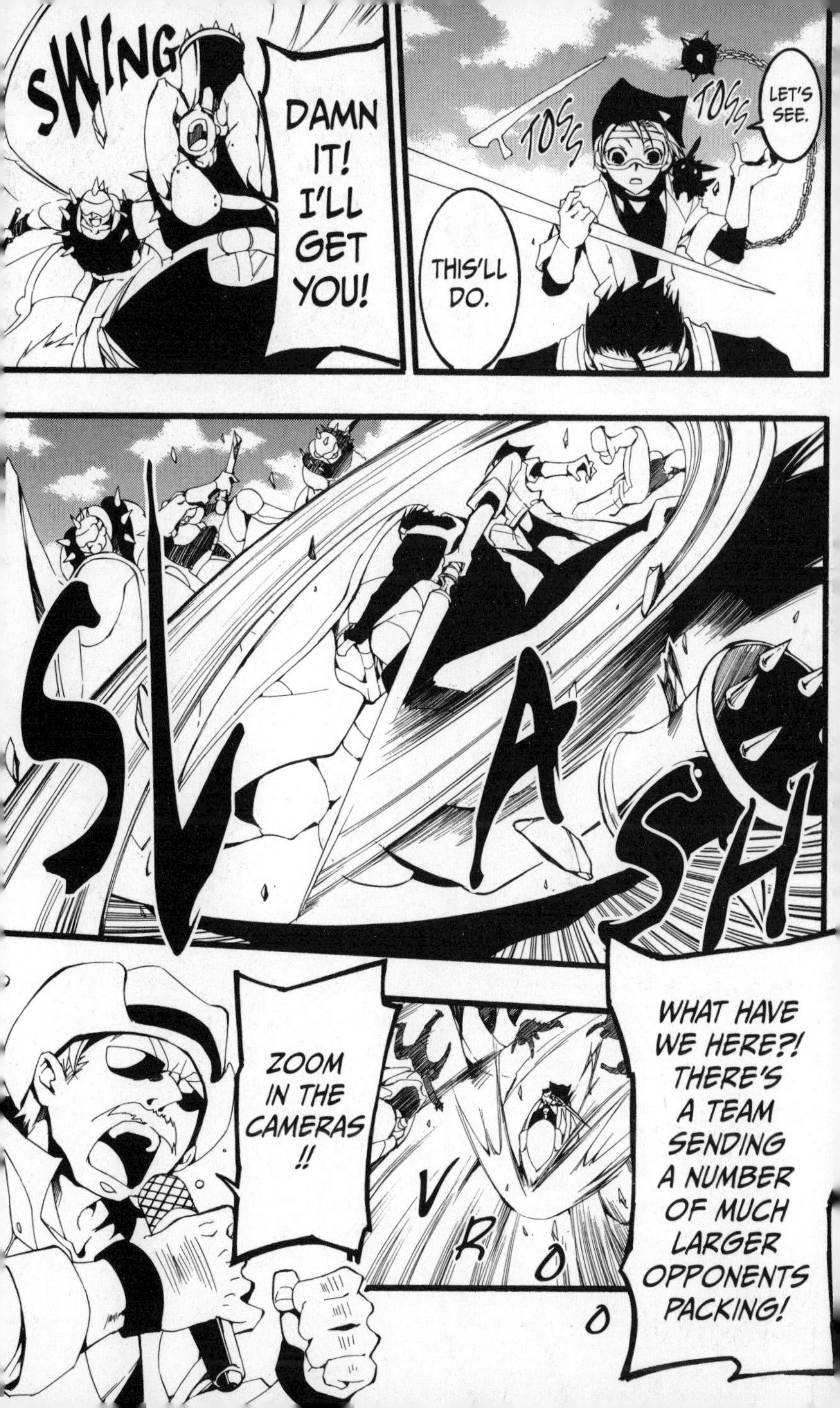
LET'S SEE.
TOSS
TOSS
THIS'LL DO.
SWING
DAMN IT! I'LL GET YOU!
SLASH
WHAT HAVE WE HERE?! THERE'S A TEAM SENDING A NUMBER OF MUCH LARGER OPPONENTS PACKING!
VROOO
ZOOM IN THE CAMERAS!!

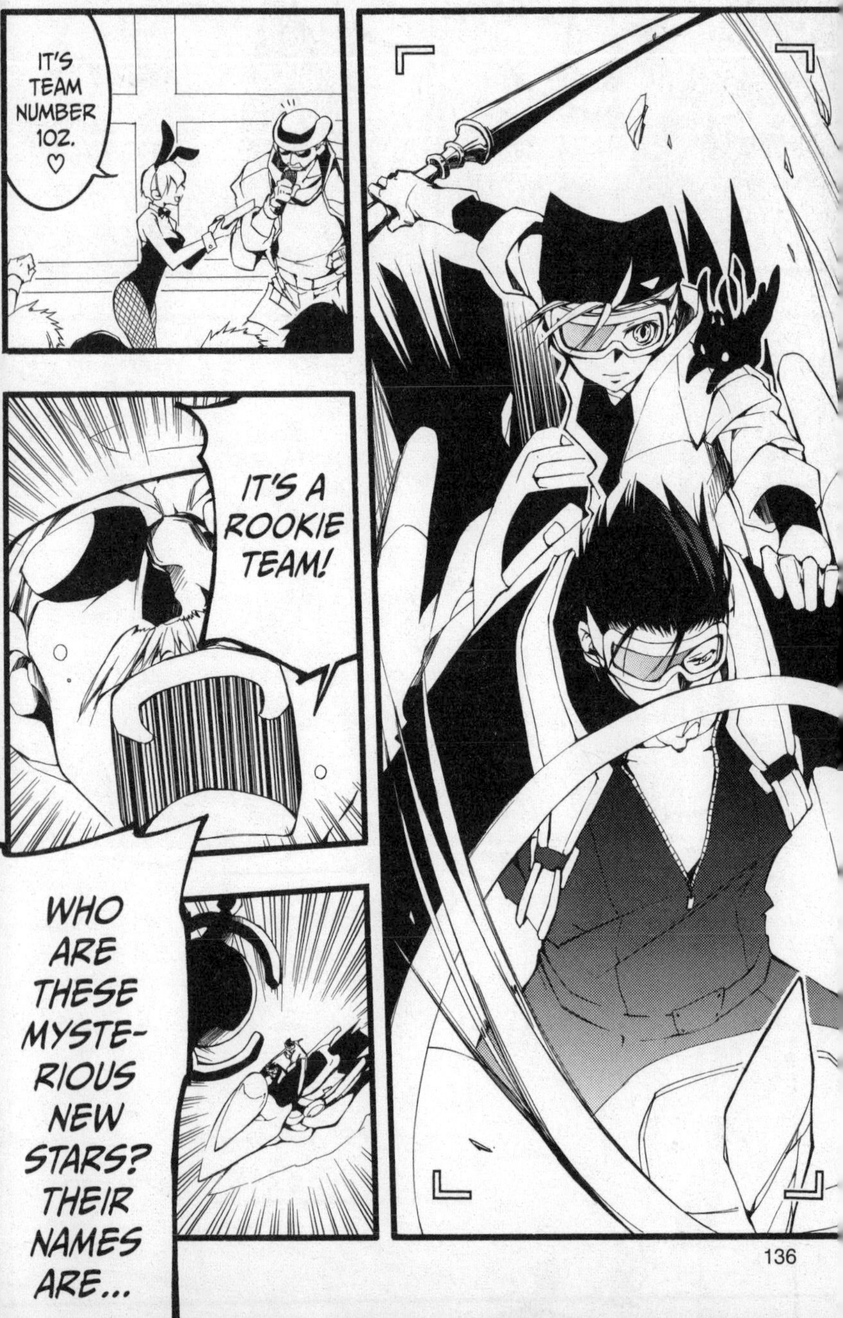
IT'S TEAM NUMBER 102. ♡
IT'S A ROOKIE TEAM!
WHO ARE THESE MYSTE-RIOUS NEW STARS? THEIR NAMES ARE...

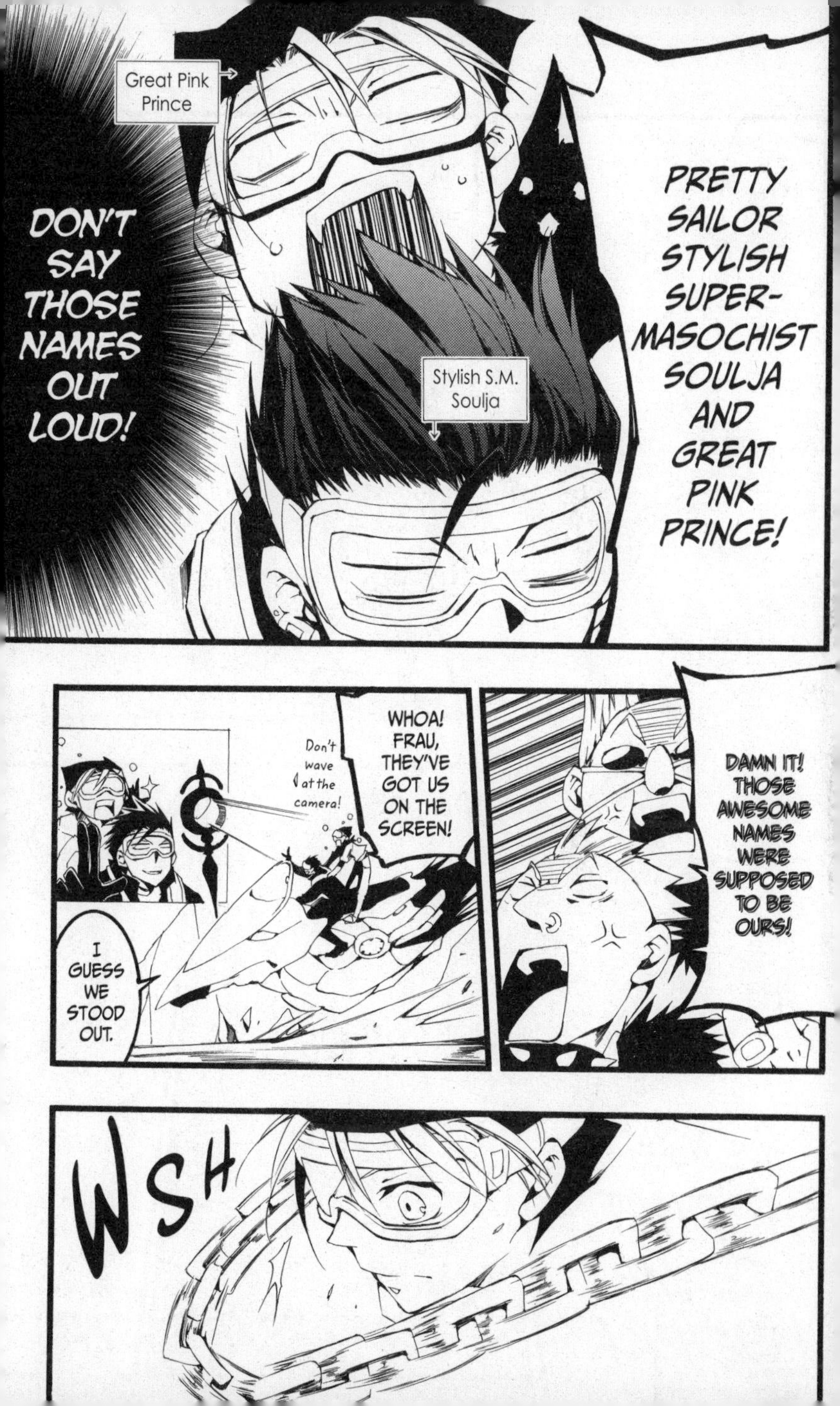

PRETTY SAILOR STYLISH SUPER-MASOCHIST SOULJA AND GREAT PINK PRINCE!
Great Pink Prince
DON'T SAY THOSE NAMES OUT LOUD!
Stylish S.M. Soulja
DAMN IT! THOSE AWESOME NAMES WERE SUPPOSED TO BE OURS!
WHOA! FRAU, THEY'VE GOT US ON THE SCREEN!
Don't wave at the camera!
I GUESS WE STOOD OUT.
WSH

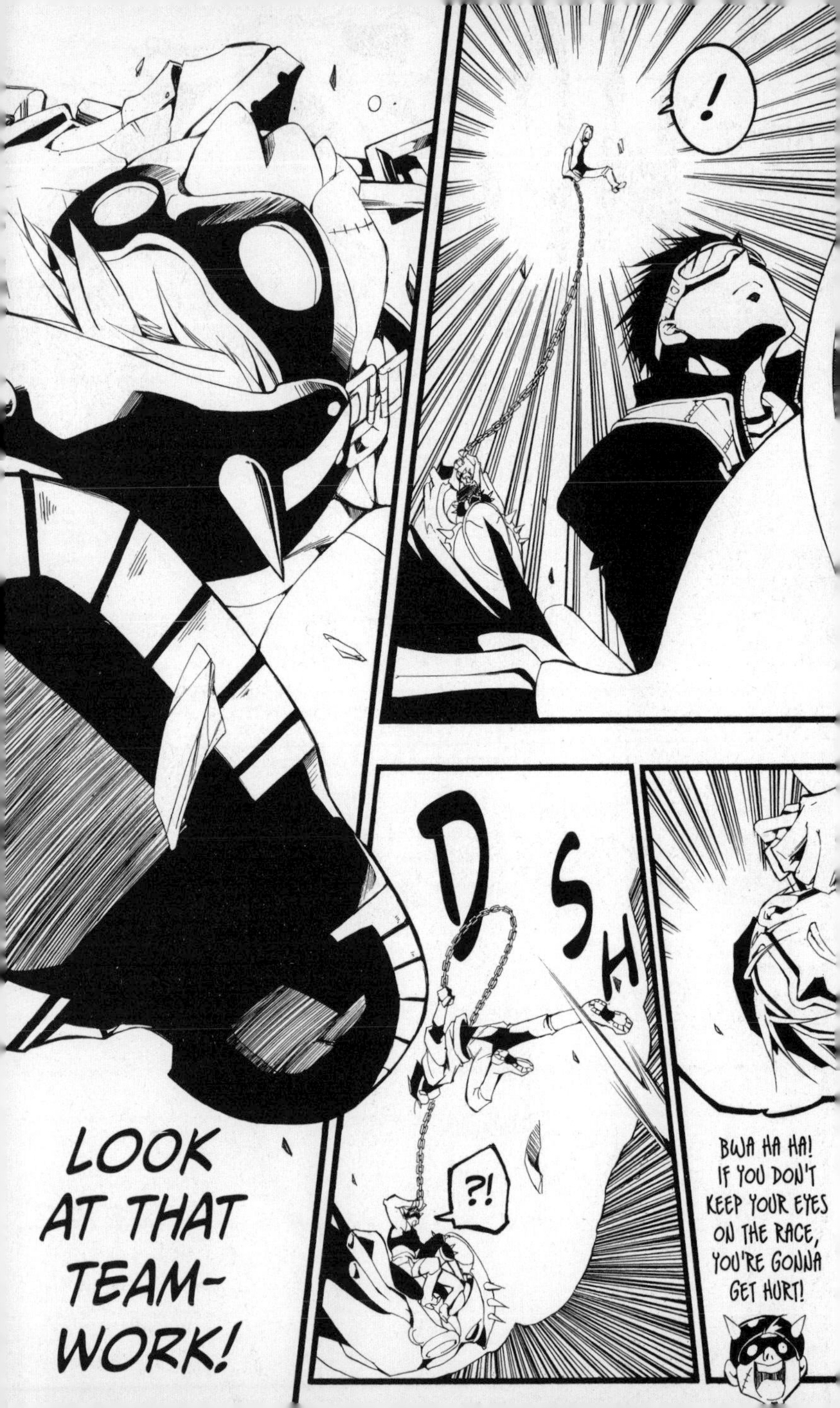
!
BWA HA HA! IF YOU DON'T KEEP YOUR EYES ON THE RACE, YOU'RE GONNA GET HURT!
DSH
?!
LOOK AT THAT TEAM-WORK!

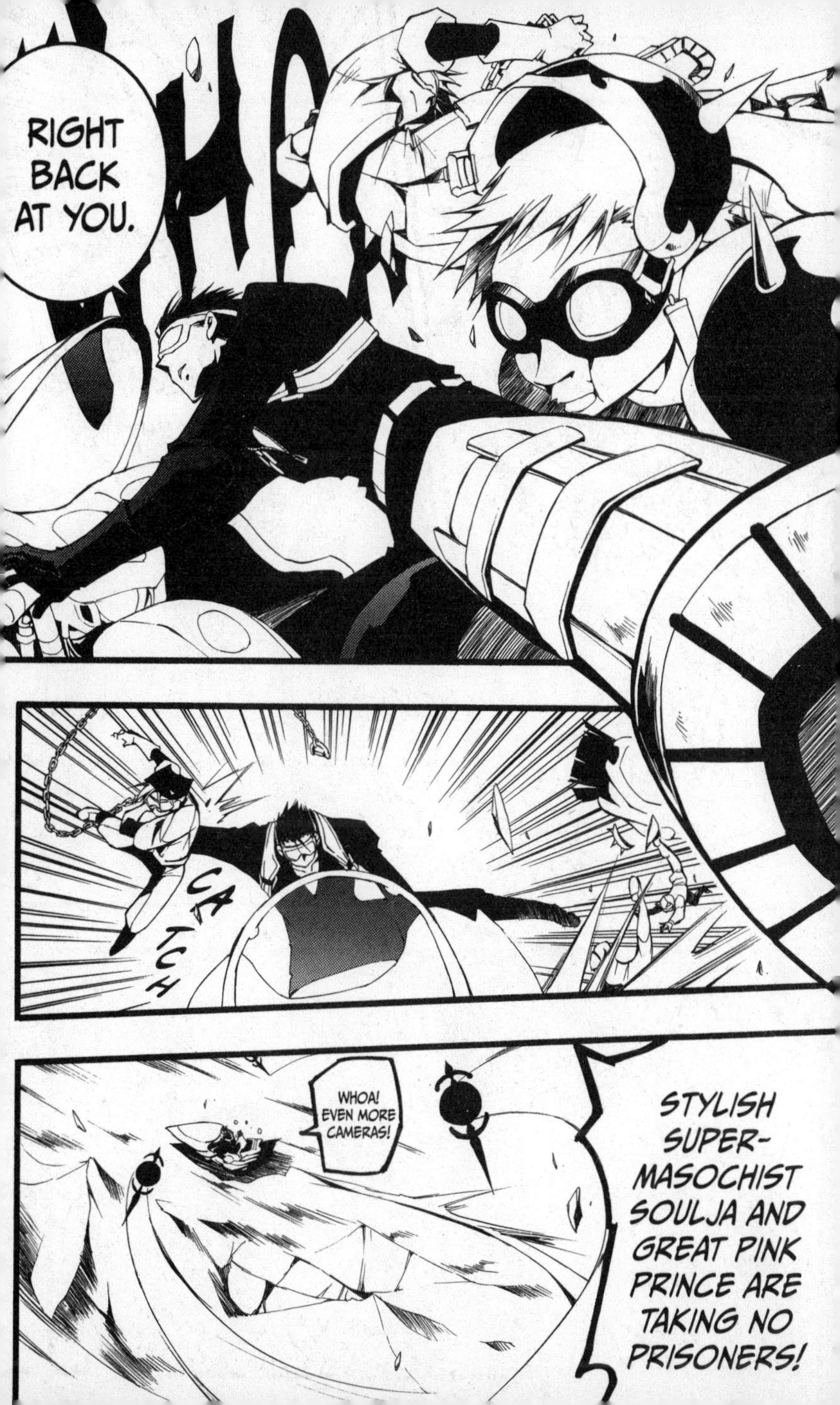
RIGHT BACK AT YOU.
CATCH
WHOA! EVEN MORE CAMERAS!
STYLISH SUPER-MASOCHIST SOULJA AND GREAT PINK PRINCE ARE TAKING NO PRISONERS!

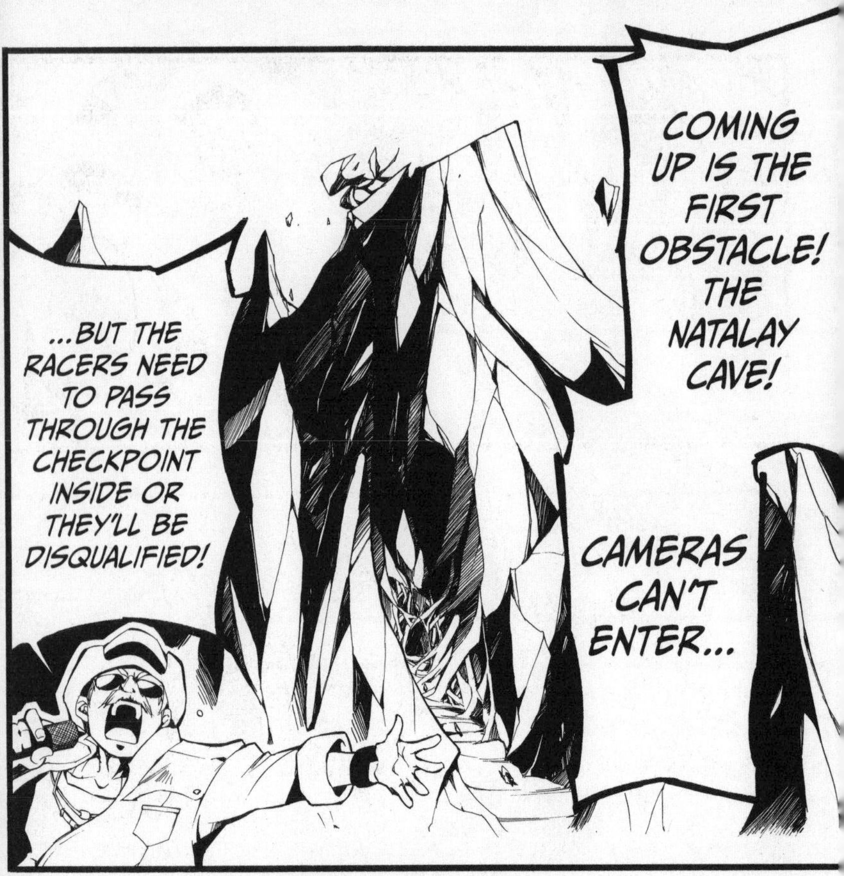
COMING UP IS THE FIRST OBSTACLE! THE NATALAY CAVE!
CAMERAS CAN'T ENTER...
...BUT THE RACERS NEED TO PASS THROUGH THE CHECKPOINT INSIDE OR THEY'LL BE DISQUALIFIED!
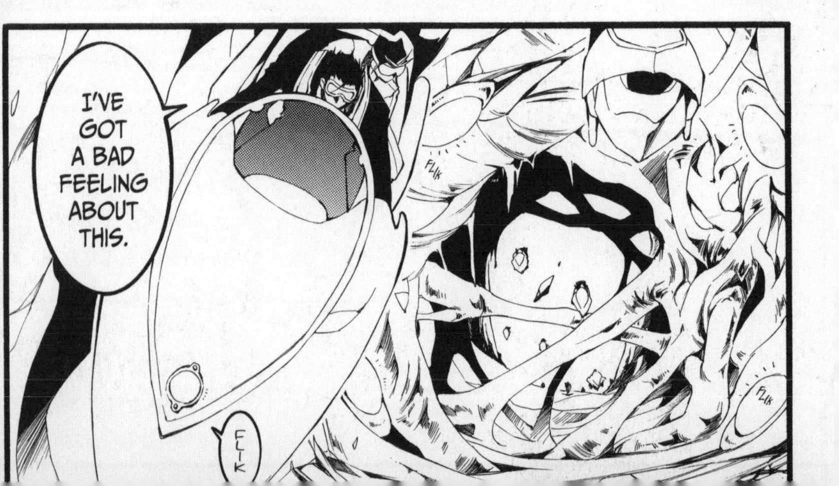
FLIK
I'VE GOT A BAD FEELING ABOUT THIS.
FLIK
FLIK

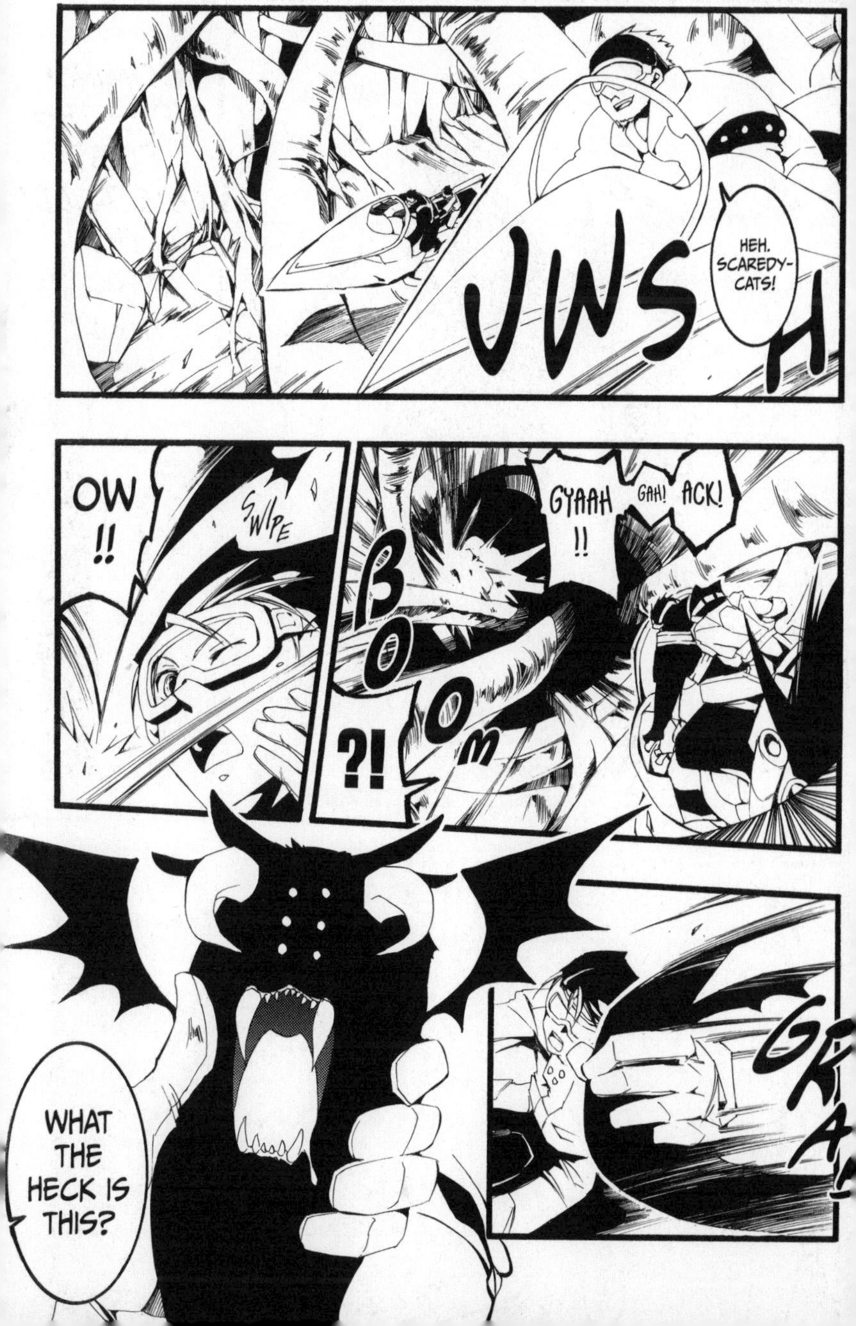
HEH. SCAREDY-CATS!
VWSH
GYAAH!!
GAH!
ACK!
BOOM
OW!!
SWIPE
?!
WHAT THE HECK IS THIS?

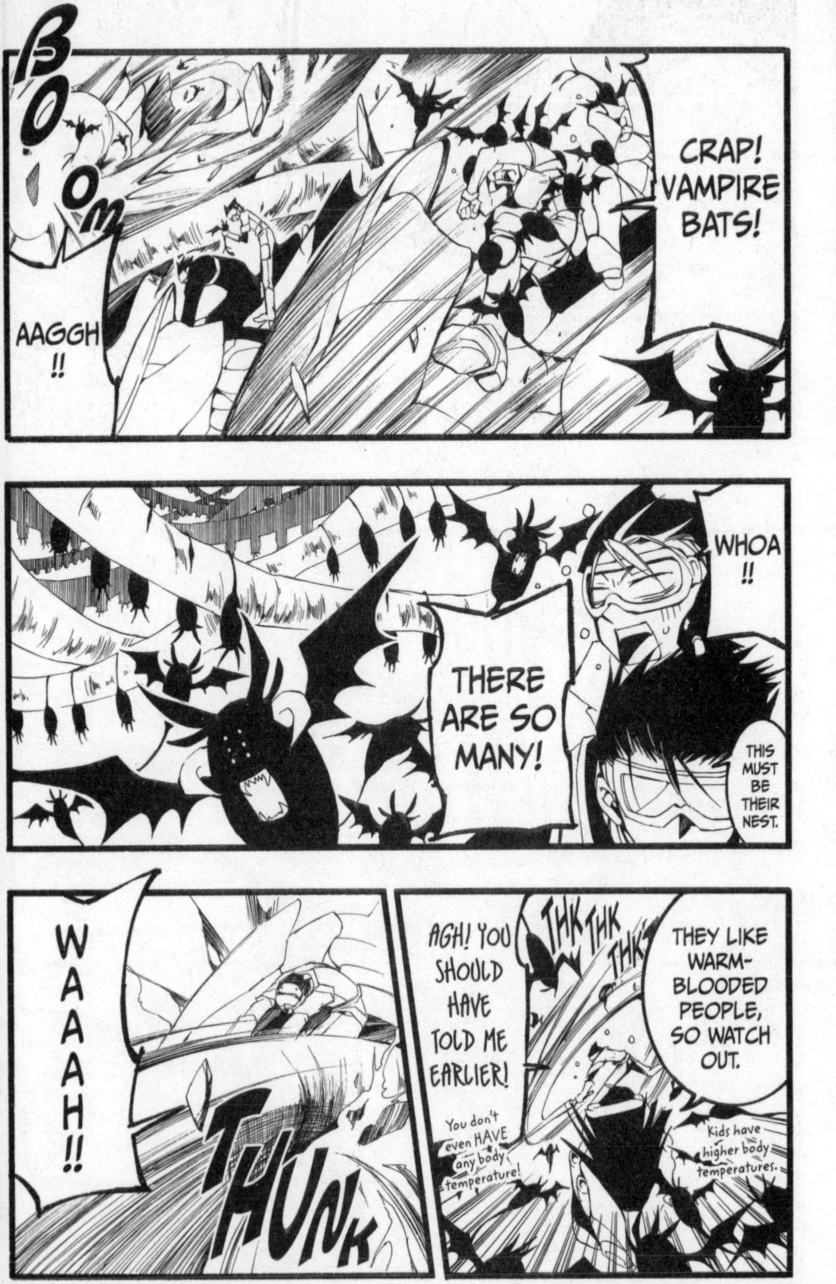

BOOOM
CRAP! VAMPIRE BATS!
AAGGH!!
WHOA!!
THERE ARE SO MANY!
THIS MUST BE THEIR NEST.
THK THK THK
THEY LIKE WARM-BLOODED PEOPLE, SO WATCH OUT.
AGH! YOU SHOULD HAVE TOLD ME EARLIER!
Kids have higher body temperatures.
You don't even HAVE any body temperature!
WAAAAH!!
THUNK

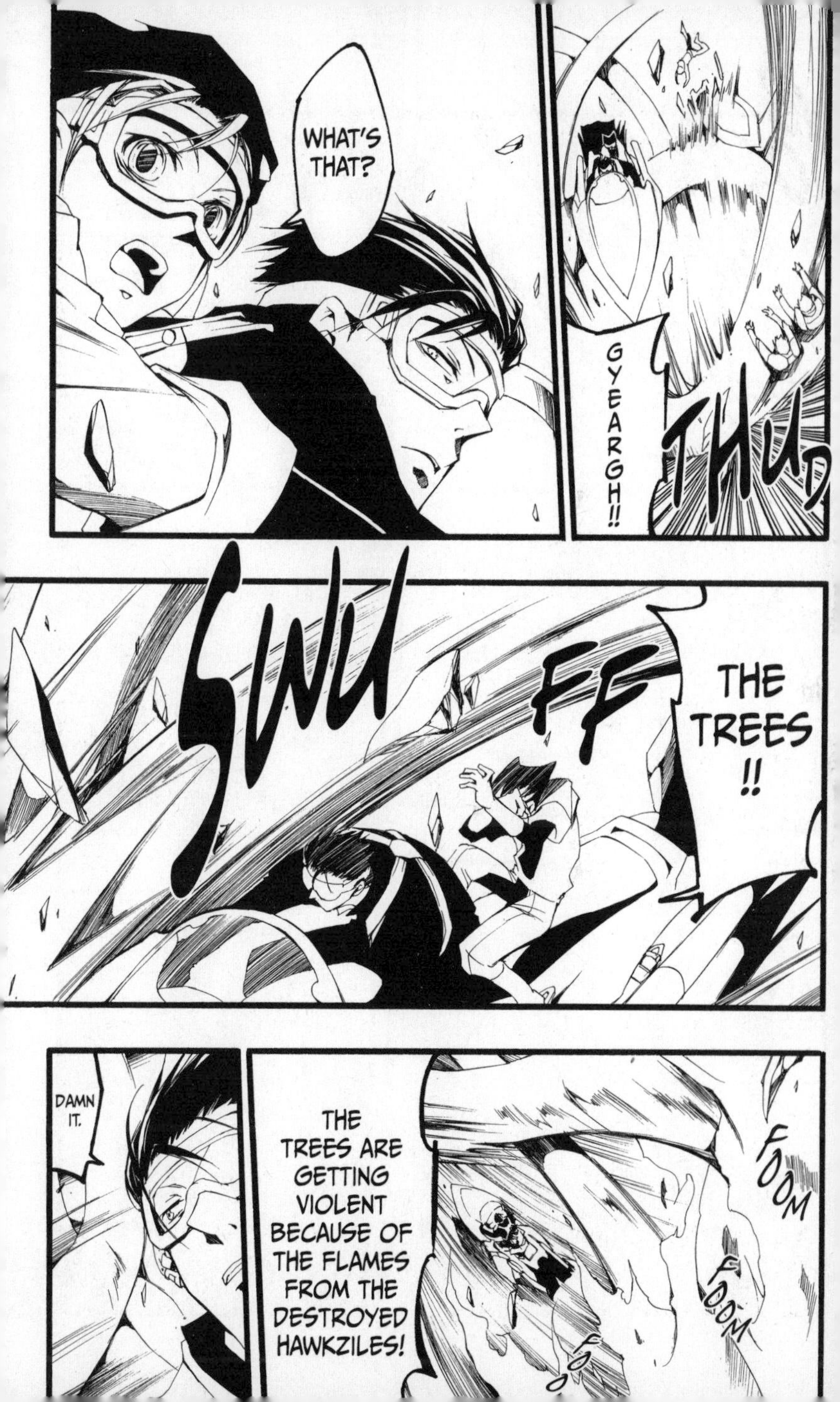
GYEARGH!!
THUD
WHAT'S THAT?
SWUFF
THE TREES!!
THE TREES ARE GETTING VIOLENT BECAUSE OF THE FLAMES FROM THE DESTROYED HAWKZILES!
FOOM
FOOM
FOOM
DAMN IT.

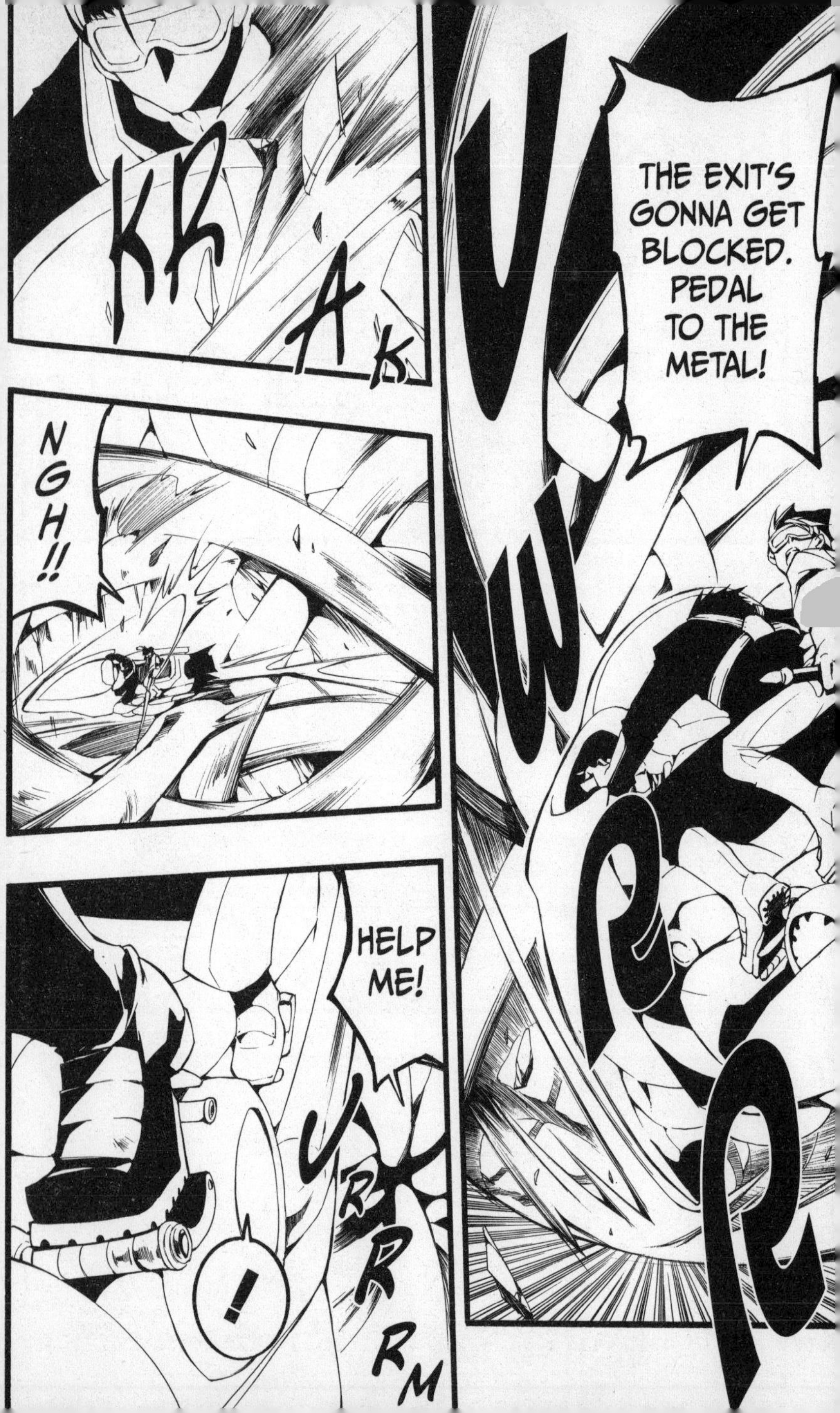
THE EXIT'S GONNA GET BLOCKED. PEDAL TO THE METAL!
KRAK
NGH!!
HELP ME!
!

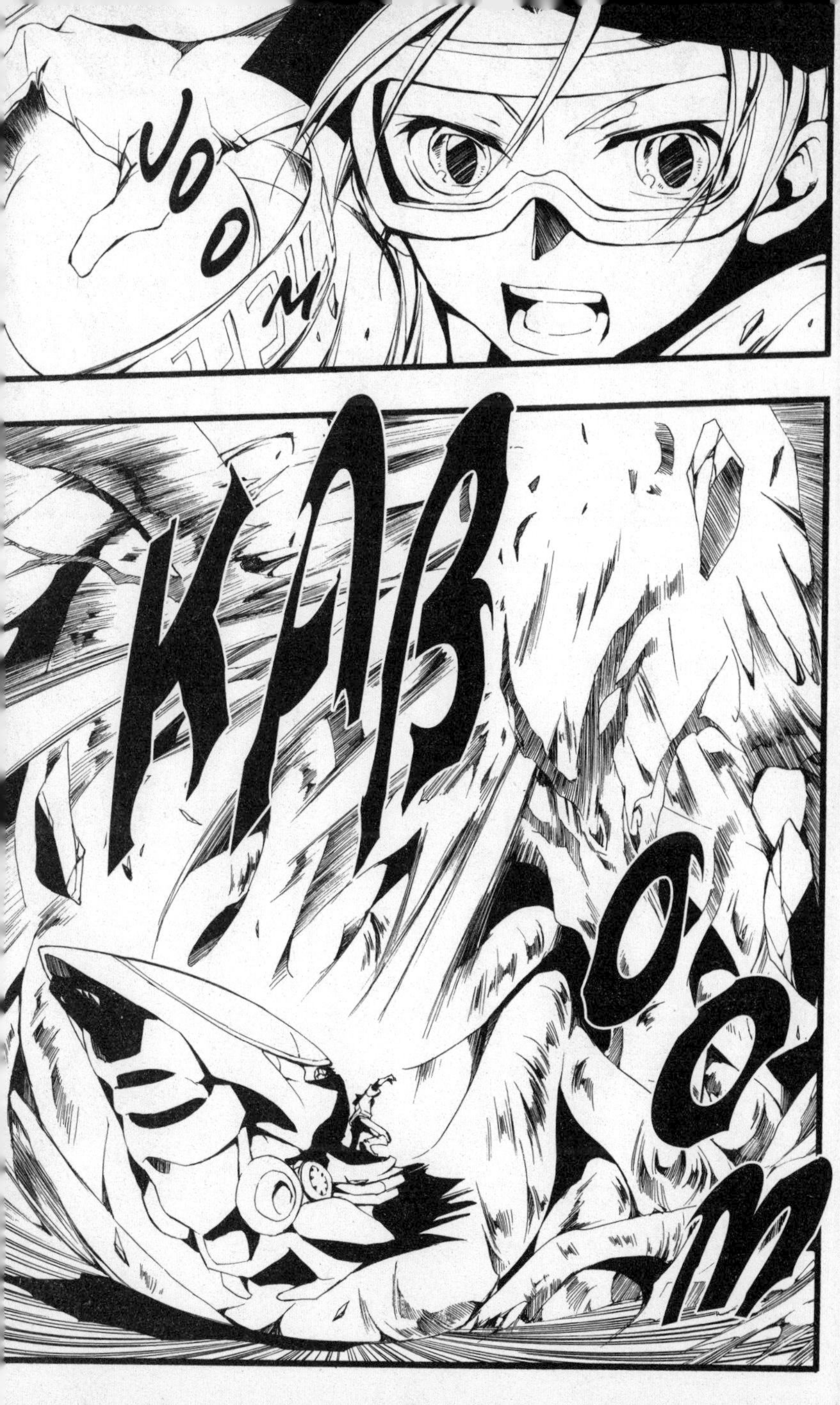
VOOM
KABOOM

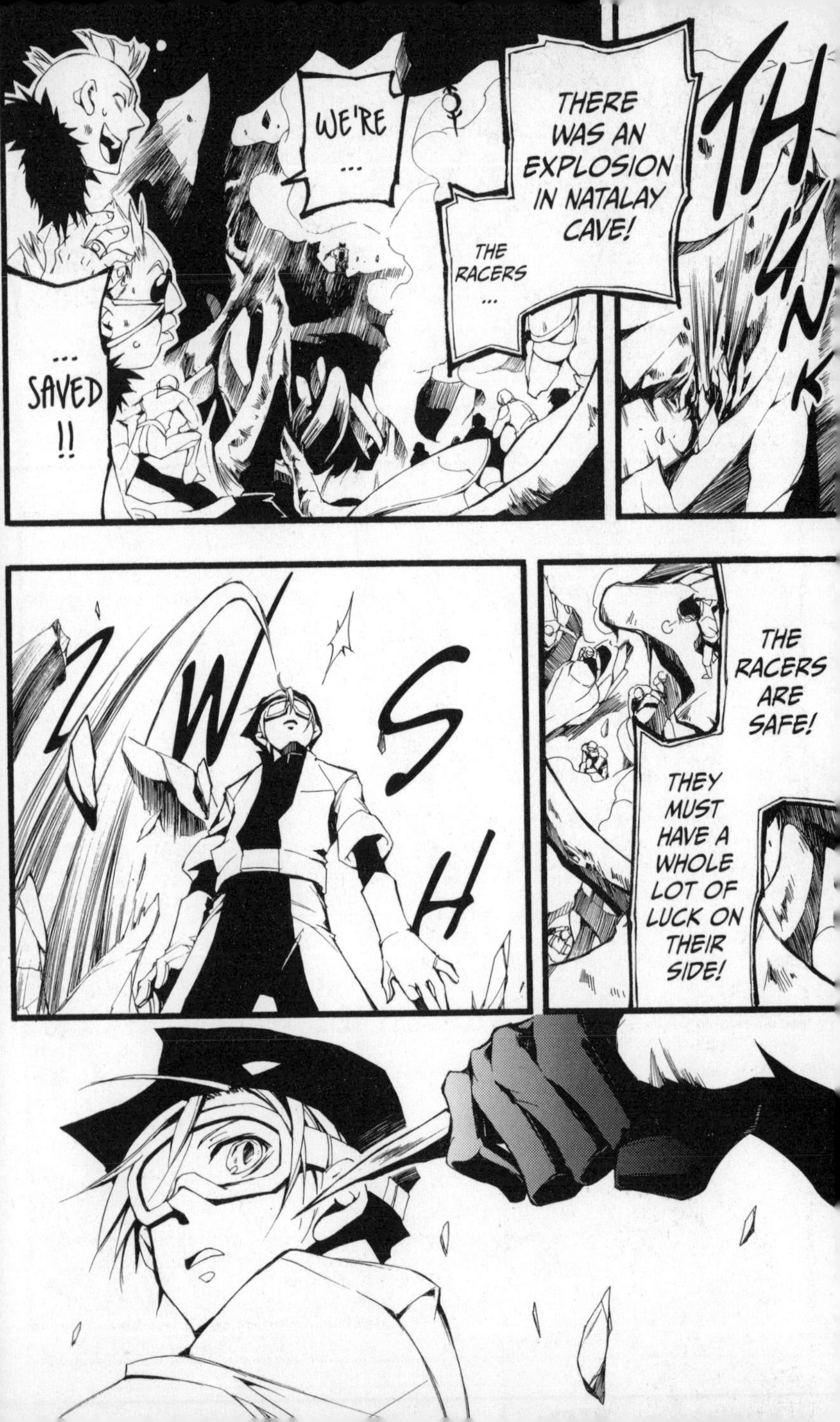
THUNK
THERE WAS AN EXPLOSION IN NATALAY CAVE!
THE RACERS ...
WE'RE ...
... SAVED !!
THE RACERS ARE SAFE!
THEY MUST HAVE A WHOLE LOT OF LUCK ON THEIR SIDE!
WSH

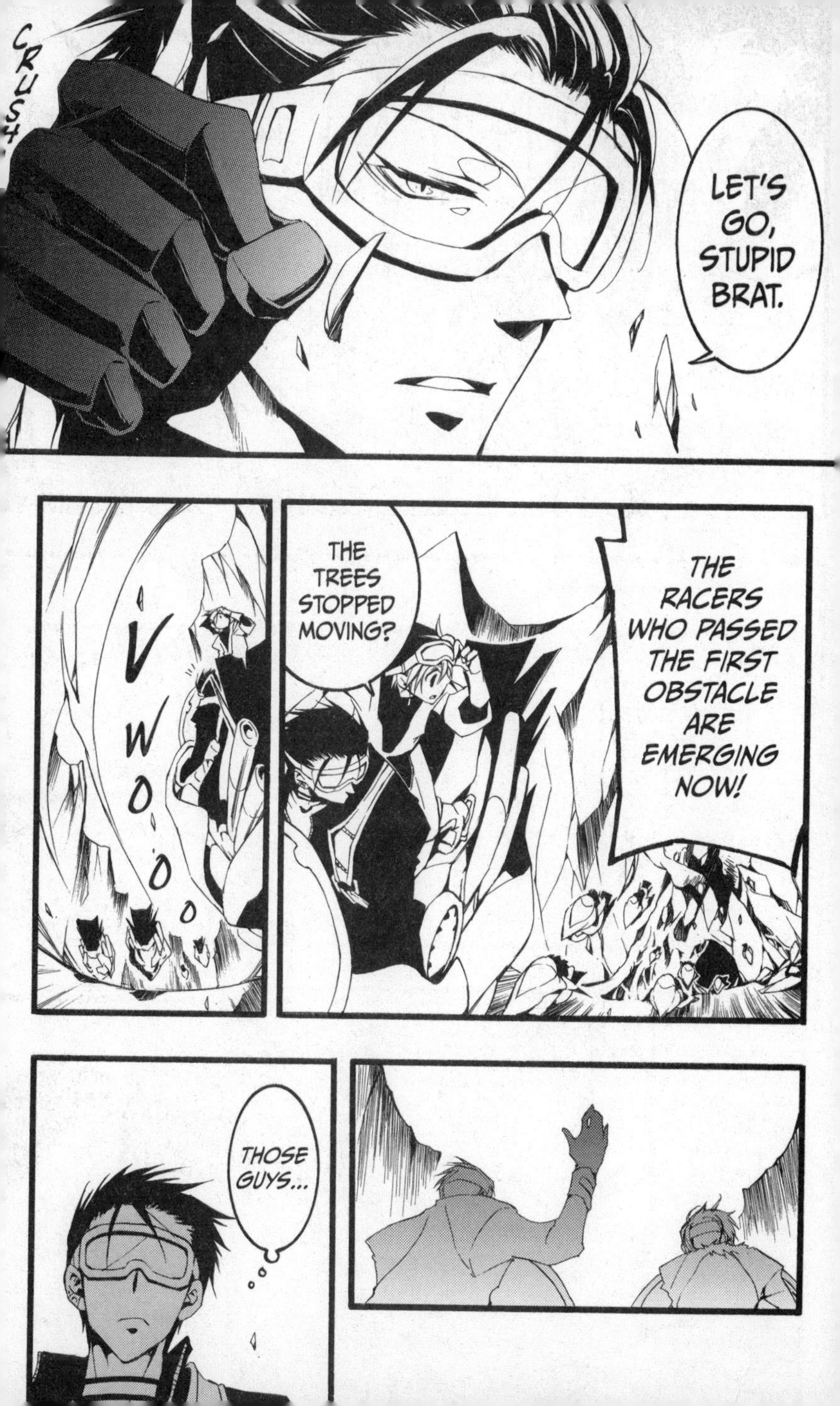
LET'S GO, STUPID BRAT.
CRUSH
THE RACERS WHO PASSED THE FIRST OBSTACLE ARE EMERGING NOW!
THE TREES STOPPED MOVING?
VWOOO
THOSE GUYS...

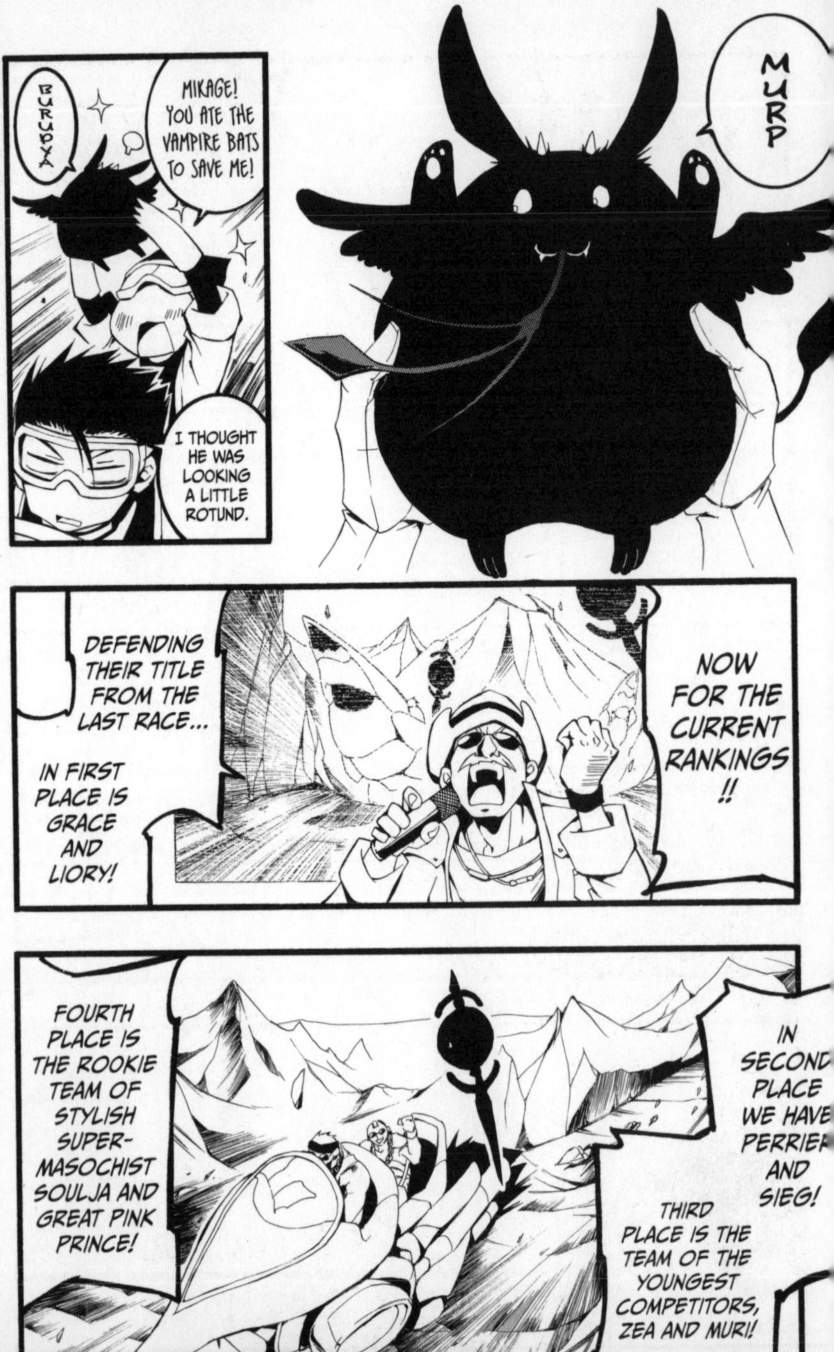
MURP
MIKAGE! YOU ATE THE VAMPIRE BATS TO SAVE ME!
BURUPYA
I THOUGHT HE WAS LOOKING A LITTLE ROTUND.
NOW FOR THE CURRENT RANKINGS!!
DEFENDING THEIR TITLE FROM THE LAST RACE...
IN FIRST PLACE IS GRACE AND LIORY!
IN SECOND PLACE WE HAVE PERRIER AND SIEG!
THIRD PLACE IS THE TEAM OF THE YOUNGEST COMPETITORS, ZEA AND MURI!
FOURTH PLACE IS THE ROOKIE TEAM OF STYLISH SUPER-MASOCHIST SOULJA AND GREAT PINK PRINCE!

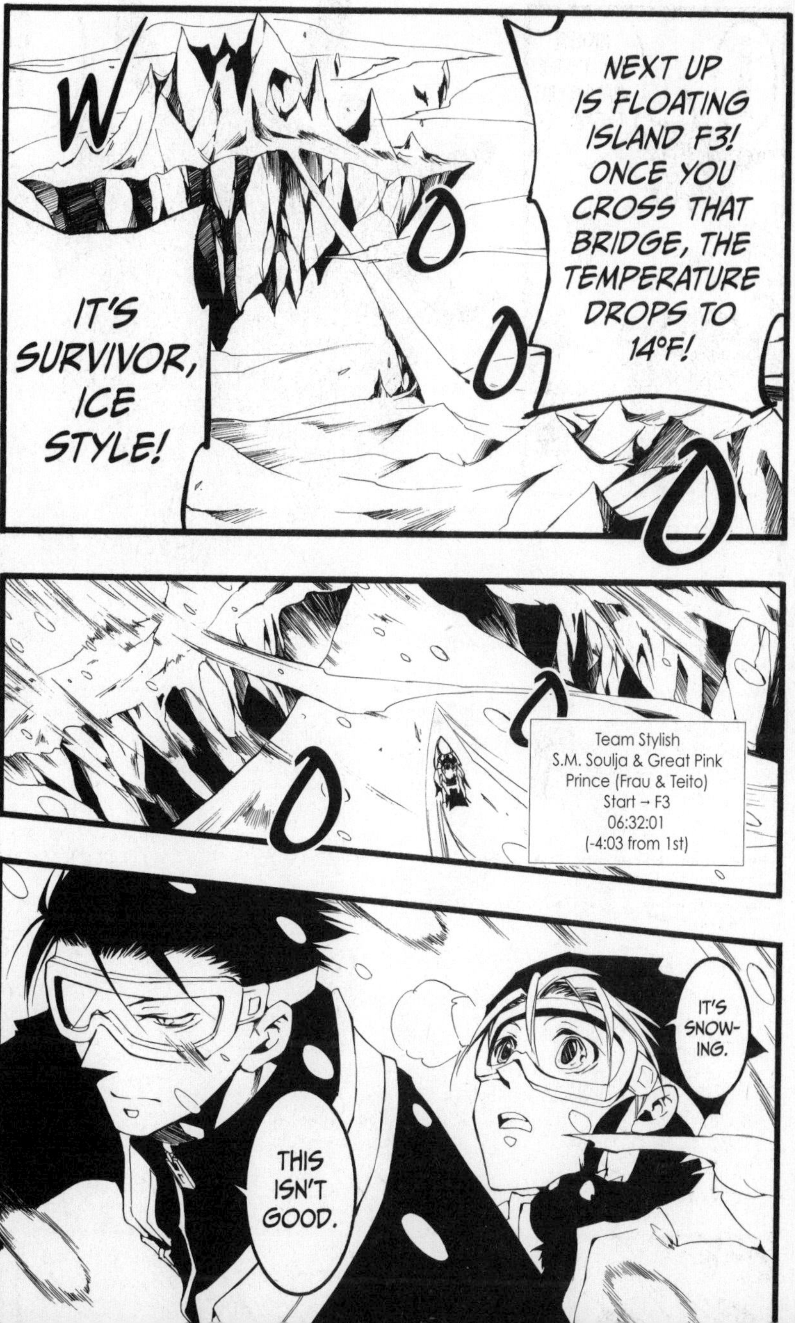
NEXT UP IS FLOATING ISLAND F3! ONCE YOU CROSS THAT BRIDGE, THE TEMPERATURE DROPS TO 14°F!
IT'S SURVIVOR, ICE STYLE!
W
Team Stylish S.M. Soulja & Great Pink Prince (Frau & Teito) Start → F3 06:32:01 (-4:03 from 1st)
IT'S SNOW-ING.
THIS ISN'T GOOD.

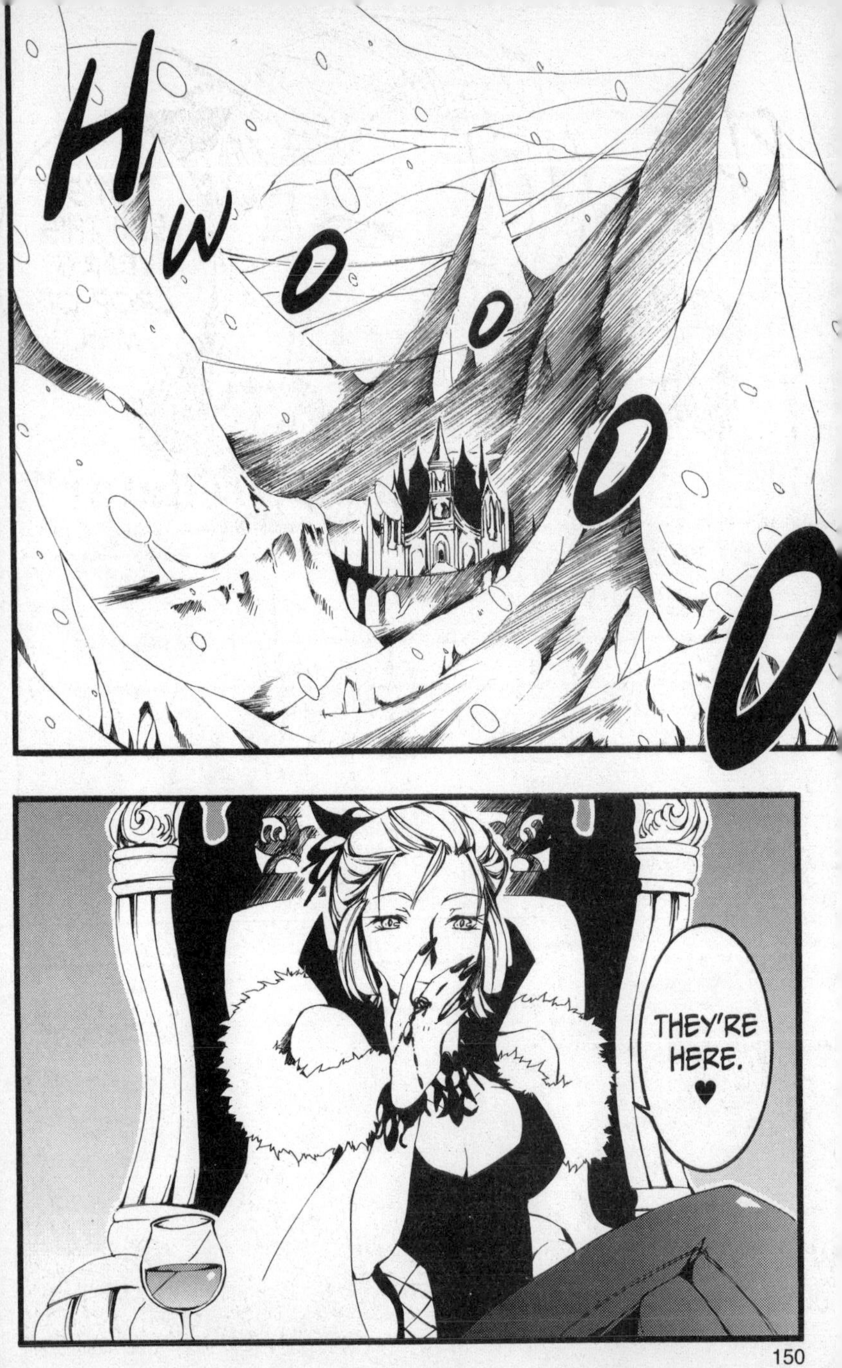
HWOOOOO
THEY'RE HERE. ♥

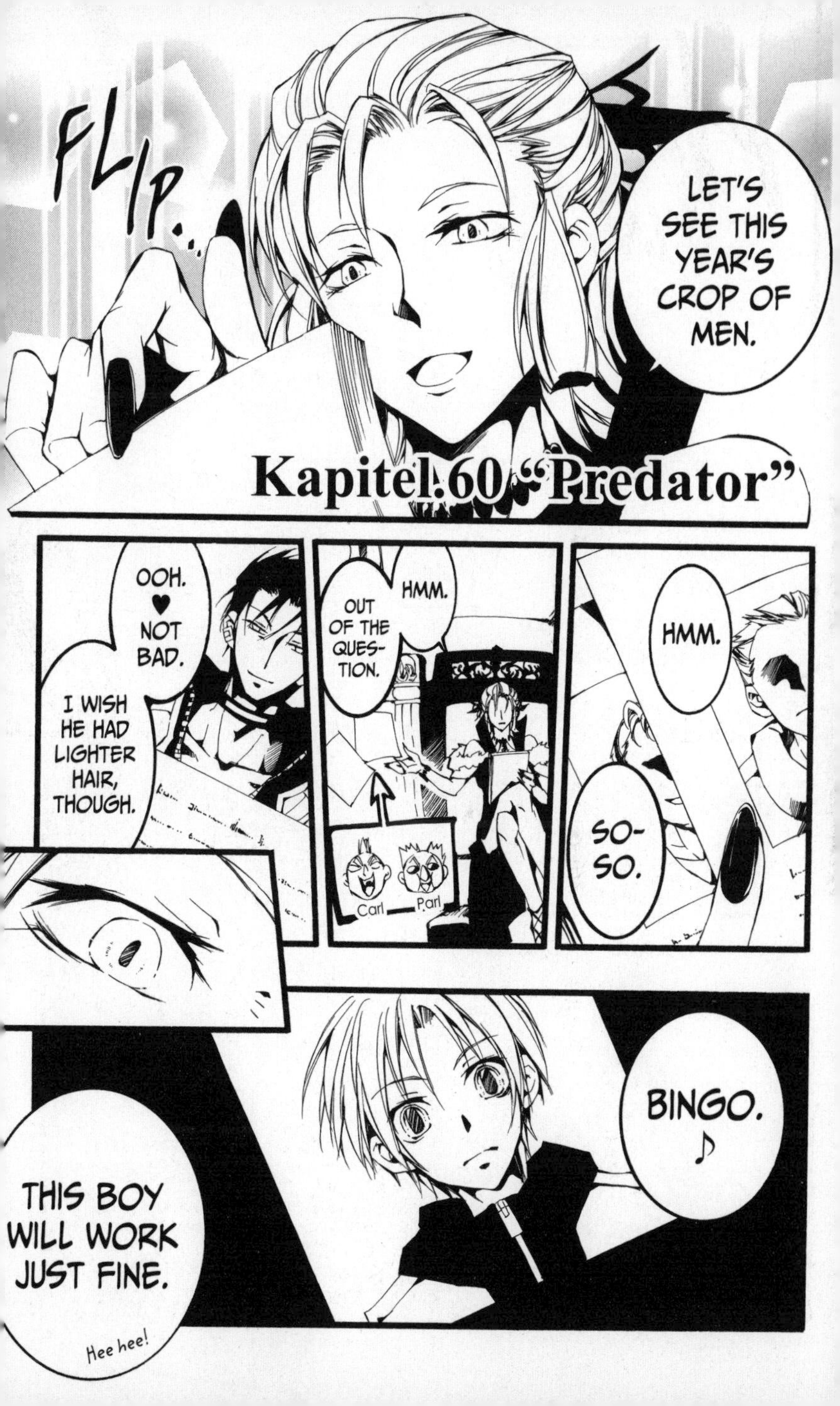
LET'S SEE THIS YEAR'S CROP OF MEN.
FLIP...
Kapitel.60 "Predator"
HMM.
SO-SO.
HMM.
OUT OF THE QUESTION.
Carl
Parl
OOH. ♥ NOT BAD.
I WISH HE HAD LIGHTER HAIR, THOUGH.
BINGO. ♪
THIS BOY WILL WORK JUST FINE.
Hee hee!

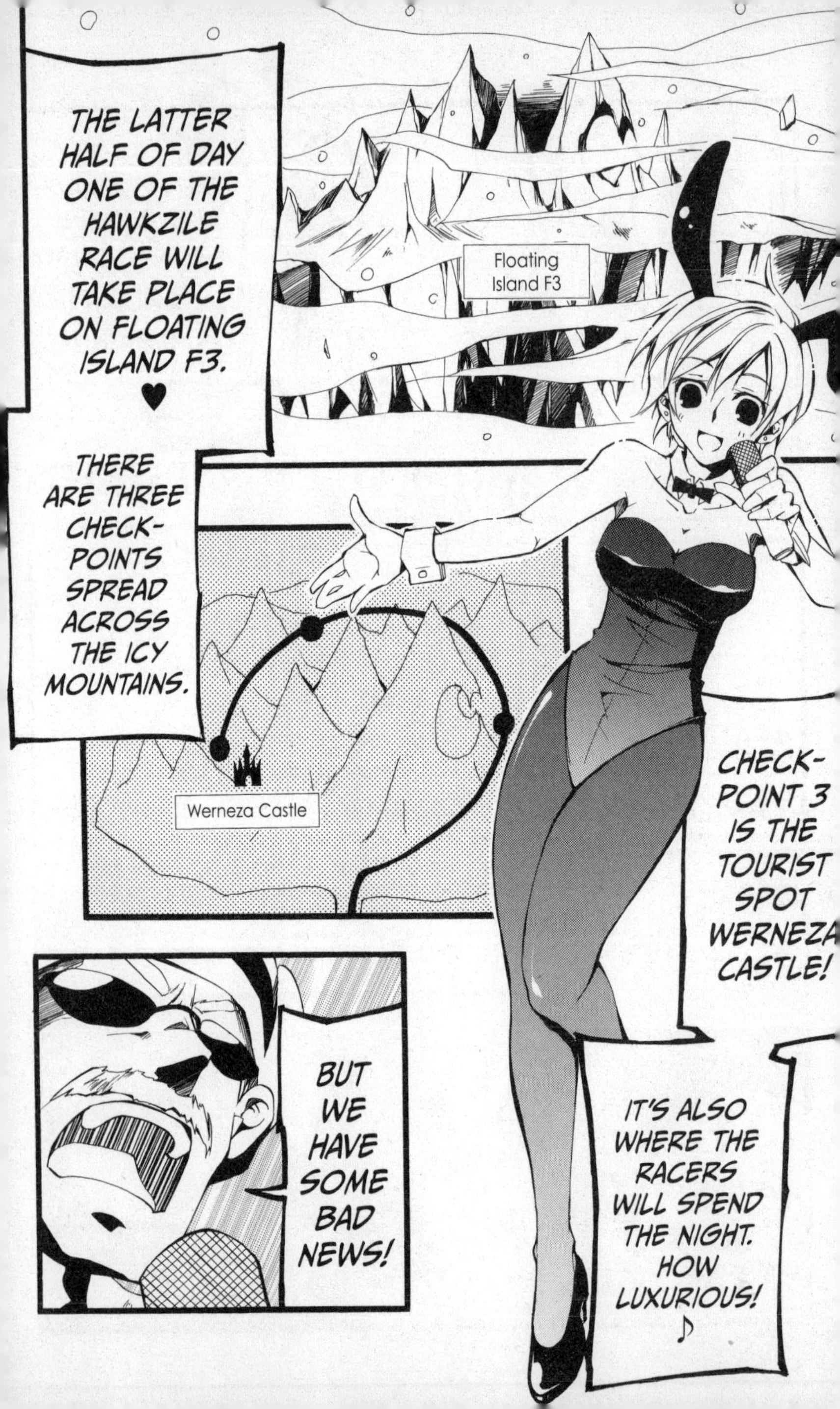
THE LATTER HALF OF DAY ONE OF THE HAWKZILE RACE WILL TAKE PLACE ON FLOATING ISLAND F3. ♥
Floating Island F3
THERE ARE THREE CHECK-POINTS SPREAD ACROSS THE ICY MOUNTAINS.
Werneza Castle
CHECK-POINT 3 IS THE TOURIST SPOT WERNEZA CASTLE!
IT'S ALSO WHERE THE RACERS WILL SPEND THE NIGHT. HOW LUXURIOUS! ♪
BUT WE HAVE SOME BAD NEWS!

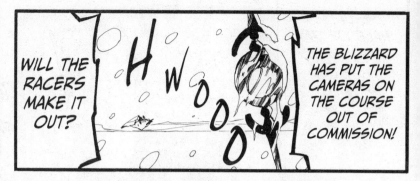

THE BLIZZARD HAS PUT THE CAMERAS ON THE COURSE OUT OF COMMISSION!
HWOOOO
WILL THE RACERS MAKE IT OUT?
I CAN'T SEE ANY-THING!
IF THE SUN GOES DOWN, PEOPLE WILL DIE.
BWA HA HA! THERE YOU ARE!
YOU GUYS ARE SO SLOW! DIDN'T YOU COLD-PROOF YOUR ENGINE?
!
VROOOM
UGH, NOT THEM!
WE SHOULDN'T HAVE HUMILIATED THEM EARLIER.

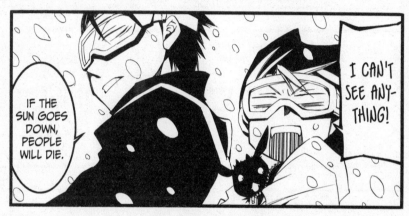

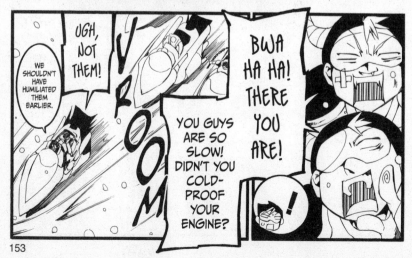

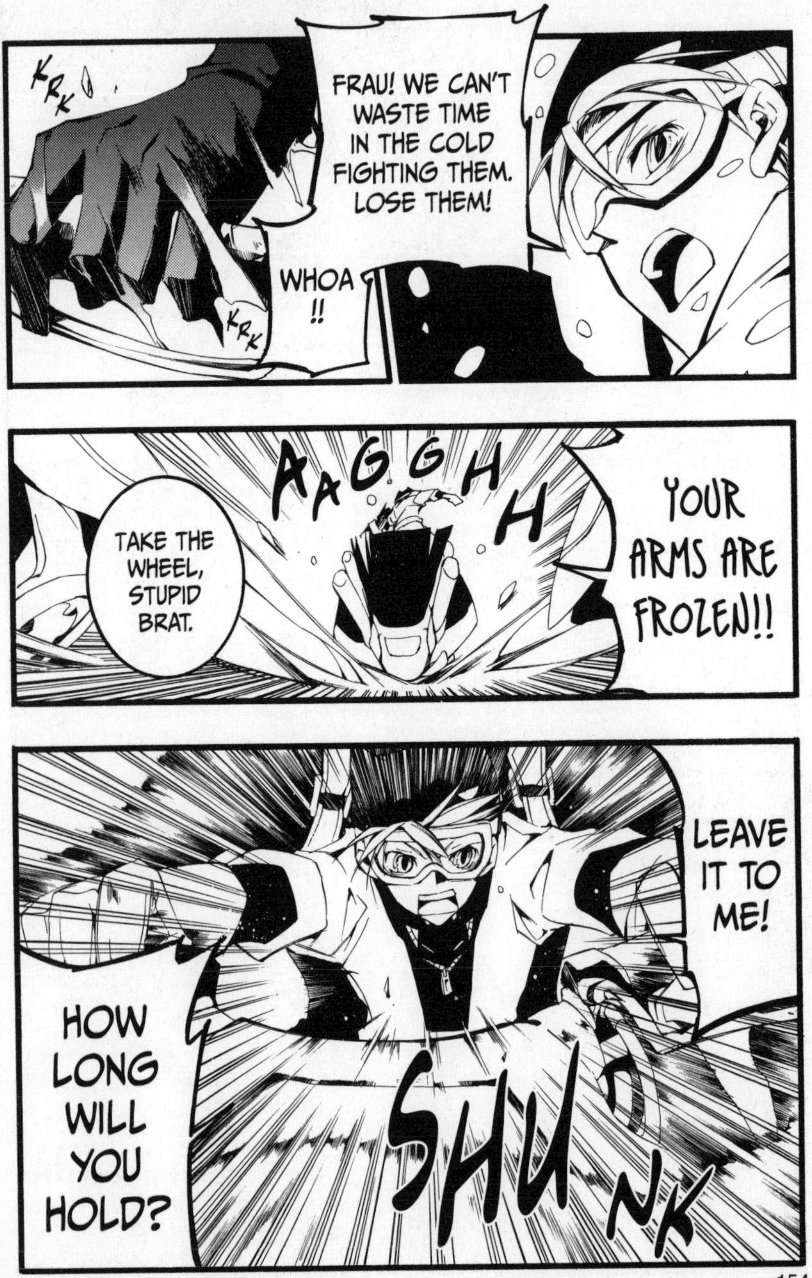
FRAU! WE CAN'T WASTE TIME IN THE COLD FIGHTING THEM. LOSE THEM!
KRK
WHOA !!
KRK
YOUR ARMS ARE FROZEN!!
AAGGHH
TAKE THE WHEEL, STUPID BRAT.
LEAVE IT TO ME!
SHUNK
HOW LONG WILL YOU HOLD?

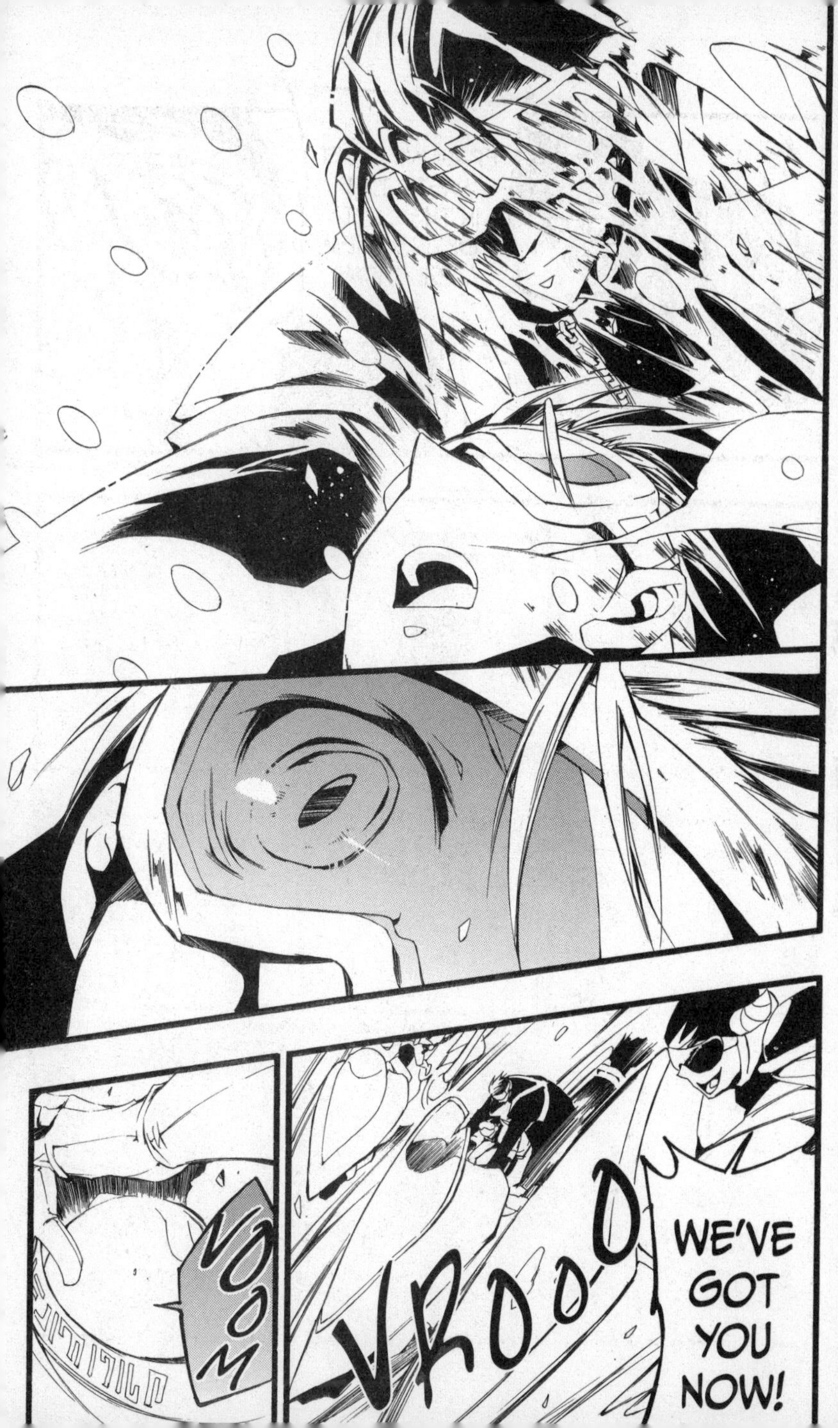
VROOOD
WE'VE GOT YOU NOW!
VOOOM

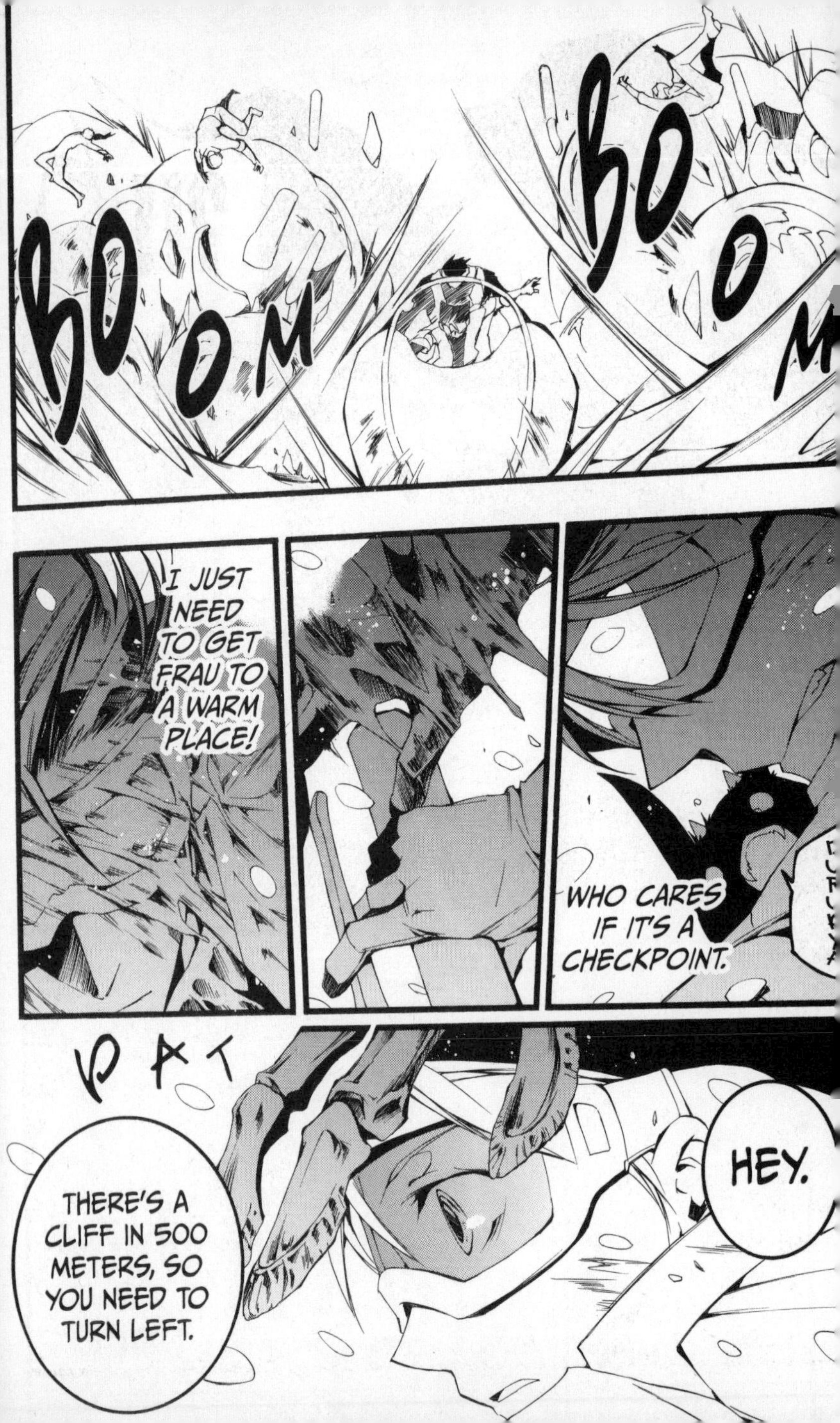
BOOM
BOOM
WHO CARES IF IT'S A CHECKPOINT.
I JUST NEED TO GET FRAU TO A WARM PLACE!
HEY.
PAT
THERE'S A CLIFF IN 500 METERS, SO YOU NEED TO TURN LEFT.

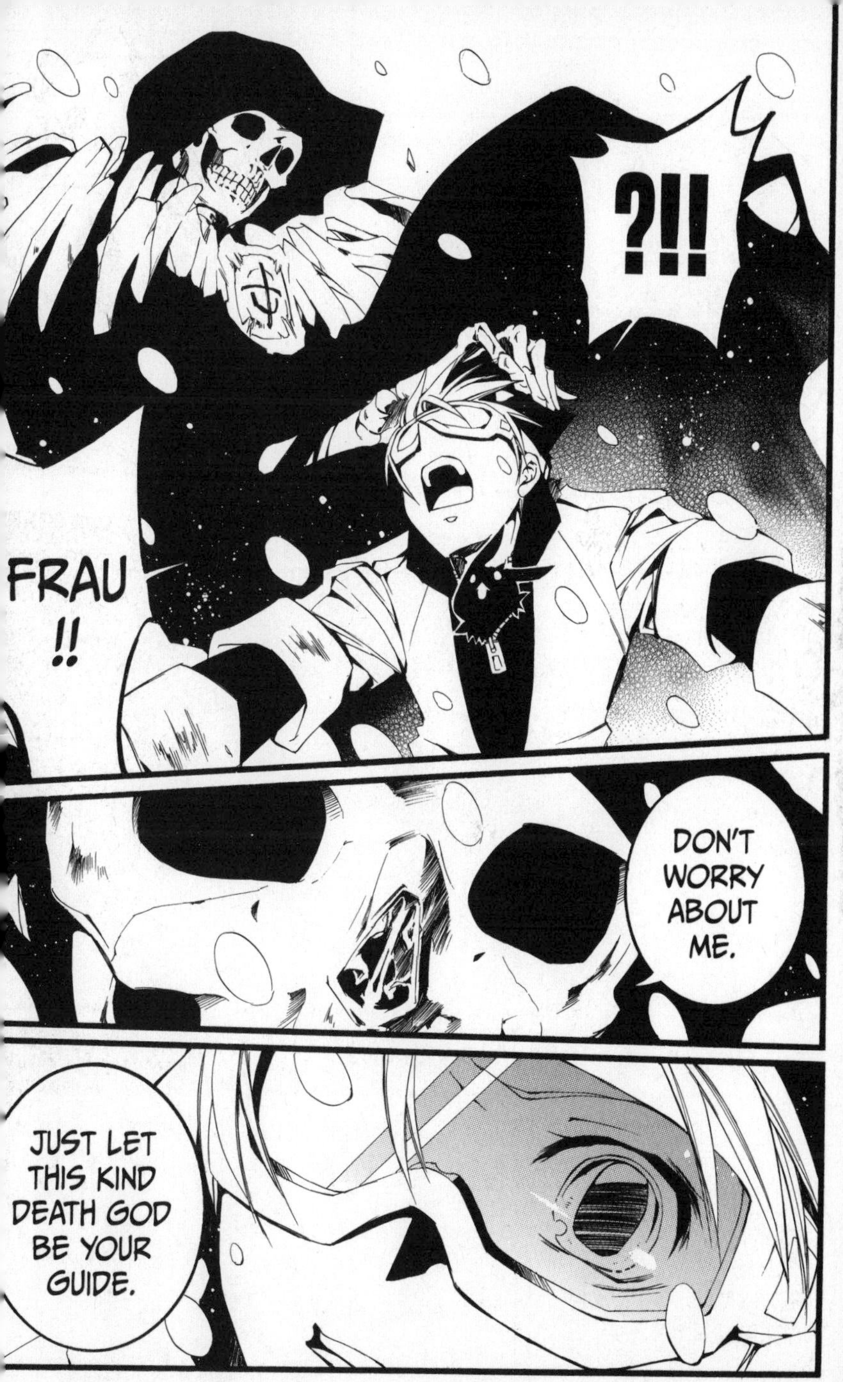
?!!
FRAU !!
DON'T WORRY ABOUT ME.
JUST LET THIS KIND DEATH GOD BE YOUR GUIDE.

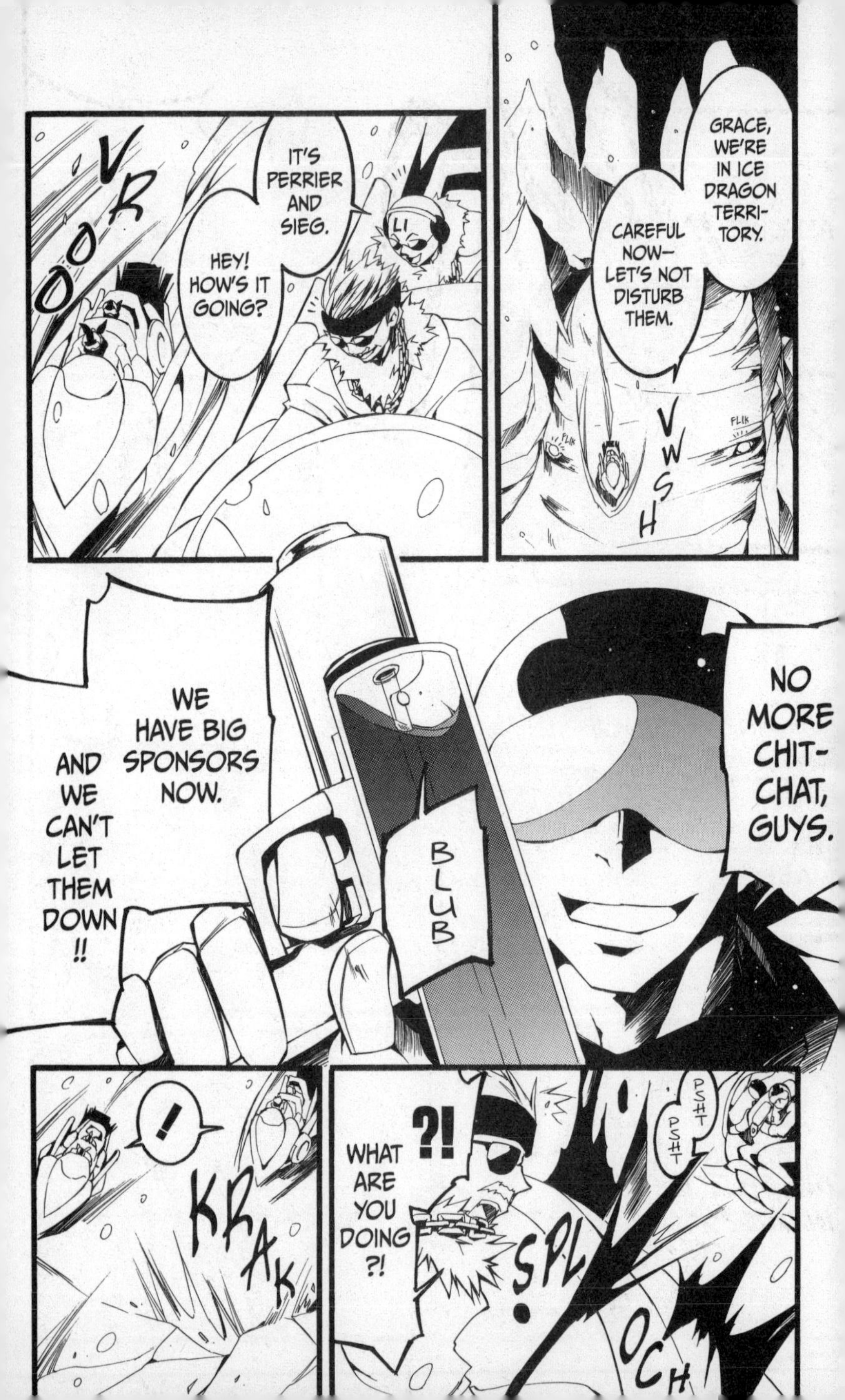
GRACE, WE'RE IN ICE DRAGON TERRITORY.
CAREFUL NOW—LET'S NOT DISTURB THEM.
FLIK
FLIK
VWSH
VROOOO
IT'S PERRIER AND SIEG.
LI
HEY! HOW'S IT GOING?
NO MORE CHIT-CHAT, GUYS.
WE HAVE BIG SPONSORS NOW.
AND WE CAN'T LET THEM DOWN!!
BLUB
PSHT
PSHT
?!
WHAT ARE YOU DOING?!
SPLOOCH
!
KRAK

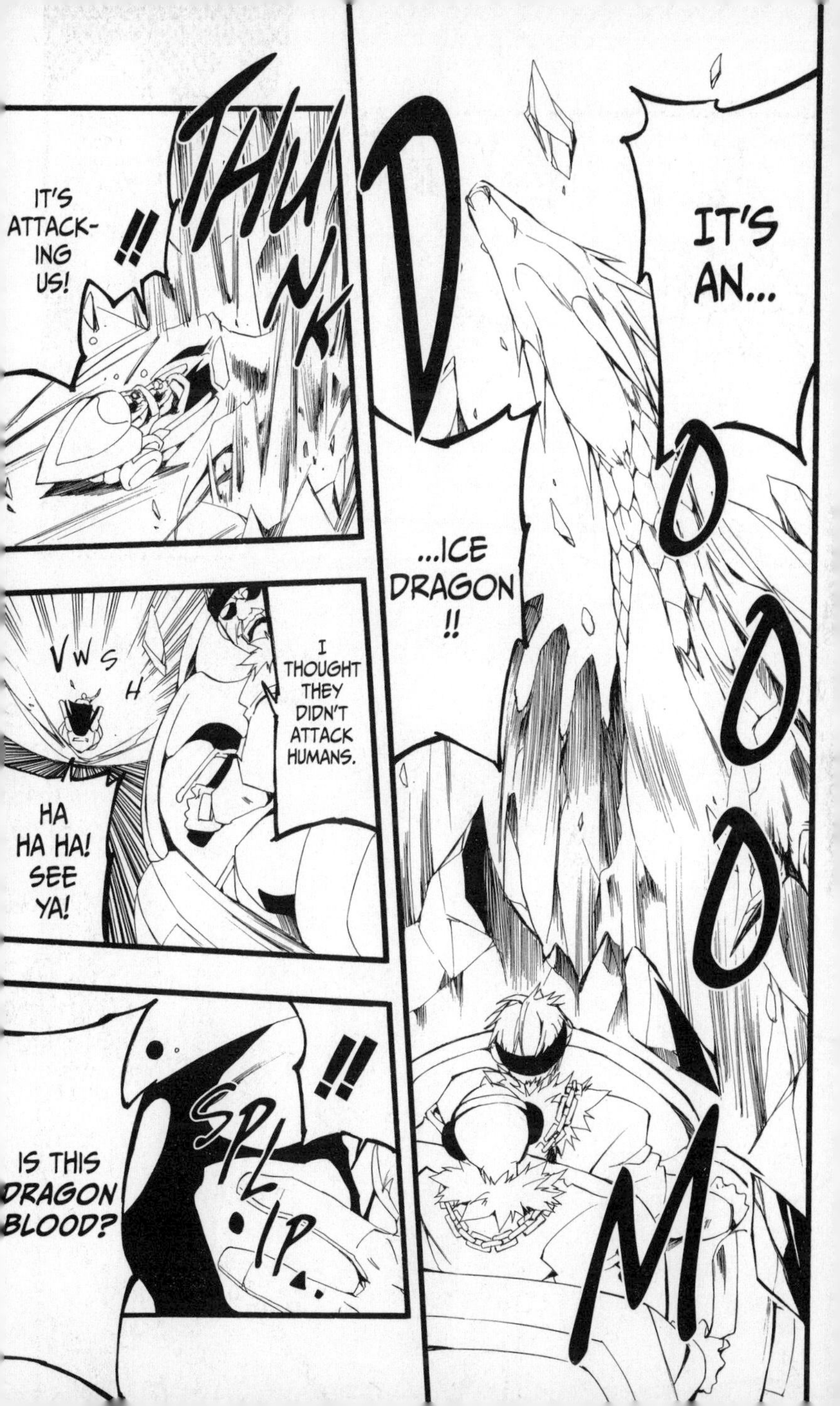
IT'S AN...
...ICE DRAGON !!
DOOOOM
THUNK
IT'S ATTACK-ING US!
!!
I THOUGHT THEY DIDN'T ATTACK HUMANS.
VWSH
HA HA HA! SEE YA!
!!
SPLIP
IS THIS DRAGON BLOOD?

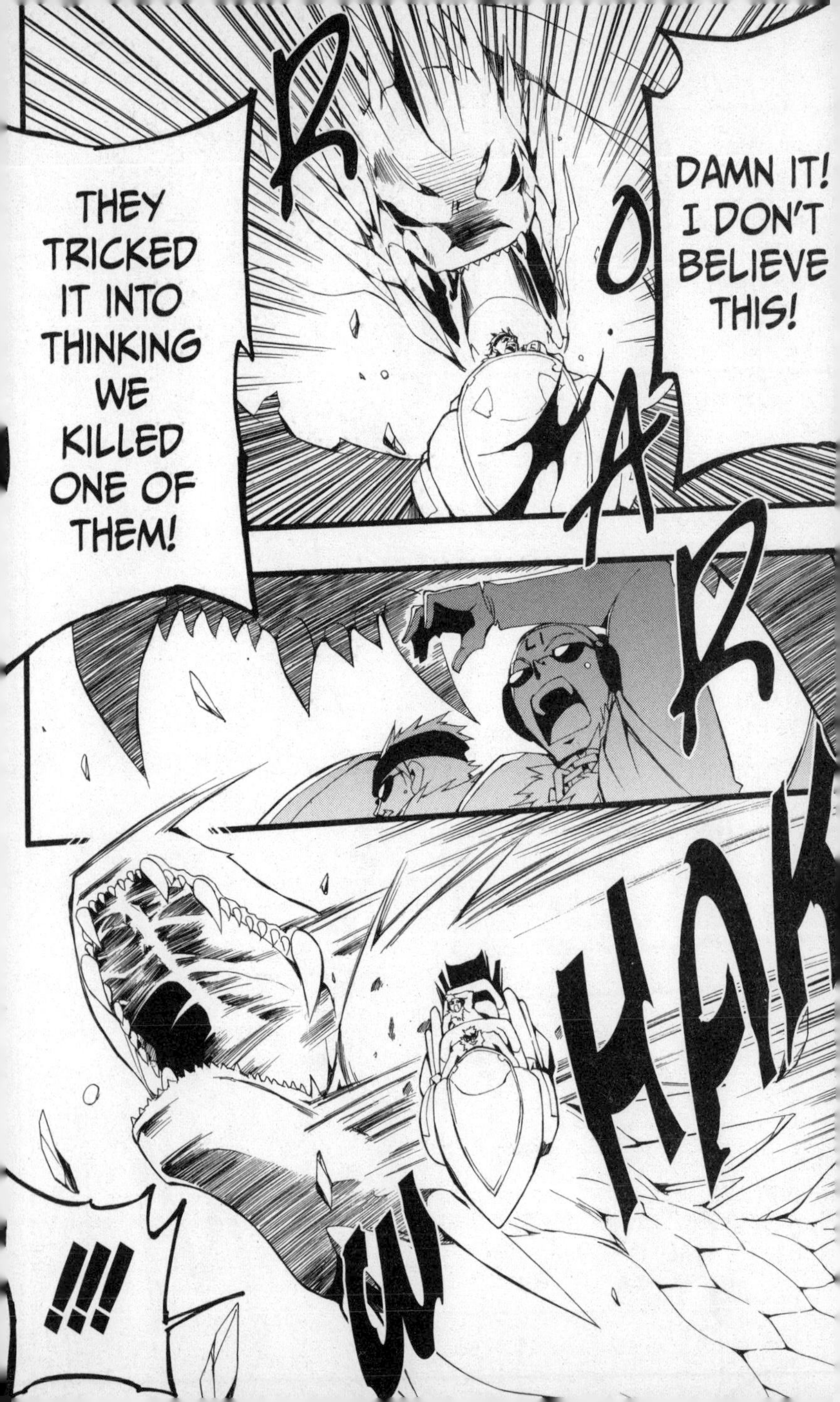
DAMN IT! I DON'T BELIEVE THIS!
THEY TRICKED IT INTO THINKING WE KILLED ONE OF THEM!
ROAR
!!!

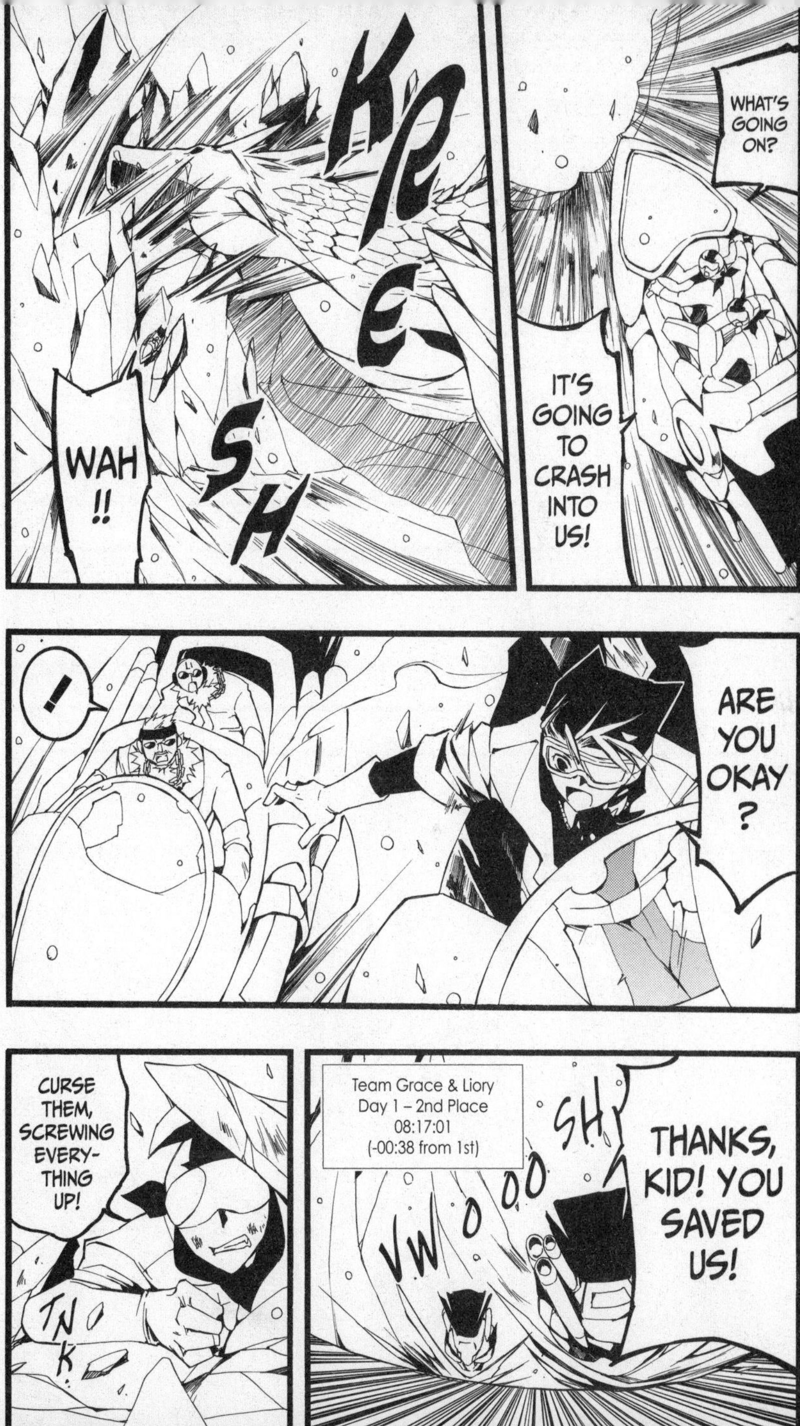
WHAT'S GOING ON?
IT'S GOING TO CRASH INTO US!
WAH!!
ARE YOU OKAY?
!
Team Grace & Liory
Day 1 – 2nd Place
08:17:01
(-00:38 from 1st)
THANKS, KID! YOU SAVED US!
VWOOOSH
CURSE THEM, SCREWING EVERY-THING UP!

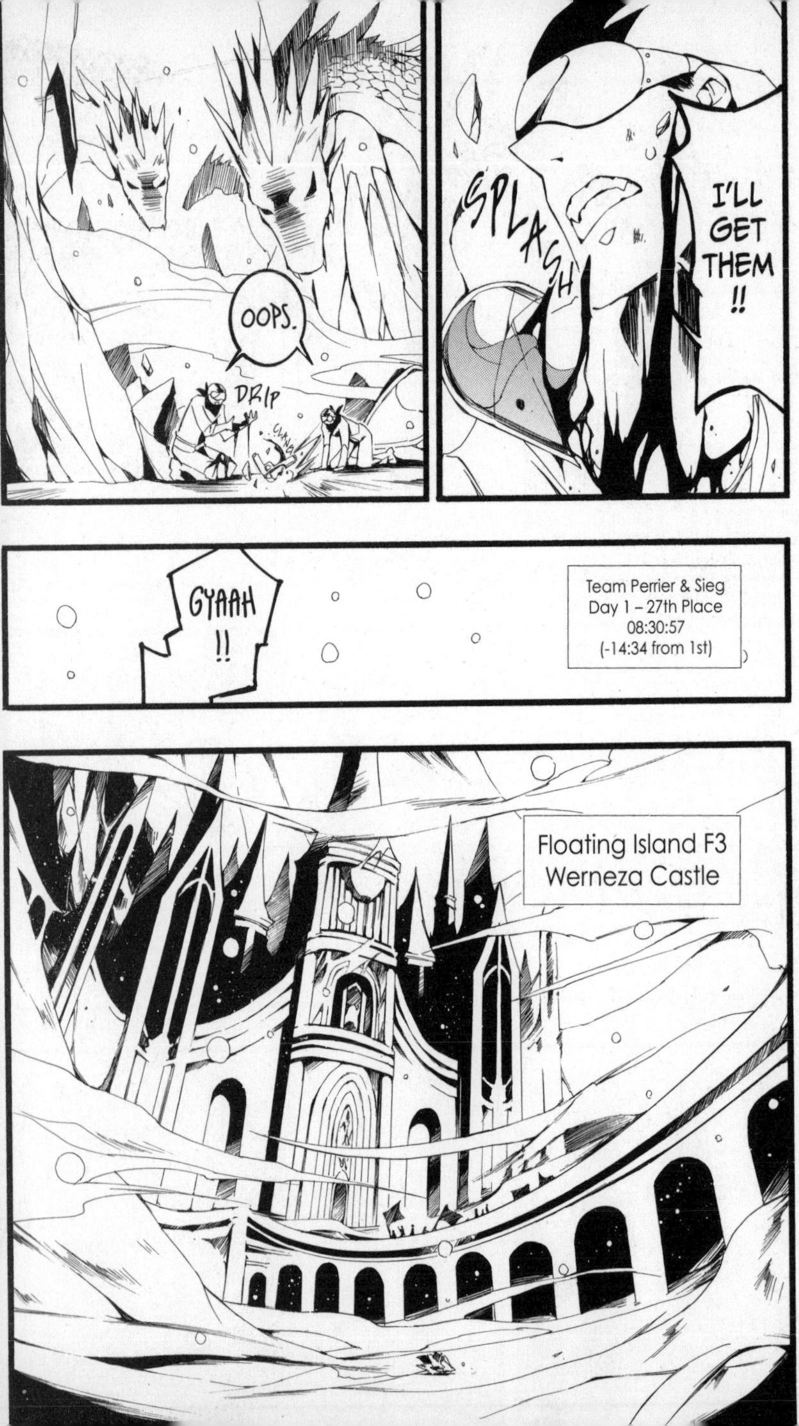
I'LL GET THEM !!
SPLASH
OOPS.
DRIP
Team Perrier & Sieg
Day 1 – 27th Place
08:30:57
(-14:34 from 1st)
GYAAH !!
Floating Island F3
Werneza Castle

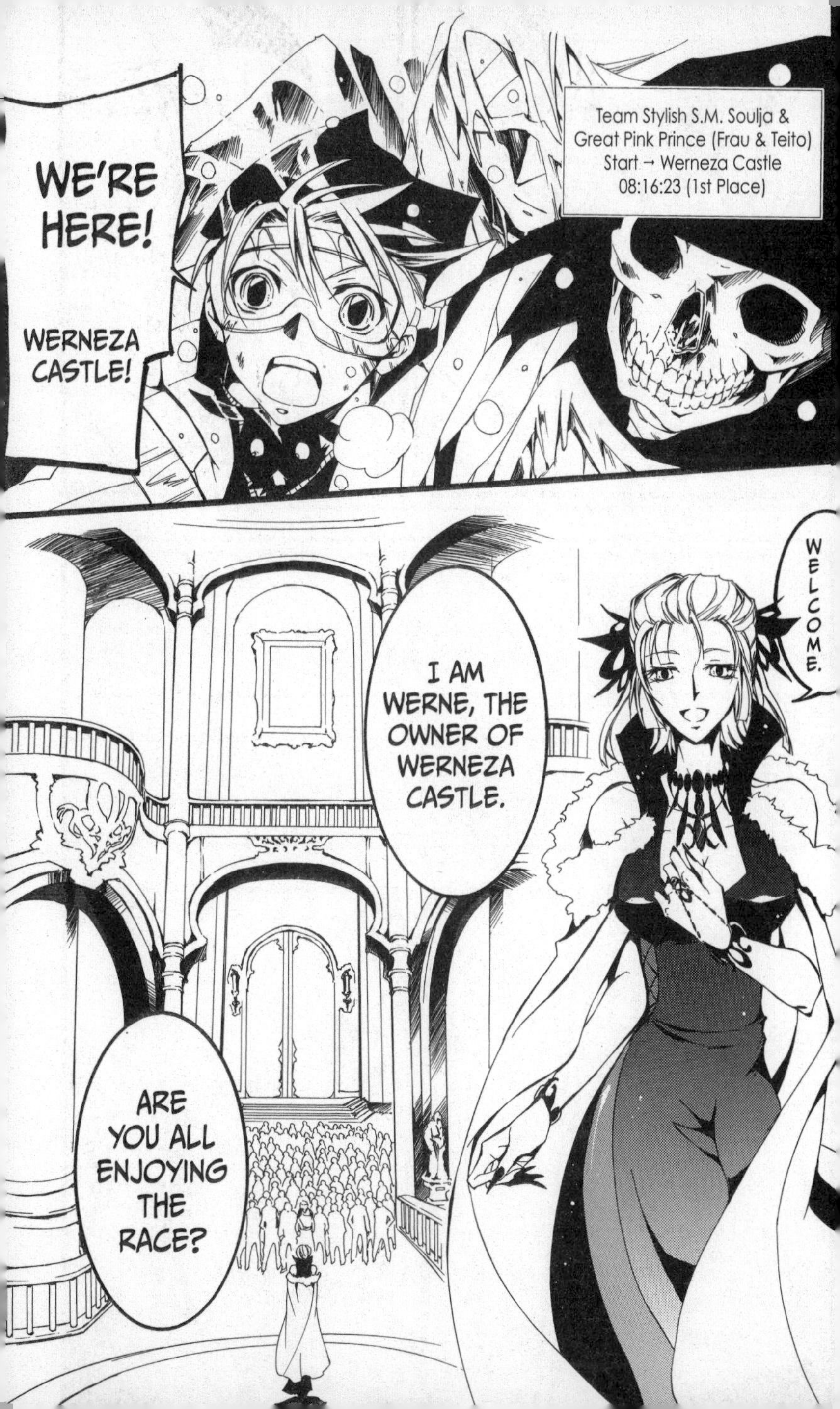

Team Stylish S.M. Soulja & Great Pink Prince (Frau & Teito) Start → Werneza Castle 08:16:23 (1st Place)
WE'RE HERE!
WERNEZA CASTLE!
WELCOME.
I AM WERNE, THE OWNER OF WERNEZA CASTLE.
ARE YOU ALL ENJOYING THE RACE?

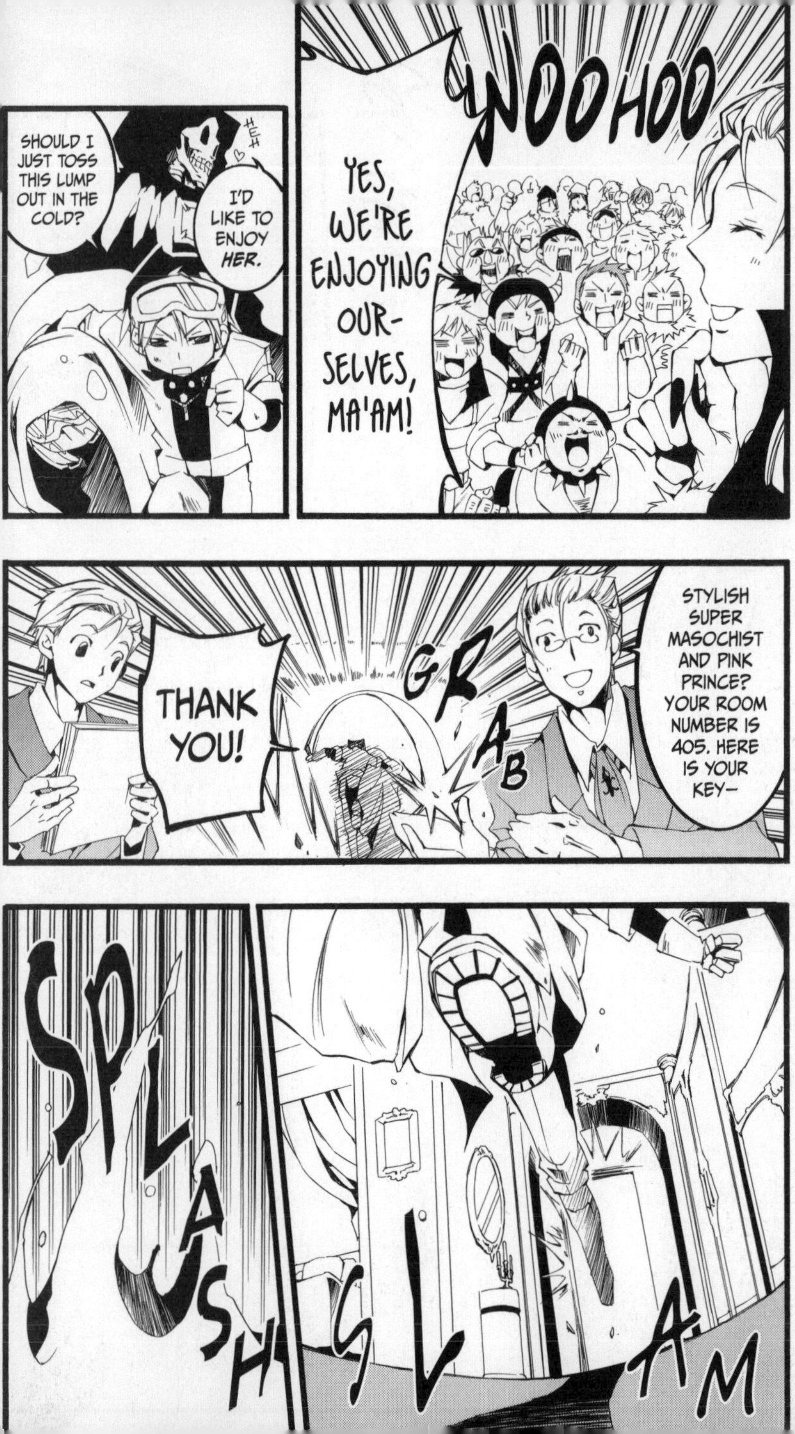
WOOHOO
YES, WE'RE ENJOYING OUR-SELVES, MA'AM!
HEH ♡
SHOULD I JUST TOSS THIS LUMP OUT IN THE COLD?
I'D LIKE TO ENJOY *HER*.
STYLISH SUPER MASOCHIST AND PINK PRINCE? YOUR ROOM NUMBER IS 405. HERE IS YOUR KEY—
GRAB
THANK YOU!
SLAM
SPLASH

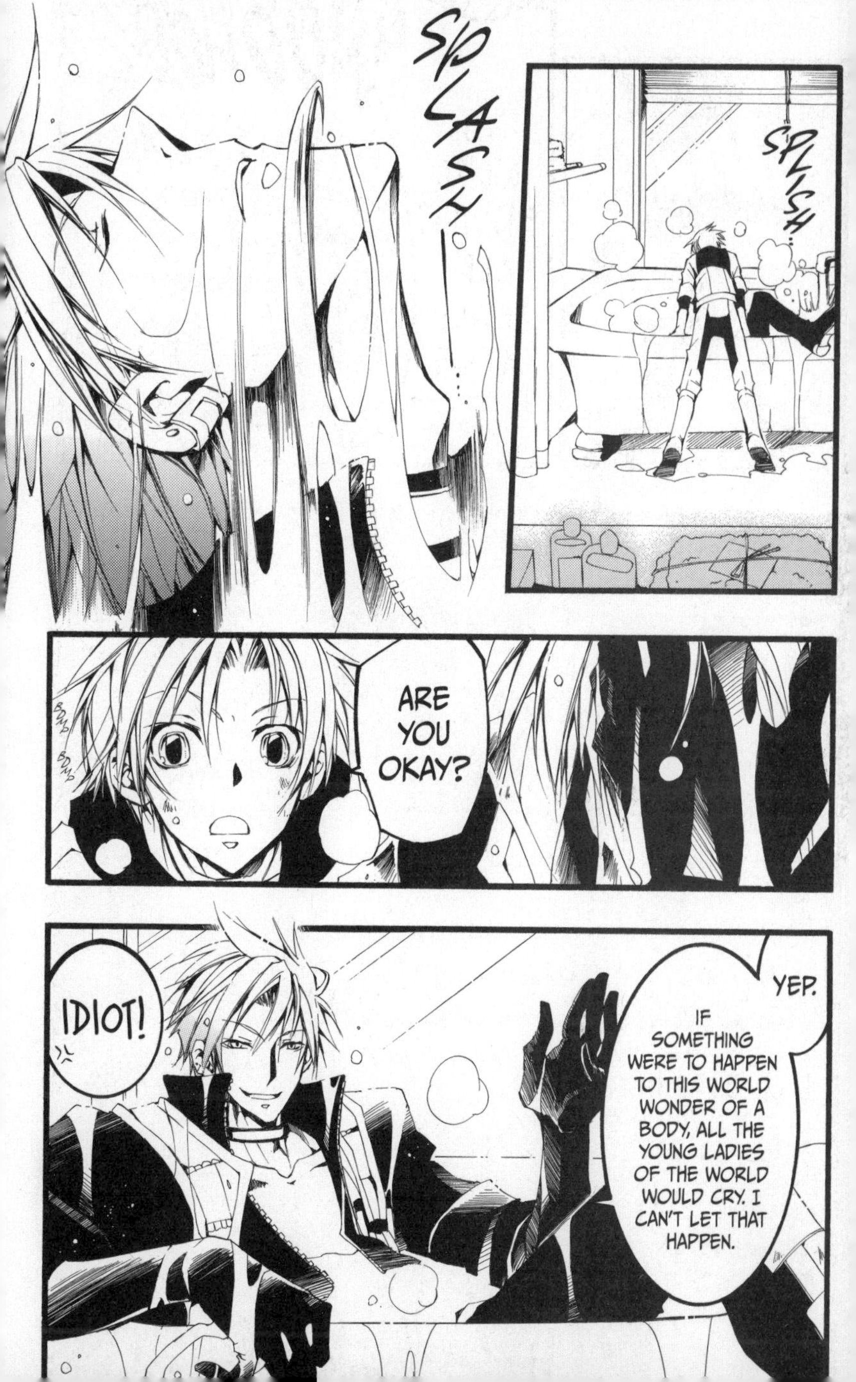
SPLISH...
SPLASH...
ARE YOU OKAY?
YEP.
IF SOMETHING WERE TO HAPPEN TO THIS WORLD WONDER OF A BODY, ALL THE YOUNG LADIES OF THE WORLD WOULD CRY. I CAN'T LET THAT HAPPEN.
IDIOT!

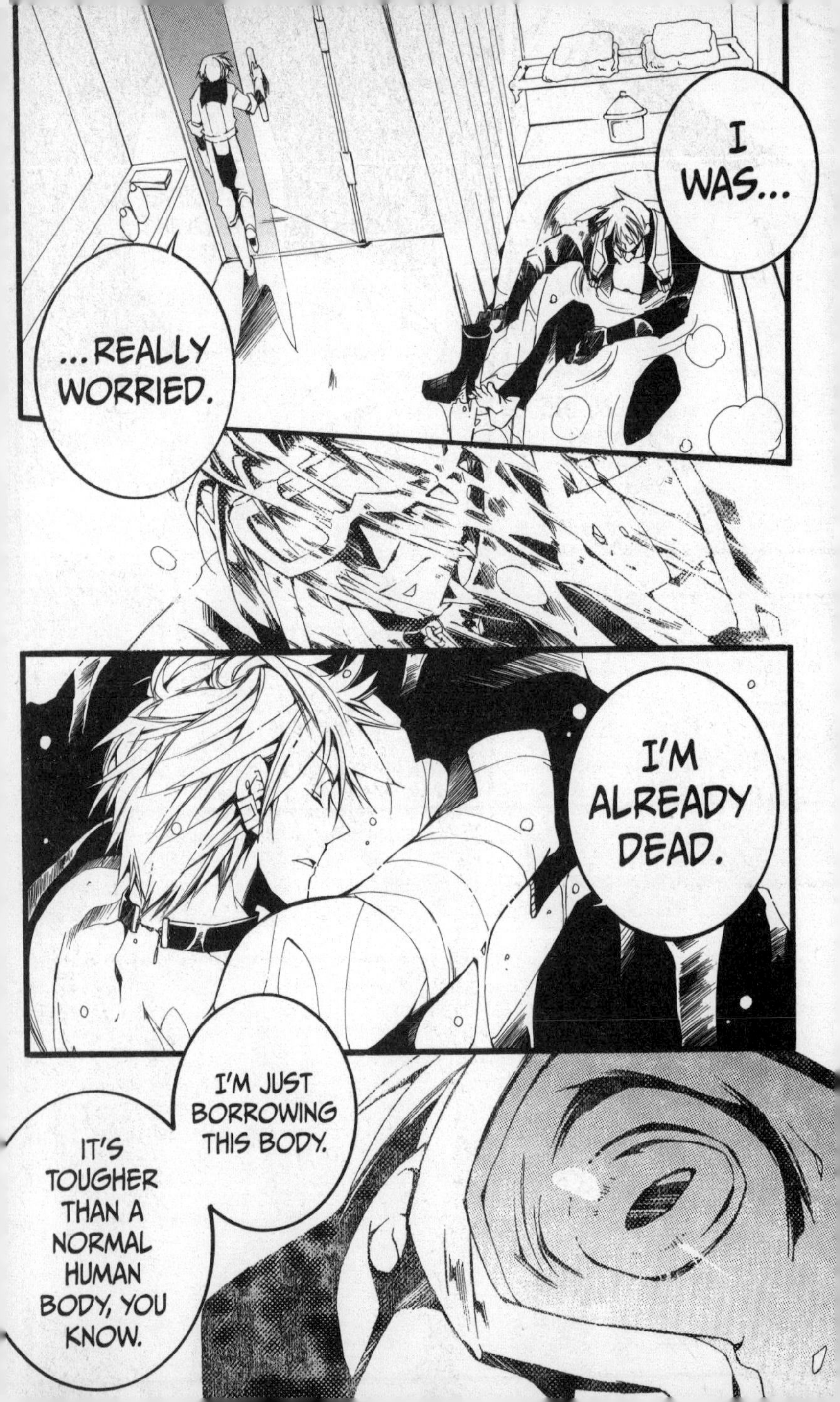
I WAS...
...REALLY WORRIED.
I'M ALREADY DEAD.
I'M JUST BORROWING THIS BODY.
IT'S TOUGHER THAN A NORMAL HUMAN BODY, YOU KNOW.

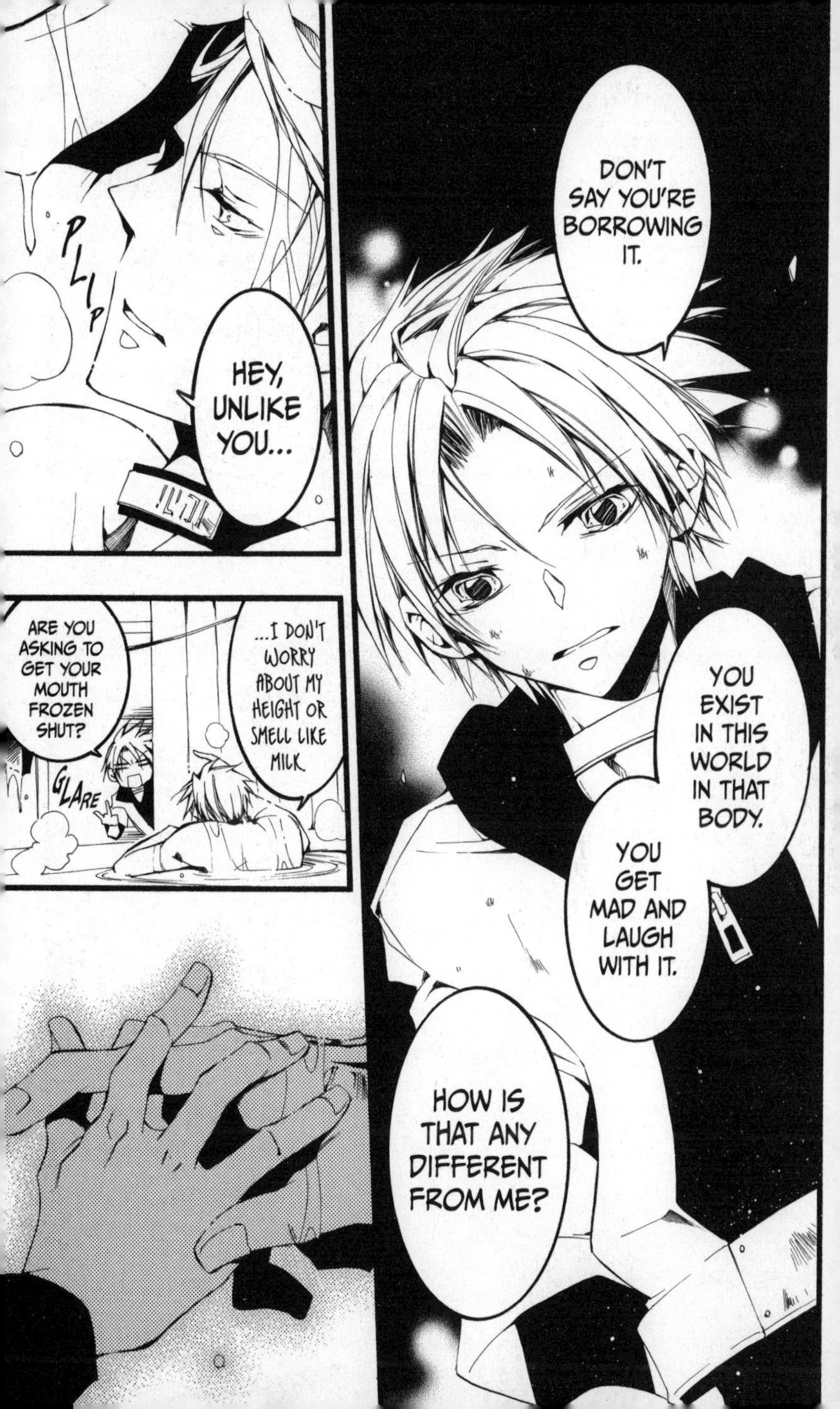
DON'T SAY YOU'RE BORROWING IT.
YOU EXIST IN THIS WORLD IN THAT BODY.
YOU GET MAD AND LAUGH WITH IT.
HOW IS THAT ANY DIFFERENT FROM ME?
PLIP
HEY, UNLIKE YOU...
...I DON'T WORRY ABOUT MY HEIGHT OR SMELL LIKE MILK.
ARE YOU ASKING TO GET YOUR MOUTH FROZEN SHUT?
GLARE

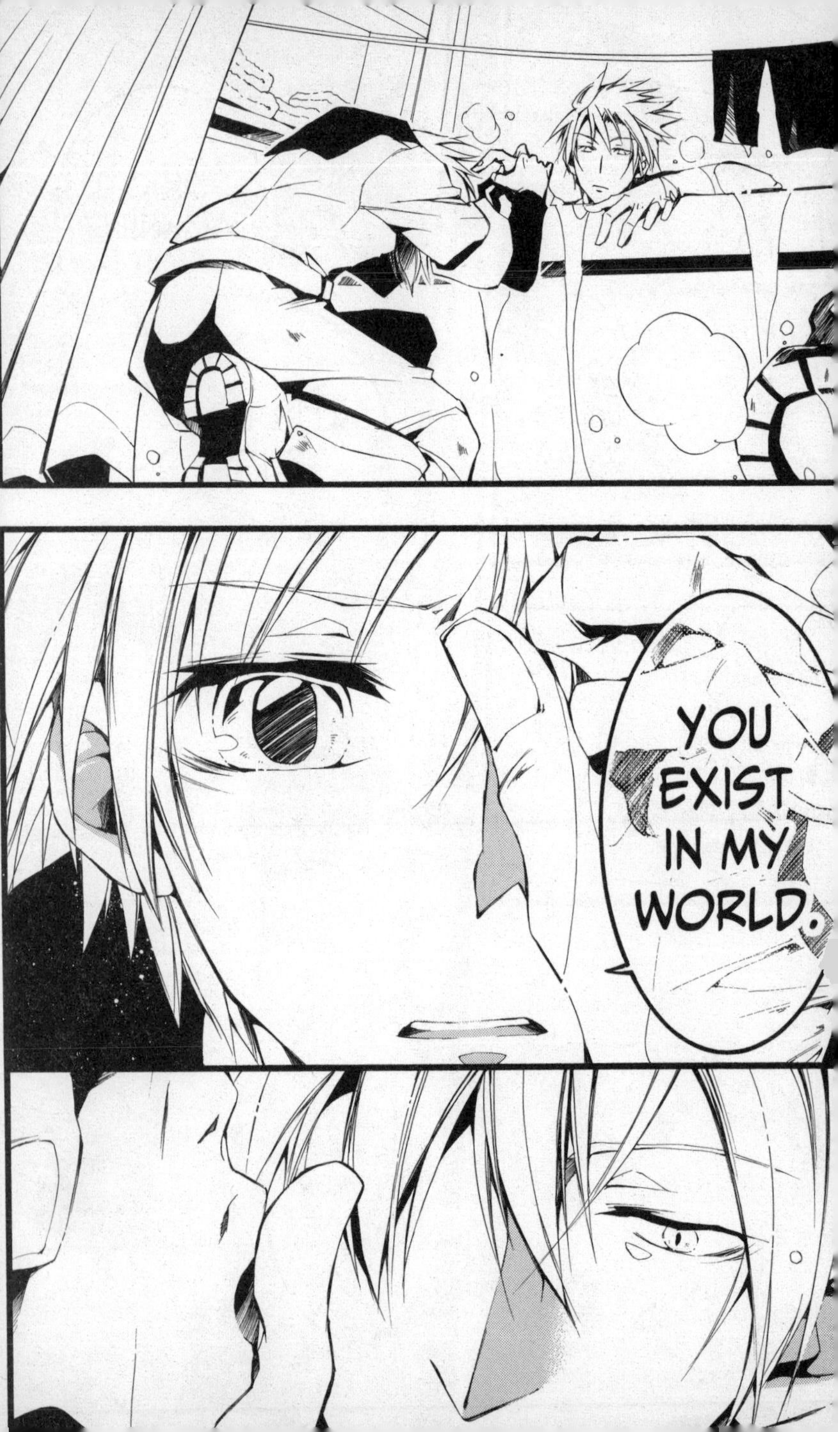
YOU EXIST IN MY WORLD.

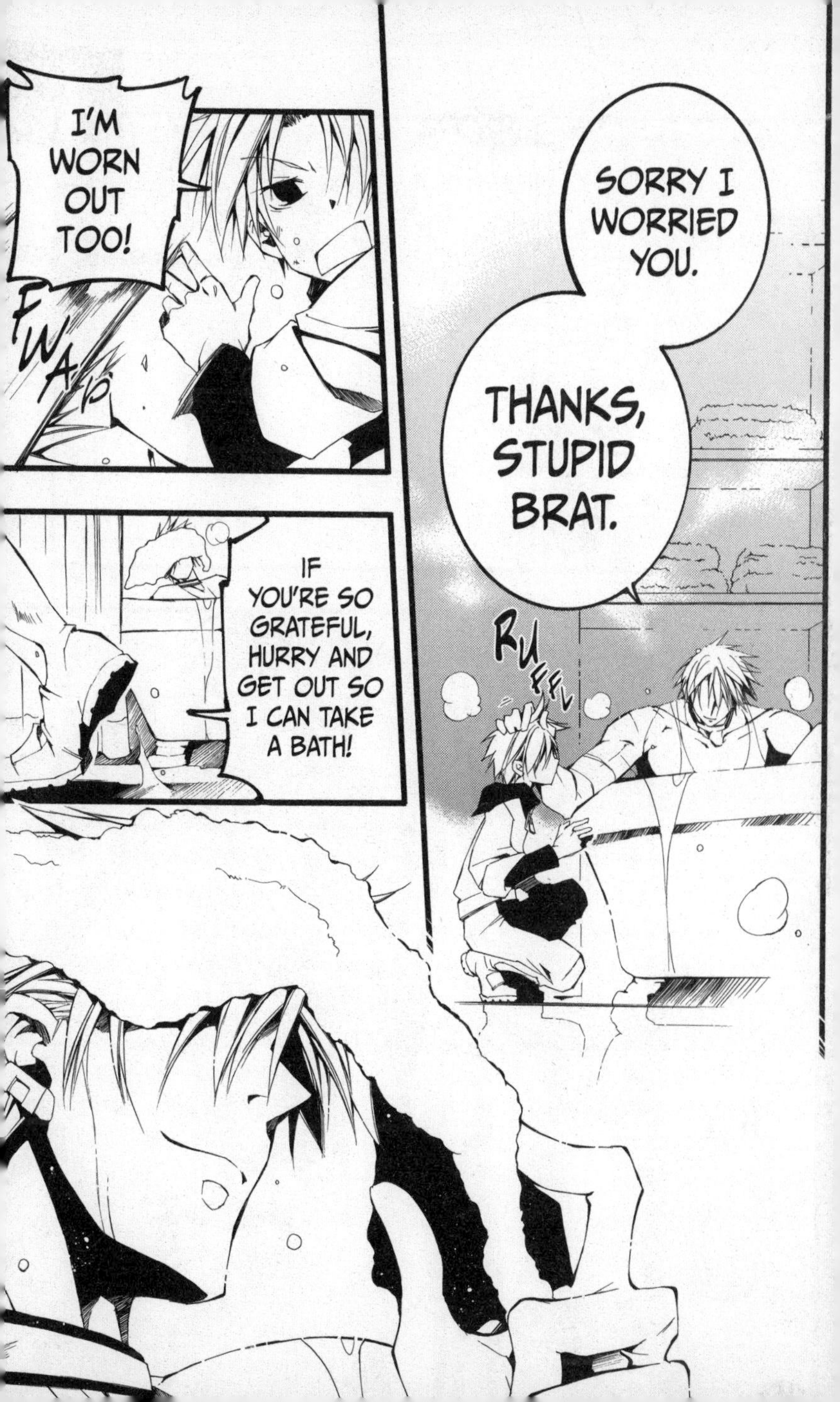
SORRY I WORRIED YOU.
THANKS, STUPID BRAT.
RUFFL
I'M WORN OUT TOO!
FWAP
IF YOU'RE SO GRATEFUL, HURRY AND GET OUT SO I CAN TAKE A BATH!

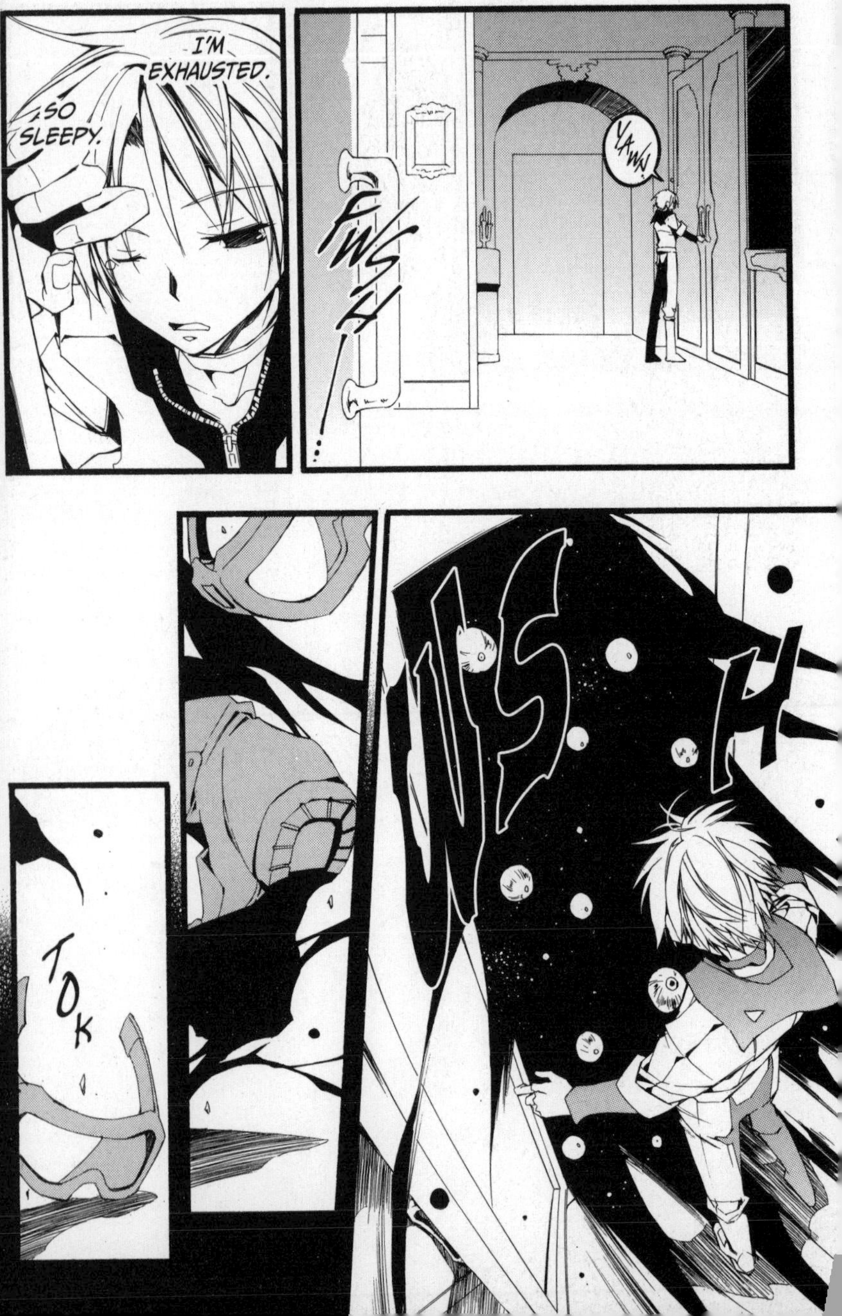
YAWN
FWSH...
I'M EXHAUSTED.
SO SLEEPY.
WHSH
TOK

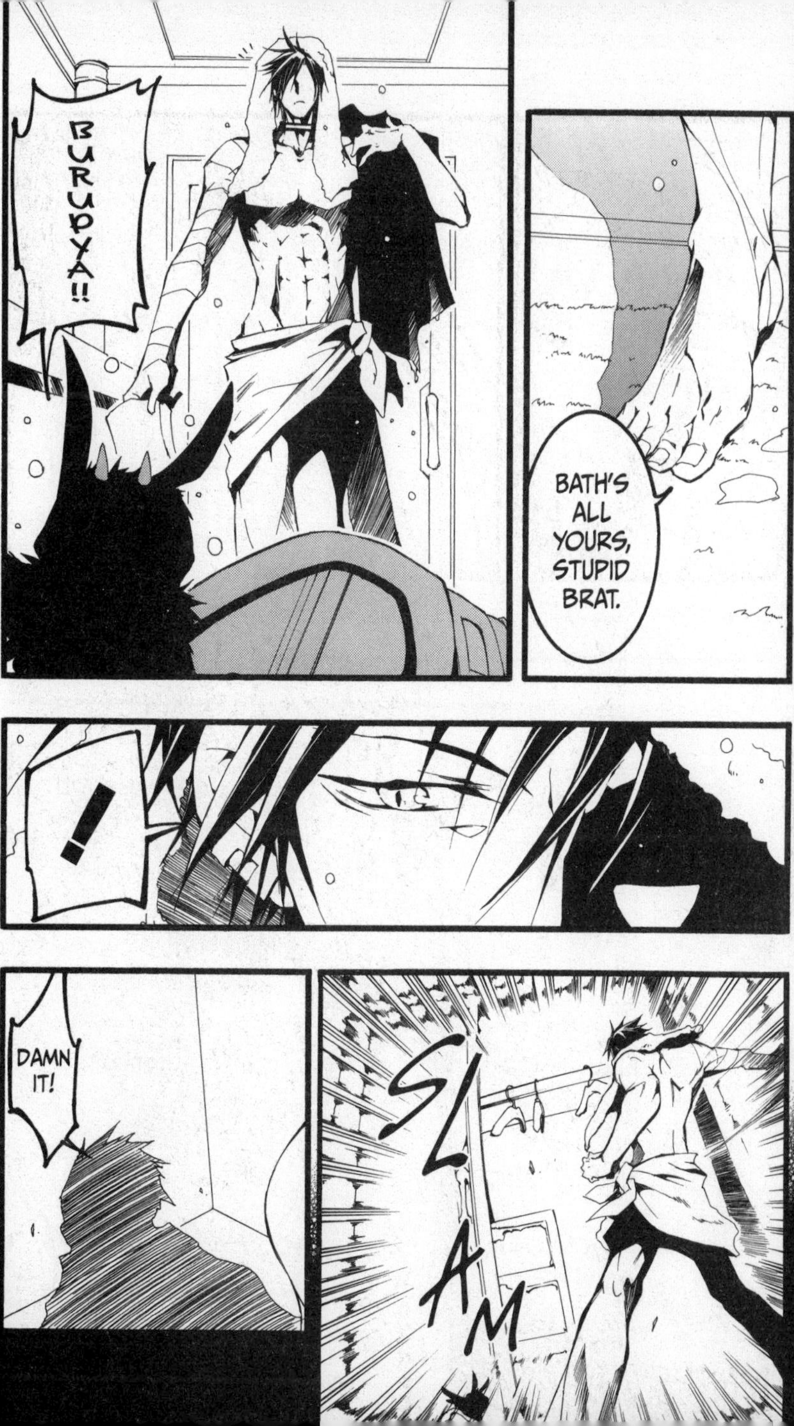
BATH'S ALL YOURS, STUPID BRAT.
BURUPYA!!
!
SLAM
DAMN IT!

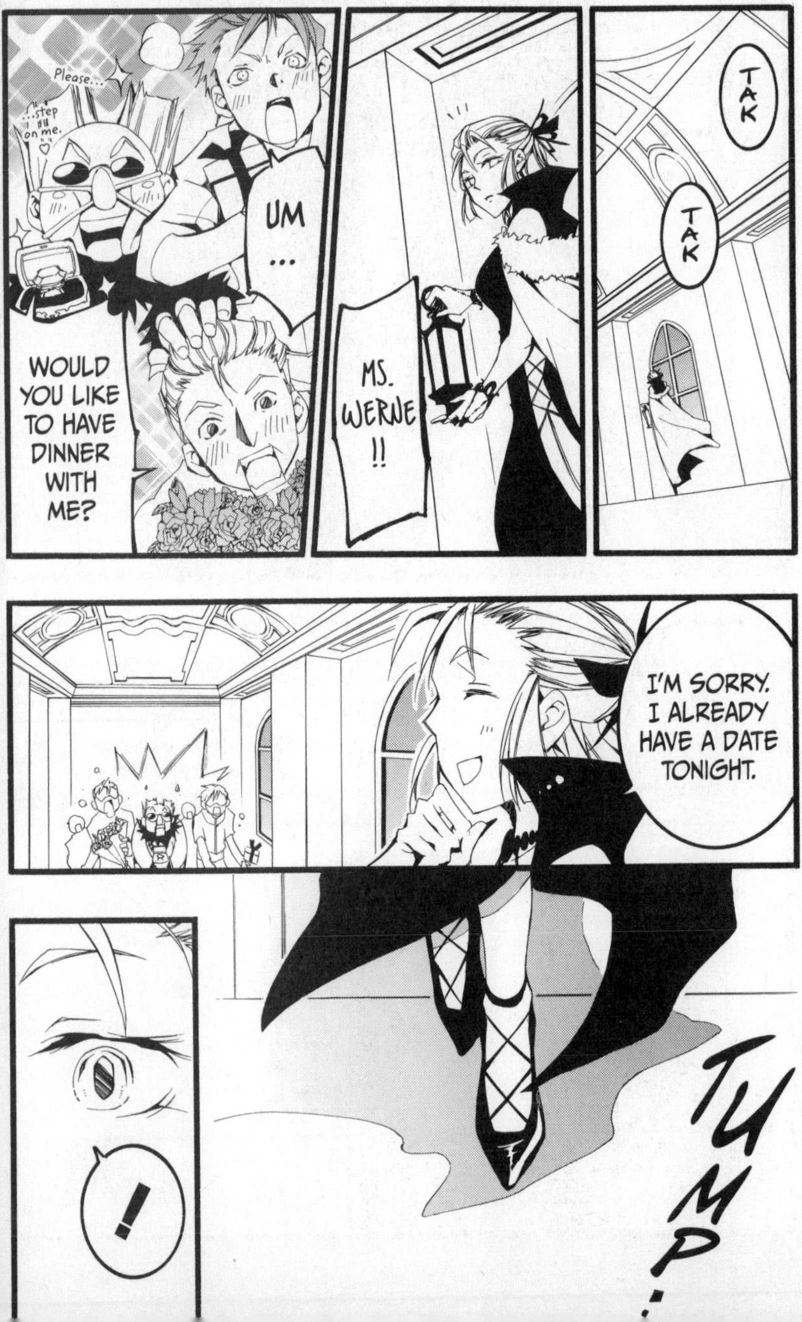
TAK
TAK
MS. WERNE !!
UM ...
Please...
...step on me.
WOULD YOU LIKE TO HAVE DINNER WITH ME?
I'M SORRY. I ALREADY HAVE A DATE TONIGHT.
TUMP..
!

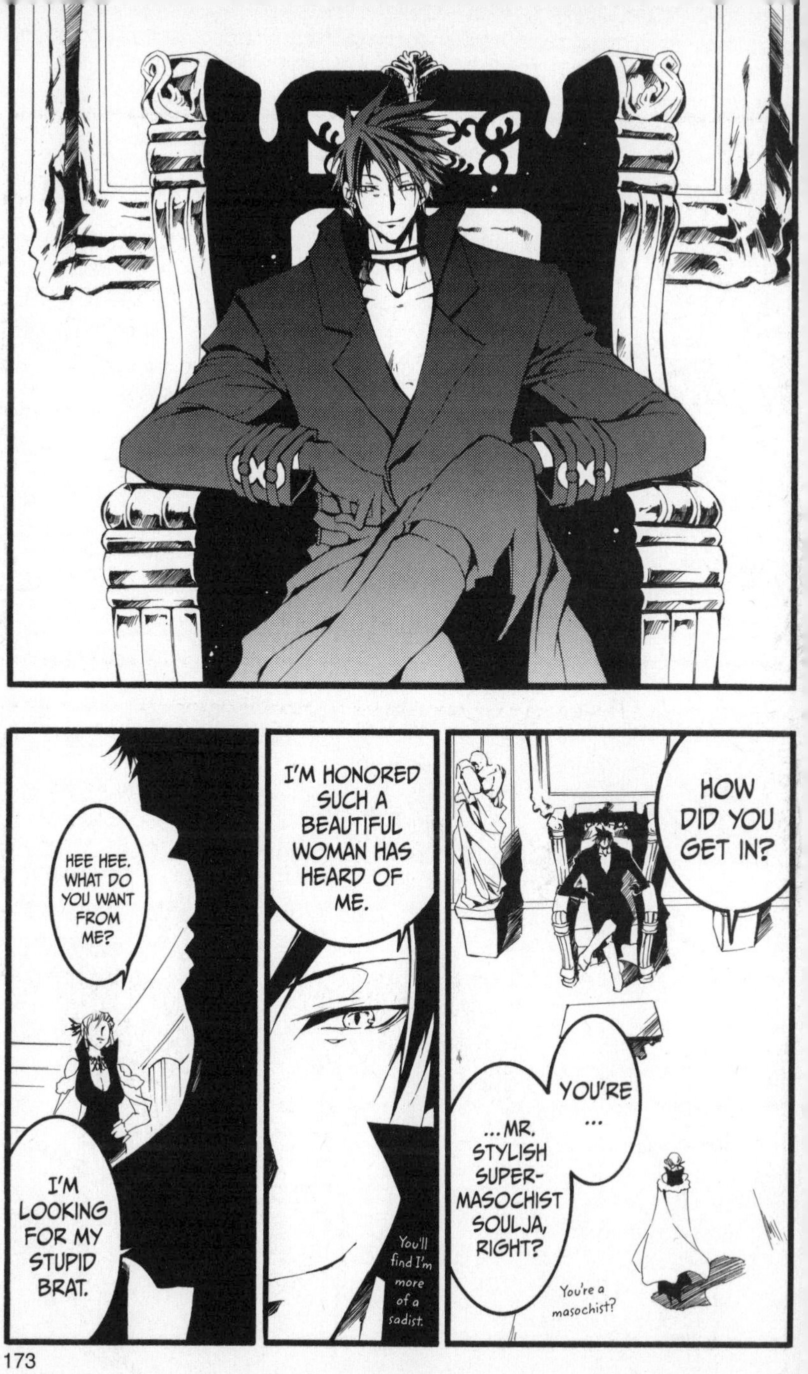
HOW DID YOU GET IN?
YOU'RE ...
...MR. STYLISH SUPER-MASOCHIST SOULJA, RIGHT?
You're a masochist?
I'M HONORED SUCH A BEAUTIFUL WOMAN HAS HEARD OF ME.
You'll find I'm more of a sadist.
HEE HEE. WHAT DO YOU WANT FROM ME?
I'M LOOKING FOR MY STUPID BRAT.

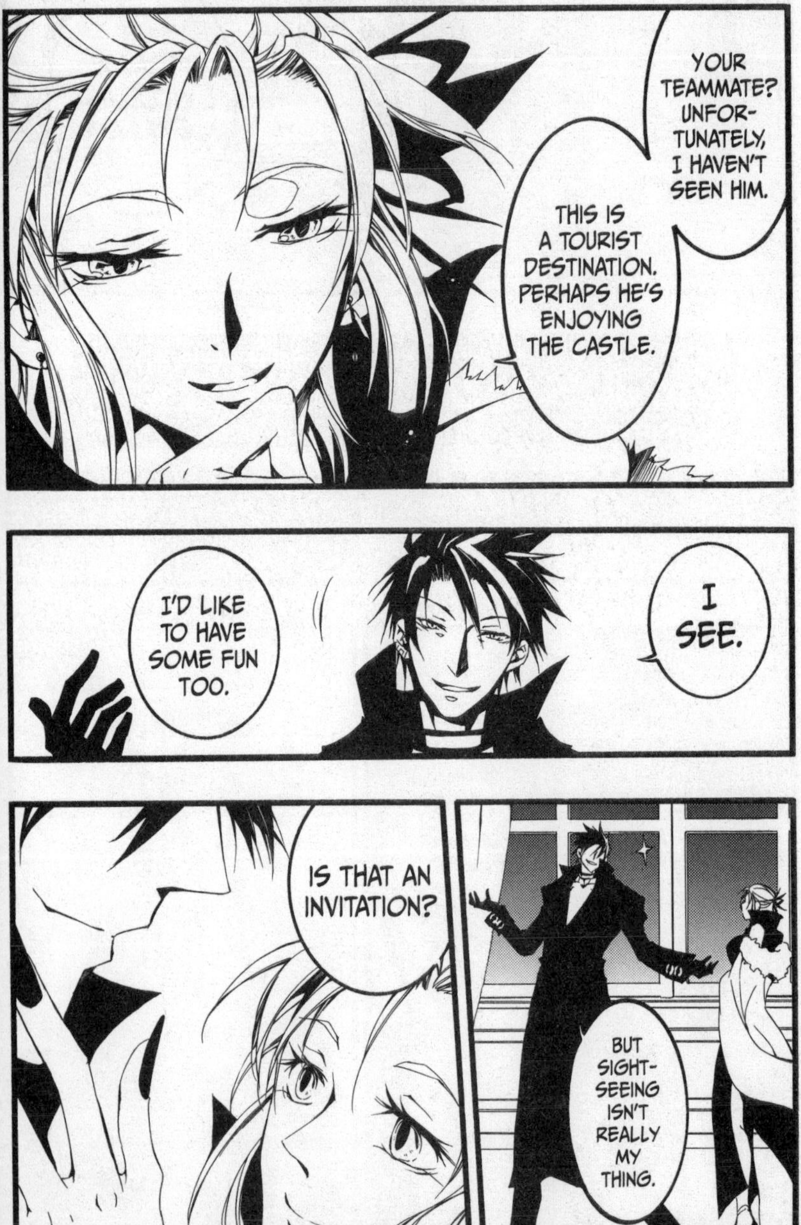
YOUR TEAMMATE? UNFOR-TUNATELY, I HAVEN'T SEEN HIM.
THIS IS A TOURIST DESTINATION. PERHAPS HE'S ENJOYING THE CASTLE.
I SEE.
I'D LIKE TO HAVE SOME FUN TOO.
BUT SIGHT-SEEING ISN'T REALLY MY THING.
IS THAT AN INVITATION?

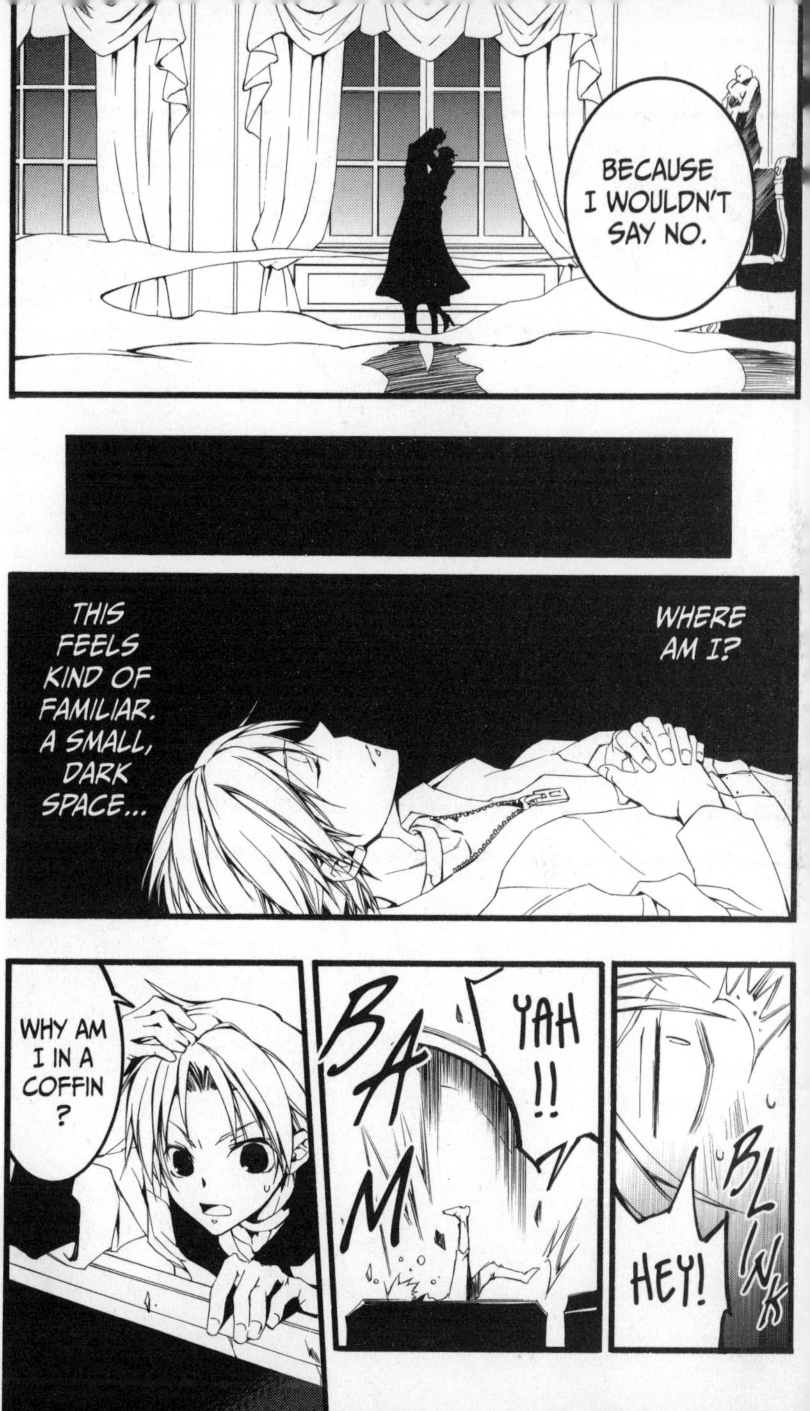
BECAUSE I WOULDN'T SAY NO.
WHERE AM I?
THIS FEELS KIND OF FAMILIAR. A SMALL, DARK SPACE...
BLINK
HEY!
YAH!!
BAM
WHY AM I IN A COFFIN?

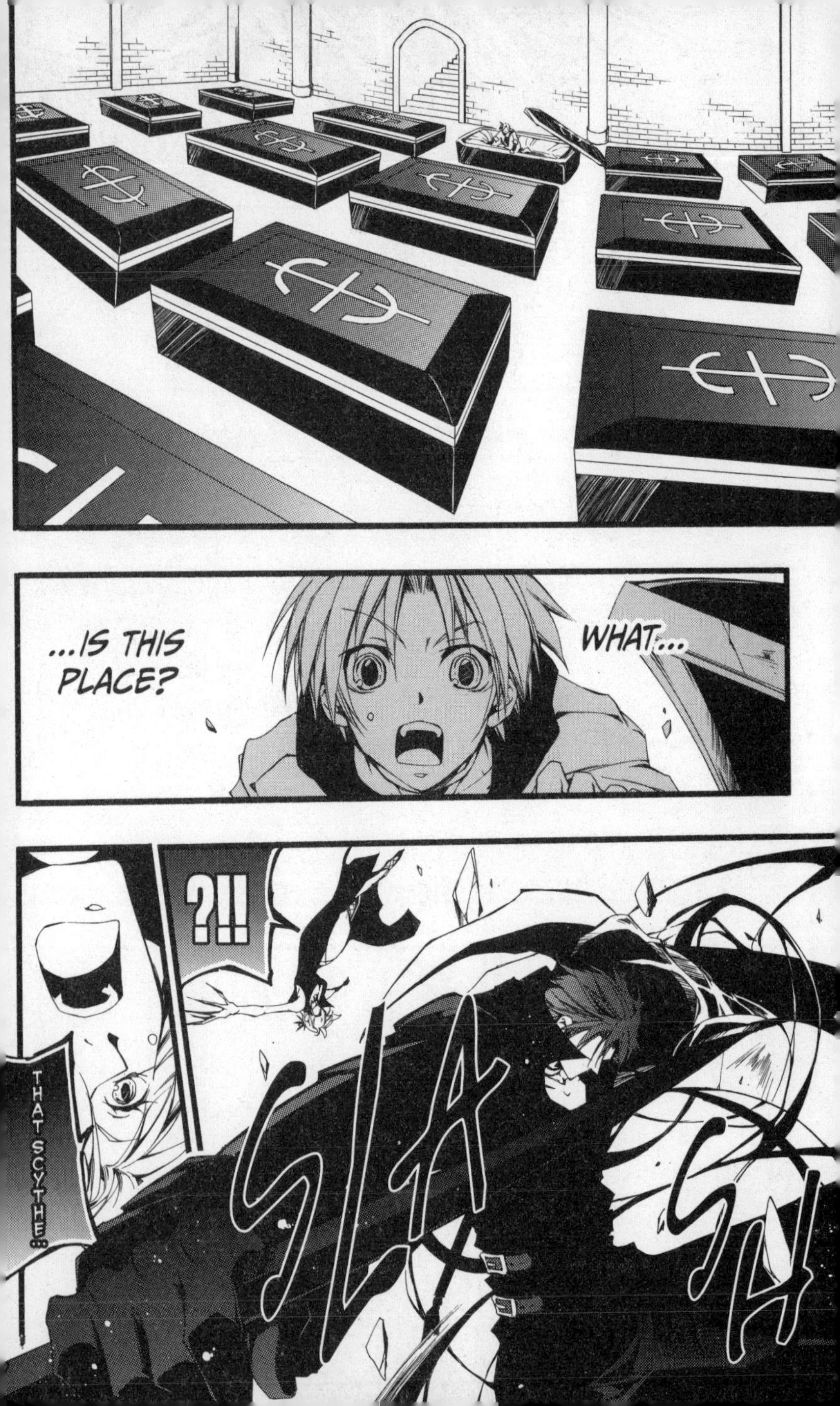
WHAT...
...IS THIS PLACE?
?!!
SLASH
THAT SCYTHE...

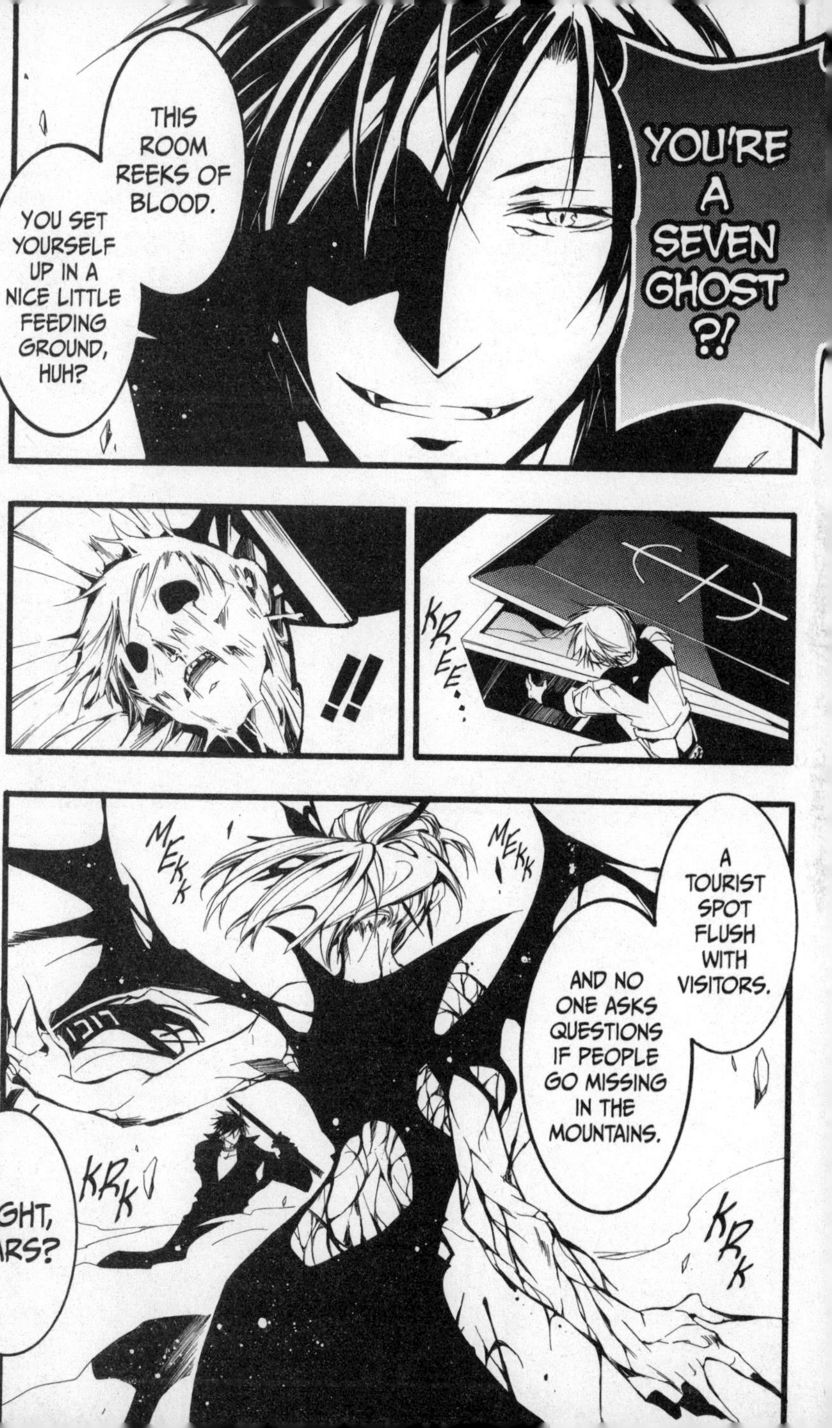
YOU'RE A SEVEN GHOST?!
THIS ROOM REEKS OF BLOOD.
YOU SET YOURSELF UP IN A NICE LITTLE FEEDING GROUND, HUH?
KREE...
!!
MEKK
A TOURIST SPOT FLUSH WITH VISITORS.
AND NO ONE ASKS QUESTIONS IF PEOPLE GO MISSING IN THE MOUNTAINS.
MEKK
KRK
KRK

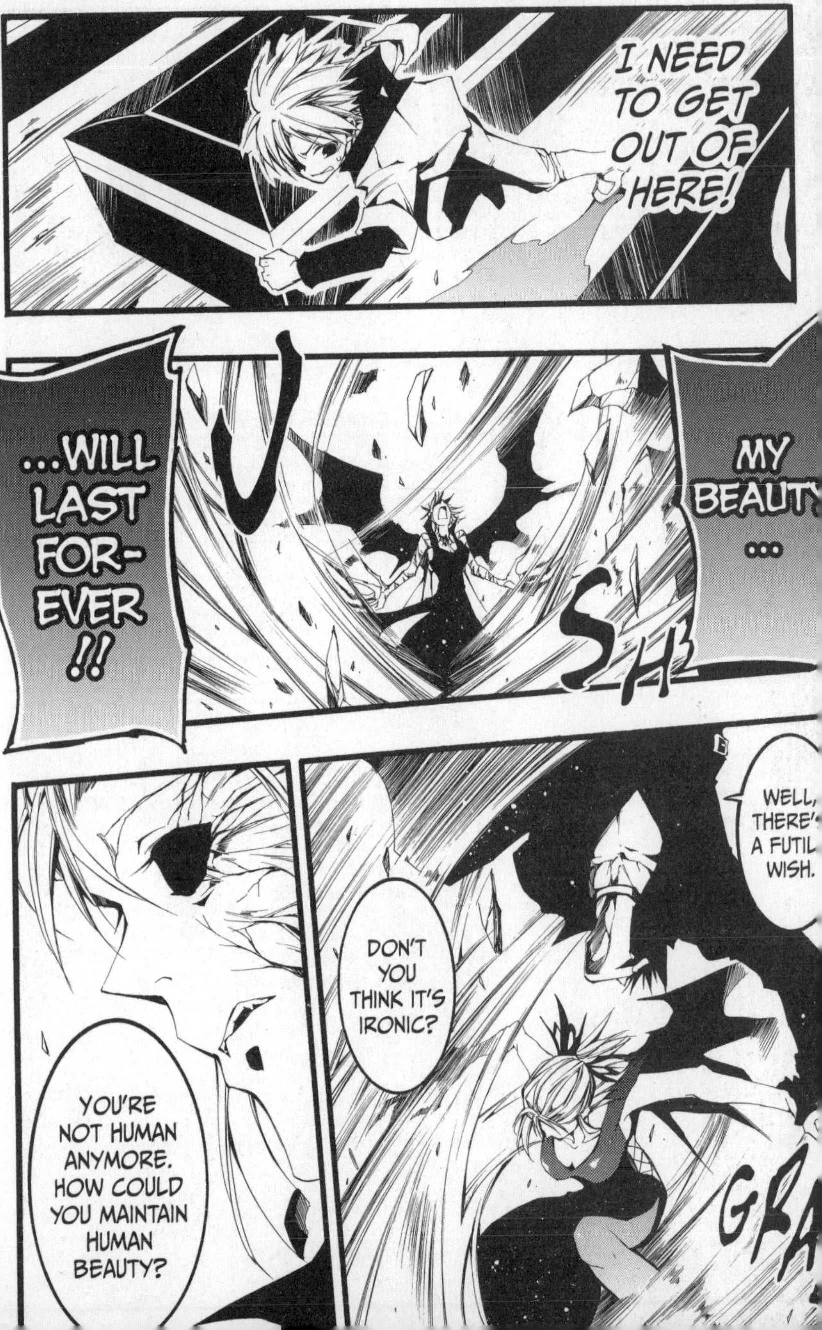
I NEED TO GET OUT OF HERE!
MY BEAUTY ...
SH
...WILL LAST FOR-EVER !!
WELL, THERE' A FUTIL WISH.
DON'T YOU THINK IT'S IRONIC?
GRA
YOU'RE NOT HUMAN ANYMORE. HOW COULD YOU MAINTAIN HUMAN BEAUTY?

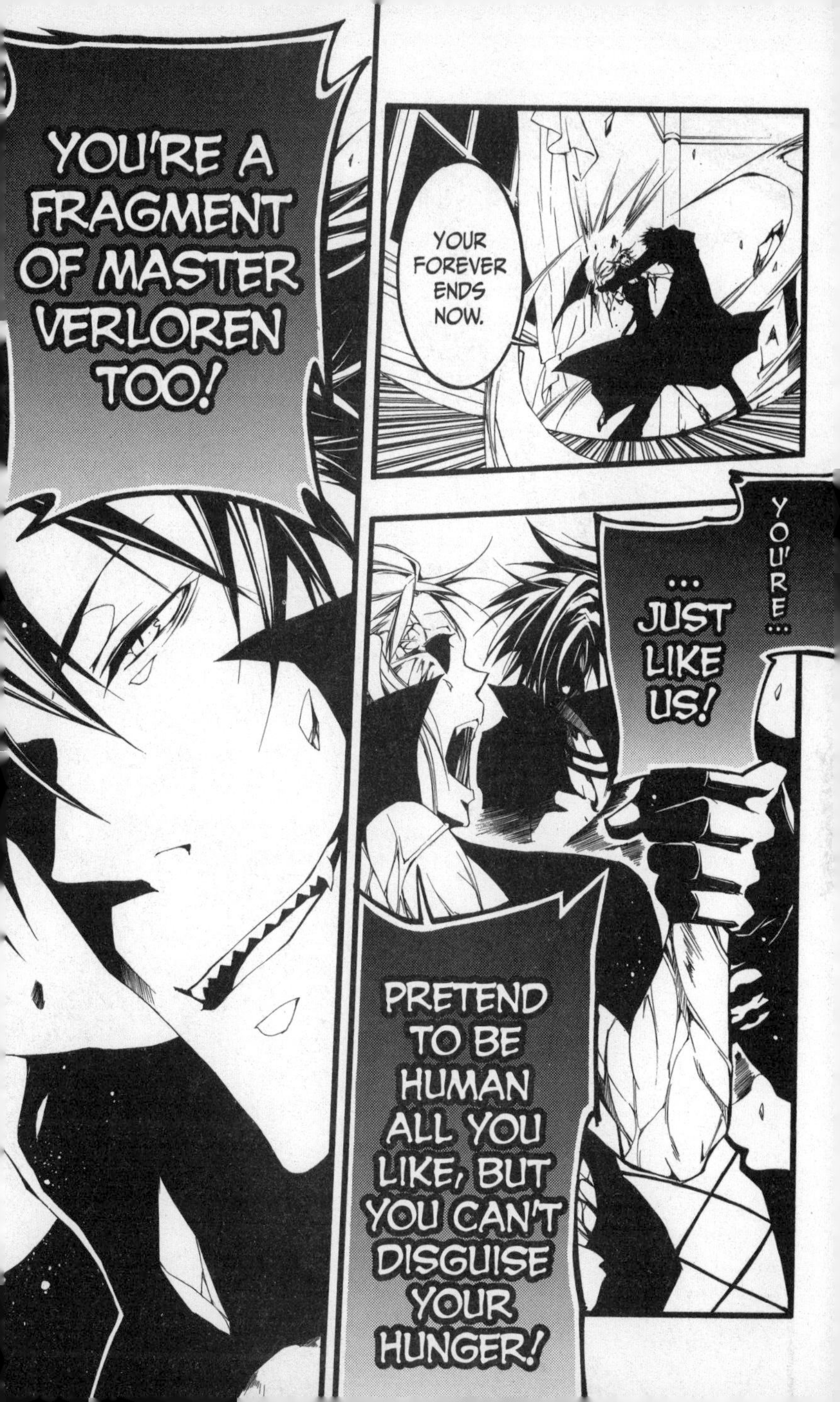
YOUR FOREVER ENDS NOW.
YOU'RE...
...JUST LIKE US!
PRETEND TO BE HUMAN ALL YOU LIKE, BUT YOU CAN'T DISGUISE YOUR HUNGER!
YOU'RE A FRAGMENT OF MASTER VERLOREN TOO!

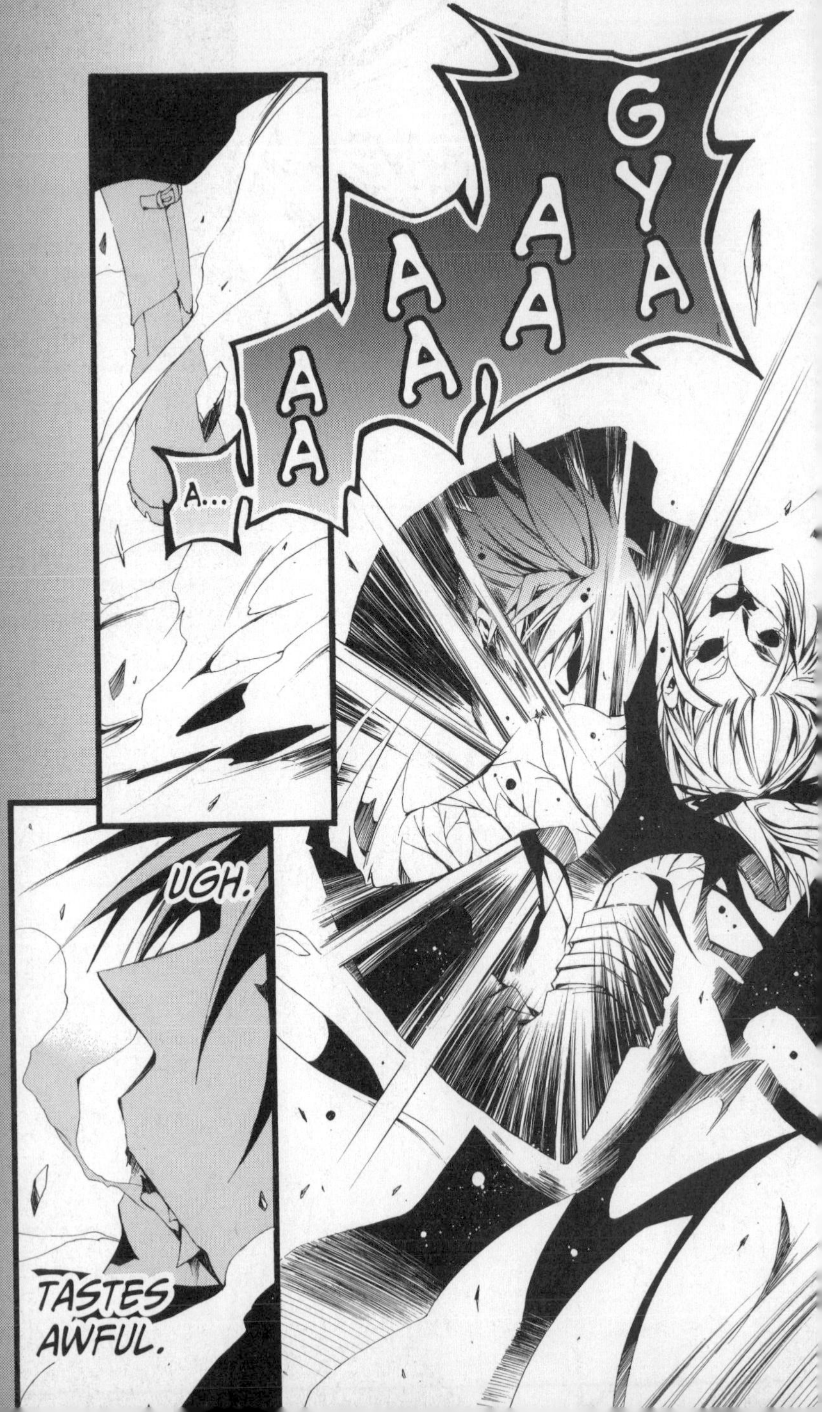
GYAAAAAAA
A...
UGH.
TASTES AWFUL.

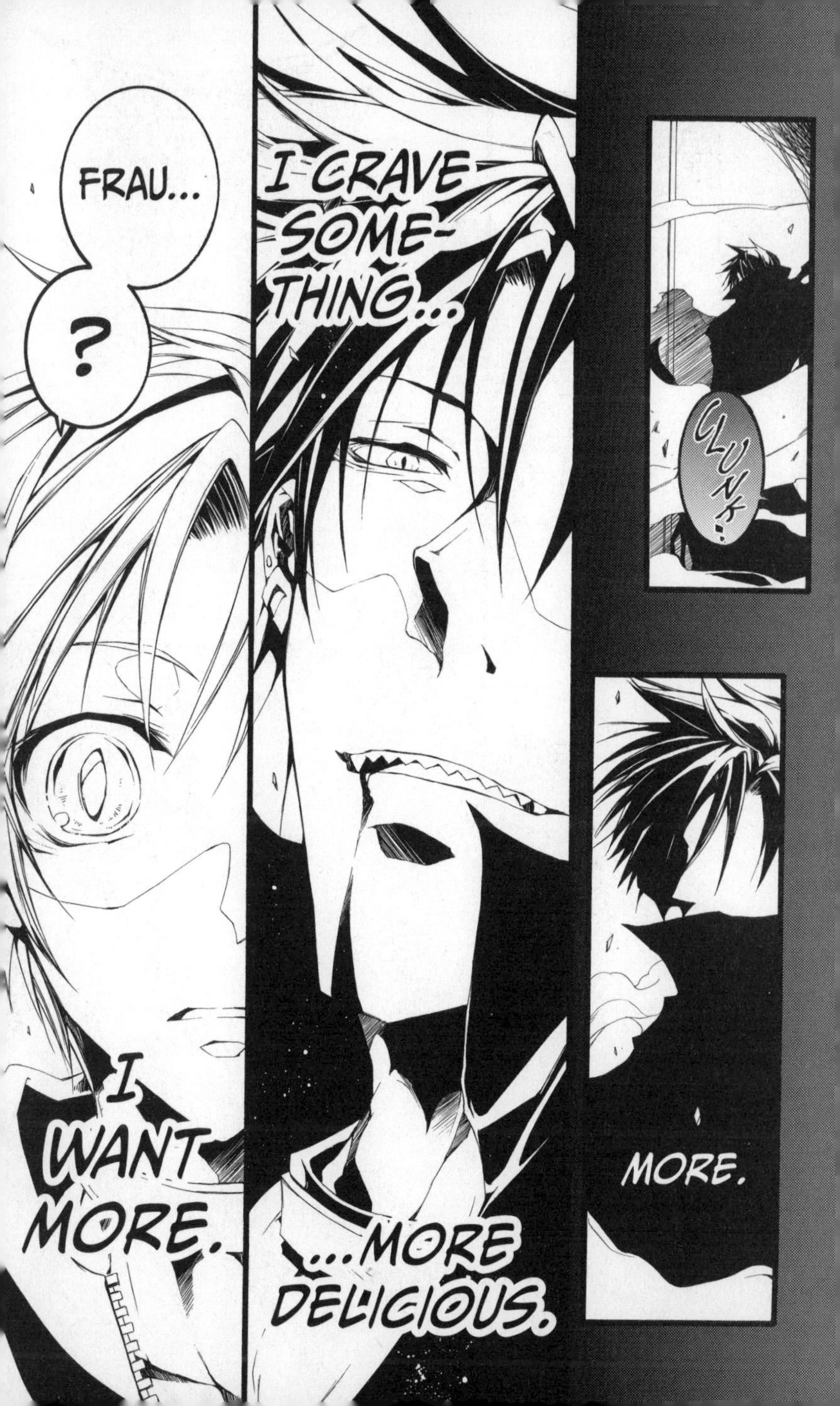
CLUNK..
MORE.
I CRAVE SOMETHING...
...MORE DELICIOUS.
FRAU...
?
I WANT MORE.

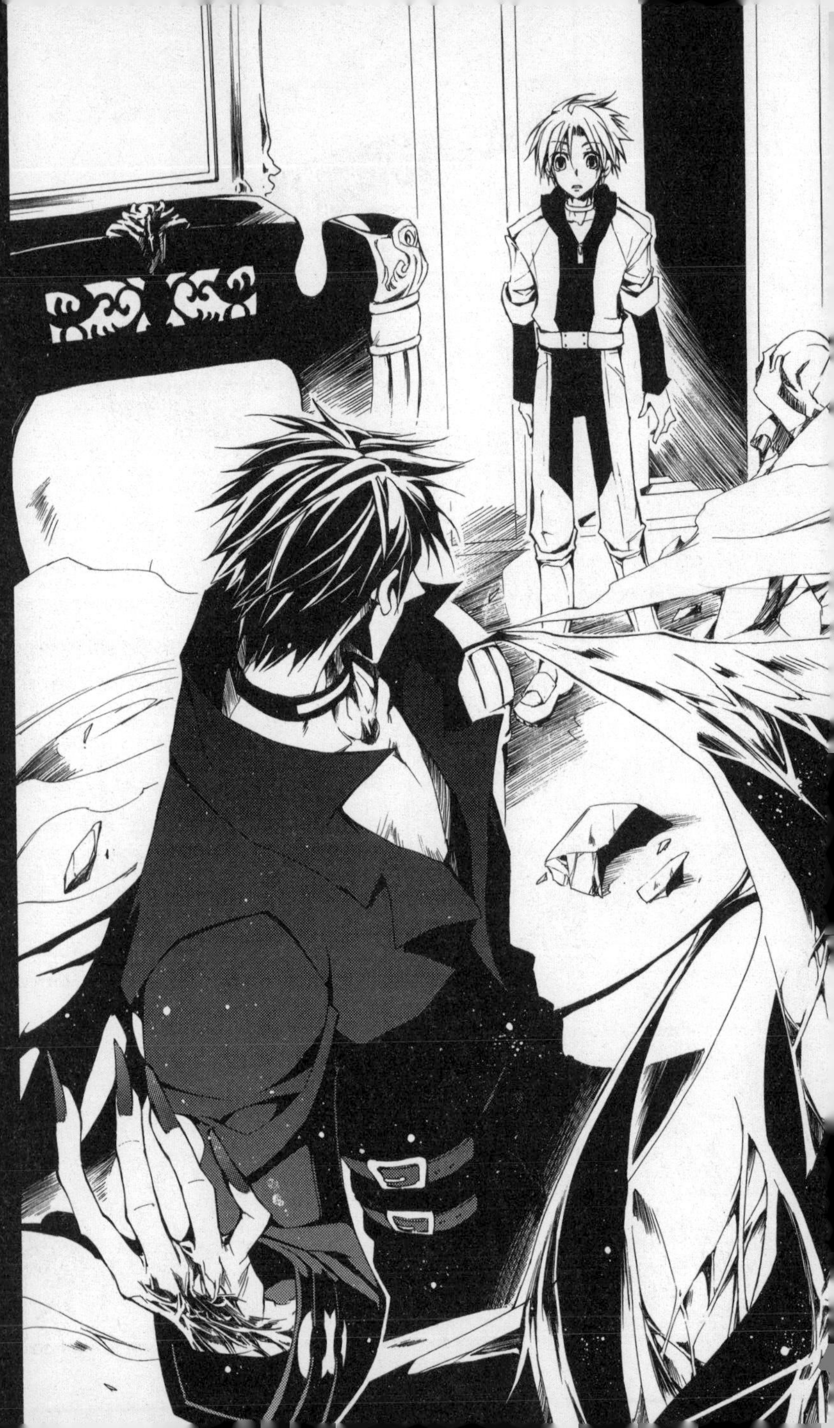

Bonus

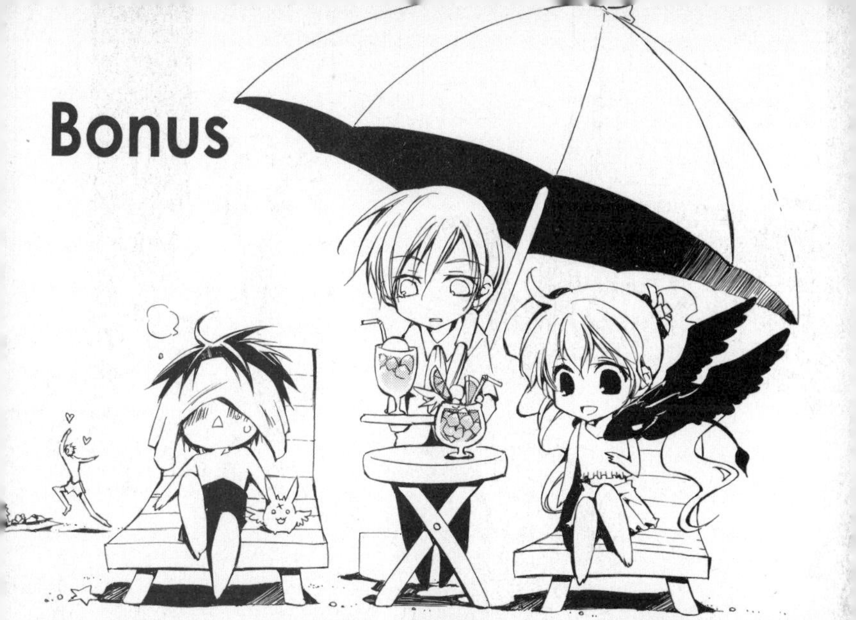

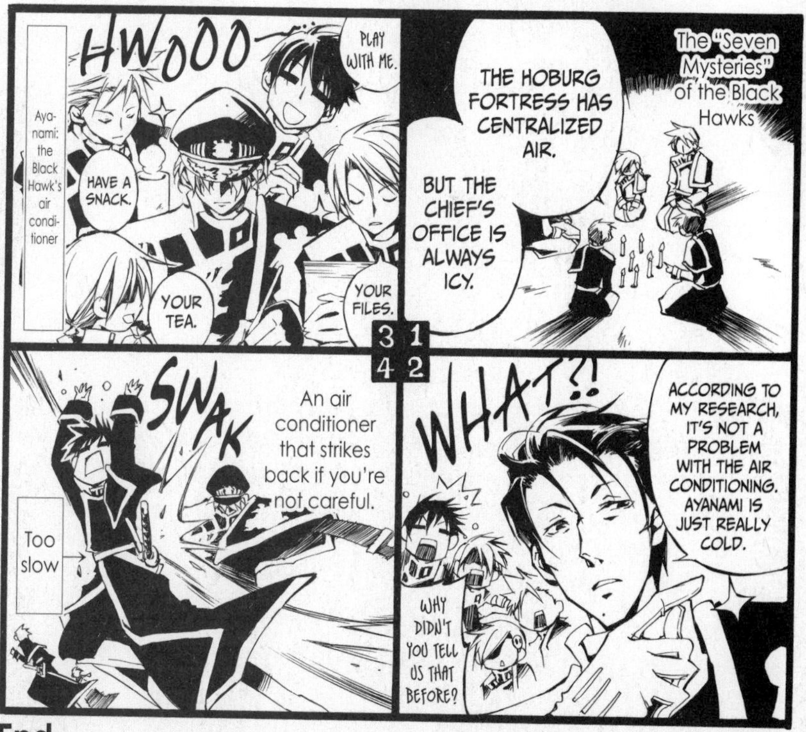

1
The "Seven Mysteries" of the Black Hawks
THE HOBURG FORTRESS HAS CENTRALIZED AIR.
BUT THE CHIEF'S OFFICE IS ALWAYS ICY.
2
WHAT?!
ACCORDING TO MY RESEARCH, IT'S NOT A PROBLEM WITH THE AIR CONDITIONING. AYANAMI IS JUST REALLY COLD.
WHY DIDN'T YOU TELL US THAT BEFORE?
3
Ayanami: the Black Hawk's air conditioner
HWOOO
PLAY WITH ME.
HAVE A SNACK.
YOUR FILES.
YOUR TEA.
4
SWAK
An air conditioner that strikes back if you're not careful.
Too slow

End

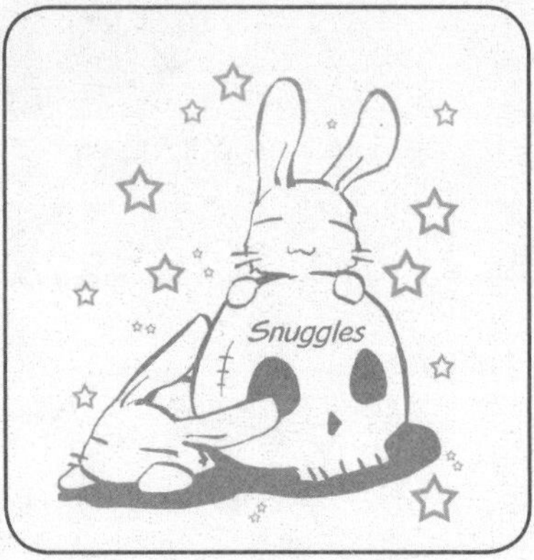
Snuggles

Weck makes the cutest jars! We just keep buying them, and our kitchen has transformed into a vibrant place. (*Yay!*)

—Yuki Amemiya & Yukino Ichihara, 2010

Yuki Amemiya was born in Miyagi, Japan, on March 25. Yukino Ichihara was born in Fukushima, Japan, on November 24. Together they write and illustrate *07-Ghost*, the duo's first series. Since its debut in 2005, *07-Ghost* has been translated into a dozen languages, and in 2009 it was adapted into a TV anime series.

07-GHOST

Volume 10

STORY AND ART BY
YUKI AMEMIYA and
YUKINO ICHIHARA

Translation/Satsuki Yamashita
Touch-up Art & Lettering/Vanessa Satone
Design/Yukiko Whitley
Editor/Hope Donovan

Printed in Canada

Published by VIZ Media, LLC
P.O. Box 77010
San Francisco, CA 94107

10 9 8 7 6 5 4 3 2 1
First printing, May 2014

www.viz.com

Enter_the_world_of_

LOVELESS

story_+_art_by_YUN_KOUGA

2-in-1 EDITIONS

Each 2-in-1
edition includes
6 color pages and
50 pages of
never-before-seen
BONUS comics,
artist commentary
and interviews!

only $14.99!
($16.99 CAN / £9.99 UK)

Available at your local book store,
comic book shop or library, or online at:

store.viz.com

RATED T FOR TEEN
ratings.viz.com

viz
media
www.viz.com

ⅥⅤⅠZMⅯⅯⅯⅯA
Read manga anytime, anywhere!

From our newest hit series to the classics you know and love, the best manga in the world is now available digitally. Buy a volume* of digital manga for your:

- iOS device (**iPad®**, **iPhone®**, **iPod®** touch) through the **VIZ Manga app**

- Android-powered device (**phone or tablet**) with a browser by visiting **VIZManga.com**

- **Mac or PC computer** by visiting **VIZManga.com**

VIZ Digital has loads to offer:

- 500+ ready-to-read volumes
- New volumes each week
- FREE previews
- Access on multiple devices! Create a log-in through the app so you buy a book once, and read it on your device of choice!*

To learn more, visit www.viz.com/apps

* Some series may not be available for multiple devices.
  Check the app on your device to find out what's available.

DEATH NOTE © 2003 by Tsugumi Ohba, Takeshi Obata/SHUEISHA Inc.
NURARIHYON NO MAGO © 2008 by Hiroshi Shiibashi/SHUEISHA Inc.
ONE PIECE © 1997 by Eiichiro Oda/SHUEISHA Inc.

viz.com/apps

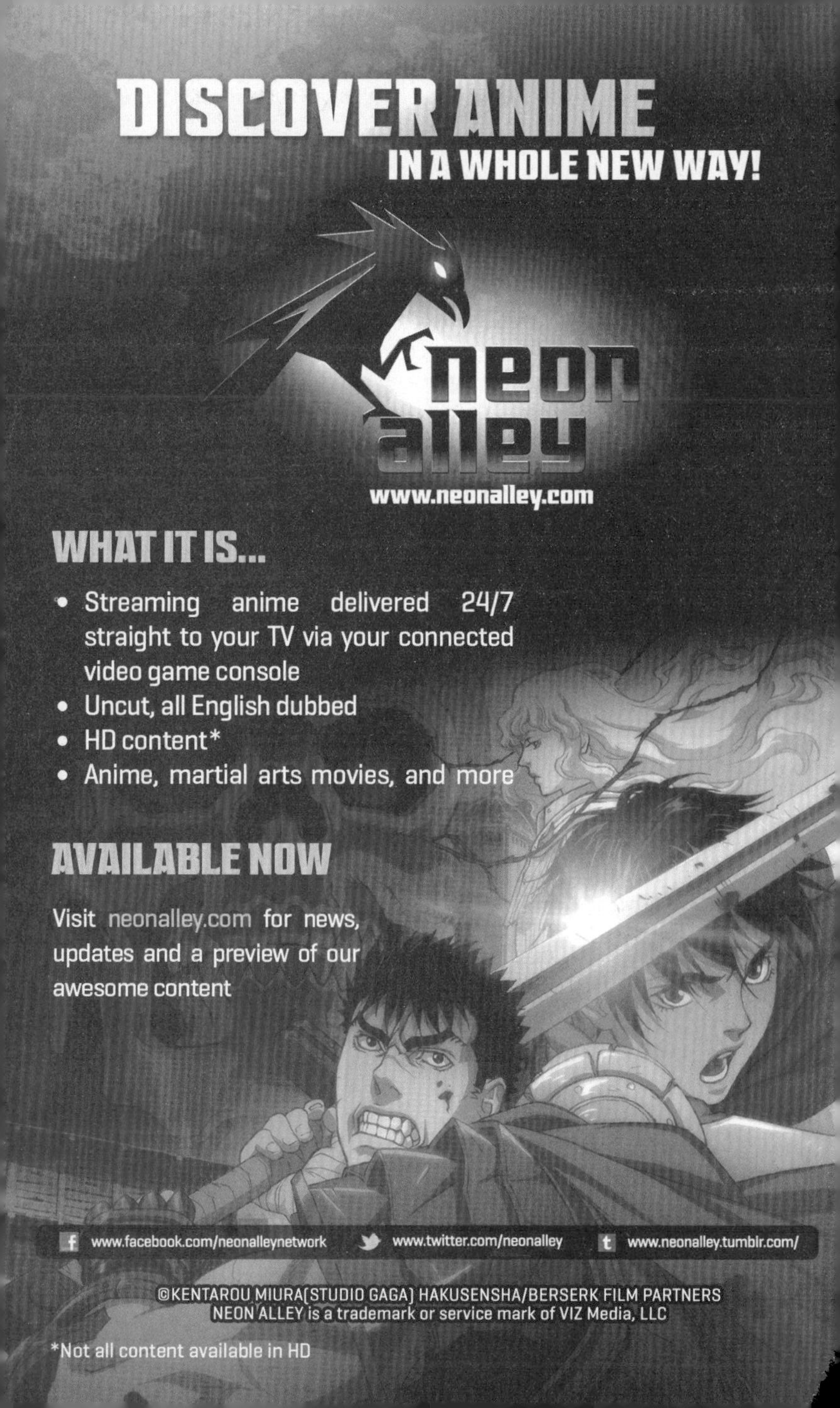
DISCOVER ANIME
IN A WHOLE NEW WAY!
neon alley
www.neonalley.com
WHAT IT IS...
• Streaming anime delivered 24/7 straight to your TV via your connected video game console
• Uncut, all English dubbed
• HD content*
• Anime, martial arts movies, and more
AVAILABLE NOW
Visit neonalley.com for news, updates and a preview of our awesome content
www.facebook.com/neonalleynetwork
www.twitter.com/neonalley
www.neonalley.tumblr.com/
©KENTAROU MIURA(STUDIO GAGA) HAKUSENSHA/BERSERK FILM PARTNERS
NEON ALLEY is a trademark or service mark of VIZ Media, LLC
*Not all content available in HD

Hey! You're Reading in the Wrong Direction!

This is the end of this graphic novel!

To properly enjoy this VIZ graphic novel, please turn it around and begin reading from right to left. Unlike English, Japanese is read right to left, so Japanese comics are read in reverse order from the way English comics are typically read.

This book has been printed in the original Japanese format in order to preserve the orientation of the original artwork. Have fun with it!

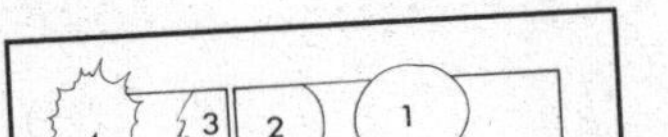
1
2
3
4
5
6
7
8
9
1
2
3
4
5
142

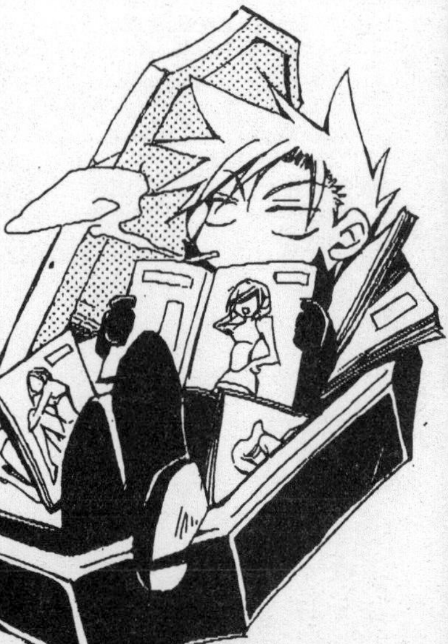

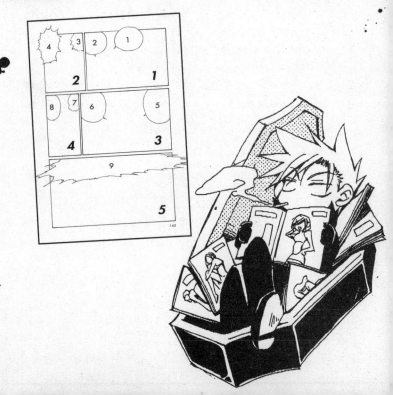